The Perennial Philosophy

Series

World Wisdom
The Library of Perennial Philosophy

The Library of Perennial Philosophy is dedicated to the exposition of the timeless Truth underlying the diverse religions. This Truth, often referred to as the *Sophia Perennis*—or Perennial Wisdom—finds its expression in the revealed Scriptures as well as the writings of the great sages and the artistic creations of the traditional worlds.

The Perennial Philosophy provides the intellectual principles capable of explaining both the formal contradictions and the transcendent unity of the great religions.

Ranging from the writings of the great sages of the past, to the perennialist authors of our time, each series of our Library has a different focus. As a whole, they express the inner unanimity, transforming radiance, and irreplaceable values of the great spiritual traditions.

Every Branch in Me: Essays on the Meaning of Man appears as one of our selections in The Perennial Philosophy series.

The Perennial Philosophy Series

In the beginning of the Twentieth Century, a school of thought arose which has focused on the enunciation and explanation of the Perennial Philosophy. Deeply rooted in the sense of the sacred, the writings of its leading exponents establish an indispensable foundation for understanding the timeless Truth and spiritual practices which live in the heart of all religions. Some of these titles are companion volumes to the Treasures of the World's Religions series, which allows a comparison of the writings of the great sages of the past with the perennialist authors of our time.

Every Branch in Me

Essays on the Meaning of Man

Edited by
Barry McDonald

World Wisdom

Every Branch in Me:
Essays on the Meaning of Man
© 2002 World Wisdom, Inc.

Library of Congress Cataloging-in-Publication Data

Every branch in me : essays on the meaning of man / edited by Barry McDonald
    p. cm. — (The library of perennial philosophy) Includes bibliographical references.
    ISBN 0-941532-39-9 (alk. paper)
    1. Philosophical anthropology. I. McDonald, Barry, 1952- II. Series.
    BD450 .E92 2002
    291.2'2—dc21

                                                        2002005225

Printed on acid-free paper in Canada

For information address World Wisdom, Inc.
P.O. Box 2682, Bloomington, Indiana 47402-2682

www.worldwisdom.com

Table of Contents

Preface

What is the vocation of man? What is the meaning of his life on earth? Like timeless streams flowing down a mountain these questions seem to have no beginning and no end. In the early morning hours and late at night they echoed in the minds of our ancestors, and they will whisper in the minds of our descendents. Profound questions which concern the deepest nature of man touch upon the very foundations of thought and throughout the centuries man has never stopped seeking answers. Perhaps, to paraphrase Rumi, within our deepest asking is the answer.

The study of the nature of human consciousness—and its deployment into our activity—has always been mostly the domain of specialists. Our ancestors took refuge in the great world religions and relied upon the teachings of the saints and sages to provide authoritative answers and spiritual guidance. Today many people seek answers from the specialized domains of science, psychology and medicine. Consequently, the world has witnessed over the past century and to the dawn of our new millennium, a chasm of separation between the sacred and the secular, and this separation has become almost as sharply differentiated as black is from white. At the center of the controversy is the question of the meaning of man.

The answer provided by the ancient sages is radically in opposition to the answer provided by the scientists and secular psychologists of our post-modern world. Most notably, the ancients placed God in the center of both macrocosm and microcosm. He was known to be the ordering Principle of the universe; the great Revelations offered a source of guidance and light to establish human norms and sanctify human life. Since the Renaissance, however, and with an ever-increasing speed, the prophets of secular humanism have sought to replace the idea of the Fatherhood of God with the brotherhood of man. Modern man—conditioned by the theories of Darwin, Freud, Marx and their intellectual progeny—now imagines himself standing in the center of creation, enjoying an almost infallible certitude that he will eventually be able to answer every question and solve every problem of the future. God is no longer a serious variable in the equation, and He has been largely forgotten—except perhaps during those moments when we are most afraid of forces which seem beyond our immediate control. The serious study of religion has been relegated to academic departments where professors lecture about great religious literature which inspired noble sentiments and heroic actions in history. They may continue to explain how the old religions established ethical frameworks which sometimes prevented our ancestors from tearing each other to pieces. Many will be quick to insist that the determinative power of metaphysical doctrines concerning the idea of Absolute Truth have been proven false by their colleagues in the science and philosophy departments.

Which world-view is correct? Is it possible for man to self-sufficiently live and enjoy the fruits of progress in a world without God? As we enter the 21st century it is of utmost importance for each of us, regardless of our specific walk of life, to come to grips with this urgent question. If we dismiss the question, we may be dismissing the most important question we could ever ask and we may be trading the wheat for the chaff. As members of the human race, and for the sake of others, it would appear that we are obligated to develop clear intellectual and moral points of reference to discern the voices of genuine authority. Seeking an answer to the fundamental question of who is qualified to answer questions concerning our essential nature and why we are on earth, returns us to the basic root of our humanity. Failing to ask this question, we run the risk of losing a central component of what constitutes the great value of the human state; we risk passing through life like a sleepwalker lost in dreams of pleasure and pain.

From whence, then, does this intelligence to discern arise? Is it through the process of transformist evolution? Do the qualities of thought evolve from the quantities of matter? Is the mind just a metamorphosis of matter? The opinion of modern science answers these questions mostly in the affirmative. Their theory asks us to believe that the most evolved man of today must *de facto* be more profound, produce greater works of genius in every field of human art and endeavor, and have the knowledge to live in closer harmony with nature and his fellow beings than did our less enlightened ancestors. This outwardly expanding myth of progress further assumes that there will be men in the future who will surpass the greatest men of our day and that these men will certainly be capable of bringing about great epochs of peace and prosperity on earth. Additionally, we are asked by philosophers and psychologists to accept the absolute Truth that there is no absolute Truth and that the only Reality is that there is no Reality, excluding of course, the reality of the physical world and the life of the senses.

Alternatively—if the ancient sages are correct—then our spiritual intelligence does not evolve; it remains an ever present source of true knowledge which takes precedence over the knowledge we gather through simple reasoning and through the senses. They affirm that objective Reality and Truth may be known through the great revelations, which are the Word of God, and through intellectual intuition which is the voice of the immortal spark of God's Being, eternally living in the depths of man's soul. Because man has been made in the image of God, the sages further affirm that there is a coincidence between the highest objective Reality and the deepest subjective Reality. Man may know the Truth because in his most profound being he contains the Truth. Man is, according to the wisdom of Sufism, a message from God to God. This message is amplified by the deepest Christian wisdom which teaches that God became man so that man might become God.

Unlike the outwardly expanding theories of modern thought which rely upon empirical evidence and material proof, the ancient wisdom leads man on an inward path to the source of his being. This path leads through the theophany of creation to the Creator. Throughout the centuries to the present day, various modalities of this wisdom have been expressed by countless saints and sages representing every religious tradition in the world. Their unanimous voices affirm that any discussion concerning the vocation of man must include God because it is only through God's Absolute Being that man possesses his existence. This metaphysical axiom is a golden thread running through the Abrahamic revelations of Judaism, Christianity and Islam and it is clearly visible in Hinduism, Buddhism, Taoism and shamanistic traditions such as the Sun Dance religion.[1] Each of these traditions has, of course, a specific

---

1. *A Treasury of Traditional Wisdom* by Whithall N. Perry (Fons Vitae, Louisville, 2000). This book is an incomparable collection of the *philosophia perennis* from diverse sources, but in its common major themes, it testifies to the remarkable unanimity of the spiritual traditions of mankind.

language which speaks to a specific human collectivity; however, it is possible to translate them into a common language which with a single voice affirms that the relative cannot exist without the Absolute and that the periphery must expand from the Center.

The various articles in this book rigorously profess a sacred world-view which links the meaning of man to the Reality of God. Touching not only upon the essence of spiritual anthropology as such, they also branch into many important aspects of human experience, including work and the sacred, the role of laughter in spiritual life, relying upon God during a time of illness, the spiritual significance of clothing and the importance of seeking a spiritual guide. The articles may be defined as perennialist in perspective, which means that the contributors—all of whom insist upon adherence to an orthodox religion—predicate their thinking upon what Frithjof Schuon has called "the transcendent unity of religions."[2] All of these authors will assert that it is of utmost importance for man to define himself in view of God. This sense of urgency was strongly emphasized by Jacob Needleman in his introduction to *The Sword of Gnosis,* a volume of essays by perennialist authors on metaphysics, cosmology, tradition and symbolism, collected from the pages of the most important 20th century journal of traditionalist studies. Needleman wrote: "On close reading, I felt an extraordinary intellectual force radiating through their intricate prose. These men were out for the kill. For them, the study of spiritual traditions was a sword with which to destroy the illusions of contemporary man."[3]

If the perennialists have set themselves the task of bursting the illusions of contemporary man, it is most important to add that they are even more committed to replacing the false idols of modernism with the liberating knowledge of God. This knowledge, which is based upon the theomorphic nature of man, is an authentically

2. *The Transcendent Unity of Religions* by Frithjof Schuon (Quest TPH, Wheaton, Illinois, 1993). Concerning this book, T.S. Eliot wrote: "I have met with no more impressive work in the comparative study of Oriental and Occidental religions". Schuon's books are essential reading.

3. *The Sword of Gnosis,* edited by Jacob Needleman (Penguin Books, Baltimore, 1974) is a collection of articles from the British journal *Studies in Comparative Religion.* Included in the collection is Titus Burckhardt's masterly "Cosmology and Modern Science," which should be of great aid in properly situating the whole body of contemporary sciences in a context free of the exaggerated awe that too often is accorded to almost anything bearing the accolade "scientific."

spiritual antidote to the impasses of despair and nihilism which are the final outcomes of the secular and relativist ideologies of our time. The perennialist perspective, which arose early in the 20th century, found its most powerful voices in Frithjof Schuon, Rene Guenon, Ananda K. Coomaraswamy and Titus Burckhardt. Their writings have proven to be—both in terms of depth and breadth— the most compelling restoration of serious metaphysical thought in the last one hundred years. The leading authors of this school of thought have illuminated the universal truths upon which all ortho-dox religions are founded, and they have done so with an adaman-tine refusal to accept anything less than the truth, the whole truth and nothing but the truth. Their writings impress upon us that the consequences of this truth branch into every aspect of human life and that its acceptance requires the totality of our being.

My hope is that *Every Branch in Me: Essays on the Meaning of Man* will serve as the trailhead on a journey of self-discovery. The subject matter of the book is unified by an underlying theme: nothing that is properly human can be separated from the deep spiritual nature of man. Additionally, to make such a separation courts disaster for the individual, the society in which we live, and for the earth upon which we spend our lives. As we begin the new century, we are still asking profound questions requiring ultimate answers. It is my wish that these essays will provide a source of hope to the serious seeker and untangle some of the knots created by the questionable axioms of the modern world. The radical secularization of the world has brought us to the brink of spiritual and ecological crises such as we have never before known. And, although modern science has made stunning discoveries in the physical world and split the atom, it will never understand the greatest mystery of all: the miracle of con-sciousness.

Barry McDonald
January 2002

Chapter 1

To Have a Center

Frithjof Schuon

To be normal is to be homogeneous, and to be homogeneous is to have a center. A normal man is one whose tendencies are, if not altogether univocal, at least concordant; that is, sufficiently concordant to serve as a vehicle for that decisive center which we may call the sense of the Absolute or the love of God. The tendency towards the Absolute, for which we are made, is difficult to realize in a heteroclite soul; a soul lacking a center, precisely, and by that fact contrary to its reason for being. Such a soul is a priori a "house divided against itself," thus destined to fall, eschatologically speaking.

The anthropology of India—which is spiritual as well as social—distinguishes on the one hand between homogeneous men whose centers are situated at three different levels,[1] and on the other hand between all homogeneous men and those who, lacking a center, are not homogeneous;[2] it attributes this lack either to a decay or to a "mixture of castes"—above all of those castes that are furthest removed from each other. But it is of the natural castes, not the social ones, that we propose to speak here: the former do not always coincide with the latter, for the institutional caste contains exceptions, to the extent that it becomes numerically very large and thereby includes all human possibilities. Thus, without wanting to concern ourselves with the castes of India, we shall describe as succinctly as possible the fundamental tendencies of which they are intended to be the vehicle, and which are found wherever there are men, with particular predominances according to the nature of the group.

There is first of all the intellective, speculative, contemplative, sacerdotal type, which tends towards wisdom or holiness; holiness referring more particularly to contemplation, and wisdom to dis-

---

1. The *brâhmana*, the *kshatriya*, the *vaishya*.
2. The *shûdra*, the *chandâla* or *panchama*.

1

cernment. Next there is the warlike and royal type, which tends towards glory and heroism; even in spirituality—since holiness is for everyone—this type will readily be active, combative and heroic, hence the ideal of the "heroicalness of virtue." The third type is the respectable "average" man: he is essentially industrious, balanced, persevering; his center is love for work that is useful and well done, and carried out with God in mind; he aspires neither to transcendence nor to glory—although he desires to be both pious and respectable—but like the sacerdotal type, he loves peace and is not interested in adventures; a tendency which predisposes him to a contemplativeness conformable with his occupations.[3] Lastly there is the type that has no ideal other than that of pleasure in the more or less coarse sense of the word; this is concupiscent man who, not knowing how to master himself, has to be mastered by others, so that his great virtue will be submission and fidelity.

No doubt, the man who finds his center only outside himself—in pleasures, without which he feels like a void—is not really "normal"; but he is nonetheless salvageable through his submission to someone better than he, and who will serve as his center. This is exactly what happens—but on a higher plane which may concern any man—in the relation between disciple and spiritual master.

But there is still another human type, namely the man who lacks a center, not because he is deprived of it through concupiscence, but because he has two or even three centers at once: this is the type known as the pariah,[4] arising from a "mixture of castes," and who bears in himself the double or triple heredity of divergent types; that of the sacerdotal type, for example, combined with the materialistic and hedonistic type of which we have just spoken. This type, who lacks an axis, is capable "of everything and nothing"; he is a mimic and a born actor, always looking for a substitute for the center, hence for a psychic homogeneity which necessarily eludes him. The pariah has neither center nor continuity; he is a nothingness eager for sensations; his life is a disconnected series of arbitrary experiences. The danger this type represents for society is evident

---

3. From the standpoint of "caste" this third type is particularly complex and unequal: it contains in fact peasants, artisans and merchants. Thus, apart from all social classifications, it includes tendencies which may be quite unequal.
4. A loan word in the European languages, derived from the Tamil *paraiyan*, "drummer."

since one never knows what kind of person one is dealing with; no one is willing to trust a leader who is at bottom a mountebank and who by his nature is predisposed to crime. This explains the ostracism of the Hindu system with regard to those who, having arisen from mixtures that are too heterogeneous, are "outcastes." We say that this explains the ostracism, and not that this excuses the abuses, or that the evaluation of individuals is always just; which indeed is impossible, in practice.[5]

Generally speaking, a man's psychological type is a matter, not of the exclusive presence of a given tendency, but of its predominance; and in this sense—or with this reservation—we may say that the first of the types enumerated is "spiritual"; the second, "noble"; the third, "upright"; the fourth, "concupiscent"; and the fifth, "vain" and "transgressing." Spirituality, nobility, uprightness: these are the fundamental tendencies of men who, according to the Hindu doctrine, are "twice born" or qualified for initiation. Concupiscence and vanity: these are the tendencies of those who a priori are not concretely qualified for a spiritual path but who, being men, nevertheless have no choice; which amounts to saying that every man can save himself in principle. As Ghazali has said, one has to drive some men into Paradise with whips.

Thus there is hope for the man who has no center, whatever the cause of his privation or infirmity may be; for there is a suprahuman Center that is always available to us, and whose trace we bear within ourselves, given that we are made in the image of the Creator. That is why Christ could say that what is impossible for man is possible for God. However decentralized man may be, as soon as he sincerely turns to Heaven his relationship with God confers on him a center; we are always at the center of the world when we address the Eternal. That is the point of view of the three monotheistic religions of Semitic origin, and also that of human distress and Divine Mercy.[6]

5. The Hindu system sacrifices the exceptional cases in the interest of the collectivity, for the sake of maintaining both quality and durability.
6. A point of view which is likewise found in Buddhism and in certain sectors of Hinduism, and necessarily so since human misery is one, just as man is one.

It is of primary importance not to confuse the absence of a center—which is abnormal—in the hylic[7] and somatic type, with the same absence—but normal in this case and situated on an altogether different plane—in the feminine sex. For it is only too evident that although as a sexual being woman seeks her center in man, she is nonetheless in full possession of her center in precisely the respect in which hylics or pariahs do not possess it. In other words: if woman as such aspires to a center situated outside herself, namely, in the complementary sex—just as the latter in the same respect seeks his vital space in his sexual complement— she nonetheless enjoys an integral personality as a human being, on condition that she be humanly in conformity with the norm, which implies the capacity to think objectively, above all in cases where virtue requires it. Too often it is thought that woman is capable of objectivity and thus of disinterested logic only at the expense of her femininity,[8] which is radically false; woman has to realize, not specifically masculine traits of course, but the normatively and primordially human qualities, which are obligatory for every human being; and this is independent of feminine psychology as such.[9]

Another point to be considered is the personal center in connection with certain racial factors. If the mixture between races too different from each other is to be avoided, it is precisely because this disparity generally has as a consequence that the individual possesses two centers, which means practically speaking that he has none; in other words, that he has no identity. But there are cases where, on the contrary, the mixture gives rise to a harmonious

---

7. Translator's note: The author uses the term "hylic," from the triad "hylic," "psychic," "pneumatic," or "materialistic," "passional," "spiritual."
8. The feminists themselves—of both sexes—are convinced of this, at least implicitly and in practice, otherwise they would not aspire to the virilization of woman.
9. Legitimate feminine psychology results from the principial prototype of woman—from the universal Substance—as well as from the biological, moral and social functions which she personifies; and this implies the right to limitations, to weaknesses, if one wishes, but not to faults. The human being is one thing, and the male is another; and it is a great pity that the two things have often been confused even in languages which—like Greek, Latin and German—make this distinction; a confusion which is due to the fact that the male is more central than the female, thus also more integral, but this reason has only a relative import, because man (*homo*, not *vir*) is one.

result, namely when each parent represents a sort of racial super-saturation, such that the racial type is limitative rather than positive; in this case, the combination with the foreign race appears as a liberation and re-establishes equilibrium; but this solution is as exceptional as are its conditions. Besides, every soul contains two poles, but normally they are complementary and not divergent.

*
* *

The practical interest of all these considerations lies in the fact that we live in a world which on the one hand tends to deprive men of their center, and on the other hand offers them—in place of the saint and the hero—the cult of the "genius." Now a genius is all too often a man without a center, in whom this lack is replaced by a creative hypertrophy. To be sure, there is a genius proper to normal, hence balanced and virtuous, man; but the world of "culture" and of "art for art's sake" accepts with the same enthusiasm normal and abnormal men, the latter being particularly numerous—to the extent that men of genius can be—in that world of dreams or nightmares that was the 19th century. That geniuses of this kind have often been unfortunate and desperate persons who have ended in disaster, does not deprive them of any prestige in public opinion; quite the contrary, people find them all the more interesting and "authentic," and let themselves be attracted by the seduction, indeed the fascination, which emanates from their siren songs and tragic destinies.

Let us take the example of a man who has two heredities and thus two equivalent centers, one intellectual and idealistic and another materialistic and self-indulgent: as an intellectual, this man will forge a philosophy, but it will be determined by his materialism and his love of pleasure; as a materialist, he will enjoy life as a *bon vivant,* but his pleasures will be intellectualized, thus he will enjoy life as an epicure and an aesthete. And he will be an elusive and inconsequential man, dominated by the pleasure of the moment which he will always justify by his hedonistic philosophy; and this is one of the most dangerous possibilities there is.

Consequently it is not astonishing that a man who is at once a man of genius and lacking a true center should easily be a psychopath—and this precisely on account of his unbridled subjectivism—whether he be a schizoid artist, a paranoiac politician or some other caricature of grandeur. It is all very well to admire the qualities of a brilliant work; its creator may have, alongside his genius, a perfectly odious character; thus the values that are manifested in his creations, or in some of them, pertain only to a single compartment of his split and heteroclite psychism, and not to a homogeneous personality.

As for profane genius as such, aside from the question of knowing whether it is normal or morbid, good or bad, it is important to know that it can be the medium of a cosmic quality, of an archetype of beauty or grandeur, and in that case it would be unjust to reject its production. Likewise it would be unjust to despise it for the simple reason that it does not pertain to traditional art, just as, inversely, it would be sheer prejudice to admire a work for the sole reason that it is traditional or sacred, since it could be badly executed and manifest unintelligence as well as incapacity. In short, cosmic values, or aesthetic and moral qualities, can manifest themselves incidentally in any human climate, to the extent that it does not set up an obstacle to them.[10]

*
* *

One has to insist, therefore, on this point: what is blameworthy in the exteriorized and worldly genius is not necessarily his production, but the fact that he places his center outside himself, in a work which in a certain manner deprives him of his real core or puts itself in place of it. Such is not the case for genius not determined by humanism: in Dante, for example, or in Virgil, their work was the providential manifestation of an immensely rich and profound center; of a "genius," precisely, in the ideal, normative and legitimate sense of the term. The criterion of such genius is that the author is as interested in his salvation as in his work, and that the latter bears the trace of the former. No doubt—speaking of literature—this cri-

---

10. It should be noted that, apart from the superior modes of talent or of genius—modes to which the great musicians and actors belong—there are also cerebral prodigies such as calculators and chess players, or prodigies of imagination and vitality such as the great adventurers; we mention them here on account of their phenomenal character, even though, since they do not produce works, they remain outside our subject.

terion could not appear in each poem nor in each tale, but it applies to every work that demands a lengthy reading and has to compensate for this intrusion by a fragrance that is spiritual and interiorizing. Every writer or artist ought to communicate—in addition to his literal message—elements of truth, nobility, and virtue, if not of eschatological ideas; the most stupid and perverse prejudice being "art for art's sake," which cannot be founded on anything whatsoever.

Indisputably, it is humanistic narcissism with its mania for individualistic and unlimited production that is responsible for this ultimately useless profusion of talents and geniuses. The humanistic perspective not only proposes the cult of man, but by that very fact also aims at perfecting man according to an ideal that does not transcend the human plane. Now this moral idealism is fruitless because it depends entirely on a human ideology; such an ideal wants man to be ever productive and dynamic, hence the cult of genius, precisely. The moral ideal of humanism is inefficacious because it is subject to the tastes of the moment, or to fashion, if one wishes;[11] for positive qualities are fully human only in connection with the will to surpass oneself, hence only in relation to what transcends us. Just as man's reason for being does not lie within man as such, so too, man's qualities do not represent an end in themselves; it is not for nothing that deifying gnosis requires the virtues. A quality is fully legitimate only on condition that in the last analysis it be linked to necessary Being, not to mere contingency, that is, to what is merely possible.

The initial contradiction of humanism is that, if one man can prescribe for himself an ideal that pleases him, so too can someone else, for the same reason, prescribe for himself another ideal, or indeed nothing at all; and in fact amoral humanism is almost as ancient as moralistic humanism.[12] The moralizing candor of a Kant

---

11. The ostentatiously human perfection of classical or academic art has in reality nothing universally convincing about it; this was noticed long ago, but only in order to fall into the contrary excess, namely, the cult of ugliness and of the inhuman, despite a few intermediary oases, certain impressionists, for example. The classicism of a Canova or an Ingres no longer convinces anyone, but that is no reason for acknowledging only Melanesian fetishes.

12. On the more or less traditionalist side one also speaks of "hominism"—with a reproving intention—no doubt because the term "humanism" still evokes "classical" associations of ideas with which one still feels obliged to make common cause.

or a Rousseau is followed by the adventurous amoralism of a Nietzsche; people no longer say "humanism is morality," they now say "I am morality"; even if morality is altogether absent.

Voltaire expressed the wish that every man should be "seated under his fig tree, eating his bread without asking himself what is in it"[13] (we quote from memory). He means: sheltered from the tyranny of dogmas and priests; and, good humanist that he is, he completely forgets that the good man he is dreaming of is potentially a savage beast, that man is not necessarily good, and that the only thing which protects man from man—or the good from the bad—is precisely religion, tyrannical or not. And religion does so even if it unleashes in turn some bad men against some good men, which in any case is inevitable and much the lesser evil compared to a world without religious discipline, a world delivered into the hands of man alone, precisely.

*

* *

Since our thesis on the human center has led us to mention that ambiguous possibility that is genius, we shall take the liberty of illustrating our preceding considerations by a few concrete examples, without wishing to get involved in "all too human" *(allzumenschlich)* blind alleys. This is not in keeping with our habit, but our subject more or less obliges us to do so. The reader should not be surprised if, in what follows, he enters as it were into a new world.

Despite the fact that Beethoven was a believer, he was inevitably situated on the plane of humanism, hence of "horizontality." And although there was nothing morbid about him, we note the characteristic disproportion between the artistic work and the spiritual personality; characteristic, precisely, for genius arising from the cult of man, thus from the Renaissance and its consequences. There is no denying what is powerful and profound about many of Beethoven's musical motifs, but, all things considered, a music of this sort should not exist; it exteriorizes and thereby exhausts possibilities which ought to remain inward and contribute in their own way to the contemplative scope of the

---

13. That is to say: without concerning himself with the supernatural, the mysteries, in short with things that are humanly unverifiable.

soul.[14] In this sense, Beethoven's art is both an indiscretion and a dilapidation, as is the case with most post-Renaissance[15] artistic manifestations; even so, compared to certain other geniuses, Beethoven was a homogeneous man, hence "normal," if we disregard his demiurgic passion for musical exteriorization.

Alongside motifs possessing all the pure beauty of the archetypes, there are necessarily in Beethoven and his successors—for example in Wagner—features denoting the megalomania of the Renaissance and thus of humanistic idealism. While appreciating particular musical motifs, and given polyphonic harmonies which throw them into relief, one cannot help noticing the disproportionate and "ponderous" side of the musical production in question; a melody may be celestial, but a symphony or an opera is excessive. It should be noted, however, that the great deviation of the *Cinquecento* had much less of an effect on music and poetry than on painting, sculpture and architecture; thus the megalomaniacal character of this or that modern music refers at bottom more directly—from the standpoint of affinity—to the plastic arts of the Renaissance rather than to its musical arts.[16]

Having spoken of music, let us pass on to another example of creations of genius, this time of a visual character but equally powerful and quasi-volcanic: namely Rodin, direct heir to the Renaissance despite the lapse of centuries. Although we cannot accept this carnal and tormented by-product of ancient naturalism as a fully legitimate expression of human art, we are compelled to take note of the titanesque dimensions of this art in its most expressive productions. As in the case of the 16th century artists—such as

14. It is quite possible that if Ramakrishna had heard the Ninth Symphony and if he could have grasped its musical language, he would have fallen into *samâdhi*, something which happened to him when he saw a lion for the first time, or when an Indian dancing girl danced before him; but we doubt very much that there are many Ramakrishnas among Beethoven's listeners, so the argument has hardly any practical value as regards the spiritual and social justification of such an exteriorized and communicative music, one which is in fact a "two-edged sword."

15. Whereas in Bach or Mozart musicality still manifests itself with faultless crystallinity, in Beethoven there is something like the rupture of a dam or an explosion; and this climate of cataclysm is precisely what people appreciate.

16. In Beethoven and other Germans, the titanism of the distant Renaissance combines with the thunder of ancient Germany, and this aside from the presence of a quasi-angelic dimension of Christian origin.

Michelangelo, Donatello, Cellini—the motivating force here is the sensual cult of the human body combined with a neo-pagan perspective,[17] thus with various abuses of intelligence and also with the Greco-Roman sense of grandeur; but a grandeur of man and not that of God.

*

* *

One of the determining causes of the blossoming of genius from the end of the 18th century onwards—but above all in the 19th century—was the impoverishment of the environment: whereas in earlier times, above all in the Middle Ages, the environment was at once religious and chivalrous, thus charged with colors and melodies, if one may say so, the Age of Philosophy and above all the Revolution, took away from the world all supra-natural poetry, all vital upward-extending space; men were more and more condemned to a hopeless horizontality, profanity and pettiness. It is this which explains in part, or in certain cases, the cries of protest, of suffering and despair, and also of nostalgia and beauty. If Beethoven, or any other great creator in the realm of art, had lived in the epoch of Charlemagne or of St. Louis, their genius might have remained more inward, they would have found satisfactions and consolations—and above all, planes of realization—more in conformity with what constitutes the reason for the existence of human life. In short, they would have found their center; or they would have perfected the center they already possessed by rendering it supernatural. Deprived of a real world, of a world which has a meaning and allows one to engage in liberating pursuits, many geniuses create for themselves an intense inner world, but one which is exteriorized on account of the need to manifest themselves; a world composed

---

17. There is a curious analogy between Michelangelo's Last Judgment and Rodin's Gate of Hell: in both cases, the sensual and tormented beauty of the bodies goes hand in hand with an atmosphere of damnation, instead of communicating the serenity of the celestial shores as do the naked and on occasion amorous divinities of India and the Far East. With Bourdelle and Maillol, the ancient naturalism is attenuated. Exact observation in art certainly has its rights, but needs the regulatory and as it were musical element of stylization; art has to remain a writing, but a legible one.

of nostalgia and grandeur, but in the final analysis with no meaning or efficacy other than that of a confession.

Such was also the case with Nietzsche, a volcanic genius if ever there was one. Here, too, there is passionate exteriorization of an inward fire, but in a manner that is both deviated and demented; we have in mind here, not the Nietzschian philosophy, which taken literally is without interest,[18] but his poetical work, whose most intense expression is in part his *Zarathustra*. What this highly uneven book manifests above all is the violent reaction of an a priori profound soul against a mediocre and paralyzing cultural environment; Nietzsche's fault was to have only a sense of grandeur in the absence of all intellectual discernment. *Zarathustra* is basically the cry of a grandeur trodden underfoot, whence comes the heart-rending authenticity—grandeur precisely—of certain passages; not all of them, to be sure, and above all not those which express a half-Machiavellian, half-Darwinian philosophy, or minor literary cleverness. Be that as it may, Nietzsche's misfortune, like that of other men of genius, such as Napoleon, was to be born after the Renaissance and not before it; which indicates evidently an aspect of their nature, for there is no such thing as chance.

This was also Goethe's misfortune, a well-balanced and, from a certain standpoint, too well-balanced genius. By this we mean to say that he was the victim of his epoch owing to the fact that humanism in general and Kantianism in particular had vitiated his tendency towards a vast and finely-shaded wisdom; he thus became, quite paradoxically, the spokesman of a perfectly bourgeois "horizontality." His *Faust*, which starts off in the Middle Ages and in mystery, comes to an end, so to speak, in the 19th century and in philanthropy, leaving aside the final apotheosis which springs from the poet's Christian subconsciousness, without being able to compensate for the Kantian and Spinozan atmosphere of the work.[19] All the same, there is unquestionably great scope in the human substance of

18. This philosophy could have been a warning cry against the peril of a leveling and bastardizing humanitarianism, thus mortal for mankind; in point of fact, it was a combat against windmills and at the same time a seduction of the most perilous kind.
19. The poet believes in the saving grace of an omnipresent divine Love, granted to whoever "strives unceasingly towards the good" (*"Wer immer strebend sich bemüht, den können wir erlösen"*); an eschatological optimism that combines in a strange fashion with 18th-century deism on the one hand, and with esoteric

Goethe: a scope manifested by the lofty and generous quality of his mind;[20] and also, in a more intimate fashion, in those poems where he makes himself the "medium" of the popular soul, in short of medieval Germany; in so doing, he continues the spring-like and delicate lyricism of Walter von der Vogelweide, as if time had come to a stop.

A particularly problematical type of talent led astray from its true vocation is the novelist: whereas in the Middle Ages novels still drew their inspiration from myths, legends, and religious and chivalrous ideals, they became from a certain period onwards more and more profane,[21] even garrulous and insignificant: their authors, instead of living their own lives, lived successively the lives of their imaginary personages. A Balzac, a Dickens, a Tolstoy, a Dostoevsky lived on the fringe of themselves, they gave their blood to phantoms, and they incited their readers to do the same: to waste their lives by burying themselves in the lives of others, with the aggravating circumstance that these others were neither heroes nor saints and, besides, never existed. These remarks can be applied to the whole of that universe of dreams which is called "culture": flooded by literary opium, siren songs, vampirizing and—to say the least—useless production, people live on the fringe of the natural world and its exigencies, and consequently on the fringe—or at the antipodes—of the "one thing needful." The 19th century—with its garrulous and irresponsible novelists, its *"poètes maudits,"* its creators of pernicious operas, its unhappy artists, in short, with all of its superfluous idolatries and all of its blind alleys leading to despair—

knowledge of hermetic and kabbalistic origin on the other hand; the incoherence is flagrant.

20. We find the same traits in Schiller, with a slightly different accentuation; it is inadmissible that people should heap sarcasms on the moving idealism of this poet—as is fashionable nowadays in Germanic countries—for there was in him a truly authentic moral elevation and sense of grandeur, as is demonstrated especially by his ballads.

21. Cervantes is in certain respects an exception—and certainly not the only one—in that his work serves as the vehicle for elements of philosophy and of symbolism, making one think of Shakespeare. As a literary genre, the theater is much less problematical than the novel, if only on account of its more disciplined and less time-consuming character. Calderón's plays prolong—to some degree—the "mysteries" of the Middle Ages and exercise a didactic and spiritual function, in the manner of the tragedies of antiquity, which were intended to provoke a catharsis.

was bound to crash against a wall, the fruit of its own absurdity; thus the First World War[22] was for the *"belle époque"* what the sinking of the Titanic was for the elegant and decadent society that happened to be on board, or what Reading Gaol was for Oscar Wilde, analogically speaking.

*
* *

Like other writers or artists, Wilde offers isolated values—we are thinking here of his tales[23]—which one would like to see in another general context but of which it may be said, at least, that beauty always communicates a celestial dew-drop, if only for an instant. Divining in him a mystical dimension—his cult of beauty was only its gilded shadow—one pities the author and one would like to save him from his morbid and futile side;[24] one may in any case suppose that his conversion *in extremis*—after so many cruel trials—was an encounter with Mercy. We can have the same sentiment in several analogous cases, where regret and hope prevail over a feeling of uneasiness, or even irritation.

Among the classic cases of self-destructive individualism we may mention the poet Lenau—half German, half Hungarian—who personifies the drama of a pessimistic narcissism sinking into melancholy and insanity. Such destinies are almost inconceivable in a religious and traditional climate; as inconceivable as the general phenomenon of a culture claiming to be an end in itself. No doubt, sadness has its beauty; it evokes a nostalgia which takes us beyond

---

22. Of which the Second World War was only a belated continuation and conclusion.

23. The best tales belong to poetry rather than to novels; they are in a way prose poems, inspired by popular tales containing an initiatory intention. We may note that Anderson does not have Wilde's capacity, but has the merit of having the soul of a child.

24. Or save him from himself, since he personifies the tragic trajectory—or the total cycle—of quasi-divinized pleasure; of ultra-refined and intellectualized hedonism wishing to live itself out, down to its ineluctable ontological consequences. As soon as enjoyment is taken for an end in itself, and in the absence of a vertical and spiritual dimension which, by supernaturalizing it, would lend it the permanence of the archetypes, it presses on fatally towards the suicide it bears within itself. In saying in his "Ballad" that "each man kills the thing he loves," the poet expresses the intrinsic tragedy, not of love, but of pleasure become idol.

13

ourselves by purifying us, and consequently it evokes distant shores far from the disappointing narrowness of our earthly dreams; as the lyricism of the *Vita Nuova* shows.

Sadness has a right to be related to the song of Orpheus, but not to that of the sirens.[25]

There are also unhappy painters, such as Van Gogh and Gauguin, who are bearers of certain incontestable values—otherwise there would be no point in speaking about them. Here too, the qualities are partial in the sense that the lack of discernment and spirituality makes itself felt—at least in certain faces—despite the prestige of the style.[26] But what counts here is not so much the value of this or that pictorial style, as the drama—typical for the modern West—of normally intelligent men who sell their souls to a creative activity which no one asks of them and of which no one has any need, they themselves no more than others; who make a religion of their profane and individualistic art and who, so to speak, die martyrs for a cause not worth the trouble.

We meet in all arts with a type of genius which, like a display of fireworks, burns itself out in a single significant work, or in two or three works born of a single burst of inspiration. This is the case with Bizet, a medium—if one may say so—of the Hispano-Provençal soul, or more particularly of the passionate and at the same time tragic romanticism of bull fighting; with accentuations which, in the last analysis, go back to heroic chivalry and to the lyricism of the troubadours; of this, however, the great majority of his listeners are scarcely aware.

To come back to literature and to its least attractive aspects: an Ibsen and a Strindberg are the very types of talent wishing to make itself the spokesman of a thesis that is excessive, revolutionary, sub-

25. Thus Saint Francis of Sales who was certainly not lacking in sensibility, could say that "a sad saint is a sorry sort of saint"; he has in mind here a melancholy which erodes the theological virtues, precisely—Krishna's flute is the very image of ascending, not descending, nostalgia; sweetness of salvation, not of perdition.
26. One should not forget—but the modernists will never admit it—that the choice of the subject matter is a part of art, and that the subject, far from being the "anecdote" of the work, as some people stupidly imagine, is on the contrary its reason for being. As a matter of fact, the subjects of portraitists are all too often lacking in interest and consequently have nothing to communicate; the landscapists are fortunate in that they avoid this pitfall.

versive, and in the highest degree individualistic and anarchic; in the 19th century, to be original at this price was like a title of nobility; and "after me the deluge." This kind of talent—or of genius, as the case may be—makes one think of children who play with fire, or of Goethe's sorcerer's apprentice: these people play with everything, with religion, with the social order, with mental equilibrium, provided they can safeguard their originality; an originality which, retrospectively, shows itself to be a perfect banality, because there is nothing more banal than fashion, no matter how clamorous.

A general remark is called for here, independent of the immediately preceding considerations: our intention is not—and cannot be—to present a survey of art and literature, so there is no point in asking why we do not mention this or that particularly conspicuous genius. A Victor Hugo, for example; if we have not spoken of this bombastic and long-winded spokesman of French romanticism, it is because neither his personality nor his destiny could motivate a substantial commentary on our part; and the same remark applies to every other typologically equivalent celebrity. We shall not say anything very notable therefore in pointing out that the author of the *Orientales*—like so many other creators of art—lives only through his productions, and that he puffs himself up and finally becomes hardened in the passionate projection of himself; all this as he encloses his readers in an intense and despairing horizontality and inculcates in them a false idea of human grandeur, or of grandeur as such. As a natural consequence, humanism—in becoming humanitarianism—likewise implies a false idea of human misery, whose whole eschatological dimension people are careful not to perceive; an idea which moreover readily opens onto demagogy. And one knows from experience that megalomaniacal idealism and moral pettiness get along well together among those who are the standard-bearers of integral humanism, especially on the political plane.

All the same, this fragile and almost dreamlike world of totally profane genius and "culture" lasted just barely two centuries; born more or less in the middle of the 18th century, it died about the middle of the 20th century, after exhausting itself like a display of fireworks in the course of the last century; this century that believed itself to be eternal. The protagonists died along with their audience, and the audience along with its protagonists.

No doubt it will be contended that the flux of culture continues, since there are always new writers and new artists, whatever may be their value or lack of value; this is true, but it is no longer the same culture; living as it does on forgetfulness, it is no longer the culture which, on the contrary, lived on remembrance.

*

*   *

A particularly problematical sector of culture with a humanist background is philosophical production, where naive pretension and impious ambition become involved in the affairs of universal Truth, which is an extremely serious matter; on this plane, the desire for originality is one of the least pardonable sins. However: apart from the fact that one should not confuse cleverness with intelligence, there is intelligence everywhere, and it is a truism to assert that the least of philosophers can sometimes say things which make sense. Irrespective of this aspect of the question, it is paradoxical, to say the least, that those who are readily qualified as being "thinkers" are not always those who know how to think—far from it—and that there are men who feel they have a vocation to think precisely because they are unable to evaluate all that this function implies.

As for doctrines—and this is an entirely different standpoint—one has to recognize that profane philosophy benefits sometimes, and even fairly often in certain respects, from extenuating circumstances, given the fact that the inadequacies of contemporary theology and confessional dissensions provoke with good reason doubts and reactions; thus philosophers are more or less the victims, at least to the extent that they are sincere. For the truths of the *philosophia perennis,* largely disregarded by average theologians, require something in the human spirit to take their place; this explains, not the whole phenomenon of modern thought of course, but its most respectable and excusable aspects.[27]

27. Leaving aside the cases of culpable negligence—in the case of liberal theologians for example—not everyone feels obliged to plunge into the ins and outs of Scholasticism, all the more so since it is not accepted by the Eastern Orthodox Church which is, after all, strictly traditional, nor by the Protestants, who intend limiting themselves to Scripture.

But there is also, over and above the vain fluctuations of specifically profane thought, the spiritualist renewal of a Maine de Biran—whose merits we cannot overlook—not to mention the prolongations of ancient theosophy in the case of Saint Martin and Baader, and partially in Schelling.

Coming back now to the flood of philosophical literature—and it is indeed to this flood that the Hegelian dialectic could be applied—the most serious reproach we can make concerning the general run of these "thinkers" is their lack of intuition of the real and consequently their lack of sense of proportion; or the short-sightedness and lack of respect with which they handle the weightiest questions human intelligence can conceive, and to which centuries of millennia of spiritual consciousness have provided the answer.

Perhaps it is worthwhile mentioning in this context a phenomenon as uncalled for as it is irritating, and that is the philosopher, or the so-called philosopher, who imagines he can support his aberrant theses by means of novels and plays, which amounts to inventing aberrant stories in order to prove that two and two make five; and this is indeed characteristic of a mentality which does not see the absurdity of intelligence denying intelligence. It is as if one were to paraphrase Descartes' *cogito ergo sum* upside down, emitting, practically speaking, the thesis that "I am; therefore I do not think."

Normally, the vocation of a thinker is synonymous with the sense of responsibility. The art of thinking is not the same thing as the joy of living; he who wishes to know how to think, must know how to die.[28]

*
* *

There is a side of "bourgeois culture" which unveils all its pettiness, and that is its aspect of conventional routine, its lack of imagination, in short its unconsciousness and its vanity. Not for an instant is it asked, "What is the good of all this?"; there is not one author who asks whether it is worthwhile writing a new story after so many other stories; it would seem as though they wrote them simply

---

28. Translator's note: Elsewhere, the author has written: "to be objective is to die a little."

because others have done so, and because they do not see why one should not do so and why one should not gain the glory that others have gained.[29] It is a *perpetuum mobile* nothing can stop, except a catastrophe or, less tragically, the progressive disappearance of readers; there is no celebrity without an audience, as we have said earlier.[30] And this is what has happened in some measure: past authors whose prestige seemed assured are no longer read; the general public has other needs, other resources and other distractions, however low they may be. More and more, culture becomes the absence of culture: the mania for cutting oneself off from one's roots and for forgetting where one comes from.

One of the subjective reasons for what we may call "cultural routine" is that man does not like to lose himself alone, consequently he likes to find accomplices for a common perdition; it is this which is the cause of a profane culture, consciously or unconsciously, but not innocently, because man bears deep within himself the instinct of his reason for being and of his vocation. The Oriental civilizations have often been reproached for their cultural sterility, that is to say the fact that they do not comprise a continuous stream of literary, artistic and philosophical production; we believe that by now there is no need for taking the trouble to explain the reasons for this fact.

Even more detestable than unimaginative conventionalism is the mania for change with the repeated acts of unfaithfulness it implies: namely the need to "burn what one has adored" and, on occasion, to "adore what one has burned."[31] Classicism, romanticism, realism, naturalism, symbolism, psychological novels, social novels, and so on; and what is most strange in all this is that at each new stage one ceases to understand what previously one had understood perfectly well; or one pretends not to understand it any longer, for fear of being left behind. One feels indeed obliged to remember Racine and Corneille—above all Molière who, as every-

29. "To be famous and to be loved," as Balzac said.
30. It was all very well for Léon Bloy to cling to the lifelines of religion, his imagination was nonetheless confined to the closed universe of literature, and it was a waste of time for him to fulminate against his colleagues and his accomplices. In too many cases, religious belief has strangely little power over the imagination, and this is still another effect of immanent humanism.
31. This is exactly what the Renaissance did in "burning" the symbolistic Middle Ages and in "adoring" naturalistic antiquity.

one knows, is always funny—or Pascal,[32] in the context of "culture" precisely; one is also obliged to accept La Fontaine and Perrault on account of children. But few are those who still know and appreciate a Louise Labé, whose sonnets are second neither to those of Petrarch, Michelangelo or Shakespeare; otherwise a poet as refined as Rilke would not have taken the trouble to translate them and in so doing turn them into new masterpieces.

No doubt, a man can grow weary of something he has busied himself with too much, or with which he has busied himself too superficially; but it does not follow from this that he has a right to despise it, especially if there is nothing in it which warrants either weariness or contempt. Weariness itself can be the sign of a warped mentality, and the tendency to arbitrary mockery certainly is; because if we have had enough of something, rightly or wrongly all we have to do is to busy ourselves with something else; there is no reason why we should speak disparagingly of it; he who has studied Aristotle too much can "go and play the violin." But it is a fact—as Schiller has said that "the world likes to blacken whatever shines, and drag the sublime in the dust. . . ."

*

* *

Whereas the traditional literatures and arts manifest all their modes and all their diversity in a simultaneous manner—with, however, differences of accentuation according to the epochs—the West, starting with the Renaissance, manifests its cultural modes in a successive manner, following a route bristling with anathematizations and glorifications. The reason for this is in the last analysis a profound ethnic heterogeneity: that is to say, a certain incompatibility, among Europeans, between the Aryan and Semitic spirits on the one hand, and between the Roman and Germanic mentalities on the other; it is a situation in a certain sense equivalent to what the Hindus call a "mixture of castes," with the difference that the constituent elements are not hierarchized, but simply disparate; the West being in addition more individualistic than the East.

---

32. To also mention a philosopher, the "most valid" one that France has known since the Middle Ages.

A characteristic trait of Western culture from the late Middle Ages onwards is, moreover, a certain feminization: outwardly, the masculine costume manifests in fact, at least in the upper classes and above all among the princes, an excessive need to please women, which is a tell-tale sign; whereas in the culture in general, we can observe an increase in the imaginative and emotive sensibility, in short an expressivity which strictly speaking goes too far and renders souls worldly instead of interiorizing them. The distant cause of this trait could be in part the respect which, according to Tacitus, the Germans had for woman—a respect we are far from blaming—but this quite normal and praiseworthy feature would have been without any problematical consequences if there had not been another much more determinative factor, namely the Christian scission of society into clerics and laymen; because of this, lay society grew into a separate humanity which came more and more to believe that it had a right to worldliness, where woman—whether she liked it or not—evidently played a leading role.[33] We mention this aspect of Western culture because it explains a certain exteriorized and hypersensitive style of genius. And let us not forget to add that all this pertains to the mystery of Eve, and not to that of Mary which pertains to ascending *Mâyâ*.

One has to take a stand against the prejudice that every man of genius, even the most eminent intellectual, is necessarily intelligent,

---

33. A sign of this lay autocracy and the worldliness resulting from it is, as regards vestimentary manifestations, the low-cut neckline of women, already criticized by Dante and paradoxical not only from the standpoint of Christian asceticism, but also from the standpoint of Semitic legalism which makes no distinction between clerics and laymen since it attributes a sacred character to society as a whole. It is not the phenomenon of denudation which is astonishing here—for it exists legitimately in Hinduism and elsewhere—but the fact that this phenomenon occurs in Christian surroundings; the same remark holds good for the prominence of the male organs in certain costumes of the late Middle Ages. It could also be said that the frivolous character of lay customs—notably the balls—is like the counterpart of the exaggerated rigorism of the convents, and that this far too ostentatious disparity points to a disequilibrium which is the fomenter of all sorts of subsequent oscillations. In India, the maharajah covered with pearls and the yogi covered with ashes are certainly dissimilar, but both are "divine images."

and that it is enough for an Einstein to be intelligent in mathematics for him to be equally intelligent in other domains—in politics for example—which in fact was certainly not the case. There are men who are geniuses in a single domain and who are all the less gifted in other respects; examples of fragmentary, unilateral, asymmetric, disproportional genius are provided above all by those writers or artists—and they are numerous—who compensate for their creative sublimity by a trivial or even odious character. In a normal world, one would readily do without their creations and the hidden poison they contain and transmit in most cases; not in all cases though, since there is the possibility of intermittent "mediumship," as we have explained above.

Among many men of varying genius we can see a "brilliant intelligence" having no connection either with metaphysical truth or with eschatological reality. Now the definition of integral or essential, and thus efficacious, intelligence is the adequation to the real, both "horizontal" and "vertical," terrestrial and celestial. A consciousness having neither the sense of priorities nor that of proportions is not really intelligence; it is at the very most a reflection of intelligence in the mirror of the mind, and we are quite willing to have it called "intelligence" in an entirely relative and provisional sense; human discernment may be exercised in a very limited theater, but the mental activity involved is still discernment. Conversely, it can happen that a spiritually—thus fundamentally—intelligent man lacks intelligence on the plane of earthly things or some of them; but that is because, rightly or wrongly, he cannot bring himself to take an interest in them.[34]

To come back to the poets: it is impossible to deny that the plays of Montherlant are quite intelligent in their way, but the fact that the author—who possessed an excessively uneven and contradictory character[35]—scarcely manifests any discernment outside dramatic art, illustrates well enough the relativity and the precariousness of

34. It is no exaggeration on our part to say that for some people, the most intelligent men are the Nobel prize winners in physics; given such blunders, it is quite excusable to say things which run the risk of being truisms.

35. That is to say that the plebeian side of his personality was opposed to the aristocratic side, just as in Heine the cynical was opposed to the lyrical; in both cases, the trouble is not in the bipolarity but in the antagonism between the two poles.

what we may call "worldly intelligence." One should not forget in this context the role of passions: pride limits intelligence, which amounts to saying that in the last analysis it slays it: it destroys its essential functions, while allowing the surface mechanism[36] to remain incidentally, as if in mockery.

In this order of ideas—and leaving aside the question of pride—we might also express ourselves as follows: in a certain sense it was very intelligent on the part of the Greeks and their emulators to have represented the human body in all exactitude and all its contingency; but more fundamentally, it was quite unintelligent on their part to have taken this trouble and to have neglected other modes of adequation, those precisely which were developed by the Hindus and the Buddhists. Intelligence as such is above all the sense of priorities and proportions, as we have pointed out above; it implies a priori a sense of the Absolute and of the hierarchy of corresponding values.

*

* *

Thus, neither efficacy in a particular domain nor the phenomenon of genius is necessarily to be identified with intelligence as such. Another error of evaluation to be refuted is the mania for seeing genius where there is none; this is to confuse genius with extravagance, snobbery, cynicism, and impertinence, and to seek an object of adoration because one no longer has God. Or again, it is to adore oneself in an artificial and illusory projection; or it is quite simply to admire vice and darkness.

Nothing is easier than to be original thanks to a false absolute, all the more so when this absolute is negative, for to destroy is easier than to construct. Humanism is the reign of horizontality, either naive or perfidious; and since it is also—and by that very fact—the negation of the Absolute, it is a door open to a multitude of sham

---

36. The meaning of human life is sanctification, without which man would not be man. "Life is no longer worthy of me," said—or thought he could say—an individualist who refused to accept a trial; whereas every man ought to say from the outset "I am not worthy of life," while accepting the trial in order to become worthy of it. Because, for man to be worthy of life is to be worthy of God; without forgetting that *Domine non sum dignus*, which expresses another relationship.

absolutes, which in addition are often negative, subversive, and destructive. It is not too difficult to be original with such intentions and such means; all one needs is a little imagination. It should be noted that subversion includes not only philosophical and moral schemes designed to undermine the normal order of things, but also—in literature and on a seemingly harmless plane—all that can satisfy an unhealthy curiosity: namely all the narrations that are fantastic, grotesque, lugubrious, "dark," thus satanic in their way, and well-fitted to predispose men to all excesses and all perversions; this is the sinister side of romanticism. Without fearing in the least to be "childlike" or caring in the least to be "adult," we readily dispense with these somber lunacies, and are fully satisfied with Snow White and Sleeping Beauty.

Literary "realism" is truly subversive because it aims at reducing reality to the vilest contingencies of nature or chance, instead of leading it back to its archetypes and consequently to the divine intentions, in short, to the essential which any normal man should perceive without difficulty, and which any man perceives notably in love, or in connection with such phenomena as provoke admiration. This is, moreover, the mission of art: to remove the shells in order to reveal the kernels; to distill the materials until the essences are extracted. Nobility is nothing else but a natural disposition for this alchemy, and this on all planes.

As for subversion: on the plane of ideologies, there are not only those which are frankly pernicious, thus negative despite their masks, there are also those which are formally positive—more or less—but limitative and poisonous and ultimately destructive in their way, such as nationalism and other narcissistic fanaticisms; the majority—if not all—being as ephemeral as they are myopic. And the worst among these false idealisms are, in certain respects, those which annex and adulterate religion.

But let us come back to the question of originality which we broached above. In order to define true originality, we shall make the following statement: art in the broadest sense is the crystallization of archetypal values, and not a literal copy of the phenomena of nature or of the soul; and that is why the terms "reality" and "realism" have another meaning in art than in the sciences; the latter record phenomena without disdaining accidental and insignificant contingencies, whereas art, on the contrary, operates by abstraction in order to extract gold from "raw material." Positive originality cannot arise from our desires; it proceeds from a combination of our traditional environment and our legitimate personality, a combination pregnant with archetypes susceptible of manifesting themselves in it, and disposed to doing so. In a word, art is the quest for—and the revelation of—the center, within us as well as around us.

*
* *

At the antipodes of the false genius exalted by people is situated the true genius of which people are unaware: among famous men, Lincoln is one such example, he who owes a large part of his popularity to the fact that people took him—and still take him—for the incarnation of the average American; as average as possible, which he absolutely was not, and could not have been, precisely because he was a man of genius; a man whose intelligence, capacity and nobility of character went far beyond the level of the average.[37]

Another case—and a rather strange one—of a genius in complete possession of his center is Gandhi; a strange case, we say, because he seems to be a borderline case from the standpoint of sanctity. Technically speaking, Gandhi can no doubt be included in the category of saints; traditionally speaking, the question remains open. "Against" him, there are his somewhat too liberal, even Tolstoian ideas, although—despite certain reservations—he rejected neither the Vedas nor the castes; "in his favor," one can insist on his practice of *japa-yoga,* which from the traditional standpoint is a good argument, but does not mean sanctity as such. We record the phenomenon without wishing to settle the question in a peremptory manner; what matters is that we have here a possibility characteristic of the cyclical period in which we live: a period of ambiguities, paradoxes and also of exceptions. Given the fact

---

37. It was during Lincoln's administration that the formula "In God we trust" was first introduced in coinage, and it was Lincoln who made Thanksgiving Day a national holiday. We should like to mention in this context the greatness of soul of another statesman, Chiang Kai-shek: at the end of the Second World War he made a declaration enjoining his compatriots not to hate the Japanese people, which was an extraordinary gesture of lucidity and courage; not in itself, because there is no people worthy of hatred, but considering human nature and the circumstances.

that Gandhi did not found anything and that he had no disciples in the strict sense of the term, the problem of the degree of his spirituality[38] can remain unanswered.

The question of normal genius, unconditioned by any cultural abuse, allows us to pass to the following considerations, which have their importance in this context. The racist argument that the whites, and among them the Europeans, have more genius than other races, obviously loses much of its value—to say the least—in the light of what we have said about humanism and its consequences; because it is all too evident that neither a hypertrophy nor a deviation constitutes an intrinsic superiority. Still, when considering genius under its natural and legitimate aspect, one has a right to ask whether this phenomenon is also met with among peoples without writing, given the fact that they do not seem to have any such examples to offer; we reply without hesitation that genius lies within human nature and that it must be possible for it to occur wherever there are men. Obviously, the manifestation of genius depends on such cultural materials as are at the disposal of a racial or ethnic group; since these materials are relatively poor among the peoples in question, the manifestations of genius must be all the more intangible and exposed to oblivion, except for legends and proverbial expressions.[39]

Non-literate ethnic groups have at their disposal three ways of manifesting genius, in keeping with their way of life: firstly, the martial and royal genius; secondly, the oratorical and epic genius;[40] and

38. But we must insist emphatically on the factor that we have just pointed out, namely that Gandhi did not exercise the function of a spiritual master; our "tolerance" thus cannot be taken as opening the door to any technical irregularity.
39. "Not every man is the son of Gaika," the Zulus say, evoking the memory of a particularly gifted and glorious chief, but who has disappeared in the mists of time.
40. There have been true Demosthenes among the orators of the Red Indians. Some of their discourses, either complete or in fragments, have been preserved in writing; they strike one by the straight-forward, generous and moving grandeur of their language. We may mention here, by way of examples, three men of genius belonging to the red race: first, Hinmaton-Yalatkit ("Chief Joseph"), chief of the Sahaptin (Nez Percés), who in the opinion of American army officers was a prodigious strategist; then the Shawnee chief Tecumseh, who lived some decades earlier—at the beginning of the 19th century—and whose qualities as a statesman and magnanimous hero are almost proverbial in the New World; and finally Tammany or Tamanend, a sachem of the Leni-

thirdly, the contemplative genius, but this one rarely leaves any traces, whereas the two preceding types leave them more easily, the second one especially. If these ethnic groups have no sense of history, it is for the same reason that they have no writing: their whole conception of life is so to speak rooted in an "eternal present" and in a flux of things wherein the individual counts for nothing; time being a spiral movement around an invisible and immutable Center.

A factor which should not be overlooked when one is astonished at the lack of "culture" among non-literate peoples is that for them the surrounding nature furnishes all the nourishment that the soul requires. These ethnic groups feel no need to superimpose on the riches and beauties of nature riches and beauties springing from the imagination and creativity of men; they feel no need to listen to human language rather than to the language of the Great Spirit.[41] On the one hand, the lack of urban culture can of course be the result of degeneration; but on the other hand, this lack can be explained by a particular perspective and a free choice; both causes can evidently be combined. It should not be overlooked that the Hindu *sannyâsi*, who lives in the forest, does not worry about "culture," any more than does a Christian hermit; this is not an absolute criterion, but it nonetheless has its importance.[42]

Lenape (Delawares)—in the 17th century—who enjoyed a reputation for wisdom and holiness not only among the Indians, but even among the whites, who went as far as venerating him as the "patron of America" and gave his name to several of their societies.

41. The remark of a Sioux chief after a visit to a museum of fine arts: "You whites are strange men; you destroy the beauties of nature, then you daub a board with colors and call it a masterpiece."

42. Translator's note: Elsewhere the author has written: "In the life of a people there are as it were two halves: one constitutes the play of its earthly existence, the other its relationship with the Absolute. Now what determines the value of a people or of a civilization is not the literal form of its earthly dream—for here everything is only a symbol—but its capacity to 'feel' the Absolute and, in the case of specially privileged souls, to reach the Absolute. So it is completely illusory to set aside this 'absolute' dimension and evaluate a human world according to earthly criteria, as by comparing one civilization materially with another. The gap of some thousands of years separating the stone age of the Red Indians from the material and literary refinements of the white man counts for nothing compared with the contemplative intelligence and the virtues, which alone impart value to man and alone make up his permanent reality, or that something which enables us to evaluate him in a real manner, as it were in the sight of the Creator. To believe that some men are lagging behind us because their

And one has to keep clearly in mind the following: the marvels of the basilicas and the cathedrals, of the iconostases and the altar pieces, as well as the splendors of the Tibeto-Mongol and Japanese art or, prior to it, those of Hindu art, not forgetting the summits of the corresponding literatures—all this did not exist in the primitive epochs of these various traditions, epochs which were precisely the "golden ages" of these spiritual universes. Thus it appears that the marvels of traditional culture are like the swan songs of the celestial messages; in other words, to the extent that the message runs the risk of being lost, or is effectively lost, a need is felt—and Heaven itself feels this need—to exteriorize gloriously all that men are no longer capable of perceiving within themselves. Thenceforth it is outward things that have to remind men where their center lies; it is true that this is in principle the role of virgin nature, but in fact its language is only grasped where it assumes traditionally the function of a sanctuary.[43] Moreover, the two perspectives—sacred art and virgin nature—are not mutually exclusive, as is shown notably by Zen Buddhism; this proves that neither can altogether replace the other.

All that we have said above concerning non-literate peoples does not mean that they have no culture in the fully legitimate sense. Integrally human culture is linked to participation in the

earthly dream takes on modes more 'rudimentary' than our own—modes which are often for the same reason more sincere—is far more naive than to believe that the earth is flat or a volcano is a god; the most naive of all attitudes is surely to regard the dream as something absolute and to sacrifice to it all substantial values, forgetting that what is 'serious' only starts beyond its level, or rather that, if there is anything 'serious' in this world, it is so in connection with that which lies beyond it . . . When people talk about 'civilization' they generally attribute a qualitative meaning to the term, but civilization only represents a value provided it is supra-human in origin and implies for the 'civilized' man a sense of the sacred: only a people who really have this sense and draw their life from it are truly civilized. If it is objected that this reservation does not take account of the whole meaning of the term and that it is possible to conceive of a world that is 'civilized' though having no religion, the answer is that in this case the 'civilization' is devoid of value, or rather—since there is no legitimate choice between the sacred and other things—that it is the most fallacious of aberrations. A sense of the sacred is fundamental for every civilization because fundamental for man. . . ." (*Understanding Islam* [Bloomington, Indiana: World Wisdom, 1998], pp. 24-26).

43. Among the ancient Aryans, from India to Ireland—except, more or less, the Mediterraneans in historic times—and in our day still among the Shamanist peoples, Asiatic and American.

sacred, and this obviously has no necessary connection with literacy or with sedentary civilization. The immense stores of oral tradition and diverse forms of artistic expression testify to a formerly prodigious richness of soul in ancient man, and this was originally linked to sacred wisdom, of which virgin nature, precisely, is the primordial expression—an expression transparent to the integral symbolist mentality, although scarcely so to modern "culturism."

*
* *

After having spoken at the beginning of this exposition of the hierarchical types of mankind—the "intrinsic" and not simply institutional castes—we next became involved in reflections on an entirely different subject, that of genius, with digressions and illustrations for which we see no reason to apologize. In both cases, that of genius as well as that of the castes, it is always a question of man and his center: either because nature has bestowed on man a given personal center and consequently a particular fundamental tendency and a particular conception of duty and happiness—this is precisely what "caste" is—or because man, whatever his basis or starting point may be, sets off in search of his center and his reason for being.

Whoever says humanism, says individualism, and whoever says individualism, says narcissism, and consequently: breaching of that protective wall which is the human norm; thus rupture of equilibrium between the subjective and the objective, or between vagabond sensibility and pure intelligence. However, it is not easy to have completely unmixed feelings on the subject of profane "cultural" genius: if, on the one hand, one must condemn humanism and the literary and artistic principles derived from it, one cannot, on the other hand, help recognizing the value of this or that archetypal inspiration, and occasionally the personal qualities of a particular author; hence one can hardly escape a certain ambiguity. And the fact that a work, by reason of its cosmic message, can transmit values graspable only by a few—just as wine can at the same time do good to some and harm to others—this fact makes our judgments in many cases, if not objectively less precise, at least subjectively more hesitant; although it is always possible to simplify the problem by specifying in what respect a given work has value.

Be that as it may, what we wish to suggest in most of our considerations on modern genius is that humanistic culture, insofar as it functions as an ideology and therefore as a religion, consists essentially in being unaware of three things: firstly, of what God is, because it does not grant primacy to Him; secondly, of what man is, because it puts him in the place of God; thirdly, of what the meaning of life is, because this culture limits itself to playing with evanescent things and to plunging into them with criminal unconsciousness. In a word, there is nothing more inhuman than humanism, by the fact that it, so to speak, decapitates man: wishing to make of him an animal which is perfect, it succeeds in turning him into a perfect animal; not all at once—because it has the fragmentary merit of abolishing certain barbaric traits—but in the long run, since it inevitably ends by "re-barbarizing" society, while "dehumanizing" it *ipso facto* in depth. A fragmentary merit, we say, because softening of manners is good only on condition that it not corrupt man: that it not unleash criminality, and not open the door to all possible perversions. In the 19th century it was still possible to believe in an indefinite moral progress; in the 20th century came the brutal awakening; it was necessary to recognize that one cannot improve man by being content with the surface while destroying the foundations.

Thus, there is no doubt that talent or genius does not constitute a value in itself. One thing is absolutely certain—so much so that one hesitates to mention it—and that is that the best way to have genius is to have it through wisdom and virtue, hence through holiness. Creative genius can certainly be added to this plenitude as a supplementary gift—for others even more than for the one who possesses it—with the mission of transmitting elements of interiorization and thereby of liberation. To be sure, pure spirituality suffices unto itself; but no one will reproach Dante for having known how to write, nor Fra Angelico for having known how to paint.

To return to the first subject of our exposition: whatever the fundamental differences may be between the hierarchized human types—from the standpoint of that central core that constitutes the substance of a person—there is what we may call, not without reservations of course, "religious egalitarianism," to which we have alluded before; in the face of God man is always man and nothing else, whether or not he possesses a valid center. And man, being what he is, is always free to choose his center, his identity and his destiny: to build his house either on sand or on a rock.

"Free to choose": but in reality, the man who is conscious of his interest and concerned with his happiness has no choice; the purpose of freedom is to enable us to choose what we are in the depths of our heart. We are intrinsically free to the extent that we have a center which frees us: a center which, far from confining us, dilates us by offering us an inward space without limits and without shadows; and this Center is in the last analysis the only one there is.

Chapter 2

Loss of Our Traditional Values

Thomas Yellowtail

In the olden days the Indians had their freedom and they followed their traditional ways. Then the whites made us settle on reservations. People had to live close together and we were not free to live in our traditional way. People also lost sight of the true meaning of these ways. It was not long until a lot of the powers and sacred things that had been given to the Indians were taken back. That is what we were told by prophecies before the time of settlement on the reservations. Many medicine men who had had good medicine, good powers, lost them. This all happened gradually over the last one hundred years, until today there are fewer men with less spiritual power and understanding. Those who still have spiritual gifts or medicine—and there are a few left—don't have as strong a power as in the days when the Indians were still free to roam the country and live in the traditional manner. As time went on, the Indians became more "civilized" and learned to live in the white man's ways, and so all of the spiritual powers were diminished. People lost sight of religion and prayer, so it seems that the old prophecies were correct. Back in the days when we were free, when our people knew more about Nature and important things, almost every man had medicine powers and the only life people knew was centered on the sacred. The real medicine man could do wonders in those days. It is really the modern world and "civilization" that is causing us to lose all these things. In olden times, the people had their values centered on spiritual concerns. The spiritual Powers, the givers of medicines, are taking those sacred things back from us because we do not know how to care for them correctly.

Modern Indians care little for spiritual things and traditional ways, so there are very few traditional people remaining with real medicine or understanding. Modern civilization has no understanding of sacred matters. Everything is backwards. This makes it even more important that young people follow what is left today.

Even though many of the sacred ways are no longer with us, what we have left is enough for anyone, and if it is followed it will lead as far as the person can go. The four rites that we have spoken of in this work[1] form the center of the religion: the sweat lodge for purification; the vision quest for the spiritual retreat; the daily prayer with the offering of tobacco smoke; and the Sun Dance itself. With all this, any sincere person can realize his inner spiritual center. I tell them to join, join the Sun Dance. Try to understand about the old sacred ways, the Sun Dance Way. Of course there are a lot of young people who do come in, but their sincerity may not be there. They just come in and out of the Sun Dance and then go away. They do not come to our prayer meetings, and we do not see them again, not until the next Sun Dance. Three or four days a year at the time of the Sun Dance is not enough.

It is important that the young people understand the difference between the traditional ways and the modern world we live in today. I have spoken before about the sacred support that was always present for the traditional Indians. With this support everywhere, from the moment you arose and said your first prayer, until the moment you went to sleep, you could at least see what was necessary in order to lead a proper life. Even the dress that you wore every day had sacred meanings, such as the bead work designs on the clothing, and wherever you went or whatever you did, whether you were hunting, making weapons, or whatever you were doing, you were participating in a sacred life and you knew who you were and carried a sense of the sacred with you. All of the forms had meaning, even the tipi and the sacred circle of the entire camp. Of course the life was hard and difficult and not all Indians followed the rules. But the support of the traditional life and the presence of Nature everywhere brought great blessings on all the people[2].

The world we live in is quite different. Young people today can't read the signs of Nature and they do not even know the names of

---

1. *Yellowtail: Crow Medicine Man and Sun Dance Chief,* recorded and edited by Michael Oren Fitzgerald, University of Oklahoma Press, 1991.
2. In the vast expanses of Nature in which the traditional Indian roamed, he was in one sense without limits on this freedom; in another sense he was always confined to the strict role placed upon him by his religious universe. In every moment and in every place, everything reinforced the sacred obligations of his heritage.

the different animals. When a bird calls, or we see the prints left by an animal, most of our people will not know the name of the animal that stands close by. If we walk down a hill, many of our grandchildren will not even know that they have walked over an "Indian turnip" or some other valuable food. What is worse, many young people do not even look, or sometimes even care, where they are walking and do not observe the beautiful things that *Acbadadea* has created. It almost makes me cry to see how some young people waste precious gifts. They will let food spoil or waste water and electricity. People do not seem to realize the value of the gifts they have been given; they think things will always be there when they need something. These same people will have a big surprise someday, because sooner or later they will be shown their errors.

Look at the way people travel and work nowadays. You always hear people say, "We are in the fast age." Everything has to be fast, according to the way people want to do things nowadays. If we are going a great distance, the destination or place we are going to isn't going to move; it is standing still, so there is no need to be in such a hurry. In addition to not being safe, there are other dangers in this fast way of life. It is a problem with their entire way of living. I think it is wise to take a little more time in whatever you're doing and do it right; then, whatever it is, it will last longer. If you do something too fast, it will deteriorate. People should ask themselves what it is that they are doing and why it is that they are doing it. So many people today don't even think; they just do something.

Many of the modern things that we have now have made everything worse. We didn't have television until a few years ago, and since the television has come into use, people have just fallen crazy for it. It is something that I don't care for myself. It makes people lazy and gives them strange ideas about life. For instance, it seems as if there isn't any modesty anymore. When people see something on television, they think it is right. They don't think for themselves; they let the television think for them. Television is something that is not good for the world. It is too bad that most people don't realize how something like television can ruin all of our true values.

It seems as if everything in today's world is set up so that everyone can keep going so fast that they never have to consider why they were given the miracle of life. It is too bad that people waste their life and their intelligence by becoming part of this fast society. If they just stopped for a moment and considered that they will all die and meet their Lord, I wonder what they would do?

One of the reasons our society is so fast is the machine. Machinery has changed the manner in which we live, and all of our values regarding this world. In olden days, it required manual labor for just about everything. Everyone had a responsibility and everyone helped each other. There was no money to keep and to possess, so you couldn't acquire more things than your neighbor. The olden-day Indians moved about the countryside and they couldn't carry more than what they needed. The qualities that a man possessed within himself were important, not what outward possessions he had. We have talked about how the Indians give away things to express their inner beliefs.

In those days, everyone knew what was expected of him and the Indian Way taught him just how to do it. Not all olden-day Indians lived up to the tribal goals, even though the sacred center was present. Today some people still pray as they should, even though the sacred center is almost gone. But the goals of the society in those days and today are different and this is something that everyone must understand. We have spoken about the manner in which we carry out our Sun Dance Religion and how everything has a meaning, a purpose. So it was with everything the olden-day Indians did, and so it should be today. You would begin to understand the mysteries of this world in which we have been placed and you would know what you must do to prepare yourself to meet death, to enter the world beyond that we cannot see.

Many of the Sun Dance ceremonies are difficult to endure; it is an ordeal to complete them. This is good and it helps us remember that there is a greater responsibility in life. Life is a gift that you are free to use as you see fit; but you also have to understand that your actions, your choices, are being observed by powers that you do not see. If everything is easy for us and if our concerns are only regarding our possessions, then we lose sight of what is important. In difficult times, we are always prepared to face death; it may come today. So it should be every day in everything we do. We must prepare ourselves today to meet our Lord, The Maker of All Things Above. People always think that there is plenty of time left to pray later. People who want to accumulate more wealth are always thinking that "I'll wait until later." The world today, and the way people do things, encourage people to be lazy in their spiritual duties.

Manual labor is not required anymore; it is all done by machinery. One man can now do a big field of hay all by himself. The hay is cut and baled by machines; they have even got machinery now that picks it up and brings it in. Without touching anything, the machine puts the bales there and they are already on the stack. Many men used to be required to work many days, but now it is practically done in one day with these machines. Sugar beet farming used to require several men; quite a few working people are all now eliminated by modern machinery. Men going around looking for farm jobs can hardly get any work now. No one needs them because the machinery they have takes care of all that.

Even in the cattle industry, it is the same way. There used to be some good cowboys who would take care of the work on the cattle ranch. A lot of them cannot find jobs anymore. There are machines now that take their place. So it looks as if we get to the time when many good men cannot find any work at all. That is not like it should be.

Nowadays men want to accumulate money and then they use the money to buy machines so that all the work can be done more quickly; then they can accumulate even more money. That is all the rich man thinks about. What about the men who want to work for a living? They have no jobs and nothing at all to do. People end up working against each other, as the people without money and machines start to hate the others. Many of the wars in the world today result from this problem. Some men will criticize our Indian boys who can't find work and say that they are lazy, that if an Indian really wants to work he can find work. In some cases this is true, but it can't be true for everyone. Think about it: If everyone on the reservation really wanted to go out and look for a job, could everyone find one? The reason the answer is "no" can be seen when you realize the problems that money and machinery cause.[3]

3. United States government estimates place unemployment on the reservation at a minimum of 60 percent, while tribal estimates put the figure at over 80 percent. Most of the economic development on the reservation is based on the tribe's natural resources, notably coal, oil, and gas. Even if the energy base of the Crow could provide sufficient one-time per capita payments to tribal members so that they could live without working, the duration of those resources

Now what happens when one good Indian boy does go out and find a job with good, hard work? Everyone should be proud of him, but they are not. Jealousy is created by the fact that people are competing against one another. On our reservations today, people are jealous of each other. No one cooperates. People blame each other for all of the problems, and criticize people who do work hard and who try to help. Many people will criticize me for talking to you. They will find some fault or try to say that I made an error in something that I have told you. "Why does that white man want to write a book about the Indian religion? What does he know?" If they find one small error, they will condemn everything we have done. This is their problem and it will only hurt them. People should think about what we have tried to accomplish with this work. Maybe people can understand that what we see in this modern world is bad, that most of the values people have today are backwards. To follow the way of the machine world will not prepare you to meet your Maker either in this life or after death.

It is true that we cannot just go back to the olden days either. What good does it do to wish you were an olden-day Indian? Why criticize your brother and try to find faults in everyone else? Will that make you a better person because you have decided that someone else has faults? Some Indians will face their problems with a bottle. This is very bad—drugs, too. It corrupts all of our youngsters. How can any of this solve problems? It just makes everything worse, because they don't try to make anything out of themselves. These same people expect that they will be given things by the tribe, the government. They think that it is the responsibility of others to take care of them. They think we should sell our coal, our water, our resources, so that they will be provided for. They don't care at all about our children. All that matters is their own welfare today. These men will certainly receive their just reward when they meet their Maker.

We have spoken about the Sun Dance Religion and what it means for us today. You can see that everything is very different today and that many of the sacred things and sacred ways that were

would be limited. Upon their depletion, the tribe's situation would be dire. The ability of tribal leaders to find long-term solutions for Crow economic development with the energy funds and to overcome pressure for excessive short-term per capita payments will determine the future welfare of the tribe.

with our Indian people in the olden days are lost. This was bound to come, for we did not deserve to keep them because we no longer had respect for them. But it does no good to blame any one person or country for our present-day situation. All these events were foreseen in sacred prophecies from all of the great religions.

No one person is to blame for our present state. Everyone who fails to live up to his spiritual duties causes further problems for everyone. Therefore, I tell people, "Don't criticize your neighbor; that will not help anyone. It is not good to fight Indian against Indian; it just makes matters worse. Work on yourself first; prepare yourself to meet your Lord."

Reprinted from *Yellowtail: Crow Medicine Man and Sun Dance Chief*, by Michael O. Fitzgerald (Oklahoma: University of Oklahoma Press, 1991), 187-193. Copyright © 1991 by the University of Oklahoma Press. Reprinted by permission of the publisher and author.

Chapter 3

Modern Psychology

Titus Burckhardt

"The object of psychology is the psychic; unfortunately it is also its subject." Thus wrote a famous psychologist of our time.[1] According to this opinion, every psychological judgment inevitably participates in the essentially subjective, not to say passionate and tendentious, nature of its object; for, according to this logic, no one understands the soul except by means of his own soul, and the latter, for the psychologist, is, precisely, purely psychic, and nothing else. Thus no psychologist, whatever be his claim to objectivity, escapes this dilemma, and the more categorical and general his affirmations in this realm are, the more they are suspect; such is the verdict that modern psychology pronounces in its own cause, when it is being sincere towards itself. But whether it be sincere or not, the relativism expressed in the words just quoted is always inherent in it. This relativism is also a kind of Prometheanism that would make of the psychic element the ultimate reality of man. It is the root of the numerous divergences within this discipline, and it dominates it to the point of contaminating everything that it touches: history, philosophy, art, and religion; all of them become psychological at its touch, and thereby also subjective, and thus devoid of objective and immutable certainties.[2]

---

1. C. G. Jung, *Psychology and Religion* (New Haven, Yale, 1938), p. 62
2. "I can find no reason to be surprised at seeing psychology exchange visits with philosophy, for is not the act of thinking, the foundation of all philosophy, a psychic activity which, as such, directly concerns psychology? Must not psychology embrace the soul in its total extension, which includes philosophy, theology, and countless other things? In the face of all the richly diversified religions, there rise up, as the supreme instance perhaps of truth or error, the immutable data of the human soul." (C. C. Jung, *L' Homme à la Découverte de son Âme* [Paris, 1962], p. 238) This amounts to replacing truth by psychology; it is totally forgotten that there are no "immutable data" outside of that which is immutable by its own nature, namely, the intellect. In any case, if the "act of thinking" is no more than a "psychic activity", by what right does psychology set itself up as the "supreme instance", since it too is but one "psychic activity" amongst others?

39

But all a priori relativism is inconsequential towards itself. Despite the admitted precariousness of its point of view, modern psychology behaves like every other science: it passes judgments and believes in their validity, and in this connection it leans unwittingly, and without admitting it, on an innate certainty: indeed, if we can observe that the psychic is "subjective", in the sense of being dominated by a certain egocentric bias that imposes on it certain limits, or by a particular "coloring", this is because there is something in us which is not subject to these limits and tendencies, but which transcends them and in principle dominates them. This something is the intellect, and it is the intellect that normally provides us with the criteria which alone can shed light on the fluctuating and uncertain world of the *psyché;* this is obvious, but it nevertheless remains totally outside modern scientific and philosophical thinking.

It is important above all not to confuse intellect and reason: the latter is indeed the mental reflection of the transcendent intellect, but in practice it is only what one makes of it, by which we mean that, in the case of the modern sciences, its functioning is limited by the empirical method itself; at the level of the latter, reason is not so much a source of truth as a principle of coherence. For modern psychology it is even less than that, for if scientific rationalism lends a relatively stable framework to one's observation of the physical world, it reveals itself as entirely insufficient when it comes to describing the world of the soul; for surface psychic movements, those whose causes and aims are situated on the plane of current experience, can hardly be translated into rational terms. The whole chaos of lower—and mostly unconscious—psychic possibilities escapes both rationality and what transcends rationality, and this means that both the major part of the psychic world and the metaphysical realm will appear "irrational" according to this way of thinking. Hence a certain tendency, inherent in modern psychology, to relativize reason itself, a tendency that is self-contradictory, since psychology cannot dispense with rational methods. Psychology finds itself confronted with a domain which on all sides overflows the horizon of a science founded on empiricism and Cartesianism.

For this reason, the majority of modern psychologists ensconce themselves in a sort of pragmatism; it is in "committed" experience, together with a coldly clinical attitude, that they see some guarantee of "objectivity". In point of fact, the movements of the soul cannot be studied from the outside, as in the case of corporeal phenomena; to know what they mean, they have in a sense to be lived, and this involves the subject of the observer, as was justly pointed out by the psychologist at the outset. As for the mental faculty that "controls" the experiment, what is this but a more or less arbitrary "common sense", one inevitably colored by preconceived ideas? Thus the would-be objectivity of the psychic attitude changes nothing in regard to the uncertain nature of the experiment, and so, in the absence of a principle that is both inward and immutable, one returns to the dilemma of the psychic striving to grasp the psychic.

The soul, like every other domain of reality, can only be truly known by what transcends it. Moreover, this is spontaneously and implicitly admitted in people's recognition of the moral principle of justice, which demands that men should overcome their individual subjectivity. Now we could not overcome it, if the intelligence, which guides our will, were itself nothing but a psychic reality; and intelligence would not transcend the *psyché* if, in its essence, it did not transcend the plane of phenomena, both inward and outward. This observation suffices to prove the necessity and the existence of a psychology deriving in a sense from above and not claiming a priori an empirical character. But although this order of things is inscribed in our very nature, it will never be recognized by modern psychology; despite its own reactions against the rationalism of yesterday, it is no closer to metaphysics than any other empirical science—indeed quite the contrary, since its perspective, which assimilates the suprarational to the irrational, predisposes it to the worst of errors.

What modern psychology lacks entirely is criteria enabling it to situate the aspects or tendencies of the soul in their cosmic context. In traditional psychology, these criteria are provided according to two principal "dimensions": on the one hand, according to a cosmology that "situates" the soul and its modalities in the hierarchy of states of existence, and, on the other hand, according to a morality directed toward a spiritual end. The latter may provisionally espouse the individual horizon; it nonetheless keeps in view the universal principles attaching the soul to an order more vast than itself. Cosmology in a sense circumscribes the soul; spiritual morality sounds its depths. For just as a current of water reveals its force and direction only when it breaks against an object that resists it, so the soul can show its tendencies and fluctuations only in relation to an immutable principle; whoever wishes to know the nature of the *psyché* must resist it, and one truly resists it only when one places oneself at a point which corresponds, if not effectively then at least virtually or symbolically, to the Divine Self, or to the intellect which is like a ray that emanates from the latter.

Thus traditional psychology possesses both an impersonal and "static" dimension (namely, cosmology), and a personal and "operative" dimension (namely, morality or the science of the virtues), and it is necessarily so, because genuine knowledge of the soul results from knowledge of oneself. He who, by the eye of his essence, is able to "objectivize" his own psychic form, by that very fact knows all the possibilities of the psychic or subtle world; and this intellectual "vision" is both the outcome and, if need be, the guarantor of every sacred science of the soul.

For the majority of modern psychologists, traditional morality—which they readily confuse with a purely social or conventional morality—is nothing but a kind of psychic dam, useful on occasion but more often a hindrance or even harmful for the "normal" development of the individual. This opinion is propagated especially by Freudian psychoanalysis, which became widely applied in some countries, where it has practically usurped the function that elsewhere belongs to the sacrament of confession: the psychiatrist replaces the priest, and the bursting of complexes that had previously been repressed takes the place of absolution. In ritual confession the priest is but the impersonal representative—necessarily discreet—of the Truth that judges and pardons; the penitent, by admitting his sins, in a sense "objectivizes" the psychic tendencies that these sins manifest. By repenting, he detaches himself from them, and by receiving sacramental absolution, his soul is virtually reintegrated in its primitive equilibrium and centered on its divine essence. In the case of Freudian psychoanalysis,[3] on the other hand, man lays bare his psychic entrails, not before God, but to his fellow. He does not distance himself from the chaotic and obscure depths

---

3. The use of the adjective is to make it clear that it is indeed the method of Freud that we are discussing here, for in our own day some forms of psychoanalysis are more neutral and less pernicious, a fact which, from our point of view, is in no wise a justification.

of his soul, which the analyst unveils or stirs up, but on the contrary, he accepts them as his own, for he must say to himself: "This is what I am like in reality." And if he does not overcome, with the help of some salutary instinct, this kind of disillusionment from below, he will retain from it something like an intimate sullying; in most cases it will be his self-abandonment to collective mediocrity that for him will play the part of absolution, for it is easier to endure one's own degradation when it is shared with others. Whatever may be the occasional or partial usefulness of such an analysis in certain cases, the state described above is its more usual result, its premises being what they are.[4]

If the medicine of the traditional civilizations knows nothing analogous to modern psychotherapy, this is because the psychic cannot be treated by the psychic. The *psyché* is the realm of indefinite actions and reactions. By its own specific nature, it is essentially unstable and deceptive, so that it can be cured only by resorting to something situated "outside" or "above" it. In some cases one will act favorably upon it by re-establishing the humoral balance of the body, commonly upset by psychic affections;[5] in other cases it is only by the use of spiritual means, such as exorcism,[6] prayer, or a sojourn in holy places, that the soul can be restored to health.

Everyone is aware of the fact that modern psychology tries to explain psychologically the spiritual means just mentioned. In its eyes, the effect of a rite is one thing, and its theological or mystical interpretation is another. The effect of a rite, arbitrarily limited to the psychic and subjective domain alone, is attributed to psychic dispositions of ancestral origin, which the form of the rite is supposed to actualize. There is no hint of the timeless and superhuman meaning inherent in the rite or symbol—as if the soul could cure itself

---

4. René Guénon has observed that the principle whereby every psychoanalyst requires to be psychoanalyzed himself before being empowered to analyze others, raises the troublesome question as to who occupied the first place in the queue.

5. Usually a vicious circle ensues, with the psychic imbalance engendering a physical intoxication, which in its turn causes the psychic imbalance to worsen.

6. Cases of diabolical possession, such as manifestly call for the application of the rites of exorcism, seem to have become rarer nowadays, doubtless because demonic influences are no longer "compressed" by the dam of tradition, but are able to spread more or less everywhere in forms that are in a fashion "diluted".

through believing in the illusory projection of its own preoccupations, whether individual or collective. There is nothing, however, in this supposition that would trouble modern psychology, since it is ready to go much further than this, when it asserts, for example, that the fundamental forms of thought, the laws of logic, merely represent a residue of ancestral habits.[7] This path is one that leads to the outright denial of intelligence and to its replacement by biological fatalities, if indeed psychology can go that far without encompassing its own ruin.

In order to be able to "situate" the soul in relation to other cosmic realities or realms, one must refer to the cosmological scheme that represents the degrees of existence in the form of concentric circles or spheres. This scheme, which makes symbolical use of the geocentric conception of the visible universe, symbolically identifies the corporeal world with our terrestrial surroundings; around this center extends the sphere—or spheres—of the subtle or psychic world, surrounded in turn by the sphere of the world of pure Spirit. This representation is naturally limited by its own spatial character, but it nevertheless expresses very well the relationship that exists between these various states. Each of the spheres, considered in itself, presents itself as a complete and perfectly homogeneous whole, whereas from the "point of view" of the sphere immediately above, it is but a content thereof. Thus the corporeal world, envisaged at its own level, does not know the subtle world, just as the latter does not know the supra-formal world, precisely because it encloses only that which has a form. Furthermore, each of these worlds is known and dominated by that which exceeds and surrounds it. It is from the immutable and formless background of the Spirit that the subtle realities become detached as forms, and it is the soul which, through its sensory faculties, knows the corporeal.

This double relationship of things, which a priori is hidden from our individual vision, can be grasped in all its reality when one considers the very nature of sensible perception. On the one hand, this truly reaches the corporeal world, and no philosophical artifice will be able to convince us of the contrary; on the other hand, there is

---

7. They will say, for example, that logic is merely an expression of the physiological structure of our brain, and forget that, were it so, this statement would also be an expression of this same physiological fatality.

no doubt that all we perceive of the world are but those "images" of it that our mental faculty is able to keep hold of, and in this respect the whole fabric of impressions, memories, and anticipations—in short, everything that for us constitutes the sensible continuity and logical coherence of the world—is of a psychic or subtle nature. It is in vain that one will try to know what the world is "outside" this subtle continuity, since this "outside" does not exist: surrounded as it is by the subtle state, the corporeal world is but a content thereof, even though it appears, in the mirror of this state itself, as a materially autonomous order.[8]

It is obviously not the individual soul, but the entire subtle state that contains the physical world. The logical coherence of the latter presupposes the unity of the former, and this is manifested indirectly by the fact that the multiple individual visions of the sensible world, fragmentary though they be, substantially coincide and are integrated in one continuous whole. The individual soul participates in this unity both by the structure of its cognitive faculties, which is in conformity with the cosmic order, and also by its nature as subject, containing the physical world in its own way; in other words, the physical world is a "world" only in relation to the individual subject, by virtue of the cleaving of consciousness into object and subject, a cleaving that results precisely from the "egoic" polarization of the soul. By this same polarization, the soul is distinguished from the totality of the subtle state—the "total" or "universal soul" of Plotinus—without, however, being separated from it substantially. For if it were separated from it, our vision of the world would not be adequate to reality; but in fact it is so, in spite of the limitations and the relativity of all perception.

It is true that we ordinarily perceive only a fragment of the subtle world—the fragment that we "are", and that constitutes our "myself"—whereas the sensible world reveals itself to us in its macrocosmic continuity, as a whole that seems to include us. This is because the subtle world is the very field of individuation; in reality, we are plunged in the ocean of the subtle world as fishes are in water, and like them, we do not see that which constitutes our own element.

---

8. Nothing is more absurd than attempts to explain the perception of the material world in material terms.

As for the opposition between the "inward" psychic world and the "outward" corporeal world, this is actualized only in relation to, and in function of, the latter. In itself, the subtle world is neither "inward" nor "outward"; it is at most "non-outward", whereas the corporeal world is outward as such, which furthermore proves that it does not enjoy an autonomous existence.

The corporeal state and the psychic state together constitute formal existence; in its total extension, the subtle state is none other than formal existence, but one calls it "subtle" inasmuch as it escapes the laws of corporeity. According to one of the most ancient and most natural symbolisms, the subtle state may be compared to the atmosphere surrounding the earth which pervades all porous bodies and is the vehicle of life.

A phenomenon can only be truly understood through its relations, both "horizontal" and "vertical", with total Reality. This truth applies particularly, and in a certain sense practically, to psychic phenomena. The same psychic "event" can simultaneously be the response to a sensory impulsion, the manifestation of a wish, the consequence of a previous action, the trace of the typical and ancestral form of the individual, the expression of his genius, and the reflection of a supra-individual reality. It is legitimate to consider the psychic phenomenon in question under one or other of these aspects, but it would be unwarranted to seek to explain the movements and purposes of the soul by one—or even by several—of these aspects exclusively. In this connection let us quote the words of a therapist who is aware of the limitations of contemporary psychology:

> There is an ancient Hindu maxim whose truth is incontestable: "What a man thinks, that he becomes." If one steadfastly thinks of good deeds, one will end by becoming a good man; if one always thinks of weakness, one will become weak; if one thinks of how to develop one's strength (bodily or mental), one will become strong. Similarly, if for years one is engaged almost daily in stirring up Hades,[9] in explaining systematically the higher in terms of the lower, and at the same time ignoring everything in man's cultural history which, despite lamentable errors and misdeeds, has been

---

9. An allusion to the words of Virgil, *Flectere si nequeo superos, Acheronta movebo* ("If I cannot bend the Heavens, I shall stir up hell"), which Freud quoted at the beginning of his *Interpretation of Dreams*.

regarded as worthwhile, one can scarcely avoid the risk of losing all discernment, of levelling down the imagination (a source of our life), and of severely reducing one's mental horizon.[10]

Ordinary consciousness illuminates only a restricted portion of the individual soul, and the latter represents only a tiny part of the psychic world. Nevertheless, the soul is not cut off from the rest of this world; its situation is not that of a body rigorously limited by its own extension and separated from other bodies. What distinguishes the soul from the rest of the vast subtle world is uniquely its own particular tendencies, which define it—if one may employ a simplified image—as a spatial direction defines the ray of light that follows it. By these very tendencies, the soul is in communion with all the cosmic possibilities of analogous tendencies or qualities; it assimilates them and is assimilated by them. For this reason, the science of cosmic tendencies—the *gunas* of Hindu cosmology—is fundamental for the knowledge of the soul. In this connection, it is not the outward context of a psychic phenomenon—the accidental occasion for its manifestation—that matters essentially, but its connection with *sattva, rajas,* or *tamas*—the "upward," "expansive," and "downward" tendencies—which confers on it its rank in the hierarchy of inward values.

Since the motives of the soul are perceptible only through the forms that manifest them, it is on these forms or manifestations that a psychological assessment must needs be founded. Now, the part played by the *gunas* in any form whatsoever can be measured only in a purely qualitative manner, by means of precise and decisive—but in no wise quantitative—criteria, such as are entirely lacking in the wholly profane psychology of our time.

There are some psychic "events" whose repercussions traverse all the degrees of the subtle world "vertically", since they touch on the essences; others—these are ordinary psychic movements—only obey the "horizontal" coming and going of the *psyché;* and finally, there are those that come from the subhuman depths. The first mentioned are not capable of being expressed entirely—they comprise an element of mystery—and yet the forms which they may

---

10. Hans Jacob, *Western Psychology and Hindu Sâdhana* (London, Allen & Unwin, 1961). The author of this work is a former disciple of Jung, who later discovered the doctrine and method—immeasurably greater—of the Hindu *sâdhana,* which enabled him to subject Western psychology to a just criticism.

from time to time evoke in the imagination are clear and precise, like those that characterize authentic sacred arts. The last mentioned, namely demonic "inspirations", are unintelligible in their very forms; they "ape" the genuinely mysterious by the nebulous, obscure, and equivocal character of their formal manifestations; examples of this are readily to be found in contemporary art.

When studying the formal manifestation of the soul, one must, however, not forget that man's psycho-physical organism can display strange caesuras or discontinuities. Thus, for instance, in the case of the somewhat "anarchical" category of contemplatives known as "fools of God", the spiritual states do not manifest themselves harmoniously and normally and do not make use of the reason; inversely, an intrinsically pathological state—and as such dominated by infra-human and chaotic tendencies—may incidentally and by accident comprise openings onto supra-terrestrial realities; this is but saying that the human soul is of an inexhaustible complexity.

Viewed as a whole, the subtle world is incomparably vaster and more varied than the corporeal world. Dante expresses this by making the entire hierarchy of planetary spheres correspond to the subtle world, whereas he makes only the terrestrial domain correspond to the corporeal world. The subterranean position of the hells, in his system, merely indicates that the states in question are situated below the normal human state; in reality, they are also part of the subtle state, and this is why some medieval cosmologists place the hells symbolically between heaven and earth.[11]

Experience of the subtle world is subjective—except in the case of certain sciences quite unknown to the moderns—because consciousness, in identifying itself with subtle forms, is affected by their tendencies, just as a ray of light is turned from its course by the form of a wave that it happens to traverse. The subtle world is made up of forms; in other words, it comprises diversity and contrast; but these forms do not possess, in themselves or outside of their projection in the sensible imagination,[12] spatial and defined contours as in the

---

11. In Islam, it is said that the throne of the devil is located between earth and heaven, a doctrine which also makes clear the temptations to which those who follow the "vertical" path are exposed.

12. If some masters have compared the subtle world to the imagination, it is the imaginative activity, and not the images produced by the imagination, that they had in view.

case of corporeal forms. They are entirely active or, to be more exact, dynamic, pure activity belonging only to the essential "forms" or archetypes that are to be found in the pure Spirit. Now the ego or individual soul is itself one of the forms of the subtle world, and the consciousness that espouses this form is necessarily dynamic and exclusive; it realizes other subtle forms only insofar as these become modalities of its own egoic form.

Thus it is that in the dream state individual consciousness, even though reabsorbed into the subtle world, nonetheless remains turned back on itself; all the forms that it experiences in this state present themselves as simple prolongations of the individual subject, or at least they appear so in retrospect and inasmuch as they verge on the waking state. For in itself, and despite this subjectivism, the consciousness of the dreamer is obviously not impermeable to influences coming from the most diverse "regions" of the subtle world, as is proved, for example, by premonitory or telepathic dreams, which many people have experienced.[13] Indeed, while the imagery of a dream is woven from the very "substance" of the subject—a "substance" that is none other than the progressive actualization of his own psychic form—it nonetheless manifests, incidentally and to different degrees, realities of a cosmic order.

The content of a dream can be considered in many different ways. If one analyzes the *materia* of which it is composed one will find that it is constituted by all sorts of memories, and in this respect the current psychological explanation, which makes the dream the expression of subconscious residues, is largely right. It is not, however, excluded that a dream may also comprise "matters" that in no wise proceed from the personal experience of the dreamer and that are like traces of a psychic transfusion from one individual to another. There is also the economy of the dream, and in this connection we can quote the following description by C. G. Jung, which is exact despite the radically false theses of the author:

> The dream, deriving from the activity of the unconscious, gives a representation of the contents that slumber there; not of all the contents that figure in it, but only of certain of them which, by way of association, are actualized, crystallized, and selected, in correlation with the momentary state of consciousness.[14]

13. Empirical psychology no longer dares to deny this phenomenon.
14. *L'Homme à la Découverte de son Âme*, p. 205.

As for the hermeneutics of dreams, this eludes modern psychology in spite of the latter's efforts in this direction, because one cannot validly interpret images reflected by the soul without knowing to which level of reality they refer.

The images one retains on waking from a dream generally represent only a shadow of the psychic forms experienced in the dream state itself. On passing into the waking state, a sort of decantation occurs—one can be aware of this—and something of the reality inherent in the dream evaporates more or less rapidly. There exists, nevertheless, a certain category of dreams, well-known to traditional oneirocrisy, the memory of which persists with an incisive clarity, and this can happen even if the profound content of these dreams appears to conceal itself. Such dreams, which mostly occur at dawn and continue until waking, are accompanied by an irrefutable feeling of objectivity; otherwise put, they comprise a more than merely mental certainty. But what characterizes them above all, and independently of their moral influence on the dreamer, is the high quality of their forms, disengaged from every turbid or chaotic residue. These are the dreams that come from the Angel; in other words, from the Essence that connects the soul to the supra-formal states of the being.

Since there are dreams of divine or angelic inspiration, their opposite must also exist, and these are dreams of satanic impulsion, containing palpable caricatures of sacred forms. The sensation accompanying them is not one of cool and serene lucidity, but of obsession and vertigo; it is the attraction of an abyss. The infernal influences sometimes ride the wave of a natural passion, which opens the way for them, so to speak. They are, however, distinguishable from the elementary character of passion by their prideful and negative tendency, accompanied either by bitterness or else by sadness. As Pascal said: "He who tries to play the angel will play the beast", and indeed nothing is so apt to provoke caricatures, both in dreams and out of them, as the unconsciously pretentious attitude of the man who mixes God with his own highly particularized ego—the classical cause of many of the psychoses studied by post-Freudian psychologism.[15]

---

15. In a general way, contemporary psychology delves into the observation of pathological cases, and views the soul only through this clinical perspective.

It was starting from the analysis of dreams that C. G. Jung developed his famous theory about the "collective unconscious". His observation of the fact that a certain category of dream images could not be explained simply on the basis of their being residues of individual experiences led Jung to distinguish, within the unconscious domain whence dreams are fed, between a "personal" zone whose contents represent basically the other face of individual psychic life, and a "collective" zone made up of latent psychic dispositions of an impersonal character, such as never offer themselves to direct observation, but manifest themselves indirectly through "symbolic" dreams and "irrational" impulses. At first sight, this theory has nothing extravagant about it, except its use of the term "irrational" in connection with symbolism. It is easy to understand that the individual consciousness centered on the empirical ego leaves on the margin or even outside itself everything which, in the psychic order, is not effectively attached to that center, just as a light projected in a given direction decreases towards the surrounding darkness. But this is not how Jung understands the matter. For him, the non-personal zone of the soul is unconscious as such; in other words, its contents can never become the direct object of the intelligence, whatever be its modality or however great its extension.

> Just as the human body displays a common anatomy, independently of racial differences, so also the psyché possesses, beyond all cultural and mental differences, a common *substratum,* which I have named the collective unconscious. This unconscious psyché, which is common to all men, is not made up of contents capable of becoming conscious, but solely of latent dispositions giving rise to certain reactions that are always identical.[16]

And the author goes on to insinuate that it is here a question of ancestral structures that have their origin in the physical order:

> The fact that this collective unconscious exists is simply the psychic expression of the identity of cerebral structures beyond all racial differences . . . the different lines of psychic evolution start out from one and the same trunk, whose roots plunge through all the ages. It is here that the psychic parallel with the animal is situated.[17]

16. C. G. Jung, *The Secret of the Golden Flower* (New York, 1931), introduction.
17. *Ibid.*

One notices the plainly Darwinian turn of this thesis, the disastrous consequences of which show themselves in the following passage: "It is this that explains the analogy, indeed the identity, of mythological motives and of symbols as means of human communication in general."[18] Myths and symbols would thus be the expression of an ancestral psychic fund that brings man near to the animal! They have no intellectual or spiritual foundation, since

> from the purely psychological point of view, it is a question of common instincts of imagining and acting. All conscious imagination and action have evolved on the basis of these unconscious prototypes and remain permanently attached to them, and this is especially so when consciousness has not yet attained a very high degree of lucidity, in other words, as long as it is still, in all its functions, more dependent on instinct than on conscious will, or more affective than rational . . .[19]

This quotation clearly indicates that, for Jung, the "collective unconscious" is situated "below", at the level of physiological instincts. It is important to bear this in mind, since the term "collective unconscious" in itself could carry a wider and in a fashion more spiritual meaning, as certain assimilations made by Jung seem to suggest, especially his use—or rather his usurpation—of the term "archetype" to signify the latent, and as such inaccessible, contents of the "collective unconscious". For though the archetypes do not belong to the psychic realm, but to the world of pure Spirit, they are nevertheless reflected at the psychic level—as virtualities of images in the first place—before becoming crystallized, according to the circumstances, in images properly so-called, so that a certain psychological application of the term "archetype" could at a pinch be justified. But Jung defines the "archetype" as an "innate complex"[20] and describes its action on the soul thus: "Possession by an archetype makes of a man a purely collective personage, a kind of mask, under which human nature can no longer develop, but degenerates progressively."[21] As if an archetype, which is an immediate and supra-formal determination of Being—and non-limitative by this very fact—could in some way cast a spell on and vampirize the soul!

18. *Ibid.*
19. *Ibid.*
20. See *L' Homme à la Découverte de son Âme* line, p. 311
21. See *Two Essays on Analytical Psychology* (Pantheon, New York, 1966), p. 234.

What is really in question in the more or less pathological case envisaged by Jung? Simply a dissociation of the possibilities inherent in the subtle form of a man, a form that includes multiple aspects, each of which has something unique and irreplaceable about it. In every non-degenerate human individual there is to be found in potency a man and a woman, a father and a mother, a child and an old man, as well as various qualities or "dignities" inseparable from the original and ontological position of man, such as priestly and royal qualities, those of a creative craftsman, of a servant, and so forth. Normally all these possibilities complete one another; here there is no irrational fund of the soul, for the coexistence of these diverse possibilities or aspects of the human form is perfectly intelligible in itself and can be hidden only from the eyes of a mentality or civilization that has become one-sided and false. Any genius-like development of one of these multiple possibilities or dispositions inherent in the human soul requires, moreover, the integration of the complementary possibilities; the true man of genius is a balanced being, for where there is no balance there is no greatness either. The opposite of such a development is a barren and pathological exaggeration of one of the soul's possibilities at the expense of the others, leading to that kind of moral caricature compared by Jung to a mask; and let it be added that it is the carnivalesque mask one must think of here, and not the sacred mask which, for its part, does indeed express a true archetype and therefore a possibility that does not bewitch the soul but on the contrary liberates it.[22]

Psychic dissociation always produces a fixation as well as a tearing apart between opposing poles, and this is rendered possible only by the clouding over of that which, in the soul, corresponds to the archetype. At the antipodes of this imbalance productive of hypertrophies, perfect virility, for example, in no wise excludes femininity, but on the contrary includes and adapts it, and the inverse is also true. Similarly, the genuine archetypes, which are not situated at the psychic level, do not mutually exclude but comprise and imply one another. According to the Platonic and hallowed meaning of the term, the archetypes are the source of being and knowledge and not, as Jung conceives them, unconscious dispositions to

---

22. See the chapter "The Sacred Mask" in *Mirror of the Intellect* (Quinta Essentia, Cambridge, England, 1987).

act and imagine. The fact that the archetypes cannot be grasped by discursive thought has no connection with the irrational and obscure character of the supposed "collective unconscious", whose contents are said to be known only indirectly through their "eruptions" on the surface. There is not only discursive thought, there is also intellectual intuition, and this attains to the archetypes from the starting-point of their symbols.

No doubt the theory according to which ancestral structures constitute the "collective unconscious" imposes itself on modern thought all the more easily in that it seems to be in agreement with the evolutionist explanation of the instinct of animals. According to this view, instinct is the expression of the heredity of a species, of an accumulation of analogous experiences down the ages. This is how they explain, for example, the fact that a flock of sheep hastily gathers together around the lambs the moment it perceives the shadow of a bird of prey, or that a kitten while playing already employs all the tricks of a hunter, or that birds know how to build their nests. In fact, it is enough to watch animals to see that their instinct has nothing of an automatism about it. The formation of such a mechanism by a purely cumulative—and consequently vague and problematical— process is highly improbable, to say the least. Instinct is a non-reflective modality of the intelligence; it is determined, not by a series of automatic reflexes, but by the "form"—the qualitative determination—of the species. This form is like a filter through which the universal intelligence is manifested. Nor must it be forgotten that the subtle form of a being is incomparably more complex than its bodily form. The same is also true for man: his intelligence too is determined by the subtle form of his species. This form, however, includes the reflective faculty, which allows of a singularization of the individual such as does not exist among the animals. Man alone is able to objectivize himself. He can say: "I am this or that." He alone possesses this two-edged faculty. Man, by virtue of his own central position in the cosmos, is able to transcend his specific norm; he can also betray it, and sink lower; *corruptio optimi pessima*. A normal animal remains true to the form and genius of its species; if its intelligence is not reflective and objectifying, but in some sort existential, it is nonetheless spontaneous; it is assuredly a form of the universal intelligence even if it is not recognized as such by men who, from prejudice or ignorance, identify intelligence with discursive thought exclusively.

As for Jung's thesis that certain dreams, which cannot be explained by personal reminiscences and which seem to arise from an unconscious fund common to all men, contain motives and forms that are also to be found in myths and in traditional symbolism, the thing is possible in principle; not that there is in the soul a repertory of types inherited from distant ancestors and bearing witness to a primitive vision of the world, but because true symbols are always "actual" inasmuch as they express non-temporal realities. In fact, under certain conditions, the soul is able to take on the function of a mirror that reflects, in a purely passive and imaginative manner, universal truths contained in the intellect. Nevertheless, "inspirations" of this nature remain fairly rare; they depend on circumstances that are, so to speak, providential, as in the case of dreams communicating truths or announcing future events, to which allusion has previously been made. Moreover, symbolic dreams are not clothed in just any traditional "style"; their formal language is normally determined by the tradition or religion to which the individual is effectively or virtually attached, for there is nothing arbitrary in this domain.

Now, if one examines examples of supposedly symbolical dreams quoted by Jung and other psychologists of his school, one notices that in most cases it is a matter of false symbolism, of the kind commonly met with in pseudo-spiritual circles. The soul is not only a sacred mirror; more often it is a magic mirror that deceives the one who views himself in it. Jung should have known this, since he himself speaks of the tricks of the *anima*, indicating by this term the feminine aspect of the soul; and some of his own experiences, as described in his memoirs,[23] should have told him that an investigator of the unconscious depths of the *psyché* exposes himself, not merely to the wiles of the egocentric soul, but also to psychic influences coming from elsewhere, from unknown beings and entities,

---

23. The kind of introspection practiced by Jung by way of psychological investigation and of which he speaks in his memoirs, as well as certain parapsychological phenomena that he provoked by this method, takes one into a frankly spiritualistic ambience. The fact that the author proposed to study these phenomena "scientifically" changes nothing in regard to the influence they in fact had on his theory of "archetypes".

especially when the methods of analysis used derive from hypnosis or mediumship. In this context must be placed certain designs executed by sick patients of Jung and which the latter tries to palm off as genuine *mandalas*.[24]

Over and above all this, there exists a symbolism, very general in nature and inherent in language itself, as for instance when one compares truth to light and error to darkness, or progress to an ascent or moral danger to an abyss, or when one represents fidelity by a dog or craftiness by a fox. Now, to explain the occurrence of a similar symbolism in dreams, of which the language is naturally figurative and not discursive, there is no need to refer to a "collective unconscious"; it is enough to note that rational thought is not the whole of thought and that consciousness in the waking state does not cover the whole domain of mental activity. If the figurative language of dreams is not discursive, this does not necessarily make it irrational, and it is possible, as indeed Jung has properly observed, that a dreamer may be more intelligent in his dreams than in the waking state. It would even seem that this difference of level between the two states is fairly frequent among men of our own time, doubtless because the frameworks imposed by modern life are particularly unintelligent and incapable of vehicling in any normal manner the essential contents of human life.

This has obviously nothing to do with the role of purely symbolic or sacred dreams, whether these be spontaneous or evoked through rites; we are thinking here of the example of the Indians of North America, whose whole tradition, as well as their vital ambience, favors a kind of oneiric prophetism.

So as to neglect no aspect of this question, the following should also be said: In every collectivity that has become unfaithful to its own traditional form, to the sacred framework of its life, there occurs a collapse or a sort of mummification of the symbols it had received, and this process will be reflected in the psychic life of every individual belonging to that collectivity and participating in that infidelity. To every truth there corresponds a formal trace, and every spiritual form projects a psychic shadow; when these shadows are all that remains, they do in fact take on the character of ancestral phantoms that haunt the subconscious. The most pernicious of

24. See the Introduction to *The Secret of the Golden Flower.*

psychological errors is to reduce the meaning of symbolism to such phantoms.

As for the definition of "unconscious", it must never be forgotten that this is eminently relative and provisional. Consciousness is capable of gradation like light and is similarly refracted in contact with the media it meets. The ego is the form of individual consciousness, not its luminous source. The latter coincides with the source of the intelligence itself. In its universal nature, consciousness is in a sense an existential aspect of the intellect, and this amounts to saying that basically nothing is situated outside it.[25] Whence it follows that the "unconscious" of the psychologists is quite simply everything which, in the soul, lies outside ordinary consciousness—that of the empirical "I" oriented towards the corporeal world—in other words, this "unconscious" is made to include both lower chaos and the higher states. The latter (which the Hindus compare to the bliss of deep sleep, the state of *prâjña*) radiate from the luminous source of the Universal Spirit; the definition of the "unconscious" thus in no wise corresponds to a particular concrete modality of the soul. Many of the errors of "depth psychology", of which Jung is one of the chief protagonists, result from the fact that it operates with the "unconscious" as if it were a definite entity. One often hears it said that Jung's psychology has "re-established the autonomous reality of the soul." In truth, according to the perspective inherent in this psychology, the soul is neither independent of the body nor immortal; it is merely a sort of irrational fatality situated outside any intelligible cosmic order. If the moral and mental behavior of man were determined behind the scenes by some collection of ancestral "types" issuing from a fund that is completely unconscious and completely inaccessible to the intelligence, man would be as if suspended between two irreconcilable and divergent realities, namely that of things and that of the soul.

For all modern psychology, the luminous point of the soul, or its existential summit, is the consciousness of the "I", which only exists to the extent that it can disengage itself from the darkness of the "unconscious". Now, according to Jung, this darkness contains the vital roots of the individuality: the "collective unconscious" would

25. Let us here recall the Vedantic ternary *Sat-Chit-Ânanda* (Being, Consciousness, Bliss).

then be endowed with a regulatory instinct, a kind of somnambulant wisdom, no doubt of a biological nature; from this fact, the conscious emancipation of the ego would comprise the danger of a vital uprooting. According to Jung, the ideal is a balance between the two poles—the conscious and the unconscious—a balance that can be realized only by the help of a third term, a sort of center of crystallization, which he calls the "self", a term borrowed from the doctrines of Hinduism. Here is what he has written on the subject:

> With the sensation of the self as an irrational and indefinable entity, to which the "I" is neither opposed nor subordinated, but to which it adheres and round which it moves in some sort, like the earth around the sun, the aim of individuation is attained. I use this term "sensation" to express the empirical character of the relationship between the "I" and the self. In this relationship there is nothing intelligible, for one can say nothing about the contents of the self. The "I" is the only content of the self that we know. The individualized "I" feels itself to be the object of a subject unknown and superior to itself. It seems to me that psychological observation here touches its extreme limit, for the idea of a self is in itself a transcendent postulate, which one can admittedly justify psychologically, but cannot prove scientifically. The step beyond science is an absolute requirement for the psychological evolution described here, for without the postulate in question I could not sufficiently formulate the psychic processes observed from experience. Because of this, the idea of a self at least possesses the value of a hypothesis like the theories about the structure of the atom. And if it be true that here too we are prisoners of an image, it is in any case a very living image, the interpretation of which exceeds my capacities. I scarcely doubt that it is a question of an image, but it is an image that contains us.[26]

Despite a terminology too much bound up with current scientism, one might be tempted to grant full credit to the presentiments expressed in this passage and to find in it an approach to traditional metaphysical doctrines, if Jung, in a further passage, did not relativize the notion of the self by treating it this time, not as a transcendent principle, but as the outcome of a psychological process:

> One could define the self as a sort of compensation in reference to the contrast between inward and outward. Such a defini-

26. See *Two Essays on Analytical Psychology,* p. 240.

tion could well be applied to the self in so far as the latter possesses the character of a result, of an aim to reach, of a thing that has only been produced little by little and of which the experience has cost much travail. Thus, the self is also the aim of life, for it is the most complete expression of that combination of destiny we call an "individual", and not only of man in the singular but also of a whole group, where the one is the complement of the others with a view to a perfect image.[27]

There are some realms where dilettantism is unforgivable.

It is the balance to be realized between the unconscious and the conscious, or the integration, in the empirical "personality", of certain forces or impulsions emanating from the unconscious, that Jung paradoxically labels as "individuation", using a term by which was traditionally designated, not some psychological process or other, but the differentiation of individuals from the starting point of the species. But what Jung understands by this term is a kind of definitive pronunciation of the individuality which is taken as an end in itself. In such a perspective, the notion of "self" plainly loses all metaphysical meaning, but this is not the only traditional notion that Jung appropriates in order to debase it to a purely psychological and even clinical level; thus he compares psychoanalysis, which he uses precisely to promote this "individuation", to an initiation in the proper and sacred meaning of the term, and he even declares that psychoanalysis represents "the only form of initiation still valid in the modern age!"[28] Whence proceed a whole series of false assimilations. and intrusions into a realm where psychology is devoid of competence.[29]

---

27. *Ibid.*
28. See psychological commentary of the *Tibetan Book of the Dead.*
29. Jung's psychological interpretation of alchemy has been expressly refuted in my book *Alchemy: Science of the Cosmos, Science of the Soul* (Element Books, Shaftesbury, England, 1986; Fons Vitae, Louisville, Kentucky, 1997). Frithjof Schuon, after reading the present chapter, sent me the following reflections in writing: "People generally see in Jungism, as compared with Freudism, a step towards reconciliation with the traditional spiritualities, but this is in no wise the case. From this point of view, the only difference is that, whereas Freud boasted of being an irreconcilable enemy of religion, Jung sympathizes with it while emptying it of its contents, which he replaces by collective psychism, that is to say by something infra-intellectual and therefore anti-spiritual. In this there is an immense danger for the ancient spiritualities, whose representatives, especially in the East, are too often lacking in critical sense with regard to the modern spirit, and this by reason of a complex of 'rehabilitation'; also it is not with much surprise, though with grave disquiet, that one has come across echoes of this kind from Japan, where the psychoanalyst's 'equilibrium' has been compared to the *satori* of Zen; and there is little doubt that it would be

Here it is not a case of the involuntary ignorance of some isolated seeker, for Jung carefully avoided all contact with the representatives of living tradition. During his visit to India, for example,
he did not wish to see Shri Râmana Mahârishi—alleging a motive of
insolent frivolity[30]—doubtless because he feared instinctively and
"unconsciously" (it is a case for saying it) a contact with a reality that
would give the lie to his theories. For him, metaphysics was but a
speculation in the void or, to be more exact, an illusory attempt by
the psychic to reach beyond itself, comparable to the senseless gesture of a man who would pull himself out of a mud hole by his own
hair. This conception is typical of modern psychologism, and this is
why we mention it. To the absurd argument that metaphysics is only
a production of the *psyché* one can immediately object that this judgment itself is but a similar production. Man lives by truth; to accept
any truth, however relative it may be, is to accept that *intellectus ade-
quatio rei*. Merely to say "this is that" is automatically to affirm the
very principle of adequation, and therefore the presence of the
absolute in the relative.

Jung breached certain strictly materialistic frameworks of modern science, but this fact is of no use to anyone, to say the least—
one wishes one could have rejoiced over it—because the influences
that filter through this breach come from lower psychism and not
from the Spirit, which alone is true and alone can save us.

easy to meet with similar confusions in India and elsewhere. Be that as it may,
the confusions in question are greatly favored by the almost universal refusal of
people to see the devil and to call him by his name, in other words, by a kind
of tacit convention compounded of optimism to order, tolerance that in reality hates truth, and compulsory alignment with scientism and official taste, without forgetting 'culture', which swallows everything and commits one to
nothing, except complicity in its neutralism; to which must be added a no less
universal and quasi-official contempt for whatever is, we will not say intellectu-
alist, but truly intellectual, and therefore tainted, in people's minds, with dogmatism, scholasticism, fanaticism, and prejudice. All this goes hand in hand
with the psychologism of our time and is in large measure its result."
30. See the preface to Heinrich Zimmer's book on Shri Râmana Mahârshi.

Chapter 4

Man in the Universe
Permanence Amidst Apparent Change

Seyyed Hossein Nasr

There is no domain in which change and transformation reign with the same supremacy and totality as in that which concerns nature and man's relation to it as well as his knowledge of it. Modern science, which has acted as a catalyst during the past centuries for change in so many other fields, is itself based upon change and impermanence. Were it to become stationary and immutable it would cease to exist in its present form. And since this is the only science of nature known to modern man, the whole relation between man and nature, as well as the nature of man himself and the Universe that surrounds him, is seen only in the light of flux and change. The view that man's position in the Universe and his knowledge of it, not to speak of the object of this knowledge, is constantly changing has come to appear as so obvious and evident as to make any other point of view seem absurd and well-nigh impossible to understand. Modern man is bewildered at even the possibility of an element of permanence in his relation with the Universe, not because such an element does not exist, but because the problem itself is never considered from the point of view of permanence.

It is often forgotten that before man began to view his relation to nature only from the aspect of change and impermanence, he had become himself inwardly detached from the immutable principle of the Intellect, the *nous,* which along with revelation is the only factor that can act as the permanent and immutable axis for the machinations of human reason. With the weakening of gnostic elements in Christianity the rational faculty of Western man became gradually estranged from the twin sources of immutability, stability and permanence: namely, revelation and intellectual intuition.[1]

1. See S. H. Nasr, *The Encounter of Man and Nature, the Spiritual Crisis of Modern Man* (London, 1968), pp. 63 ff.

The result was on the one hand the nominalist trend, which destroyed philosophical certainty, and on the other this reduction of man to the purely human, cut off from any transcendental elements, the man of Renaissance humanism. Such a concept of man itself implied sheer change and becoming—which are apparent even outwardly during that period in those rapid transformations of Western society which have given the Renaissance its transitional character. But even then man's concept of the Universe had not as yet changed. His science of nature was still essentially medieval, comprised of Hermetic and Scholastic elements. It is only his conception of himself that had changed, leading in turn to a change in his concept of the Universe and his own place in it.

It is always essential to bear in mind the time-lag between the religious and metaphysical revolt at the end of the Middle Ages expressing an attempt on the part of Western man to cut himself away from his celestial and immutable archetype and to become purely terrestrial and human, and the scientific revolution which carried this secularized vision of man to its logical conclusion by creating a purely secular science. Man, once he came to consider himself a predominantly secular being, developed a science that considers the changing aspect of things alone, a science that is concerned solely with becoming rather than being, and this is a most logical happening if we remember that even etymologically *secular* is derived from the Latin *secularis* one of whose meanings is change and temporality. The destruction of the sacred vision of man and the Universe is equivalent to the destruction of the immutable aspect of both man and the Universe. A secular science could not have come into existence without being wholly concerned with change and becoming.

If we keep in mind the historical factors that brought into being a world-view in the West based solely on the changing aspect of things, it should be possible for us to reconstruct and bring back to light permanent elements in the vision of modern man without appearing to speak of absurdities; but this can only happen if there is an understanding of traditional metaphysics and the language of symbolism through which the metaphysical truths have always been revealed.[2] Metaphysics, or the science of the permanent, can be

---

2. See F. Schuon, *The Transcendent Unity of Religions*, trans. by P. Townsend (London, 1953), pp. 9 ff., and R. Guénon, *La métaphysique orientale* (Paris, 1951

ignored or forgotten; but it cannot be refuted precisely because it is not concerned with change *qua* change. That which deals with permanence cannot become "out of date," because it is not concerned with any date as such. The permanent elements in the relation between man and the Universe remain as valid now as ever. Only they must become known once again after the long period during which the West did not search for permanent elements in change and even sought to reduce permanence itself to change and historical process.

*
* *

From the point of view of traditional metaphysical and cosmological doctrines there are several elements of permanence in the relationship between man and nature and in man's own situation in the Universe. The first and most basic element is the fact that the cosmic environment that surrounds man is not ultimate reality but possesses the character of relativity and even illusion. If one understands what is meant by the Absolute then by the same token one understands the relative and comes to realize that all that is not Absolute must of necessity be relative. The aspect of the world as *mâyâ*, to use the Hindu term or *samsâra* in the Buddhist sense, is itself a permanent element of the cosmos and man's relation to it. The Universe, in its cosmic aspect, was always *mâyâ* and will always be *mâyâ*. The Absolute is always the Absolute and the relative the relative, and no amount of historical process and change can turn one into the other. Historical process can cause a people or even a civilization to forget for a while the distinction between the Absolute and relative and therefore to take the relative for the Absolute as modern science seems to have done. But wherever and whenever metaphysical discernment appears, the distinction becomes clear and the world becomes known for what it is, namely *mâyâ*. The changing element of the world which the concept of *mâyâ* implies is itself a permanent feature of the world. It is in the nature of the world to be changing, to undergo generation and corruption, to experience life and death. But the meaning of this

[See "Oriental Metaphysics" in *Sword of Gnosis*, ed. by J. Needleman (Baltimore, Maryland, 1974), pp. 40-56. *Ed.*])

change can only be understood in terms of the permanent. To have understood that the world is *mâyâ* is to have understood the meaning of *Âtman* or *Brahman* that transcends *mâyâ*. To know that the world is impermanent or *samsâric* in nature is to know by extension the prescience of the *nirvânic* state beyond it.[3] The changing character of the world reveals metaphysically the permanent reality that transcends it. To realize the relativity of things is to know, by extension of the same knowledge, about the Absolute and the Permanent. Throughout history, in all periods of human culture, this metaphysical distinction has existed. It lies in the nature of things and so is there for all to see, provided they turn their vision towards it. Only, in certain periods such as ours the relative has come to be idolized as the Absolute. Today, one often hears the claim that all is relative. But the same people who make such a claim often bestow an absolute character on the domain of the relative itself. Without always being fully aware of it they have mistaken both *Brahman* and *mâyâ*, due to a lack of discernment and true knowledge, an ignorance which itself stems from *mâyâ*. But when there is metaphysical knowledge there is also awareness of the relativity of things in the light of the Absolute, and this fundamental truth is a permanent element in man's situation in the Universe, and concerns his destiny as a being who is called upon to seek to transcend the cosmic crypt into which he has fallen and to return from the domain of the relative to the Absolute.[4]

Another element of permanence in the relation of man to the Universe is the manifestation of the Absolute in the relative in the form of symbols understood in the traditional sense of the word.[5] A symbol is not based on man-made conventions. It is an aspect of the ontological reality of things and is as such independent of man's perception of it.[6] The symbol is the revelation of a higher order of

---

3. See F. Schuon, *In the Tracks of Buddhism,* trans. by M. Pallis (London, 1968 [Revised and augmented as *Treasures of Buddhism* (Bloomington, Indiana, 1993), *Ed.*]) where the relation between *nirvâna* and *samsâra* is discussed in all its amplitude and depth.
4. Concerning this theme in its Islamic setting, see S. H. Nasr, *An Introduction to Islamic Cosmological Doctrines* (Cambridge, Mass., 1964), chapter XV.
5. The meaning of traditional symbols cannot be treated here. This question has been amply dealt with in the writings of F. Schuon, R. Guénon, T. Burckhardt, and A. K. Coomaraswamy as well as H. Zimmer and M. Eliade.
6. "The science of symbols—not simply a knowledge of traditional symbols—proceeds from the qualitative significances of substances, forms, . . . , we are not

reality in a lower order through which man can be led back to the higher sphere. To understand symbols is to accept the hierarchic structure of the Universe and the multiple states of being.

During phases of the historical process symbols which are given special significance and power in a revealed religion through the revelation itself can gradually lose their efficacy either partially or completely, as a result of the weakening of the spiritual basis of that religion as can be seen in the case of the de-mythologizers of our day. Nevertheless, the symbols of nature are permanent and immutable. What the sky signifies symbolically, as for example the dimension of transcendence and the Divine throne (*'arsh*), to use the Islamic image, is as permanent as the sky itself. The sun symbolizes the Universal Intellect as long as it goes on shining and the tree with its extended branches is a symbol of the multiple states of being as long as trees grow on the surface of the earth. That is why one may speak of a *cosmologia perennis,* of a qualitative science of nature which is always valid and which reveals an aspect of nature which is, to say the least, no less real than the changing aspect studied by modern science.[7] The main difference between the traditional and modern sciences of nature lies in the fact that modern science studies change with respect to change, whereas traditional science studies change in the light of permanence through the study of symbols which are nothing but the reflection of permanence in change.

A civilization may develop a science which turns its back upon the qualitative aspect of things revealed through symbols to concentrate upon the changes which can be measured quantitatively; but it cannot destroy the symbolic reality of things any more than can a qualitative and symbolic study of natural phenomena destroy their weight or size. Today through the destruction of the "symbol-

dealing here with subjective appreciations, for the cosmic qualities are ordered both in relation to Being and according to a hierarchy which is more real than the individual . . ." F. Schuon, *Gnosis, Divine Wisdom,* trans. G. E. H. Palmer (London, 1959), p. 110.

7. On the *cosmologia perennis,* see T. Burckhardt, *Scienza moderna e saggezza tradizionale* (Torino, 1968 [See "Traditional Cosmology and Modern Science," in *Mirror of the Intellect* (Cambridge, England, 1987), pp. 17-67. *Ed.*]), see also his *Alchemie, Sinn und Weltbild* (Olten, 1960 [See *Alchemy: Science of the Cosmos, Science of the Soul* (Louisville, Kentucky, 1997). *Ed.*]), which deals with permanent values of Hermetic cosmology.

ist spirit",[8] men in the West have lost the sense of penetrating into the inner meaning of phenomena which symbols alone reveal. But this impotence does not mean that natural symbols have ceased to exist. The symbolic significance of the homocentric spheres of Ptolemaic astronomy, which the immediate appearance of the heavens reveals, remains valid, whether in the theoretical Newtonian absolute space or in the curved space of relativity the earth moves around the sun or the sun around the earth. The homocentric spheres symbolize states of being above the terrestrial sphere in which man is presently placed. The states of being remain true whether we understand and accept the natural symbolism which the heavens themselves reveal to us in our immediate and direct contact with them, or whether we destroy this immediate appearance and the symbol in the name of other theoretical considerations.

In fact even new scientific theories, if they conform to any reality at all, possess their own symbolic meaning. To correspond to reality means to be symbolic. If the Ptolemaic spheres symbolize man's position with respect to higher states of being, the galactic space of modern astronomy itself symbolizes the indefinitude of the relative, the vastness of the ocean of *samsâra*. It is itself proof of the fact that man's intelligence was created to know the Infinite rather than the indefinite. But in a more direct sense, the symbolic meaning of the phenomena of nature, not to speak of scientific theories based upon them, represents a permanent aspect of things and of man's relation to the cosmos. It is upon this permanent character of the symbolic content of the phenomena of nature that one can construct a symbolic science of nature, a traditional cosmology which remains of perennial value and permanent importance, and which is of particular significance today when the purely quantitative sciences of nature and their manifold applications threaten the existence of both man and nature.[9]

Yet another permanent feature of the relation between man and the Universe, at least according to a certain aspect of the situation, is the way that nature presents itself to man. Today man seeks to

8. Concerning the "symbolist spirit" see F. Schuon, "The Symbolist Outlook" in *Studies in Comparative Religion*, Winter, 1966, pp. 50 ff [Also in *The Feathered Sun: Plains Indiana in Art and Philosophy* (Bloomington, Indiana, 1990), pp. 3-13. Ed.].

9. The author has dealt fully with this question in his *Encounter of Man and Nature*.

change all his social, political and even religious institutions with the excuse that nature itself is always changing and therefore man must change likewise. In fact just the reverse holds true. It is because man's mentality has lost its anchor in the permanent and become itself a fleeting river of ever-changing ideas and images that man sees only change in nature. If modern man has read evolution into nature, he had begun to believe in evolution in his mind before observing it in nature itself. Evolution is primarily not the product of natural observation but of a secularized mentality cut off from every avenue of access to the immutable, which then began to see its own fleeting nature in outward nature. Man always sees in nature the reflection of his own being and his conception of what he himself is.

If we study the world about us we see that in fact the terrestrial environment in which men saw permanence for millenia has not changed in its general features. The sun still rises and sets the same way now as it did for ancient and medieval man, who looked upon it as the symbol of the Divine Intellect. The natural forms still reproduce themselves with the same regularity and through the same processes as in older historical periods. Neither the petals of the rose nor its scent have changed since Dante and Shakespeare wrote about them. Nor in fact has man himself evolved biologically since there has been a recorded or even unrecorded human history. Today's man is biologically the same as the men of old who believed in permanence and transcendence. If modern men have ceased to so believe they had better find some other excuse than their own biological or natural evolution.

In this question of the permanence of natural phenomena as they appear to man there is a diametrical opposition between the traditional and that modern point of view which is its direct inversion. Today all things are considered to be changing, yet the hypothesis of uniformitarianism is used with such certainty in geology, paleontology and even anthropology that one would think it was a proven law. On the one hand it is said that laws have been uniform and so we speak of events having taken place millions and billions of years ago without considering precisely what it is that we mean by a "million years." On the other hand we say that nature changes all the time, without considering the possibility that what appears as a "law of nature" today may itself have changed over the ages or under particular circumstances and conditions. If we cannot walk on water, there is no logical reason why such and such a medieval saint could never have done so.

The traditional view of nature reverses this situation completely. In place of change it substitutes permanence and in place of uniformity and immutability of natural conditions, qualitative change. The changing processes of nature are viewed as permanent patterns which through repetition integrate time and process into the image of eternity.[10] The apparent uniformity of nature is in turn modified by the theory of cycles, the *yugas* of Hinduism or *adwâr* and *akwâr* of certain schools of Islamic thought, which do not mean mere repetition of the same patterns but rather bring out the qualitative difference between different epochs both in the cosmos and in human history. The modern inversion of these two realities has destroyed the vision of permanence in nature as well as the realization of the qualitative differences in the various cycles. In fact this inversion is itself proof of the reality of the cosmic cycles and only confirms what all authentic traditions teach about them.[11]

For this reason alone older works of natural history and mythology have become closed books and at best are interpreted in a purely psychological manner, whereas they can be understood in the light of the fact that there is a qualitative difference between the cosmic milieu of the ancient natural environment and our own. There was not the same crystallization and condensation, the same separation of matter from spirit. The water of Thales was still full of the animating spirit of nature and in fact symbolized the psychophysical substratum of things. It was very far removed from the post-Cartesian dead matter with which Lavoisier was experimenting twenty-four centuries later.

Yet, between this change and that permanence and across this inversion of views there remains one immutable element: that is,

10. On the relation between linear and cyclic time as it effects both history and cosmology, see M. Eliade, *The Myth of the Eternal Return*, trans. by W. Trask (New York, 1954); see also, A. K. Coomaraswamy, *Time and Eternity* (Ascona, 1947), where the metaphysical relationship between time and eternity in different traditions is elucidated.
11. The downward tendency of the Kali Yuga or Dark Age which itself obliterates the vision of qualitative time for most men is admirably treated by R. Guénon in many of his writings, especially *The Reign of Quantity and the Signs of the Times*, trans. by Lord Northbourne (London, 1951).

the way in which the phenomena of nature appear to man. The sky, the sea, the mountains, the seasonal cycles, these realities manifest themselves now as in the millenia before, except for certain qualitative differences involved, and they are the majestic testament of the Immutable manifested in the process of becoming. Men who love nature are essentially in quest of the permanent, and nature in fact itself gives the lie to those who want to limit all reality to change and becoming. Such philosophies never arose among people who lived close to nature but have always been the products of sedentary environments where an artificial atmosphere has enabled men to forget both nature and the permanent elements which she reveals to man, elements which evoke in man those factors that are permanent and anchored in the immutable strata of man's own being.

As far as the present sciences of nature are concerned, much though they differ from the various traditional cosmologies, even here there is an element of permanence if one takes modern science for what it really is. Of course by the very fact that modern science has consciously turned its back upon the metaphysical and symbolic aspect of things, it is cut off from the traditional view of nature through its own point of view and must ignore any metaphysical significance that its own discoveries may possess. Yet, these discoveries, to the extent that they have a connection with the reality of things, do possess a symbolic significance, For example the fact that order repeats itself in all planes of material reality from the galaxy to the atom, or the fact that with whatever unit science deals with, whether it be the biological cell or the atom, there is a harmony of parts within a whole, represent permanent features of any science of nature whether one bothers to take these facts into consideration or not.

Even in a more evident manner, one sees the repetition of certain patterns and problems throughout the history of science, a fact which more than any other has attracted many modern scientists to its study. No matter how much science changes, the encounter of man's mind with nature seems to produce certain permanent features. Take for example the problem of continuity and discontinuity of bodies, which had occupied Aristotle and the Greek atomists, the Muslim Peripatetics and theologians as well as the modern physicists; or the relation of the One to the manifold, or between order and disorder or between chance and determinism; these are all problems that recur perennially in all forms of science. Many scientists turn today to the history of science to find inspiration for new methodologies in order to face problems of contemporary physics or biology which are basically related to the problems of the ancient and medieval sciences. The recurrence of these patterns and problems is yet another element of permanence in a domain that is the most changing and fluid of all fields, just because men have turned their backs upon Unity to view multiplicity, to study the contingent without considering the Principle.

But perhaps the most important permanent element in man's relation to the Universe is his "existential" situation in the hierarchy of universal existence. Traditional man knew with certainty where he came from, why he lived and where he was going. Modern man, however, for the most part knows neither where he comes from nor what his end will be and therefore, most important of all, why he is living. Nevertheless, like the traditional man he faces the two points which determine the beginning and end of his terrestrial life. He is born and he dies. This fact has not changed one *iota* nor will it do so through the cheap form of would-be immortality that modern man seeks, if unconsciously, through such artificial means as heart transplantations. The only difference is that what was once certainty has become today doubt and fear. But the reality of birth and death remains, and no amount of modern science can unravel the mysteries of these two "eternities" between which stands the flickering moment of earthly life.[12]

It is these two "infinities" which determine the character and meaning of the finitude that stands between them. With respect to these two "infinities" the situation of man has not changed at all even if the destruction of the medieval cosmologies has destroyed for most men the metaphysical doctrine of the states of being which that cosmology symbolized so beautifully. Man is still a finite being with an intelligence made to understand the Infinite and the Absolute and not merely the indefinite and the relative, whereof the total grasp lies forever beyond the ken of any human science. With

---

12. "Modern Science, which is rationalist as to its subject and materialist as to its object, can describe our situation physically and approximately, but it can tell us nothing about our extra-spatial situation in the total and real Universe". F. Schuon, *Light on the Ancient Worlds*, trans. by Lord Northbourne (London, 1965), p. 111.

respect to the Absolute and all the states of being which comprise the Universe man is what he has always been and will always be, an image of the Absolute in the relative, cast into the stream of becoming in order to return this becoming itself to Being. Today there is so much talk of change that men are hypnotized by their own phrases and forget that just beneath the surface of these ever moving waves of change lies the immutable and permanent sea of man's real nature. The situation of this permanent nature which man carries within himself wherever he comes face to face with the Real, in its metaphysical sense, has never changed nor can it ever alter. The ontological situation of man in the total scheme of things is forever the same; it is, more than all the other elements of cosmology and the sciences that relate man to the Universe, a situation of permanence midst apparent change.

Chapter 5

Lucifer

Tage Lindbom

The biblical narrative of the Fall of man has an important double aspect. The fruit that the serpent offers to the first human beings is succulent and attractive; the serpent's offer poses the delights of the external and sensory world and excites the merely vegetative and animal aspects of man's nature—it is the appeal of materialism. But the Fall of man also has a deeper meaning; the serpent urges a more excellent promise than mere experience of sensory delights. The Tree of Knowledge offers man insight; his eyes will be opened, and he will be enlarged and leave behind his state of confident innocence. He will be given an intellectual capacity; he will become "like God."

The serpent's seduction, therefore, has a double meaning. He will show man the route to unreflecting animal lust, to a sensualism whereby man will become a slave to materialism. But something far more dangerous is added to this: man repudiates the fidelity that he owes to God and gives himself up to the greatest of all sins, *superbia*, spiritual pride. He tries to raise himself up to become the equal of the Creator, "to be like God." This self-idolization by man is Luciferism pure and simple. For to ungoverned sensuality is added a haughty, narcissistic self-deception whereby man falsifies, distorts, and manipulates fundamental constituents of his existence and that of the world: namely, the truth that the world comes from the Creator, that the creature can never himself become God or "like God"; but rather that he, man, has the vocation of viceregency and trusteeship under the aegis and law of God.

Because of progressive secularization—and the confusion that results from it—the West has been ensnared in a Luciferism that has had disastrous consequences in many areas of Western life, and not least in theology. We encounter Luciferism in varying, fluctuating, and often seductive forms; for example, in the "beautiful" system that we call idealism. Idealism presents itself as an elevated, ennobled form of the best in humanity; and thereby it can be interpreted as a line of argument negating materialism and hedonism. But the incense on the altar of idealism has the function of concealing the fundamental fact that idealism, in its anthropomorphic guise, is a form of humanism and thus of Luciferism. It is not at all in contradiction to materialism and sensualism but, on the contrary, is one of the double aspects of the Fall of man. Idealism is the complement to materialism.

The sensual temptation toward the beautiful but forbidden fruits of the Garden of Eden leads to a seduction less dangerous than the Luciferian promise that man will be "like God." To yield to all things in the sensual world that attract is not intrinsically unpardonable—after all, we live in a world of material and sensible objects. If the disobedience of the first human beings had been limited to the consumption of delicious fruit, correction would have been possible. But to revolt against the Creator, in effect to dethrone him—*quod fieri non potest*—by idolizing oneself, this is a catastrophe and is the deeper aspect of the Fall of man. For Luciferism is much more dangerous than the concupiscence that one feels before the attractions of the material world. Moral decay is never so disastrous as pride, the properly Luciferian intention. Yielding to concupiscence (and, in the first instance, allowing it to assume unmanageable proportions) is a breaking of norms, a degradation, a degeneration that God can counter and heal with his pardon and grace. Pride is a denial, a negation of the divine order itself, a falsification of revealed truth.

Draped in the shining garment of idealism and humanism, the West has accomplished a manipulation whereby the deepest meaning of the Fall of man is concealed. In the name of idealism and humanism, secularization is legitimized. More and more, Western man is living in a world in which he listens only to his own voice, which begins as the voice of rationalism; and listening to this voice, he is able to refer continuously to the "legitimation" that he believes the idealist and humanist pseudo-spirituality confers on him. In this world, secularization progresses because man can be represented as a higher being, carrying "the eternal" in his breast, conquering all creation, and at last proclaiming himself as universal sovereign.

What we call "Western" attitudes, perspectives, and ways of thinking have their sources in Greek thought, and Greek thought was rationalist, at least in its classical form. In Greek thought, we encounter a Luciferian element. The Greek conception of reality, at least in its rationalist posture, excludes transcendence; the perfect is reached through the limited, the finite. Being is the highest category, and the infinite and the eternal are excluded[1]. According to an apocryphal tale, a party of ancient Greeks were on a boat at sea; when one of them maintained that beyond the formal and closed world of received wisdom, there must be something that we are incapable of grasping with our rational faculties, he was thrown overboard.

In the Renaissance, the Luciferian temptation advances on a wave of "liberation," even though we are less conscious of this as a road (albeit a winding road) leading to a further Fall of man. Idealism and humanism, regarded as bearers of spiritual light to a secularized world, are so much stronger in the consciousness of the time. And we must note the fact that advancing secularization has and must have the support of a narcissism that promises "self-realization" under the lodestar of everlasting progress.

The nineteenth century is the culmination of Luciferism, and in that century we see three fields of Luciferian conquest. The first can be compared to a cultivation: the opening and exploitation of a mighty landscape, wherein all forms of humanistic, nonmaterial cultivation are brought together in homage, not to the Creator but rather to constitute a celebration of the "human spirit." Culturalism, indeed, is like a tremendous mirror in which man regards himself and in which, in the name of idealism and humanism, the image in this mirror will always be immaculately pure.

The second field of Luciferian conquest is theology. Pietism, with its intimate and sentimental character, undergoes a displacement in the eighteenth century; its center of gravity shifts from the theocentric to the Christocentric.[2] The theologians of the nineteenth century, with the German Protestant Schleiermacher in the

---

1. It must be noted, however, that this "ontic" aspect of classical Greek thought is far different from and inferior to the genuinely metaphysical ontology of the medieval Scholastics and must not be confused with the latter perspective— Alvin Moore, Jr. [co-translator and editor of *The Myth of Democracy*, the book from which the present article derives. *Ed.*]
2. That is, a reduction of the Logos to merely human dimensions. Needless to say, such reductionism is heretical—especially if compared to that of the Christology of the Greek Fathers or that of the High Middle Ages. Cf. John

vanguard, transform the Son of Man into an ideal human model, thereby placing physical or sensory experience at the center of religion. Nineteenth-century theology deals less and less with God and more and more with man; the transcendent is progressively replaced by the earthly and horizontal. More and more, religion becomes religiosity: intimacy, brotherhood, welfare, consolation, social and mental therapy. The new theology considers that its first duty is collaboration with secular institutions to offer prescriptions—moral in the first instance—favoring strength and viability, liberty and loftiness. No longer a *scientia sacra,* theology strives blindly to achieve a Luciferian goal and regards itself as a collateral, collaborating element among other social forces. The Spanish philosopher Juan Donoso Cortés harshly remarks: They offer God worship, but they do not obey him.

The third field of Luciferian conquest is science (the natural sciences), that "son of pride"—*le fils de l'orgeuil,* in the expression of Joseph de Maistre. For science, the nineteenth century is the epoch of triumphal progress. Knowledge in the Luciferian dream-world has now assigned itself a double mission: it must, through scientific research, discover the forces that govern the Universe; and, by bringing mankind into conformity with this discovered law, it will assure man a position of omnipotence in the world. It is only a matter of time for this position to be reached, and it is significant that the definitive literary formulation of this view was published by the German zoologist Ernst Haeckel in his popular *Das Welträtsel* (published in English translation in 1899 in London as *The Riddle of the Universe*).[3] Very soon, Professor Haeckel assures us, the last blanks on the map of knowledge will be filled in. Then the great day of Luciferian triumph will arrive.

It is in the last trembling minutes of the nineteenth century that Luciferism believes it can claim victory The liberalization of the Western world and confidence in rational thinking were regarded as guarantees against any possible reversion to former barbarian

---

16:7: "It is better for you that I depart"; that is Christ in his humanity—Alvin Moore, Jr.

3. In that heyday of scientific triumphalism and in his zeal to advance the cause of evolution, Professor Haeckel saw fit to fabricate evidence in the drawings he prepared for this purpose. "Schematize" was the word he used when this was discovered—Alvin Moore, Jr.

times. Western secularized man was not at all prepared, therefore, for the bitter Luciferian crisis that would overtake him shortly thereafter.

We must admit that nonmaterial creations, rich emanations of fantasy and of artistic form and elaboration, did give the nineteenth century great aesthetic riches; and it should not surprise us if people of the time were filled with self-esteem. We must understand, however, that in all of this achievement we encounter the last radiations from a spiritual source, a higher, divine wisdom akin to that which everywhere has been given to men throughout the centuries. Already in the early nineteenth century there are clear warning signs: certain penetrations into the nervous system forebode a coming mental crisis. Ambiguous, *outré* romanticism makes inroads into the human psyche; the music of Richard Wagner, for example, manifests a morbidity in its peristatic, tropistic upheavals. Culturalism, the idolization of cultural pursuits, had promised to bring the human spirit to a higher level, mobilizing "the eternal" in man's breast; but now we begin to see suggestions that this spiritual journey is in fact going in the opposite direction.

Aggiornamento, so widely heralded at the beginning of the Second Vatican Council—*aggiornamento,* the accommodation of theology to a more and more secularized world—does not mean that the City of God is vanquishing Lucifer. It means, on the contrary, that the troops of doubters and deniers are increasing. Nor does it help when muddled and anarchic "theologians," in the name of a distorted brotherly love, preach that they will realize the City of Well-being. Those in the West who are on the side of God have to face the brutal fact of largely losing a whole social class, namely, the industrial proletariat. In one sense, the encyclical *Rerum novarum* of Pope Leo XIII was in vain: the working class opted for socialism.

One of the fundamental assumptions of Luciferian rationalism is that the world is a solid, continuous, law-bound unity, and this unity is the object of human knowledge. This is a mathematical and causal conception, formulated by Newton. But already in the last years of the nineteenth century physicists began to call into question this picture of the material world; and during the first decades of the new century, the "classical" Newtonian interpretation was no longer considered valid. Modern particle physics and structural investigations into matter provide a description of empirical reality much more like Heracleitus' *panta rei*. And as this incessant flux does not provide solid local and causal connections, we cannot reach conclusive answers by structural analysis. It is not in a "downward" direction that man must seek stable and changeless truth, and even among scientists it is sometimes realized that, conceivably, we have to look inward and upward in this quest. More than one of the great physicists of our time have openly declared that we have to reckon with the possibility of a higher, divine order. Lucifer's power begins to waver.

Man can live indefinitely as consumer of the fruits that the Creator has given him, and he can consume these fruits even when he has forgotten whence they come; he even begins to praise himself, as if he were himself the creator of these goods. But in the beginning of our century we are confronted with the bitter harvest of Luciferism. Let us consider art, where the first indicators are clear and distinct by the turn of the century. In Cubism, for example, art is no longer pictorial. Portraits and landscapes are no longer objects for the artist. The aesthetic, creative process is now purely subjective; it must be purified of all external objects and models. Now the artist really is a "creator," as everything comes from an inner process, from which all outward sense is eliminated—and beauty first and foremost. In his famous letter to Émile Bernard in 1904, Cézanne writes: "We must interpret nature with cylinders, cones and spheres." Beyond time and space and beyond all aesthetic rules, the artist is now creating "his own" reality as a model or as models, using geometric figures among other things. Man as artist puts himself in the place of God, for he declares that he creates *ex nihilo*, from nothing and without models external to himself.

Beauty is now an extinct star. Art becomes aesthetic autism, delivered from every rule or norm. The artist and his product are an aesthetic unity; art is a process of creation, going on only inside of the artist. The artist begins from a *tabula rasa*, a clean slate; there is no model, there are no canons, no aesthetic standards or legitimate attitudes. The artist tells us that what he is originating is a creation in its most profound meaning, and that his production is therefore real per se; this reality is in itself the aesthetic dimension. The artist, as personality, is apotheosized, according to Guillaume Apollinaire. In this sense the aesthetic product is said to be "pure," untainted by any outside influence. Art is real because it is identical with the artist himself; art is true because it springs from the artist's personality.

The aesthetic revolution—for it is a revolution—broke out at the beginning of the twentieth century. If we accept literally what the leading theorist of this revolution, Guillaume Apollinaire, says in his little book *Les Peintres Cubistes*, the essential is that Luciferism is pushed to its utmost consequences. But just as Haeckel's work, *Das Welträtsel*, derives its epitaph from a ruined philosophy of natural science, the same is true for the aesthetic revolution. In the apparent moment of triumph, the revolution opens the door to Luciferian destruction. Every rule, every norm, every model, all well-rooted criteria are denied. First and foremost, when beauty is not perceived as an emanation from a divine and archetypal model—when everything is reduced to the dimensions of the sensual world of man, then this world of unfounded and chaotic impressions and fantasy is very soon emptied of all content and meaning.

The process of destruction whereby the beautiful and the ugly, the good and the bad, have lost their distinction and meaning happens at an accelerating tempo and expands over vast areas. James Joyce's *Ulysses* contains eight hundred pages of senseless monologues and dialogues, senseless in content and in aesthetic significance. The essential as regards this novel is that it destroys everything built up in respect of literary form; and in that destruction of form, the shadow figures we meet in the Joyce novel carry on with their equilibrist nonsense.

Let us consider another domain of art, music. Music is a form of art that acoustically turns the senses toward the heart. Nevertheless, in spite of its freedom from every plastic model, music is bound to time by rhythm; and it is bound to space in its architectonic structure, the linear and vertical tone sequences, melody and harmony. Music formed its major and minor tonality in its meanderings through Europe's cultural life. The musical revolution also occurred at the beginning of the twentieth century with Arnold Schönberg as its first protagonist, but initially it did not entail a break with every form. Atonalism, however, opens the door to the liquidation of what has been traditionally considered Western music. In the ongoing musical revolution, the leap into a world without norms leads to electronic or industrially produced music, which lacks an essential element of traditional music: namely, the overtones.

Another leap forward is in the multifarious "popular" forms of music, wherein we have to listen to an industrial rattle combined with a rhythmic intensification to the extent of sleep-producing monotony, even while it is being elevated acoustically to insupportable levels. In this "popular" and "industrial" form, music has the important function of both stimulating and anesthetizing the listener's nerves and of dulling his higher faculties.

What man as a sensual, biological creature has to offer to art is soon exposed. The paucity, the impoverishing effect of secularization becomes increasingly evident, and it becomes urgent to find new forms for sensory stimulation. The ugly, the distorted, the morbid, the malicious are mobilized; representational art becomes anti-art; the novel becomes anti-novel; musical consonance is replaced by dissonance. The divine source of art, beauty as the heavenly model for all that is beautiful on earth, is denied and forgotten. The beautiful in creation, all that we look on as a reflection of the beauty of heaven, has no place in the "creative process" as it is envisaged by the Luciferian artists.

When the divine is totally denied, the ineluctable consequence is that there is nothing else to take its place but the spirit of negation, the satanic. And this is what we must now face up to. Anti-art, anti-novel, anti-music—all have sensual stimulation as their aim, the double purpose being to further weaken vitality and to still anxiety. In these stimuli, in these encounters with the ugly, the distorted, the morbid, the satanic is lurking. The cult of sexuality, for example, can be presented as a hymn to life; but we need to be aware that the biological sex function can become an act of aggression and thereby deeply linked with violence. Moralists the world over lament the explosion of promiscuous sex and violence; but this is more than a moral problem, for the two are interconnected and can easily be engaged as servants of the satanic. "Rock" music, for example, has the dual function of evoking and stilling tensions, and it can simultaneously lead to devil worship.

The Luciferian lies along the road to the satanic. Secularized man proclaims himself as light-bearer; instead, he is prisoner of the Lord of Darkness. Here the Luciferian "progress" loses its sure sign of victory. Science, for example, faces a positivistic crisis; it cannot offer the Archimedean point where we can place our foot and move the world. And in its final stages, culturalism mobilizes a host of functionaries, administrators, and advisors under the banner of UNESCO to legitimize us as cultural beings. But the muse has departed, for reality speaks another language. When the inward, spiritual Light is denied, man is no longer disposed to a vision of God's revealed beauty as reflected in creation and as constituting the genuine source of all cultural creation.

The Luciferian process has an inner logic. Power is not sought in an upward direction; on the contrary, the road leads downhill, and along this road are many telltale signs. One of these is widespread mental disharmony. The Luciferian promise is to produce a free, happy, strong, and harmonious man. Instead we encounter neurosis as mass phenomena. Never before has there been so much talk of "healing," never, before so many practitioners of the healing arts. How could it be otherwise? No one affirms more explicitly the downward direction of attention and consciousness in the modern world than the father of psychoanalysis, Sigmund Freud, who chose as motto for his *Die Traumdeutung* (published in English as *The Interpretation of Dreams*) Virgil's sinister *Flectere si nequeo superos, acheronta movebo*[4]—if I cannot move the gods, I will stir up hell.

But what of theology? Has not Western theology seen the falsehood of the promises of everlasting progress and of all of the dreams associated with this myopia? I will answer the question briefly and to the point. Theocracy, the affirmation of God's sovereignty and omnipotence over his creation, has slowly diminished and credence has moved in the direction of an emphasis on the humanity of Jesus Christ. The next step is taken when the anthropocentric is unashamedly proclaimed. One hears less and less that the Creator will at some point take back his own creation. Rather, it is widely believed and proclaimed that existentially the world is everlasting and that within this context man must concentrate his powers on achieving a terrestrial and social paradise—notwithstanding mounting evidence that man's best efforts are having pre-

---

4. Notably, these words were spoken by Dido in a fit of rage and frustration when she realized she was unable to thwart Aeneas in the accomplishment of his heaven-given vocation. See *The Aeneid*, Bk. VII—Alvin Moore, Jr.

cisely the contrary effect. What Platonism taught us—that creation
is both fontal from and inflowing to the Sovereign Good—is now
forgotten. Two pagan thinkers, the Germans Karl Marx and Martin
Heidegger, promise that this world will never have to answer to the
Lord. Theology, more and more defenseless vis-á-vis these philosophers and others like them, is a virtual prisoner in a hardened
Luciferian grasp.

Fundamental for an understanding of our situation is to be conscious of the fact that existentialism, especially as formulated by
Heidegger, is the definitive philosophical formulation of
Luciferism. A higher, transcendent Reality is denied; the highest
reality is Being, the "ontic" itself, and on this immovable and inaccessible Being reposes our existence.[5] Every idea of creation is
excluded, and in this existential world man lives completely
deprived of norms. His life has no profound meaning; he has only
to preserve himself as best he may in the fleeting, existential flow,
which he does by continuous activity. Man is, as Heidegger says, *ent-
worfen*—dispossessed. The good and the bad, the true and the
false—these notions are of no significance; all proceeds from restless and meaningless human activity. This means, in effect, that man
creates his own solipsistic spiritual world.

Marxism belongs to the nineteenth century, to the epoch of
closed ideological systems. With its Hegelian dialectic and its materialistic interpretation of history, Marxism was an "orthodoxy," one
now quite out of fashion. The Luciferian man-of-today is more and
more heterodox; for this reason existentialism has been advanced
as a more adequate philosophy, the philosophy of the City of Man.
Existentialism is a kind of "laughing gas" for the theological *aggiornamento*; it offers endless possibilities for dissolving orthodox systems and for interpreting them in "new" ways. First and last,
existentialist philosophy delivers modernist theologians from the
"burden" of transcendence. Heaven is a charming story for little
children, but "the man who has come of age" has a "deeper" insight;
God is "down here," included in our earthly existence and manifested only in human beings and in human activity. The contention

5. It cannot be overemphasized that the "ontology" of Martin Heidegger is not
that of the Judeo-Christian tradition (nor of the Islamic tradition, for that matter), notwithstanding a certain commonality of terms which is itself a continuing source of confusion for the unwary. See note 2 above—Alvin Moore, Jr.

between rationalism and faith can now be ended, for faith has been reduced to sentimentality, if not altogether vanquished.

Marxism was always involved in conflict with Western scientific positivism; and here, too, existentialist philosophy dissolves all conflicts. Culturalism also can enjoy unlimited freedom and possibilities. Surely existentialism is the perfect philosophy for Luciferian man in the late twentieth century. But is Lucifer the victor? The world can be covered in darkness, cathedrals can lie in ruins, people can be thrown into confusion and led astray, the light of the Spirit can be obscured. But the false light-bearer, Lucifer, cannot destroy the Spirit. The Luciferian man of our times confronts a sign of the inner truth, and this sign is guilt.

The great secular promise has always been the same: that man— free, strong, and happy—would deliver himself from the burden of guilt. But always, from the Garden of Eden to our own time, man has striven in vain for this impossible deliverance, as if he could run away from his own shadow. This is what Franz Kafka tells us in his novel *The Trial.* The leading character in the story, Joseph K, an insipid and melancholy bank employee, is accused by a shadowy bureaucratic authority of an undefined crime of which he is ignorant. Imprisoned, he meets the chaplain in the prison chapel. The pastor reminds Joseph K of the fact that the law has not only an outward, imperative order, but also an inward order. Not everyone has understood this, even if they have obeyed the law every day of their lives. We always meet differing opinions about the law, and these can even be contradictory. Who in this world is free, and who is bound? The pastor's answer is that to be bound to the law in one's calling, even if only as a porter, is infinitely more precious than to live "free in the world."

This tale has a profound message as well as a plain and direct pedagogical meaning. Reality has a double dimension, the outward and the inward. Consequently, man lives in a two-sided reality. As creation is an order, a cosmos, God has given us a law that has an inward, invisible force as well as one that is external. Even the ordinary servant under the law is superior to the Luciferian hero of liberty, who in his psychic inflation imagines himself to be free in the world—even if this ordinary servant has no profound insight into the Spirit as the inward reality of the law. This is what the prison chaplain tries to tell poor Joseph K, tormented by a guilt the meaning and basis of which he does not understand.

Secularized Western man, incarnated as Joseph K in Kafka's novel, is ignorant of the truth that man has two sources of knowledge, *ratio* and *intellectus*, and that man has within him as it were a fragment, or a reflection, of God's infinitely precious immortal Spirit, and therefore he has a soul. *Duo sunt in homine*, there are two in man—this was a maxim of sacred anthropology in the West until the Renaissance. Within the heart of man resides a spiritual light, and he has intellectual knowledge, an intuitive knowledge of divine Reality. Joseph K cannot understand that he can disavow his presumed Luciferian liberty and freedom from guilt. When therefore a court functionary informs him that he must stand trial, he declares that he does not know the law on which the charge against him is based and he insists that he is innocent. But the court servant points out that if he says he is innocent, then there must be a law confirming this innocence. And when Joseph K insists that he is a free man, the functionary says that there must also exist an absence of freedom.

The Luciferian man believes that he has delivered himself from all guilt and judgment, that he is capable of living strong and free in his jovial heathendom. But the guilty man has intrinsic feelings toward his Creator that he can neither throw off nor escape. He does not understand that creation has a double meaning. First, all creation is an outpouring stream of the divine goodness, and we cannot repay all that we are given of this goodness no matter how many sacrifices we may offer. God's love, his beneficence, is greater than the sum of all human striving; and therefore we are always in debt to our Creator. Second, creation is a cosmos, an order, a divine law that determines the nature of things. If we run counter to this law, it is inevitably to our injury and we are guilty before our Creator. This guilt is twofold: It denies God's love and it denies the right order of God's creation, of which we are part.

Guilt is an existential fact that we have no choice but to acknowledge and accept. We know that in the nature of things, we cannot make recompense; but in our inward light, we have the intuition that God places his infinite grace on our side of the scale, thrown out of balance by our guilt. Through his grace our scale is brought back into balance, and we reach a state of gratitude and inward peace. Secularized man, however, believing that he can rid himself of his burden of guilt—as if he could successfully evade his shadow—encounters not grace but the onus of his uneasy conscience. In our time, one of the indicators of this increasingly widespread sense of guilt is the upsurge of neurotic disorders. This is what Kafka's novel tells us, under the symbol of a trial.

A growing feeling of guilt is, then, one of the many signs of the inward crisis in the City of Man. The helplessness of Western theology is often expressed in essays that seek to justify it as a psychotherapeutic institution, instead of telling the truth about God, his nature, his work, and what is required of us. But God's spirit lives, even in the midst of a fallen world, and even if it is denied, concealed, and forgotten. Amid Luciferian confusion, amid a growing burden of guilt, beyond a ruinous Western theology, every day man can meet God.

Man's encounter with God is an encounter with the holy. We meet God in inward and outward meaning, and this meeting is like a point of crystallization of the holy in earthly life, a manifestation of the uncreated Absolute in the relative and the contingent. We have some experience of the holy when, inwardly quiet, we encounter connatural substance. This meeting place is at the center of man's being: the heart; and the quiet of the heart lends to our soul the character of a mirror in which, with the "eye of the heart," we can see rays of the divine Sun. The restlessness and hyperactivity of the world lead us away from the holy; but in a quietened heart, the door opens that leads to the holy.

Our terrestrial existence is a continuous wandering between dream and reality. Life's contradictions prompt secularized man to seek refuge in dreams, illusions, utopias, ideological castles in the air. In his self-deception, profane man thinks that what he receives in his mental consciousness is the real and the objective; at the same time, he hopes that by his dreams, utopias, ideologies, and so forth, he can change the world and make it better. This self-deception is twofold. What he calls real or objective is only the outermost layer of creation, that which is accessible to sensory observation. And what man hopes to do and to achieve in the world is founded on subjectivism: on impressions, dreams, speculations.

Man achieves objectivity only when he goes beyond the limits in which he lives as a sensual ego. In the inner light of our heart we can escape from the labyrinth of existence and, with discipline, effort, and the aid of heaven, become aware of divine Reality. Through objectivity, we can encounter the holy in the world; we can conceive of creation as a gigantic symbol of God's omnipotence; we can distinguish between the real and the illusory. In this objectivity, man is conscious of his own position and limitations, but also of his spiritual possibilities by means of which he can receive God's ineffable grace.

We can encounter the world by means of the holy and through objectivity, but with a third element also: through love, God's love. As Creator, he is generous; and this generosity is love, beneficence. As the Absolute, he has given spirituality to man, a reflection of his eternal Spirit. We were created by the Father, and in the innermost depths of our soul we are immortal; in this twofold meaning, we are bound to God. All that we have is from him; all that we have, we have received as an emanation of his love. Therefore, we say that God is love. Therefore, the world, and man in the world, must bear witness to God's love.

The holy is presence, and it is also attraction. We seek the holy because the holy means purity and perfection. Objectivity is presence, but objectivity is also attraction. We seek objectivity because we desire Reality and Truth, not illusions and lies. Love is presence, but love is also attraction. We seek love because we will not be isolated or abandoned. We seek God, the very Source of our being.

Chapter 6

The Mystery of the Two Natures

James S. Cutsinger

> The things we are going to say seem to some of the multitude to be
> different from the Scriptures of our Lord. But let these know that
> it is by the Scriptures themselves that these things live and breathe;
> from them they draw their whole grounding, but from them they
> take only the spirit and not the language.
> —St Clement of Alexandria

From the very start it was clear that this was something extraordinary. As a college professor of religion, I had read fairly widely
and deeply before, and had made it my aim to assimilate many of
the greatest philosophical and theological works. But nothing had
prepared me for my first encounter with a book by Frithjof Schuon.
I vividly recall reading the opening page, and then reading it again,
and then a third and fourth time, before proceeding. The words
themselves were certainly not difficult, nor was the style at all complex. Indeed, compared to many a modern philosopher's work,
Schuon's books are noted for their simple, and often poetic, beauty. And yet for some reason I found myself unable to move with the
speed I was accustomed to. It was like running along the beach and
then into the ocean. Here was a new medium, no less able to support my movement, but requiring an altogether different engagement. There would be no more running now. I would have to swim.

This initial sense that Schuon was different—that there is an
intensity or depth in his message unlike any other—has since been
many times confirmed, both in my continued study of his books and
through a number of personal contacts which I was privileged to
have with the man himself during the last decade or so of his life. It
is hard for me to know quite what to say, how to convey the significance of these encounters. Others have spoken about Schuon in the
most exalted terms. Comparing him to figures like Shankaracharya
and Meister Eckhart, they have said that he was a paragon among
religious authorities, perhaps the *qutb* or spiritual axis for our age,

whose work was of a cyclic or Eleatic importance—a *jivan-mukta*, blessed with the vision of the cosmic Intellect itself. While I have seen no reason to discount such judgments, and many good reasons to suppose them true, I myself prefer to be more circumspect. It seems to me that Schuon's books are not in need of any special praise or promotion and can be left to speak for themselves, and I heartily commend them to the attention of every serious seeker. As for our personal relationship, I shall simply say that Frithjof Schuon is one of the greatest men I have ever known, and I am profoundly grateful to have had his friendship.

What is the most important thing that Schuon taught me? This is the question I have posed to myself for the purpose of writing this chapter. As soon as I ask it, however, I am struck by the extent to which virtually everything I believe and think has been shaped by his perspective. Someone has said that it was Schuon's aim, not only to promulgate a doctrine and teach a method, but to create a civilization, and as one who has endeavored to enter into that civilization as fully as circumstances permit, I now find that it is almost impossible to recall my initial experience of its borders, or to rank my many discoveries. I can say this, though: On the doctrinal side, very few points have turned out to be more decisive or fruitful than Schuon's teachings on Christ, and it is upon these that I would like to concentrate here.

I am myself a Christian, a member of the Eastern Orthodox Church, and as a professor of theology at a large university in the American South, I teach mostly Christian students. It is only natural that other Christians should from time to time become aware of my sympathy for Schuon's perspective, and when they do so it is understandable that many of them should be surprised, and in some cases dismayed—especially those who learn that Schuon was a universalist and a leading exponent of the *sophia perennis*. They wonder what I could possibly be thinking. How could I compromise my allegiance to Christ and my fidelity to His Church by supposing that other religions are equally true, and by looking to Schuon as a spiritual guide? I do not here wish to go into the second part of this question, except to say that when I once asked a very high ranking and well-known hierarch of the Orthodox Church for his comments on my friendship with Schuon, he replied by referring me to a passage in *The Way of a Pilgrim* which permits the Christian, in the absence of an Orthodox *starets*, to seek direction "even from a Saracen". There is also this to be added: In my first meeting with Schuon, almost his very first words to me were an admonition that "Christ is your master".

But what about the larger matter of other spiritual forms? How in good conscience can a traditional Christian accept the idea that there is a "transcendent unity of religions"?[1] The first thing to stress about Schuon's answer to this question is that it requires no diminution in our convictions as to the stature of Christ. Unlike certain modernist theologians, who in the interest of fostering harmony among the religions are prepared to jettison the Incarnation and to reduce Jesus to purely human and historical categories, Schuon is adamant in his defense of the traditional doctrine. "The mainspring of Christianity," he insists—borrowing as he so often does the familiar Patristic formulation—"is that 'God has become man so that man may become God.'"[2] Indeed, "the whole of Christianity hangs on these words: Christ is God."[3] As his readers know very well, he had nothing but the most withering scorn for those who would call into question this and other traditional doctrines by acting as if they had in some way been ruled out by a currently fashionable, and unreflective, materialism, and who have determined accordingly to purge the Gospels of the supernatural. "Scientific discoveries prove nothing to contradict the traditional positions of religion,"[4] Schuon writes, and many pages of his prose are dedicated to criticizing the pretensions of modern scientism and historicism, and to chastising

---

1. I refer here to the title of one of Schuon's earliest works, and perhaps his best known, *The Transcendent Unity of Religions* (Wheaton, Illinois: The Theosophical Publishing House, 1984).
2. Schuon, *Esoterism as Principle and as Way*, trans. William Stoddart (London: Perennial Books, 1981), p. 37. "In Christianity, the Patristic formula of saving reciprocity is a priceless jewel: 'God became man that man might become God'; it is a revelation in the full sense, of the same rank as scripture, which may seem surprising, but which is a 'paracletic' possibility" (*Survey of Metaphysics and Esoterism*, trans. Gustavo Polit [Bloomington, Indiana: World Wisdom Books, 1986], p. 116).
3. Schuon, *Gnosis: Divine Wisdom*, trans. G. E. H. Palmer (London: Perennial Books, 1990), p. 108. Elsewhere he writes, "A Christianity that denies the Divinity of Christ denies the reason for its own existence" (*Transcendent Unity*, p. 99).
4. Schuon, *Light on the Ancient Worlds*, trans. Lord Northbourne (Bloomington, Indiana: World Wisdom Books, 1984), pp. 37-38.

those who feel obliged to reduce their religions in the interest of making them relevant. As for a more recent and somewhat more nuanced suggestion that we might as good Biblical critics nonetheless allow for Christ's having been a kind of shamanistic healer—though still, of course, without His being God—there is this pointed reply: "The miracles of Christ are not 'occult powers' (*siddhis*) that can be exercised or not exercised, but Divine manifestations, therefore facts that elude all psychological evaluation, and Christ is not a man who became wise, but Wisdom become man."[5] My aim here is not to defend these assertions against the objections of the demythologizers. They have only to investigate such works of Schuon's as *Logic and Transcendence*, or perhaps the excellent chapter on "Orthodoxy and Intellectuality" in his *Stations of Wisdom*, to discover why scholarly integrity in no way necessitates a sacrifice of traditional faith. But my interlocutors for the moment are my fellow Orthodox and other conservative Christians, and my aim is to emphasize how fully traditional are this perennialist's Christological teachings.

Nor are they traditional by accident or inadvertently. As with every religion about which he wrote, Schuon made it his business to penetrate deeply into Christianity. He knew its scriptures, its liturgies, its art, its leading authorities, the lives of its saints, its denominational divergences, and its conciliar formularies. And when it came to Christian teaching on Christ, he always wrote with a full knowledge of the early Church and its historical controversies. He was well aware, for example, of the anathemas which Dyophysites, Monophysites, Aphthartodocetae, Phthartolatrae, Agnoetae, Akistetae, and Ktistolatrae hurl at one another over the question of knowing whether Christ is of an incorruptible substance or whether, on the contrary, his was like other bodies, or whether there was a part of human ignorance in the soul of Christ, or whether the body of Christ is uncreated while being at the same time visible, or whether it was created, and so on. And Schuon was able, like the Church Fathers before him, to find the essential balance between these competing extremes. He realized, in other words, that Christ, "as living form of God, had to show in His humanity supernatural prerogatives which it would be vain to seek to enumerate, but that

---

5. *Gnosis*, pp. 56-57.

inasmuch as He was incontestably man, He was bound to have certain limits, as is proved by the incident of the fig tree whose sterility he did not discern from afar".[6] We shall be looking more closely at certain particulars later. My immediate purpose in citing this passage is simply to show that Schuon's Christology was by no means uninformed by the classic Christian sources. On the contrary, he was fully aware of what he called in one of his most important chapters "The Mystery of the Two Natures",[7] and he was tireless in demonstrating its manifold implications.

But it is here precisely that a certain dilemma arises. If Schuon really believed that Christ is God, how could he at the same time have defended the "spiritual equivalence of the great revelations"?[8] This seems to many a sheer contradiction. If Christ is both true God and true man—if the early creeds are right that Jesus of Nazareth was the incarnate, only-begotten, and eternal Son of God—then it is surely impossible to condone those religions which ignore or dismiss His Divinity. Is it not obvious that they must be rejected as false? Or alternatively, if these other religions are true, does it not follow that in order to honor them, we should reject instead the early creeds? Must we not admit, no matter how grudgingly, that the doctrine of the two natures was a bit of pious excess, a speculative luxury conditioned by the now outmoded philosophical categories of late antiquity, and unjustified in any case by the life of the historical Jesus?

The first of these alternatives—the repudiation of other religions—has of course always been common among traditional Christians, and it may take either of two basic forms. Some will say that the non-Christian is necessarily damned, that there can be no salvation apart from a conscious, explicit, and active faith in Jesus Christ and membership in His visible Body, the Church; whereas

---

6. Schuon, *In the Face of the Absolute* (Bloomington, Indiana: World Wisdom Books, 1989), pp. 65-66.
7. Schuon, *Christianity/Islam: Essays on Esoteric Ecumenicism*, trans. Gustavo Polit (Bloomington, Indiana: World Wisdom Books, 1985), pp. 55-66. It is important to add that Schuon's knowledge of Christianity came from more than just books. His own brother was a Trappist monk, and his many other contacts included the Orthodox Archimandrite Sophrony, a noted disciple of St Silouan of the Holy Mountain.
8. Schuon, *Spiritual Perspectives and Human Facts*, trans. P. N. Townsend (London: Perennial Books, 1987), p. 121.

others will allow that the non-Christian may in certain cases be saved, but only in spite of the religion he practices and only through the mercy of a God who overlooks his ignorance in this life and permits him to submit to the lordship of Christ after death. As for the second alternative—the repudiation of the early creeds—this as we know is the more typical modern approach, an approach which presumes that believing in the Divinity of Christ necessarily goes hand in hand with religious prejudice and exclusivist bigotry. In recent conversation with a prominent member of the much-discussed Jesus Seminar, I was told that while the previous generation of scholars was doubtless wrong in imposing an Enlightenment worldview on the New Testament texts, they were nonetheless right in rejecting the claim that Jesus is God. This is required in part for various textual and historical reasons, the scholar claimed, but his admitted first concern was to avoid causing offense to those of other faiths.

But are these really the only options? Are we obliged to choose between an "exclusive dogmatism", on the one hand, which has admittedly become "untenable and dangerous in a universe where everything meets and interpenetrates", and a "blind and dissolvent ecumenism",[9] on the other, which forgets that "the religions and their orthodox developments are inalienable and irreplaceable legacies to which nothing essential can be added and from which nothing essential can be subtracted"?[10] Schuon thinks not, and a large part of his work was devoted to showing a way out of this dilemma.

The solution for him lies in an esoteric ecumenism—an ecumenism which is based upon a sacred science of symbols and which is designed to reveal the inward meaning of traditional religious doctrines and rites. "When a man seeks to escape from dogmatic narrowness," he writes, "it is essential that it be 'upwards' and not 'downwards': dogmatic form is transcended by fathoming its depths and contemplating its universal content, and not by denying it in the name of a pretentious and iconoclastic ideal of 'pure truth'".[11]

9. Schuon, *Logic and Transcendence*, trans. Peter N. Townsend (London: Perennial Books, 1975), pp. 4, 5.
10. Schuon, "No Activity without Truth", *The Sword of Gnosis: Metaphysics, Cosmology, Tradition, Symbolism*, ed. Jacob Needleman (London: Routledge and Kegan Paul, 1986), pp. 34-35.
11. Schuon, *Stations of Wisdom* (Bloomington, Indiana: World Wisdom Books, 1995), p. 4.

A legitimate and spiritually profitable dialogue among the religions is one which recognizes, paradoxical though this may seem, that the traditions are closest to each other and most alike at their centers, not along their circumferences, and it will therefore always take as its starting point those dogmas and symbols which are the most distinctive or characteristic in a given religion. Instead of apologetic and half-embarrassed dismissals, it will be noted for its serious and sympathetic engagement with each tradition's most essential and original teachings, for "that which in each religion provides the key for total or non-dualist esoterism is not some secret concept of a heterogeneous character, but is the very presiding idea of the religion."[12] In the case of Christianity, of course, no teaching is more central or presiding than the Incarnation, and it was therefore always in full view of this doctrine, understood in its own traditional terms, that Schuon wrote about the Christian faith, whether with respect to some historical or denominational question, or in connection with metaphysics and *gnosis*.[13] But what exactly does this doctrine say?

*

* *

The Christian believes that God became man in Jesus Christ. It must be understood at once, however, that the Incarnation is a considerably more subtle affair than this highly elliptical formulation suggests—however much Christian piety may have sometimes wished to simplify, and however often the modern critics have reacted to this simplification with an equal disregard for the doctrine itself. God became man, it is true. But as the Fathers of the early Church helped to clarify, it was not just any aspect of God, or God as such, who was incarnate in Jesus; nor was it some particular man, but man as such, that He became; and in becoming man He never

12. *Esoterism*, pp. 25-26.
13. Since "Christianity is founded on the idea and the reality of Divine Manifestation" (*Logic and Transcendence*, p. 98), and since "for the Christian, the overwhelming argument is the Divinity of Christ, and, flowing from this, the fact that there is an intermediary between God and man in the form of God made man" (*Gnosis*, p. 13), it follows that if there is to be a "Christian *gnosis*", it must find "its support a priori, and of necessity, in the mysteries of the Incarnation and the Redemption, and thus in the Christic Phenomenon as such" (*Esoterism*, p. 26).

ceased to be God. It is crucial that we not lose sight of these three important distinctions. Let me restate them in the classic language of the ecumenical councils.

The tradition teaches us first that it was the Son or *Logos*, the second Person of the Holy Trinity, who was incarnate in Jesus, not the first Person of the Father. On the contrary, the Father is the *aitia* or cause of both the Son and the Spirit, whether by filiation or spiration; He is the Unity, according to St Gregory the Theologian, "from whom and to whom the order of the Persons runs its course",[14] and He remains forever, therefore—despite the Incarnation—a transcendent and inaccessible mystery. The three Persons are indeed *homoousios* or consubstantial, all of them sharing in the common essence of Divinity. But Christianity explicitly repudiates the notion that they are therefore the same or interchangeable. To suppose that they are, to confuse or confound or equate the Persons, is in fact a heresy—the heresy of modalistic monarchianism or Sabellianism.

The second distinction pertains to the human dimension of Christ. According to many early Christian authorities, especially those associated with the Alexandrian school, the Son's human nature is to be regarded as generic, not specific, for it was not the historical particularity of an individual man, but the essence of man as such, which was assumed into God when "the Word became flesh" (Jn 1:14). The humanity of Jesus was in this sense impersonal or "anhypostatic"—or perhaps "enhypostatic", to use the technical parlance of Leontius of Byzantium, who preferred to say that while Jesus had no uniquely human *hypostasis*, His humanity shared in the *hypostasis* of the Divine Son of God. In any case, although Christ fully participated in every aspect of our *physis* or nature, sin only excepted, He was unlike us in not having a human personality, or substantial agency, as such. What He was, was both Divine and human, but who He was, was the *Logos*—His Person being in fact none other than the eternal second Person of the Trinity, who had existed from before the foundation of the world. To suppose otherwise, to think that Divinity had been projected somehow into an independent, and otherwise unexceptional, human being named

14. *Theological Orations*, XLII.15.

Jesus, is also a heresy—the heresy of adoptionism or dynamic monarchianism.

Finally a third point, equally essential to a correct understanding of the traditional doctrine, pertains to the relationship between the two natures in Christ. While the first two distinctions have to do with the parallel planes of Christ's Divinity and humanity, the third concerns the vertical junction or intersection between them, and in this case the tradition explicitly forbids all attempts to confuse or identify the Divine and the human. Because of the Incarnation, the two natures are said to be "hypostatically" or substantially linked in Christ's Person, to such a degree that each shares the other's properties in a *communicatio idiomatum.* And yet it is impermissible to think that either nature was effaced by the other in the Person of the incarnate Word. To suppose that one of the natures could have been subsumed or eclipsed, to act in particular as though the humanity of Jesus had been overwhelmed by the Divinity that was manifest in Him, is to court yet another heresy—in this case, the heresy of monophysitism.

Schuon was well aware of these technical points. In fact, he seems to have understood them much better than many traditional Christians, including even certain doctors of the Church, who in their zeal to insure our conviction as to Christ's Divinity have often risked merging or confusing the God whom "no man hath seen at any time" (Jn 1:18) with the historical particularity of Jesus of Nazareth. This remark will probably come as a surprise to some of my readers, either because they were unaware of the subtlety in the early Church's pronouncements or because they are new to the Schuonian vocabulary. Nevertheless, once one understands his terms it is clear that Schuon's teaching on Christ, while perhaps controversial in certain particulars, is well within the bounds of Chalcedonian orthodoxy. Let me try to substantiate this claim.[15]

15. My readers will understand that I do not pretend to be complete. What follows is only a brief and somewhat elliptical sketch of essentials, touching on but a few of the many relevant passages in Schuon's work. The allusion above is to the Definition of Chalcedon, promulgated in A.D. 451 by the fourth of the Ecumenical Councils. In summing up the distinctions which were touched on above, this classic statement of faith has since been a standard for the orthodox understanding of Christ, "the only-begotten Son, who is in two natures, unconfusedly, immutably, indivisibly, and inseparably, without the distinction of natures being taken away by the union" (*The Seven Ecumenical Councils*, ed.

Like every aspect of his message, Schuon's Christology must be seen in light of his metaphysics, and the place to begin is with the principial distinction he so often makes in his work between the Absolute and the Relative, or *Âtmâ* and *Mâyâ*. On the one hand there is That which cannot not be, the necessary, but on the other hand there is also that which need not be, the contingent or possible. "All other distinctions and valuations derive from this fundamental distinction."[16] As his readers know, this is a distinction which gives rise above all to the polarity of transcendence and immanence. To know that there is an Absolute, and to understand what It is, is to know that It is the only Reality. Only the Absolute is absolute, and in Its utter transcendence It completely eclipses the Relative, which in comparison is but an illusory nothingness. And yet to know that this Absolute is the only Reality is to know also that everything else is in some fashion It, for in Its independence and freedom from limits, It is equally infinite, and by virtue of this Infinitude It cannot but give rise to the Relative, in which It is immanent. Only *Âtmâ* truly is, but *Mâyâ* is the deployment and manifestation of *Âtmâ*. Nothing truly exists except God, and yet whatever exists truly is God.

According to Schuon, a full grasp of this teaching will oblige us to recognize that Relativity actually begins within the Divine Principle Itself: hence what he calls "the key notion of *Mâyâ in divinis*".[17] This in fact is one of the most important and characteristic features of his message. The Principle is not a monolithic Reality,

---

Henry R. Percival, Vol. XIV of *The Nicene and Post-Nicene Fathers* [Grand Rapids, Michigan: Eerdmans, 1983], pp. 264-65). It might be added, for those familiar with the early Christian schools and major Patristic figures, that Schuon's perspective is primarily Alexandrian, not Antiochene, and that his reading of Chalcedon is largely along Cyrilian lines—in keeping, that is, with the teaching of the Patriarch St Cyril of Alexandria. I do not however mean to suggest that Schuon was operating deliberately or self-consciously in these terms. He was a metaphysician and esoterist, not a theologian, and his point of departure was the nature of things, not the exoteric doctrines of any given religion. Doctrines were of interest to him insofar as they might serve as intellectual keys or methodic supports for those who would know what is.

16. Schuon, *Survey of Metaphysics*, p. 7.
17. *Survey of Metaphysics*, p. 121. This "key notion", which Schuon calls "apparently absurd but metaphysically essential", is a hallmark of his perspective. For a fuller treatment of the idea of dimensions or levels in God, see Chapter 5, "The Degrees of Reality", in my *Advice to the Serious Seeker: Meditations on the Teaching of Frithjof Schuon* (Albany, New York: State University of New York Press, 1997).

but comprises instead an inward or intrinsic differentiation between two distinct degrees. There is on the one hand the Absolute as such, the Supreme Reality or "pure Ipseity";[18] but there is also a second level of Divinity, wherein the pure Absolute, while transcending all determinations and categories, makes Itself known in a determinate way, thus anticipating or prefiguring the world. By virtue of this determination, metaphysically necessary, the Absolute becomes subject in that measure to *Mâyâ*; it is precisely this Divine self-subjection to Relativity which gives rise to the difference, in Hindu teaching, between *Nirguna Brahman* and *Saguna Brahman*, or in Meister Eckhart's doctrine between *Gottheit* and *Gott*. In Schuon's vocabulary it is the difference between Beyond-Being and Being, or again between the Divine Essence and the Divine Person. But whatever language we use, the distinction itself is universal and inescapable. On the one hand, there must be an Absolute, utterly independent and sovereign, conditioned by nothing, not even by Itself; and yet, given the very nature of this Absolute, which cannot but be Infinite, there must also arise a determinate, and subordinate, dimension within the Divine Principle, which, though absolute with respect to the world, is nonetheless relative with respect to Its Essence. However paradoxical the formulation may seem, there must also be a "relative Absolute".[19]

Even those with no experience in reading Schuon will quickly see the implications which these distinctions have for Christology. If one has understood the necessity of levels or dimensions in God, it should come as no surprise to discover that these dimensions are directly related, in Christian terms, to the Persons of the Holy Trinity. Nor should we be surprised to discover that for Schuon it is the First Person alone who is purely the Absolute, while the Son and the Holy Spirit—called by St Irenaeus the two "hands" of the Father—are at the level of the relative Absolute.[20] What this means,

18. This is a formulation to be found in a number of Schuon's unpublished texts.
19. Schuon, *The Play of Masks* (Bloomington, Indiana: World Wisdom Books, 1992), p. 35. See also *Stations of Wisdom*, p. 16.
20. St Irenaeus, *Against the Heresies*, 4.20.1. Schuon points out that God the Father may be pictured as a central point, the Holy Spirit as the radii projected out from this point, and the Son as the resulting circle. See *From the Divine to the Human*, trans. Gustavo Polit and Deborah Lambert (Bloomington, Indiana: World Wisdom Books, 1982), p. 40. Since my interest here is specifically in Schuon's Christology, I must set aside an investigation of his teaching on the

of course, is that a certain subordinationism is a necessary ingredient in any adequate understanding of Christ's Divinity. Even apart from His historical incarnation in Jesus, the *Logos* or Word of God must be acknowledged as precisely God's Word, His primal expression and self-determination, and as such, says Schuon, this *Logos* cannot help but partake of the metaphysically Relative. The Second Person cannot escape being the second person. Although absolute with respect to His creatures, He remains subordinate even so, from all eternity, to the First Person of "God the Father almighty" (Nicene Creed). Christ's Divinity is that of the "lesser Absolute".[21]

I realize that traditional Christians will at first be uneasy with this line of thinking, especially when they hear the word "subordinationism", which continues to this day to be associated with the much-maligned Origen. It is only natural that upon reading this exposition many will "hasten to deny Relativity *in divinis* with the intention of safeguarding the absoluteness of God"[22] and thus, they suppose, the Divinity of the Son—in spite of the fact that neither is under attack. But as Schuon often pointed out, in so doing these Christians are forgetting their own scriptures, where the subordination of the Divine Son is quite clear. It is certainly true that Jesus proclaimed His Divinity: "I and my Father are one" (Jn 10:30), and "He that hath seen Me hath seen the Father" (Jn 14:9); and the Nicene Creed therefore obliges the Christian to affirm the consubstantiality of these Persons. Nonetheless, the Son also asserted, in no uncertain terms, that "my Father is greater than I" (Jn 14:28),[23] a relationship which we readily see, a multitude of other proofs

---

Trinity as such, which is considerably more subtle than I have suggested above. Here I have in mind only what he has called the "vertical perspective", which "envisages the Hypostases [or Persons] as 'descending' from Unity or from the Absolute". But there are also two "horizontal" perspectives. See Schuon, *Understanding Islam* (Bloomington, Indiana: World Wisdom Books, 1994), p. 53.

21. *Face of the Absolute*, p. 40.
22. *Logic and Transcendence*, pp. 106-107.
23. It might be well to remind the reader that I am writing as an Orthodox Christian for other traditional Christians. I realize that the many quotations from St John will prove of little value to modern Biblical critics, who question the authenticity of many of Christ's sayings in this Gospel and find it the least reliable portrait of the "historical Jesus". But one cannot do everything at once, and a critique of these critics' assumptions, alluded to earlier, lies beyond the scope of this article. My specific aim in using John at this point is to accentuate the fact that even in the Gospel with the "highest" Christology, subordination remains.

aside, in the Son's frequent prayers to the Father. Clearly there is One who is greater than Christ, and we must therefore conclude that there is a kind of hierarchy within God Himself.

Some traditional Christians, in hopes of protecting our faith in the Second Person from the corrosive effects of the Arian heresy, which denied His Divinity, have tried to make sense of this hierarchy by identifying any hint of subordination with Christ's human nature alone. When reference is made to the superiority of the Father, or when prayers are directed to the First Person, it is simply "Jesus the man", they contend, who is talking. But as the history of Christian doctrine makes clear, this is to risk falling prey in turn to the views of Nestorius, who divided Christ into two separate persons, assuming falsely that the Son's human "half" could act independently of His Divinity, and it is to forget what the Council at Ephesus so forcefully taught in response to this heresy: that the two natures cohere undividedly in the single Person of the *Logos*. To put the matter in less technical terms, the conciliar formulations require us to say that whatever deeds Jesus may have performed, and whatever words He spoke, were deeds done and words spoken by the eternal Son of God. When Jesus was born, it was God the Son who was born, so that the Virgin Mary may be addressed as the *Theotokos* or Mother of God. Similarly when Jesus wept and when He died, it was the Second Person who wept and died, albeit in a manner befitting Divinity and hence impassibly.

Schuon is therefore perfectly orthodox in explaining that "if Christ addresses a prayer to His Father, it is not solely by reason of His human nature; it is also by reason of the Relativity of the uncreated *Logos*".[24] He continues:

> The words of Christ announcing His subordination are often attributed to His human nature alone, but this delimitation is arbitrary and interested, for the human nature is bound by its Divine content; if it is part of the Son, it must manifest that content. The fact that this human nature exists and that its expressions manifest its subordination, and by the same token the hypostatic subordination of the Son, shows that the interpretation of the Son as the first Relativity confronting the purely Absolute Father is not contrary to Scripture and is inherently irrefutable.[25]

24. *Face of the Absolute*, p. 79.
25. *Logic and Transcendence*, pp. 98-99.

Nor is this interpretation in any way contrary to Patristic tradition, which forbids (as we have seen) any modalistic confusion of Persons, and which in so doing implicitly acknowledges that the Persons are intrinsically different—different, that is, independently of their extrinsic roles in the Divine economy. And if they are intrinsically different, they must also be hierarchically different. For unless words have no meaning it is absurd to think that the Son and Holy Spirit could be as absolute as their *cause*, or that the two *hands* could be on the same level as the person who wields them, or yet again that a *son* should be as original as the one who begat him. It is absurd in other words to suppose that the infinite simplicity of the pure Absolute could be repeated in an equally infinite and absolute duplicate. We must admit instead that Christ's Divinity is derivative, and that what one encounters in Jesus is not the Divine Essence Itself, but Its self-determination at the level of Being.

I turn now to the second and third of our Christological distinctions, which may I think be usefully treated together. Our task at this point is to examine more closely the mode of Christ's humanity and the nature of its union with the *Logos*. As explained earlier, two dogmatic points are essential to the traditional view on these questions. When God the Son became man, say the Fathers, it was not some particular man, but man as such, that He became, and in becoming man in this sense He never ceased to be God. The Divine humanity was not limited to the individual order, and yet the difference between the two natures was not eclipsed by their union. Here once more a careful reading of Schuon makes it clear that his teaching was in full accord with the Christian tradition.

Before we examine the specific terms of that tradition, however, another short metaphysical excursus is in order. I have called attention to the distinction which Schuon makes within the Divine Principle between the Absolute as such and the relative Absolute, and have explained that the Divinity of the Son corresponds to the latter. The Second Person takes second place to the First, and for this reason the *Logos* must be situated below the Divine Essence at the level of Being—a level which anticipates or prefigures the domain of creation or manifestation. For "all things were made by Him, and without Him was not anything made that was made" (Jn 1:3). A similar discrimination must now be established between two additional degrees of Reality, this time within the formal or created universe. This is a distinction, in the Schuonian vocabulary, between the manifested Principle and manifestation as such. Even as manifestation is prefigured in the Principle, so the Principle is projected or prolonged in manifestation, and the result is "the celestial order", or simply "Heaven". Finally, beneath this heavenly level, there is a fourth and final degree, and this is the "natural" or "profane" world, or simply the "Earth".[26] According to Schuon, any metaphysically adequate understanding of the Incarnation will have to take into account both of these manifested degrees. For in entering the world of becoming as man, the Son of God became what we are, but without in any way ceasing to be what He is, and it can therefore be said that He was still in Heaven though He was present on Earth. He was at once the Principle manifest, and the manifest Principle. "It is not as man," says Schuon, "that Christ is God; but on the other hand the fact that He is man does not prevent His being really God."[27] Let us look now to see whether the tradition says the same thing.

According to the Bible "the Word became flesh" (Jn 1:14). But just what does this mean? It means, the Fathers say, that the Divine Son of God condescended to live the life of a real human being, becoming "consubstantial with us as to His humanity, being like us in every respect apart from sin" (Definition of Chalcedon). Whatever additional fine points we shall have to insist on, any attempt to deny this humanity must be rejected as heresy. Schuon was well aware of this point, concurring fully—as we shall see momentarily—with the Church's repudiation of docetism and heretical gnosticism. He too rejects the claim, in other words, that Christ was a pure spirit and only seemed to be man. But at the same time he was also of one mind with the Fathers in realizing that a bare admission of Christ's manhood still leaves open the important question of its mode, and it was obvious to him, as it was to the early Church, that however genuine the Son's human nature might be, it was nevertheless "of a different essence from that of the ordinary man, and this by reason of the intimate penetration of all His modalities by the Universal". For the "very substance of the individuality"—the very thing which distinguishes each of us as human

---

26. *Survey of Metaphysics*, p. 19.
27. *Eye of the Heart*, pp. 153-54.

egos and agents—was "transmuted by the Real Presence" of Divinity.[28]

Thinking only of these and other similar passages in Schuon's writings, some Christian readers have charged their author with ignoring the historical particularity of the Incarnation, and with focusing too exclusively on the supra-temporal *Logos* or cosmic Christ. But is this really fair? Schuon was doubtless less inclined than many contemporary Christian scholars to emphasize the "historical Jesus"—but then so were the Bible and other orthodox sources, with which he was in complete unanimity. One recalls, for example, the words which Christ spoke to Nicodemus: "No man hath ascended up to Heaven but He that came down from Heaven, even the Son of Man which is in Heaven" (Jn 3:13). However else we might wish to gloss this remarkable text, there is no escaping the fact that a celestial Man, who could be simultaneously present on two distinct planes of Reality, must have differed from the rest of us in much more than degree. Or consider Christ's miracles, especially perhaps those involving His manipulation of material substances and those effected by contact with His physical body. Here, too, it seems obvious that the human dimension of His incarnate Person, although truly human—and although subject, at some important level, to the conditions of a fallen environment—must have retained nonetheless at least some of the powers and privileges of Eden. Or yet again one thinks of the incarnate Word's ability to render Itself invisible and weightless, disappearing in the midst of crowds (Lk 4:30) and walking on water (Mt 14:25). In these and numerous other such cases, it is obvious that Christ was free from terrestrial and temporal constraints in some way—certainly to an extent we are not—and hence that the properties and powers of His manhood, genuine though it was, were ontologically affected by its union with the *Logos*.

"The Divine man is 'true God and true man.'" With this claim no orthodox Christian will wish to quarrel. But Schuon is surely right to add that "being 'God', and despite being 'man', He is not 'man' in the same way as other men are who are not 'God'".[29] No less a figure than St Athanasius concurs:

28. *Eye of the Heart*, pp. 104, 105.
29. *Eye of the Heart*, p. 106.

> A man cannot transport things from one place to another merely
> by thinking about them; nor can you and I move the sun and stars
> by sitting at home and looking at them. With the Word of God in
> His human nature, however, it was otherwise. His body was for
> Him not a limitation, but an instrument, so that He was both in it
> and in all things, and outside all things, resting in the Father alone.
> At one and the same time—this is the wonder—as man He was liv-
> ing a human life, and as Word He was sustaining the life of the uni-
> verse.[30]

I have referred to Christ's words and mentioned His miracles, but
the wonder of which the saint is here speaking can be apprehend-
ed most clearly perhaps in the Transfiguration, when "His face did
shine as the sun, and His raiment was white as the light" (Mt 17:2).
What we see in this account, say the Orthodox Fathers, is resplen-
dent and irrefutable evidence of what Christ always was in Himself.
For the transformation on Tabor involved no change in Him whose
eternal and celestial glory persisted throughout His earthly life; it
was a transformation instead in the eyes of His apostles, who were
now able to see His human nature as it had always been. Thus
Schuon's observation:

> To recognize that the humanity of Christ is the vehicle of the
> Divine nature amounts to saying that if the human side is in one
> respect truly human, it is so in a way that is nonetheless different
> from the humanity of ordinary men. In a certain sense and a priori
> the Divine Presence transfigures, or transubstantializes, the human
> nature; the body of Christ is already, here below, what celestial bod-
> ies are, with the sole difference that it is nevertheless affected by
> some of the accidents of earthly life.[31]

God became man. But since it was God who was this man, the man
cannot but have shimmered with the Divinity of His other nature,
and for this reason we are obliged to affirm that even His human
nature was not quite the same as our own. In becoming man, says St
Gregory of Nyssa, the Word of God "took our nature within

---

30. *On the Incarnation*, XVII. Some may object that despite its saintly provenance,
   this passage comes too close to the Apollinarian heresy, which denied that
   Christ had a real human soul. It is clear, however, that the "body" is for St
   Athanasius what the "flesh" is for St Paul: the psychosomatic ensemble of the
   individual man as a whole.
31. *Christianity/Islam*, pp. 56-57.

Himself, so that the human should be deified by this mingling with God. The stuff of our nature was entirely sanctified by Christ."[32]

There remains, however, one final distinction. The Person of Christ's Divinity and the unique mode of His manhood having been underscored, we are still faced with the question as to the union between them. As we have just seen, the tradition insists that the Son's humanity was not of an ordinary or purely limited order. But it must now be added that the Fathers also eschew the opposite extreme: the Christian is not permitted to believe that Jesus was a man like all others, a man merely chosen and empowered by God, but neither may he deny that He was a man altogether. For even though the human nature of Christ was transmuted, transfigured, or "transubstantialized" through its union with God, that nature remained truly and recognizably human. The Son of God really lived as a man, and His willing submission to the accidents and contingencies of the terrestrial order was not an illusion—or in any case no more an illusion than that order itself.[33] This, too, Christianity affirms and requires.

What is true for the tradition is also true for Schuon. It is evident once again, from his many references to the Incarnation, that he was thoroughly steeped in the classic sources and arguments, and that he too was prepared to emphasize a real human nature in Christ. As I mentioned earlier, some Christians appear to have concluded from the fact that Schuon was an esoterist and a teacher of *gnosis* that he was a gnostic in the ancient sectarian sense, and perhaps for this reason they have been unwilling to study him closely enough to see how consistent his teaching is on this point with the Church. Jesus Christ, Schuon says unequivocally, "was incontestably man", and therefore "He was bound to have certain limits",[34] the claims of heretical docetists notwithstanding. "There is no doubt," he continues, "that the Man-God is, in a certain respect and by definition, a human individual; otherwise He would not be a man in

---

32. *Against Apollinarius*, II.
33. The point of this qualification is to remind us that everything below the level of the pure Absolute partakes to some extent in the illusory nature of *Mâyâ*. At the same time, however, there is no denying "the objective homogeneity of the cosmic environment" (*Spiritual Perspectives*, p. 114). "A mountain is a mountain and not a dream, or it would be in the void that ants would be crossing rocks and climbing slopes" (*Gnosis*, p. 57).
34. *Face of the Absolute*, p. 66.

any sense, and it would be impossible to speak of Him in any way." Being ourselves of a formal and individual order, an individual form is necessary to ensure us access to God. This in effect was the whole point of the Incarnation: God became man precisely "for us men and for our salvation" (Nicene Creed). Moreover, this "individuality—the presence of which, in some mode or other, is an obvious thing in every man, since the human state is an individual one— cannot but be what it is by definition", namely a condition of limitation. It is in the nature of things, says Schuon, that any human being must possess "the limitative attributes which constitute his essential definition, and failing which he would not be a human individual but something else".[35] Man is not God, to say the least; he is one kind of creature, and his distinction both from God and other creatures will necessarily exhibit itself in his human form and his manner of being. There should therefore be nothing unexpected in the fact that Jesus was limited in various ways, whether we think of His admitted ignorance in certain situations—the episode of the fig tree has been mentioned already—or the physical hardships to which His body was subject, or His real human emotions.

Nor is it strange that He should have said of Himself, speaking by virtue of His human nature, "Why callest thou Me good? There is none good save one, that is God" (Mt 19:17). "We may compare these Gospel words," Schuon observes, "with the following saying from an Upanishad: 'the essence of man is made of desire.'" Schuon's point is by no means that Christ, a celestial and sinless man, was subject to unruly passions; nevertheless He did assume a real human soul, "which, as such, necessarily comprises all the constituent elements and all the essential attributes of individuality". Since to be a man means to have a mind which can reason, a will which can choose, and emotions which are able to feel, it must be said as a consequence that Christ possessed a genuine human "psychism", which included something "analogous to what in ordinary mortals we call 'desire'". While admittedly we "cannot know the dimensions which individual facts, thanks to their transcendent quality, have for the 'human God'",[36] it is very clear from the Bible

---

35. *Eye of the Heart*, pp. 103, 105.
36. *Eye of the Heart*, pp. 104, 105. It is of interest to note that after more than fifteen hundred years, many Orthodox authorities have concluded that the division between them and the Copts on these very delicate points may have been strict-

that Jesus could truly think and feel as a man, being "tempted as we are, and yet without sin" (Hebrews 4:15). Whether therefore we look at the matter as metaphysicians or simply as readers of Holy Scripture, the inadequacies of monophysitism should be obvious: Christ was truly human, or else the Incarnation is a meaningless term. In all this, once again, Schuon agreed with the Fathers.

*

* *

Schuon was of one mind with the Fathers in much more than the details, however. He was like them as well in his recognition that the Incarnation presents the human mind with a puzzle or paradox, which no discursive analysis will ever suffice to resolve. The Christian tradition has always insisted that the Reality behind its central beliefs infinitely transcends the categories and terms that have been fixed in its dogmas; and in the case of Christology in particular, the dogmatic formulas of the Councils have a largely apophatic or koanic function, telling us primarily what should *not* be taught regarding the incarnate Son. No unilateral affirmation may be fully acknowledged, for whatever is said about Christ must be at once taken back—and we are left to wonder in silence. In the words of the Orthodox Vespers for Christmas, "A marvelous wonder has this day come to pass. Nature is made new, and God becomes man. That which He was, He has remained, and that which He was not, He has taken upon Himself, while suffering neither confusion nor division."[37]

The mystery of the two natures is a wonder indeed, and it would be foolish to think that one might give it a conclusive or definitive explanation or discern the full range of its meaning. Indeed, for all his dialectical efforts, Schuon was the first to admit the impossibility of ever finding the appropriate words: "One may indeed try, in human language, to specify in what manner the Divine man is indi-

---

ly terminological. In recent conversation with an Orthodox monk—and reader of Schuon—the Coptic Patriarch, His Holiness Pope Shenouda III, admitted for his part that the Orthodox and Oriental Christologies are "merely points of departure and are not contradictory". The Copts, long thought to be monophysite, had never meant to deny Christ's continuing humanity in its incarnate union with the *Logos*, but only to stress its Divine uniqueness.

37. *The Festal Menaion*, p. 291.

vidual and in what manner He is not"—or, we might add, in what manner He is Divine and in what manner not—"but it will always be impossible to express this adequately and completely, because the infinitely complex and apparently paradoxical realities involved transcend the bounds of simple human reason, of which language is the instrument".[38] Metaphysically, the Incarnation means that the Principle has entered manifestation in order to become what It is not. But since this Principle is on the one hand the only thing that exists, and since on the other hand whatever exists is the Principle, the boundaries to be crossed in Its apparent descent are as it were in constant movement, shifting and vanishing according to perspective and spiritual strategy. There is certainly a pattern or rhythm to this movement, and it can be discerned by the Intellect; but it can never be adequately put into words.[39]

It therefore goes without saying that my aim in this chapter is by no means to fathom the full depth of the doctrine, nor is it even to present a complete picture of the Schuonian teachings on Christ. Not the least of the matters that must remain unexamined are the far-reaching implications of Christology for the spiritual life. We get just a taste of these in Schuon's observation that "the function of the historical Christ is to awaken and actualize the inward Christ, the Heart-Intellect", which itself is "true man and

---

38. *Eye of the Heart*, p. 106. For those with the need to know and the ears to hear, there is an important lesson here *mutatis mutandis* when it comes to assessing the precise stature of any great saint or sage. Since "every spiritual master, by his knowledge and his function and by the graces attaching to them, is mysteriously assimilated to his prototypes and, both through them and independently of them, to the primordial Prototype, the founding *Avatâra*" (*Logic and Transcendence*, p. 227), it is to be expected that the genuine master, whether Christian or otherwise, should participate at some level in the antinomic or paradoxical qualities resulting from that "union without confusion" which is the mystery of the two natures. We should never be surprised at finding in such a figure certain puzzling or even scandalous features, and we should realize that it will never be an easy task to determine whether in any given instance these are a part of the foolishness with which the Divine Wisdom must appear in the world, or the result instead of the inevitable limitations which are marks of the human condition. In a sense this entire article is meant to underscore this lesson.

39. "'God became man in order that man might become God': the Absolute became Relativity in order that the relative might become absolute. This paraphrase of the Patristic formula suggests, with no more and no less felicity than the formula itself, a metaphysical situation which it would be difficult to express in a few words" (*Logic and Transcendence*, p. 104n).

true God",[40] and that "the Son, Second Person of the Trinity, is man universalized" while "Jesus Christ is God individualized",[41] or again that "man's problem is that he is at one and the same time accident and Substance and that he needs to know exactly in what respect he is the one or the other, and how he must turn this double nature to account".[42] The mystery of the two natures is a mystery inherent in our own deepest selves, and Christology is a matter finally of esoteric anthropology. Here however, in the concluding section of this chapter, I would like to direct our attention, not to the spiritual path as such, but to the multiplicity of spiritual forms—not to Christ and the Self, but to Christ and the non-Christian religions.

As I explained at the outset, my fellow Orthodox and other traditional Christians are often surprised when they learn that I share the Schuonian perspective. How can a Christian accept the idea that other religious traditions are true while at the same time remaining faithful to Jesus? Many are convinced, without even reading his books, that Schuon—in typical modernist fashion—must have somehow ignored or distorted their tradition, and that the doctrine of the Incarnation in particular has been misrepresented or misunderstood. Do the Fathers not tell us that Jesus is "the only-begotten Son of God, begotten of His Father before all ages" (Nicene Creed)? And did not He Himself say that "I am the way, the truth, and the life: no man cometh unto the Father but by me" (Jn 14:6)? Surely, many Christians would argue, this is decisive proof that no other path to salvation is possible.

It is with such objections and protests in mind that I have devoted the largest part of this discussion to a detailed treatment of Schuon's teaching on Christ, and I hope it is clear by now that whatever else one might say about his message in general, it is absurd to think that his Christology came from neglect or misinformation. By moving back and forth between his own words and those of the Church, one can see very clearly that his understanding of the two natures, based upon a close acquaintance with the traditional sources, was perfectly orthodox in all the dogmatic essentials, even

---

40. *Esoterism*, pp. 38-39.
41. *Transcendent Unity*, p. 109.
42. *Logic and Transcendence*, p. 84.

judging the matter according to strictly exoteric criteria. This of course is precisely what we would expect of the genuine esoterist, who knows that the "truth does not deny forms from the outside, but transcends them from within".[43] However he may assist us in deepening or interiorizing our comprehension of a given spiritual world, or a given traditional doctrine, his message will be distinguished by its orthodoxy, and hence by its fidelity to the central and presiding ideas of that world.

But if all this is true—if the Christological teachings of Schuon are essentially orthodox—one begins to wonder, in view of his explicit and distinctive universalism, why so many Christians have nonetheless thought that a traditional faith in Christ obliges them to repudiate the possibility of other saving religions; and it is difficult to avoid the conclusion that they themselves must have failed to understand the actual terms of the doctrine. In fact, although Schuon never put it this way, one is inclined to go further yet: not only have such Christians failed to comprehend the deepest significance of their most important dogma; the understanding they *do* claim to have—however shocking it may sound for me to level this charge—is itself heretical. It is the result in fact of three heresies all wrapped into one.

Consider what the Christian exclusivist says. Salvation is impossible, he asserts, apart from a conscious, explicit, and active faith in Jesus Christ, for Jesus is the only man in history who at the same time was God, and it therefore follows that He alone can rescue men from sin and death. This reasoning can be expressed in the form of a syllogism: God alone can save; Jesus is God; therefore,

43. *Spiritual Perspectives*, p. 118. In emphasizing that Schuon's Christology is in accord with the letter of the Patristic formulas, I do not wish to imply that he accepted all the opinions of the Church Fathers, nor all the more that most of them would have approved of his universalism. Even allowing for the fact that the Fathers knew very little *de facto* about other authentic traditions apart from Judaism, we must admit in most cases that a *de jure* exclusivism marks their writing. The words of St Justin the Philosopher are by no means unique, but like those of St Nikolai Velimirovich in our own time (see note 61 below), they are exceptional. According to Justin, "We have been taught that Christ is the First-begotten of God, the *Logos* of which every race of man partakes. Those who lived in accordance with the *Logos* are Christians, even though they were called godless, such as, among the Greeks, Socrates and Heraclitus. . . . Those who lived by the *Logos*, and those who so live now, are Christians, fearless and unperturbed" (*First Apology*, 46).

only Jesus can save. Now certainly the Schuonian will not object to the first proposition, for it is undeniably true that there is no possibility of salvation apart from Divine grace and the initiative of Heaven. The problem arises with the exclusivist's understanding of the second claim, the minor premise of the syllogism. Jesus Christ *is* certainly God, but the exclusivist takes the further step of supposing that the verbal copula functions like the sign of identity in a mathematical equation, and hence that the nouns in the minor premise can be reversed: not only is Jesus God, but God is also Jesus. As a result, the unique and eternal nature of the Son's Divinity is transposed onto the plane of history; the one-and-only quality of Him who was incarnate, "the only begotten Son of God", is confused with the temporal and spatial particularity of His incarnation in Jesus, and His singularity *in divinis* is conflated with an event of a strictly factual or historical order.[44] Now of course, to affirm that God is fully present in Christ is by no means false, and there is no question as to the formula's great rhetorical power. But the homiletic or kerygmatic value of this expression should not blind us to its dialectical weakness, for as an ellipsis it risks identifying the Beyond-Being of the pure Absolute with the individuality of a particular human being.

Such an identification is the consequence of three very serious errors, each the result of collapsing an important distinction, and all strongly condemned—as we have seen—by the Christian tradition. To use Schuon's terms, those who thus reason have confused the relative Absolute with Its principial Essence, they have failed to distinguish between the Principle and manifestation, and they have forgotten that the manifest Principle is not the same as manifestation as such. They have not understood, in other words, that orthodox Christology is a "combination of three polarities—man and God, terrestrial man and Divine man, hypostatic God and essential God".[45] Or again, in the language of the early Church, they have identified the First and Second Persons of the Holy Trinity, they have

44. The truth is that "only the Divine manifestation 'is the Self', to the exclusion of every human counterfeit". But this is reduced to meaning: "only such and such a Divine manifestation—to the exclusion of all others—is the Self" (*Gnosis*, p. 68). This of course is not to deny a certain symbolic resonance between the historical singularity of Jesus's life and the eternal uniqueness of the *Logos*.
45. *Face of the Absolute*, p. 74.

failed to discriminate between Christ's Divinity and His humanity, and they have forgotten that Jesus was no ordinary man. Reverting to the technical vocabulary used by historians of doctrine, we must conclude that the exclusivist's point of view is the product of three major heresies: modalistic monarchianism, monophysitism, and dynamic monarchianism. Ironically enough, it is only because he is three times a heretic that he believes himself to be so orthodox!

Now I realize that this is quite a bold allegation, and I must confess at once that I have somewhat overstated my case. In truth I am very far from supposing that, at the level of pious practice, there is anything wrong with an exclusive fidelity to Jesus as the "only Son", and I am in no way proposing that the tenets of the *sophia perennis* should be adopted as *de fide* dogmas. I recall in this regard a very serious and pious priest who once told me that if he did not believe that Jesus of Nazareth was the only way to be saved, he could not believe in Jesus at all. Whether or not we are metaphysicians, there is clearly no point in disparaging such a faith, or in deliberately distracting such a person from the "one thing needful" (Luke 10:42) by suggesting that he should concern himself with philosophical and theological subtleties. Schuon always said that the whole point of his books and other writings was the salvation of souls, and he would never have countenanced that pseudo-intellectual one-upmanship which presumes to tell people what they have no need of knowing; he would also have been adamant in reminding the *jñâni* or intellectual that "intelligence and metaphysical certainty alone do not save, and do not of themselves prevent titanic falls".[46]

Furthermore, in asserting that the exclusivists have misunderstood the Incarnation, I do not mean to suggest that the whole of the Christian tradition can be reduced to this single doctrine, central and indispensable though it is. A religion is much more than any one, or even all, of its dogmatic beliefs; as Schuon often observed, religions are like planets or worlds, each bearing the imprint of a Divine archetype and each serving to mold, not just the arts and sciences of a given civilization, but the very souls of those who inhabit it. Much of his work was devoted to explaining the vari-

---

46. *Spiritual Perspectives*, p. 145. Elsewhere he writes, "Even if our writings had on the average no other result than the restitution for some of the saving barque that is prayer, we would owe it to God to consider ourselves profoundly satisfied" (*Play of Masks*, p. vii).

eties of religious partisanship which inevitably result from this fact, especially in the climate of the Abrahamic traditions, and he was always the first to allow for the existence of a "human margin",[47] where the believer has a certain right to his ego and hence to certain sentimental predispositions and individual preferences. Schuon taught, moreover, that what is true of the human beings in a given traditional collectivity must be true in a sense of that tradition itself. In the interest of saving as many men as possible, religions take on something of the individuality of their adherents, and therefore "every religion by definition wants to be the best, and 'must want' to be the best".[48] There is thus considerably more to the exclusivist's attitude toward other faiths than any given believer's comprehension (or not) of traditional Christology, and it is in no way surprising that a majority of Christians, like their counterparts in other religions, should wish to cling to the notion that they alone have the keys of the Kingdom.

Indeed, this is all the more understandable, according to Schuon, when one considers the esoteric and initiatic nature of the central Christian mysteries, and when one measures them against the capacity and expectations of the average believer, who needs to see things in terms of clear-cut choices between God and the world. The "simultaneity of antinomic aspects"[49] in any adequate formulation of Christ's two natures must unavoidably elude such a person, and for this reason, in order to appeal to "a mentality more volitive than contemplative", the Christian theologian has in most cases settled for "a logic that is dogmatically coagulative and piously unilateral"[50]—one that accentuates "the most important truth to the detriment of essential metaphysical shades of meaning".[51] Of course,

---

47. *Face of the Absolute*, pp. 65-105.
48. *Christianity/Islam*, p. 151.
49. *Logic and Transcendence*, p. 106.
50. *Logic and Transcendence*, p. 96.
51. *Face of the Absolute*, p. 75. That the two natures are indivisibly but unconfusedly united in the one Person of Christ (see note 15 above) is a quintessentially dialectical formula, in the very saying of which one must conflate complementary opposites, neither of which is true on its own. In order to approach the doctrine discursively, the theologian is therefore obliged, in any given rhetorical moment, to stress either the unity or the diversity, giving the appearance of a competition between the two truths, and traditionally a kind of victory has always been accorded to the relatively more important half-truth of unity. "'The Father is greater than I', but 'I and the Father are one'. Theology does not draw

if Christianity "were not a religion but a sapiential doctrine, it might rest content with describing why and how the Absolute manifests Itself. But being a religion," Schuon observes, "it must enclose everything within its fundamental idea of manifestation".[52] And so it is that the Absolute in Itself becomes reduced to the level of historical fact: Jesus is God, and therefore God is Jesus—completely, uniquely, and irrevocably. From this point, of course, it is but a very small step to the claim that a conscious and sacramental connection with this particular fact is the condition *sine qua non* for salvation.

Nevertheless, having conceded the rights of the Christian faithful to their simplifications, and thus their exoteric exclusivism, I must at the same time continue to insist that the conciliar formulas of the early Church by no means require the Christian to adopt an exclusivist stance. Truth has its rights, greater indeed than those of any man, and the truth in this case means calling the bluff on those theologians and other Christian believers who would presume to criticize Schuon for neglecting or misinterpreting their tradition. Other justifications and explanations aside, it means facing up to the fact that there is simply no good Christological reason for thinking that Christianity is the only means of salvation.[53] Charity cer-

all of the consequences implied by the former, and it draws too many from the latter" (*Divine to the Human*, p. 40n).

52. *Logic and Transcendence*, p. 98. According to Schuon, there has always been a kind of tension between "the eminently esoteric character of primitive Christianity" and the fact that it was providentially destined to be a world religion, and therefore open to all men. "The essentially initiatory character of Christianity is apparent from certain features of the first importance, such as the Doctrine of the Trinity, the Sacrament of the Eucharist, and more particularly, the use of wine in this rite, or again from the use of purely esoteric expressions such as 'Son of God' and especially 'Mother of God'. If exoterism is 'something that is at the same time indispensable and accessible to all' [René Guénon], Christianity cannot be exoteric in the usual sense of the word, since it is in reality by no means accessible to everyone, although in fact, by virtue of its outward application, it is binding upon everyone" (*Transcendent Unity*, pp. 137, 132).

53. The exclusivist will perhaps respond that there are other scriptural and traditional reasons for arguing that a rejection is called for, and this I concede, though I cannot even begin addressing them here. I can only briefly mention Schuon's comments on two frequently cited Biblical texts. When it is written (says Schuon) that there is "none other name under Heaven given among men whereby we must be saved" (Acts 4:12), either the phrase "under Heaven" is meant to indicate the "providential sphere of expansion and life of the Christian civilization", or else the name *Jesus* must be regarded as "a symbolic

tainly demands that we be indulgent toward a simple piety, but when the admitted virtues of simplicity become the pretext for a pretentious fideism, the esoterist has every right to object. For nowhere do the Ecumenical Councils require us to think that the uniqueness of the Word in His eternal relation with the Father is to be attributed to the temporal or spatial facticity of His incarnation in Jesus, and nowhere therefore does the traditional understanding of Christ's Person and natures require the repudiation of other spiritual worlds. If anything, the implications are just the reverse. As preposterous as this may sound to many of my fellow Christians, what a truly orthodox Christology "requires"—if such a word is permissible in this context—is a full acknowledgment of the transcendent unity of all orthodox religions.

I have gone to considerable lengths to demonstrate that Schuon's teachings on Christ are compatible with those of the early Church, and that his universalism is therefore—at the very least—a legitimate Orthodox *theologoumenon* or theological opinion. But in the final analysis it is not a question of compatibility alone; it is not just the case, in other words, that the doctrine of the double nature can be conveniently reconciled with the perennialist perspective through some sort of artificial or Procrustean adaptation. On the contrary, the mystery of Christ is at the very heart of that perspective, serving in a sense as a key to Schuon's entire approach to the world's religions. God has become man in order that man might become God; the Absolute has become relative in order that the relative might become Absolute; the Self has become ego in order that the ego might become the Self; *Nirvâna* has become *samsâra* in order that *samsâra* might become *Nirvâna*. As his readers know, we

designation of the Word Itself, which would imply that in the world there is one name only, the Word, by which men can be saved, whatever the Divine manifestation designated by this name in any particular case, be it 'Jesus', 'Buddha', or any other". One must of course remember that the scriptural term "name" signifies primarily authority and is not to be confused in such contexts with the proper name of a given individual. As for Christ's words that "this Gospel of the Kingdom shall be preached in all the world for a witness unto all nations, and then shall the end come" (Mt 24:14), Schuon points out that this saying relates to "cyclic conditions in which separating barriers between the different traditional worlds will have disappeared", and that from this point of view "'Christ', who for the Hindus will be the Kalki *Avatâra* and for the Buddhists the Bodhisattva *Maitreya*, will restore the Primordial Tradition" (*Transcendent Unity*, pp. 80, 85).

have here a continuing theme that runs throughout this author's teaching. For wherever one looks, "Reality has entered into nothingness so that nothingness might become Real",[54] and "the Essence has become form in order that the form may become Essence; all Revelation is a humanization of the Divine for the sake of the deification of the human".[55]

What we thus find are repeated reminders of the decisive and universal significance of the Incarnation. My fellow Christians have sometimes told me that the real meaning of this dogma is distorted in the work of Schuon and other perennial philosophers, and that in spite of all their protestations to the contrary, they end up ignoring the real importance of Christ. But I have never understood how one could possibly take this criticism seriously. Far from being constricted or reduced in its scope, Christ's significance is so far expanded in the Schuonian vision that one might well have wondered instead, apart from a careful reading of his books, what role is left for the other religions. If anything, it is their adherents who might ostensibly have had better cause to complain. For Schuon leaves no doubts on this score: "All genuine religions are Christian";[56] or again, "every truth is necessarily manifested in terms of Christ and on His model",[57] for "there is no truth nor wisdom that does not come from Christ".[58] Now of course what he means is that "the other religions are 'Christian' inasmuch as they have the universal Christ, who is the Word that inspires all Revelation".[59] Schuon is not saying, in other words, that in order to be a true Muslim or Hindu, one must identify the man Jesus with God; but then, as we have seen, neither should the discerning Christian acquiesce in so simple an equation. God and man have been united in Jesus Christ, but unless we choose to be heretics, the Christian tradition forbids us to think that the manhood in question

---

54. *Stations of Wisdom*, p. 133.
55. *Face of the Absolute*, pp. 71-72. Taking just the Abrahamic religions, for example, and considering "the revelation on Sinai, the Messianic redemption, [and] the descent of the Koran", in every case what one sees are "so many examples of the 'Subjectivizing objectivation'" by virtue of which "*Âtmâ* is 'incarnated' in *Mâyâ*, and *Mâyâ* expresses *Âtmâ*" (*Spiritual Perspectives*, p. 107). See also *Light on the Ancient Worlds*, pp. 140-41.
56. *Gnosis*, p. 67.
57. *Stations of Wisdom*, p. 49.
58. *Gnosis*, p. 105.
59. *Transcendent Unity*, p. 81.

was merely that of a historical individual, or that the Divinity was that of the pure Absolute. Rather we ourselves are that man in our essential humanity, and the God who assumed us into Himself was the Divine *Logos* or Word, in and through whom the inaccessible Essence makes Itself known to all.

As I have noted so often, Schuon was a master not only of *gnosis* but of the Bible and other traditional sources, and he knew in this case that Christ is "the true Light which lighteth every man that cometh into the world" (Jn 1:9)—that He who "in the beginning" was "with God" and "was God" (John 1:1), and who therefore *is* "before Abraham was" (John 8:58), must also be the One "from whom arise all the ancient wisdoms".[60] Schuon knew, in other words, that it is the Second Person of the Holy Trinity through whom are revealed "the invisible things" of the Divine Principle, "even His eternal power and Godhead" (Rom 1:20), and that it is therefore He alone who accounts for the truth in any given tradition. It follows, however—if we have understood the subtleties of the doctrine—that every orthodox religion must be regarded as a kind of Incarnation and as possessing "two natures". For in each of the world's orthodox traditions, the Divinity of the *Logos* is indivisibly but unconfusedly manifest in an individual form, becoming fully present on earth, but without compromise to either Its principial or Its celestial integrity.

The terrestrial modalities will naturally differ, of course, and in the case of religions with central human supports, the names will vary: Jesus, Gautama, Muhammad, and so on. In each of these traditions, writes Schuon, the proper name "indicates the limited and relative aspect of the manifestation", whereas the traditional titles of these several figures refer to their corresponding celestial prototypes. Thus the term "'Christ'—like 'Buddha' and '*Rasûl Allâh*'— indicates the universal Reality of this same manifestation, that is to say, the Word as such".[61] In an alternative formulation, Schuon points out elsewhere that even the term *Logos* or "Word" is a kind of

---

60. *Light on the Ancient Worlds*, p. 70.
61. *Transcendent Unity*, p. 92. It is in this light that St Nikolai Velimirovich (see note 43) could speak of the Divine Word as revealing "precious gifts in the East". He writes: "Glory be the memory of Lao-Tse, the teacher and prophet of his people! Glory be the memory of Krishna, the teacher and prophet of his people! Blessed be the memory of Buddha, the royal son and inexorable teacher of his

name, colored by a specific religious world; it is a name—to use again his technical metaphysical terminology—for the "relative" or "lesser" Absolute, and thus it refers to a level of Reality which, while subordinate to the Absolute as such, is nonetheless independent, not only from the particularities of certain historical forms, but even from Its own universal prolongations at the level of Heaven— just as Christ's degree of Divinity remains unconfused with His celestial humanity. Thus "in Itself," says Schuon, "the *Logos* is neither 'Word' nor 'Son' nor 'Book' nor 'Buddha', but appears as one of these according to Its mode of earthly manifestation".[62] In this way It anticipates the distinctive role of Jesus for Christians or of Muhammad for Muslims or of Gautama for Buddhists. The most important point to notice, however, is that in each of these religions, whether Christianity or Islam or Buddhism, the essential metaphysical discriminations are precisely the same: there remain in each case the same sets of distinctions and the same pattern of "union without confusion"—whether between the Absolute and the Relative, or between the Principle and manifestation, or between the manifest Principle and manifestation as such. Wherever we look we see the mystery of the two natures of Christ, expressed anew in many dialects.

The Christian may feel the need to raise a final objection. Far too great an emphasis has been placed, he may say, on "the principial, non-human, and non-historical *Logos*",[63] and there is thus a risk of ignoring the actual, concrete facts of salvation. What about the baby born in Bethlehem, the Baptism in the Jordan, the healing of the man born blind, and all the many other specific events in Jesus's life? Most importantly, what about "Christ and Him crucified" (1 Cor 2:2)? As I have already stressed, however, Schuon had no intention of denying the reality of Christ's individual manhood, and unlike the demythologizers and other Biblical reductionists of our day, he never supposed that the miraculous details of the Gospels were anything but literally true. On the other hand, he would have been quick to remind his exclusivist critics that, according to the teaching of the Christian tradition itself, the eternal *Logos*

---

people!" (*Prayers by the Lake* [Grayslake, Illinois: Free Serbian Orthodox Diocese of the United States and Canada, n.d.], XLVIII, XLIX).

62. *Spiritual Perspectives*, p. 65.

63. *Esoterism*, p. 36.

is the one and only *hypostasis* of Christ's Divine humanity; in placing his own emphasis upon that *Logos*, Schuon is simply following the lead of the ancient Church, modern historical and psychological sensibilities notwithstanding. There is no doubt, certainly, that Jesus was truly human, that He truly spoke to other men, and that He truly acted in and upon this world; but we are not to forget that the underlying subject of all His words and actions, however temporal their mode of manifestation, remained the eternal Son of God. The exclusivist wishes to cling to "Jesus the man" as the only means of salvation. But Schuon is surely right that "in naming Himself the way, the truth, and the life in an absolute or principial sense", there is no reason to think that Christ was "trying to limit the universal manifestation of the Word" to a particular earthly form or to a specific series of historical actions. On the contrary, He was "affirming His own essential identity with the *Logos*, the cosmic manifestation of which He Himself was living in subjective mode".[64] It remains true, of course, that "no man cometh unto the Father" (Jn 14:6) except by way of His Word; but what this means metaphysically is that there is no entry into the Divine Essence except through the Divine Person—however or wherever that Person may have chosen to be present on Earth.

The Schuonian perspective thus provides us with a way of understanding the Son's earthly deeds which fully honors their saving importance, but without restricting their operation or "efficient causality" to any given temporal or spatial context. We are asked, like every Christian, to admit the historical reality of the great redemptive events of Christ's Passion and Resurrection: Jesus really died—in a particular way, in a particular place, and at a particular moment—and He really rose from the dead in His body. But at the same time, while remaining perfectly faithful to the conciliar dogmas, Schuon assists us in seeing that these actions, if they are to have the salvific power that Christians claim, could not have been those of some isolated human individual, nor could their cosmic effect have come from a purely temporal cause. On the contrary, the only reason that Good Friday and Easter are of lasting significance is that they are the reverberations in time of eternity. For He who died on the cross was not some specially chosen man, but the Divine Son of

64. *Transcendent Unity*, pp. 27-28.

God, and if that Son, who is eternal, can be truly said to have died—as the Christian tradition explicitly teaches—then His death must have been eternal as well: the Lamb of God must have been "slain from the foundation of the world" (Rev 13:8), and not only on Golgotha. And if that same Son really rose from the dead, then His rising, too, must be eternal: if He came forth from the Tomb at a particular moment of time, it is only because His is a light that has always shone "in the darkness", though "the darkness comprehended it not" (Jn 1:5). Thus Schuon writes

> The Divine Redemption is always present; it pre-exists all terrestrial alchemy and is its celestial model, so that it is always thanks to this eternal Redemption—whatever may be its vehicle on earth—that man is freed from the weight of his vagaries and even, *Deo volente*, from that of his separative existence; if "my Words shall not pass away", it is because they have always been.

"A consciousness of this," Schuon concludes—that is, a perception of the true dimensions of the Son's saving work—"far from diminishing a participation in the treasures of the historical redemption, confers on them a compass that touches the very roots of existence."[65]

Far from diminishing our full participation in Christ, prayerful reflection on the mystery of His two natures cannot but do Him great honor, for whatever a man's traditional path toward salvation might be, it is one and the same *Logos* that is the true Savior of all. His scope is unlimited, extending far beyond the boundaries of the Christian religion to "other sheep which are not of this fold" (Jn 10:16), and His treasures are bequeathed to us all.

---

65. *Light on the Ancient Worlds*, p. 70. Schuon adds elsewhere, "The Redemption is an eternal act which cannot be situated in either time or space, and the sacrifice of Christ is a particular manifestation or realization of it on the human plane" (*Transcendent Unity*, 21). Schuon was under no illusions, of course—no matter the scriptural and other classic proofs—that his perspective would be acceptable to all traditional Christians. "Within the framework of Christianity, the idea that the Redemption is a priori the timeless work of the principial, non-human, and non-historical *Logos*, that it can and must be manifested in different ways, at diverse times and places, and that the historical Christ manifests this *Logos* in a given providential world, without its being either necessary or possible to define this world in an exact manner, is an idea that is esoteric in relation to Christian dogmatics, and it would be absurd to demand it from theology" (*Esoterism*, p. 36).

Chapter 7

Do Clothes Make The Man?
The Significance of Human Attire

Marco Pallis

"If a man does not honour his own house, it falls down and crush-
es him"
—Greek Proverb

During an exchange of letters that took place between the late
Ananda K. Coomaraswamy and the present writer during the war
years, discussion once happened to turn on the question of traditional dress and its neglect, a subject which had frequently occupied
my mind in the course of various journeys through the Himalayan
borderlands. We both agreed that this question was of crucial
importance at the present time, a touchstone by which much else
could be judged. Dr. Coomaraswamy (who henceforth will usually
be denoted simply by his initials A.K.C.) then informed me that his
own earliest publication on any subject other than Geology was precisely concerned with this question of dress; the paper referred to
bore the title of "Borrowed Plumes" (Kandy, 1905) and was called
forth by its author's indignation at a humiliating incident he witnessed while staying in a remote district of Ceylon. He further suggested that I might some day treat the same theme in greater detail;
the opportunity came for complying with his wishes when I was
asked to add my personal tribute to a world-wide symposium in
honour of the seventieth birthday of that prince of scholars, whose
rare insight had made him the qualified interpreter and champion
of the traditional conception of life not only in India but everywhere. All that remained, therefore, was for me to apply to the subject chosen that dialectical method, so typically Indian, with which
A.K.C. himself had made us familiar in his later works: that is to say,
the question at issue had first to be presented under its most intellectual aspect, by connecting it with universal principles; after which
it became possible, by a process of deduction, to show the develop-

ments to which those principles lent themselves in various contingencies; until finally their application could be extended, as required, to the field of human action, whether by way of doing or undoing. In the present chapter appeal will be made, all along, to the parallel authority of the Hindu and Islamic traditions, as being the ones that between them share the Indian scene; such reference being primarily intended as a guarantee of traditional authenticity, as against a merely human, personal and private expression of opinion on the part of the writer.

*
* *

Fundamentally, the question of what kind of clothes a person may or may not wear (like any other similar question) is a matter of *svadharma,* an application of that law or norm of behavior which is intrinsic to every being in virtue of its own particular mode of existence *(svabhava).* By conforming to his norm a man "becomes what he is," thus realizing the full extent of his possibilities; in so far as he fails, he accepts a measure of self-contradiction and disintegrates proportionally.

The late Sir John Woodroffe, in *Bharata Shakti* (Ganesh, 1921)— a work that ought to be in the hands of every Indian and more especially the young—quotes George Tyrrell as having once written: "I begin to think that the only real sin is suicide or *not being oneself.*" That author was probably thinking in individual terms only; nevertheless, his statement contains echoes of a doctrine of universal scope—from which all its relative validity at the individual level is derived—namely, that the ultimate and only sin is "not to be One Self", ignorance *(avidya)* of "What one is", belief that one is "other" than the Self—indeed, on that reckoning we, one and all, are engaged in committing self-murder daily and hourly and we shall continue to do so, paying the penalty meanwhile, until such time as we can finally "recollect ourselves", thus "becoming what we are".[1]

---

1. Following Tyrrell, we have used the word "suicide" here in its more usual and unfavorable sense, as denoting an extremity of self-abuse; it can however, be taken in a different sense, when it is far from constituting a term of reproach: we are referring to the voluntary self-immolation implied in a phrase like that of Meister Eckhart when he says that "the soul must put itself to death" or in the Buddhist *atta-m-jaho* (= "self-noughting" in Medieval English) which coin-

Do Clothes Make the Man?

It has been said that there are three degrees of conformity *(islam)* to the truth; firstly, everyone is *muslim* from the very fact of being at all, since, do as he will, he cannot conceivably move one hairs-breadth out of the orbit of the Divine Will that laid down for him the pattern of his existence; secondly, he is *muslim* in so far as he recognizes his state of dependence and behaves accordingly— this level is represented by his conscious attachment to a tradition, whereby he is able to be informed of what he is and of the means to realize it; and thirdly, he is *muslim* through having achieved perfect conformity, so that henceforth he is identical with his true Self, beyond all fear of parting. In Hindu parlance this same doctrine might be expressed as follows: every being is *yogi* in that any kind of existence apart from the Self is a sheer impossibility, even in the sense of an illusion; that being is a *yogi*—called thus by courtesy, as it were—in so far as he, she or it strives, by the use of suitable disciplines *(sadhana),* to realize Self-union; the selfsame being is *the Yogi* in virtue of having made that union effective. No element in life can therefore be said to lie outside the scope of *yoga.*

What individual man is, he owes, positively, to his inherent possibilities and, negatively, to his limitations; the two together, by their mutual interplay, constitute his *svabhava* and are the factors which make him uniquely qualified *(adhikari)* for the filling of a certain part in the Cosmic "Play" *(lila),* for which part he has been "cast" by the Divine Producer. Neither possibilities nor limiting conditions are of his own choice—not his either to accept, select or evade. The

cides, on the other hand with *bhavit' atto* (= "Self-made-become"). This whole doctrine, and ultimately our basic thesis in this essay, rests on the principle that "as there are two in him who is both Love and Death, so there are, as all tradition affirms unanimously, two in us; although not two of him or two of us, nor even one of him and one of us, but only one of both. As we stand now, in between the first beginning and the last end, we are divided against ourselves, essence from nature, and therefore see him likewise divided against himself and from us." This quotation is taken from A.K.C.'s two-pronged essay *Hinduism and Buddhism* (New York, 1943); the section dealing with Theology and Autology is strongly recommended to all who wish to understand the meaning of the universal axiom *duo sunt in homine* ["There are two (natures) in man." *Ed.*]. We say "Be yourself" to someone who is misbehaving: it is in fact, only the carnal self *(nafs)* or soul that can misbehave, the Self is infallible. Hence for the former an ultimate suicide is essential. As between the outer and inner man, only the latter is the Man (the image of God), the outer man being the "shadow" or "vehicle" or "house" or "garment" of the inner, just as the world is the Lord's "garment" (Cp. *Isha Upanishad* I, and Philo, Moses II, 135).

relative freedom of will which he enjoys within the limits assigned to him is but a translation, into the individual mode, of that limitless and unconditional freedom which the Principle enjoys universally.

Individual responsibility, therefore, applies solely to the manner of playing the allotted part; this, however, presupposes some opportunity of comparing the individual performance throughout with its pattern as subsisting in the intellect of the dramatist; but for some means of access to this standard of comparison, all judgment must be exercised at random. The authentic source of such information can only be the dramatist himself, so that its communication implies the receiving of a favor or "grace" at his hands, by a handing-over of the required knowledge, either directly or through some indirect channel—in other words, an act of "revelation" is implied. As for the carrying out of the task in practice, by faithful imitation of the pattern as traditionally revealed, that is a question of using the tools one has been given, never of forging new ones. Furthermore, in so far as one has been led, from any reasons of contingent utility, to extend the range of one's natural tools by artificial adjuncts, these too must, in some sort, be treated as supplementary attributes *(upadhi)* of the individuality: whatever equipment or "ornament" (the primary meaning of both these words is the same) may be required, it must be of such a character and quality as to harmonize with the general purpose in view, which is the realization, first at an individual and then at every possible level, of what one is.

*
* *

Of the many things a man puts to use in the pursuit of his earthly vocation there are none, perhaps, which are so intimately bound up with his whole personality as the clothes he wears. The more obviously utilitarian considerations influencing the forms of dress, such as climate, sex, occupation and social status can be taken for granted; here we are especially concerned with the complementary aspect of any utility, that of its significance, whence is derived its power to become an integrating or else a disintegrating factor in men's lives. As for the actual elements which go to define a particular form of apparel, the principal ones are shape or "cut", material, color and ornamental features, if any, including fastenings and also trimmings of every sort.

The first point to be noted is that any kind of clothing greatly modifies the appearance of a person, the apparent change extending even to his facial expression; this can easily be proved by observing the same individual wearing two quite distinct styles of dress. Though one knows that the man underneath is the same, the impression he makes on the bystanders is markedly different. It is evident, therefore, that we have here the reproduction of a cosmic process, by the clothing of a self-same entity in a variety of appearances; on that showing, the term "dress" can fittingly be attached to any and every appearance superimposed upon the stark nakedness of the Real, extending to all the various orders of manifestation which, separately or collectively, are included in the "seventy thousand veils obscuring the Face of *Allâh*". In view of this far-reaching analogy, it is hardly surprising if, at the individual level also, dress is endowed with such a power to veil (or reveal) as it has.[2]

For the human being, his choice of dress, within the limits of whatever resources are actually available to him, is especially indicative of three things: firstly, it shows what that man regards as compatible with a normal human state, with human dignity; secondly, it indicates how he likes to picture himself and what kind of attributes he would prefer to manifest; thirdly, his choice will be affected by the opinion he would wish his neighbors to have of him, this social consideration and the previous factor of self-respect being so closely bound up together as to interact continually.

According to his idea of the part he is called upon to play in the world, so does a man clothe himself; a correct or erroneous conception of the nature of his part is therefore fundamental to the whole question—the common phrase "to dress the part" is admirably expressive. No better illustration can be given of the way dress can work on the mind than one taken from that little world of make-believe called the theater: it is a commonplace of theatrical production that from the moment an actor has "put on his motley" and applied the appropriate "make-up", he tends to feel like another person, so that his voice and movements almost spontaneously

---

2. The concepts of change of clothes and becoming *(bhava)* are inseparable: Being *(bhuti)* only can be naked, in that, as constituting the principle of manifestation, it remains itself in the Unmanifest. Ultimately, the whole task of "shaking off one's bodies" (or garments) is involved—these including all that contributes to the texture of the outer self "that is not my Self."

begin to exhale the flavor *(rasa)* of the new character he represents. The same individual, wearing the kingly robes and crown, paces majestically across the stage; exchanging them for a beggar's rags, he whines and cringes; a hoary wig is sufficient to impart to his voice a soft and quavering sound; he buckles on a sword and the same voice starts issuing peremptory commands. Indeed, if the "impersonation" be at all complete, the actor almost becomes that "other" man whose clothes he has borrowed, thus "forgetting who he is"; it is only afterwards, when he is restored "to his right mind" that he discovers the truth of the saying that, after all, "clothes do not make the man".

Shri Ramakrishna Paramahamsa has paid a tribute to this power of dress to mold a personality in the following rather humorous saying: "The nature of man changes with each *upadhi*. When a man wears black-bordered muslin, the love-songs of Nidhu Babu come naturally to his lips and he begins to play cards and flourishes a stick as he goes out for a walk. Even though a man be thin, if he wears English boots he immediately begins to whistle: and if he has to mount a flight of stairs, he leaps up from one step to another like a *sahib.*"

This testimony of the Sage can be matched by evidence drawn from a very different quarter. When one studies the history of various political tyrannies which, during recent centuries, have deliberately set out to undermine the traditional order with a view to its replacement by the "humanism" of the modern West, one is struck by a truly remarkable unanimity among them in respect of the policy both of discouraging the national costume and at the same time of eliminating the Spiritual Authority as constituted in their particular traditions. These dictators were no fools, at least in a worldly sense, and if they have agreed in associating these two things in their minds and in making them the first target for their attack, even to the neglect of other seemingly more urgent matters, that is because in both cases they instinctively sensed the presence of something utterly incompatible with the anti-traditional movement they wished to launch. As they rightly divined, the costume implied a symbolical participation *(bhakti)* in that "other-worldly" influence which the Spiritual Authority was called upon to represent more explicitly in the field of doctrine.

The Tsar Peter I of Russia seems to have been about the first to perceive how much hung upon the question of dress, and when he decided that his country should "face West", politically and culturally, he made it his business to compel the members of the governing classes to give up their Muscovite costume in favor of the coat and breeches of Western Europe, while at the same time he seriously interfered in the constitution of the Orthodox Church, with a view to bringing it under State control on the model of the Protestant churches of Prussia and England. Likewise in Japan, after 1864, one of the earliest "reforms" introduced by the modernizing party was the replacement of the traditional court dress by the ugly frock-coat then in vogue at Berlin, by which the Japanese officials were made to look positively grotesque; moreover, this move was accompanied by a certain attitude of disfavor towards the Buddhist institutions in the country, though government action concerning them did not take on an extreme form. In many other countries of Europe and Asia reliance was placed rather upon the force of example from above; the official classes adopted Western clothes and customs, leaving the population at large to follow in its own time, further encouraged by the teaching it received in westernized schools and universities.

The classical example, however, is that afforded by the Kemalist revolution in Turkey, a distinction it owes both to its far-reaching character, and to the speed with which the designed changes were effected as well as to the numbers of its imitators in neighboring countries: in that case we have a military dictator, borne to power on the crest of a wave of popular enthusiasm, as the leader in a *jihad* in which his genius earned him (falsely, as it proved) the title of *Ghazi* or "paladin of the Faith", who no sooner had overcome his foreign enemies in the field than he turned his power against the Islamic tradition itself, sweeping the *Khalifat* out of the way like so much old rubbish and plundering the endowments bequeathed to sacred use by ancient piety; while under the new legislation *dervishes* vowed to the Contemplative life were classed with common vagabonds. It was another of Kemal's earliest acts to prohibit the Turkish national costume, not merely in official circles but throughout the nation, and to impose in its place the shoddy reach-me-downs of the European factories. Some thousands of *mullahs,* who dared to oppose him, earned the crown of martyrdom at the hands of the hangmen commissioned by an arak-drinking and godless *Ghazi*. Meanwhile, in the rest of the Moslem world, hardly a protest was raised; in India, where the movement to defend the *Khalifat* had been of great political service to Kemal in his early days, only the red Ottoman *fez*, adopted by many sympathizers with the Turkish cause, still survives (though proscribed in its own country) as a rather pathetic reminder of the inconsistencies to which human loyalties sometimes will lead.

*

* *

It may now well be asked what, in principle, determines the suitability or otherwise of any given form of clothing, and indeed what has prompted Man, in the first place, to adopt the habit of wearing clothes at all? It is evident that a change so startling as this must have corresponded to some profound modification in the whole way of life of mankind. To discover the principle at issue, one must first remember that every possibility of manifestation—that of clothing for instance—has its root in a corresponding possibility of the Unmanifest, wherein it subsists as in its eternal cause, of which it is itself but an explicit affirmation. Metaphysically, Being is Non-Being affirmed, the Word is but the uttering of Silence; similarly, once Nakedness is affirmed, clothing is "invented". The principle of Clothing resides, therefore, in Nakedness. In seeking to throw light on this fundamental aspect of the doctrine, one cannot do better than refer to the Cosmological Myth common to the three branches issued from the traditional stem of Abraham, of *Seyidna Ibrahim*. According to the Biblical story, Adam and Eve, that is to say, primordial mankind in the Golden Age *(Satya yuga)*, were dwelling in the Garden of Eden at the center of which grew the Tree of Life or World Axis *(Meru danda)*. The Axis, which "macrocosmically" is assimilated to a ray of the Supernal Sun *(Aditya)* and "microcosmically" to the Intellect *(Buddhi)*, occupies the *center* of human existence, all other faculties of knowledge or action being grouped hierarchically round the Intellect as its ministers and tools, none encroaching, each keeping to its allotted work in conformity with its own norm *(dharma);* this state of inward harmony being, moreover, externally reflected in the peaceful relations existing between Man and all his fellow-creatures around him, animals, plants and others.

It is also recorded that Adam conversed daily and familiarly with God, that is to say, the individual self was always immediately receptive of the influence emanating from the Universal Self, "one-pointed" *(ekagrya)* concentration being for it a spontaneous act requiring the use of no auxiliary means. Such is the picture given of the state of normal humanity, or the Primordial State as the Taoist doctrine calls it, which corresponds to that state known as "childlikeness" *(balya)* in the Hindu or "poverty" *(faqr)* in the Islamic doctrine, the latter term betokening the fact that the being's Self-absorption is free from all competing interests, here represented by "riches"; for this state "nakedness" would not have been an inappropriate name either.

The Bible story goes on to describe the loss of that condition of human normality by telling how Eve, corrupted by the Serpent (an embodiment of the *tamasic* or obscurantist tendency), persuaded her husband to taste of the forbidden fruit of the Tree of Knowledge of Good and Evil, with fatal results; that is to say, the original unity of vision gives way to *dualism,* a schism takes place between self and Self, in which essentially consists the "original sin" of Christian theology, containing as it does the seed of every kind of opposition, of which "myself" versus "other" provides the type. And now comes a detail which is of particular interest for our thesis: the very first effect of Adam and Eve's eating of the dualistic fruit was a feeling of "shame" at their own nakedness, a self-consciousness by which they were driven to cover their bodies with fig-leaves, thus fashioning the earliest example of human clothing.[3]

The rest of the symbolism is not hard to unravel. For one still in the state of *balya* the thought never could arise "I must be clothed", because *balya,* by definition, implies the clear recognition that the individuality, including all its sheaths *(kosha)* variously diaphanous or opaque, is itself but a cloak for the true Self; to clothe it would

---

3. In connection with Adam's "shame" a Jewish traditional commentary. (Philo, IA 11.55 f.) offers a strikingly concordant testimony, as follows: "The mind that is clothed neither in vice nor in virtue (i.e. does not partake of the fruit of the Tree of Knowledge of Good and Evil), but is absolutely stripped of either, is naked, just as the soul of an infant *(=balya)."* It should likewise be noted that in Judaism the High Priest entered *naked* into the Holy of Holies— "the noblest form, if stripping and becoming naked," noblest, that is to say, as distinguished from e.g. Noah's nakedness, when he was drunk. In the same connection Shri Krishna's theft of the *gopis'* clothes *(vastraharana)* has an obvious bearing.

be tantamount to piling dress upon dress. From this it follows that, for one who has realized that primordial state, the most natural proceeding would be to discard all clothes; one is on sure ground in saying that the unclothed ascetic or *nanga sannyasin* adequately represents the position of one who is intent on rejoining the Self.

Once there has been a departure from the indistinction of this primitive nakedness, the various traditional ways part company thus producing a wide diversity of types in each of which certain aspects of the symbolism of clothing are predominant, to the partial overshadowing of others; this, indeed, is the general principle of distinction as between any one traditional form and another, by which each is made to display a "genius" for certain aspects of the truth, leaving to its neighbors the task of emphasizing the complementary aspects.

Space does not allow of a detailed study even of the main types into which clothing can be classified; there are, however, one or two which must be mentioned: the first of these, as a letter received from A.K.C. himself once explained, represents the most characteristic constituent of Hindu clothing both ancient and modern, and consists of a length of material woven all of a piece, without joins—the "tailored" styles, as worn by Indian Muslims for instance, come into another category. In this type of single-piece wrap as commonly worn by Hindus, therefore, we are dealing with a "seamless garment", like that of Christ.

It will be remembered that at His Crucifixion the soldiers who stripped Jesus of His raiment were unwilling to tear the seamless robe, so they cast lots for it. As for the Savior Himself, He was raised naked on the Cross, as was only fitting at the moment when the Son of Man was discarding the last remaining appearance of duality, assumed for "exemplary" reasons, and resuming the principial nakedness of the Self. Christian theologians have often pointed out that the symbolical garment of Christ is the Tradition itself, single and "without parts", like the Supreme *Guru* who reveals it; to "rend the seamless garment" is equivalent to a rupture with tradition (which must, of course, not be confused with an adaptation of its form, in a strictly orthodox sense, to meet changing conditions).

Tradition is a coherent whole, though never "systematic" (for a "system" denotes a water-tight limitation of form); once torn, the seamless garment cannot be "patched" simply by means of a "hereti-

cal" (literally "arbitrary") sewing on of elements borrowed at random—those who think of saving their tradition by compromising
with a secularist outlook might well take note of the words of Christ:
"No man putteth a piece of new cloth into an old garment, for that
which is put in to fill it up taketh from the garment, and the rent is
made worse" (St. Matthew, ix, 16).

Some mention must also be made of what might be called the
"monastic habit", founded on a general type consisting of some
plain material shaped to a rather austere design or even deliberately put together from rags, as frequently occurs in Buddhism. These
forms of apparel are always meant to evoke the idea of poverty and
may be taken to symbolize an aspiration towards the state of *balya*.
To the foregoing category might be attached, but in a rather loose
sense, the self-colored cotton homespun *(khaddar)* which, in
Gandhi's India, had become the emblem of a certain movement. In
this case, too, the idea of poverty had been uppermost; but it must
be said, in fairness, that some of its supporters, possibly affected by
an unconscious bias towards westernization, often were at pains to
disclaim any other purpose for their hand-spinning than a purely
economic one, that of helping to reclothe the many poor people
who had been deprived of their vocational life and reduced to dire
want under pressure of modern industrialism. This was tantamount
to admitting that *khaddar* had a utilitarian purpose but no spiritual
significance and that the movement to promote its use was essentially "in front of (= outside) the temple", which is the literal meaning of the word "profane". It is hard to believe, however, that such
could have been the whole intention of the saintly founder of the
movement, since he had never ceased to preach and exemplify the
doctrine that no kind of activity, even political, can for a moment be
divorced from faith in God and self-dedication in His service, a view
which, more than all else, earned for him the hatred of the "pro-
gressives" of every hue, who were not slow in applying to him the (to
them) opprobrious epithets of "medieval", "traditional", and "reac-
tionary".

Apart from the two special examples just given, we must confine
ourselves to a few quite general remarks on the subject of traditional dress, for all the great variety of types it has displayed
throughout the ages and in every part of the world. By calling a
thing "traditional" one thereby relates it immediately to an idea

which always, and necessarily, implies the recognition of a supra-human influence: to quote a phrase from A.K.C.'s writings: "All traditional art can be 'reduced' to theology, or is, in other words, dispositive to a reception of truth." Thus, the costume which a man wears as a member of any traditional society is the sign, partly conscious and partly unconscious, that he accepts a certain view of the human self and its vocation, both being envisaged in relation to one Principle in which their causal origin *(alpha)* and their final goal *(omega)* coincide. It is inevitable that such a costume should be governed by a *Canon*, representing the continuity of the tradition, the stable element, Being; within that canon there will, however, be ample room for individual adaptation, corresponding to the variable element in existence, impermanence, Becoming.

In tribal civilizations, which are most logical in these matters, the art of dress and self-adornment is carried to a point where the details of human apparel are almost exact symbolical equivalents of the draperies, head-dress and jewels that indicate its *upadhis* in a sacred image *(pratima)*; moreover, such costume is usually covered with metaphysical emblems, though its wearers are by no means always aware of their precise significance; nevertheless, they reverence them greatly and undoubtedly derive a form of spiritual nourishment and power *(shakti)* from their presence. Furthermore, it is at least rather suggestive that tribal costume often entails a considerable degree of nudity, and is, in appearance, extremely reminiscent of the dresses of gods and goddesses, as portrayed in the ancient paintings and sculptures; so much so, that a friend recently suggested that the forms of tribal life in general constitute survivals from a period anterior to our present Dark Age *(Kali-yuga)*. It is not surprising that both "Christian" missionaries and the apostles of modern materialism (the two seemingly contradictory motives being, indeed, not infrequently found in the same person) should be glad whenever they succeed in inducing some simple-minded peasant or tribesman to forego the natural safeguards provided for him by his native dress and customs; for after that he is only too easily demoralized and will fall a ready victim to their properly subversive persuasions.

*
* *

One last type of clothing now remains to be considered, that specific to modern Europe and America, which is also the type that is threatening to swamp all others, to the eventual abolition of every distinction, whether traditional, racial or even, in more extreme cases, individual. This "modern dress", through its development parallel with that of a certain conception of Man and his needs, has by now become the recognized uniform to be assumed by all would-be converts to the creed of "individualism", of mankind regarded as sufficing unto itself; it is somewhat paradoxical that partisans of a violent nationalism (which in itself is but an offshoot of individualism) have often been sworn opponents of their own national costume, just because of its silent affirmation of traditional values; some examples illustrating this point have already been given in the course of this chapter, and readers can easily find other similar cases if they but care to look around in the contemporary world.

In this context some mention should be made of a variant on human clothing of recent occurrence, that of "party uniform" as introduced in the totalitarian states of the last decades. One has but to remember the "Blackshirts" of Mussolini's Italy or the "Brownshirts" of Hitler's Germany, for instance, whose respective uniforms were so designed as to suggest ruthlessness and brutality together with a kind of boisterous "camaraderie", indicative of party loyalties. In totalitarianism of another hue, it is a wish to affirm the "proletarian ideal" that has been uppermost. A striking example of party uniform having this idea in view is provided by that in vogue among members of the Chinese Communist party which in its calculated drabness expresses its purpose in a way that verges on genius: nothing could better indicate the total subordination of the human individual to the party machine than that shapeless tunic-like jacket, buttoned up to the chin, sometimes with a most hideous cap to match such as lends a peculiarly inhuman character to any face which it happens to surmount. The most interesting point about this type of costume is that it amounts, in effect, to the parody of a monastic habit; that is to say, where the austerity of monastic dress, in all its various forms, is imposed for the purpose of affirming a voluntary effacement of the individual in the face of the Spiritual Norm, the party uniform in question likewise is meant to suggest an effacement of individuality, but one that operates in an inverse sense, in the face of the deified collective principle known as "the

Masses", supposed source of authority as well as admitted object of all human worship and service. It is the ideal of a humanity minus Man, because none can be truly human who tries to ignore his own symbolism as reflecting the divine image in which he has been fashioned and to which his whole existence on earth should tend by rights. Moreover, it is no accident that all these types of uniform have been derived from Western, never from a native form of clothing.

The above admittedly represent extreme perversions, not less instructive for that. When one turns again to Western dress, however, under its more ordinary forms, it is at least fair to recognize that it has lent itself, more than other forms of clothing, to the expression of profane values: this has been true of it, in an increasing degree, ever since the latter half of the Middle Ages, when the first signs of things to come began to show themselves, in the midst of a world still attached to tradition—or so it seemed. It took a considerable time, however, before changes that at first were largely confined to "high society", and to the wealthier strata generally, were able seriously to affect the people as a whole. Over a great part of Western Europe the peasant costume remained traditional, and even with all the extravagances that had begun to affect the fashions of the well-to-do a certain "aristocratic" feeling remained there that it took time to undermine completely.

Now if it be asked which are the features in modern dress which correspond most closely with the profane conception of man and his estate, the answer, which in any case can but be a rather tentative one, will include the following, namely: the combining of pronounced sophistication, on the one hand, with "free and easiness", on the other, coupled with the frequent and gratuitous alterations introduced in the name of "fashion", of change for the sake of change—this, in marked contrast with the formal stability of traditional things—without forgetting either the manifold effects of machine production in vast quantities by processes which so often denature materials both in appearance and in their intimate texture—unavoidable or not, all these are factors that tell their own tale. Also chemical dyes, which have now swept across the world, are playing their part in the process of degradation and even where traditional costume still largely prevails, as in India, they and the excessive use of bleaching agents have together done much to offset such quality as still is to be found in the forms themselves; in most of the East the same would apply. Nor must such factors as the enclosing of feet formerly bare inside tight shoes or the disturbance to the natural poise of the body resulting from the introduction of raised heels be underrated. These and many other more subtle causes have operated in turning Western dress into a vehicle of great psychological potency in a negative sense. Besides, there is the fact that wherever ornamental features occur in modern clothing, these never by any chance exhibit any symbolical character; in other words, ornament, at its best as at its worst, has become arbitrary and therefore profane.

An objection might, however, be raised here which is as follows: the Western dress of today is, after all, but a lineal development of what formerly had been, if not a specifically Christian form of costume, at least one that was habitual in Christian Europe, one that could therefore claim to be in a certain degree traditionally equivalent to whatever existed elsewhere; it may be asked, how comes it then that its present prolongation is opposable to all other known types, so that it alone is compelled to bear the stigma of providing a vehicle for anti-traditional tendencies? Historically the fact just mentioned is incontrovertible, no need to deny it; but far from invalidating the foregoing argument it but serves to render it more intelligible: for it must be remembered that error never exists in a "pure" state, nor can it, in strict logic, be opposed to truth, since truth has no opposite; an error can but represent an impoverishment, a distortion, a travesty of some particular aspect of the truth which, to one gifted with insight, will still be discernible even through all the deformations it has suffered. Every error is *muslim*, as it were in spite of itself, according to the first of the three degrees of conformity as defined in a preceding section, and it cannot be referred back to any separate principle of its own, on pain of accepting a radical dualism in the Universe, a ditheism, a pair of alternative, mutually limiting realities. Anything can be called "profane" in so far as it is viewed apart from its principle, but things in themselves will always remain essentially sacred.

In the case of dress, this it is that explains the fact that many Westerners, though now wearing a costume associated with the affirmation of secularist values, are less adversely affected thereby (which does not mean unaffected) than Asiatics, Africans or even

135

Eastern Europeans who have adopted that same costume; with the former, alongside anti-traditional degeneration there has been some measure of adaptation bringing with it a kind of immunity—the disease is endemic, whereas in the second case it has all the virulence of an epidemic. Furthermore, since, as we have seen, some positive elements, however reduced, must needs persist through every corruption, those to whom this form of dress properly belongs are enabled, if they will, to utilize whatever qualitative factors are still to be found there; though the reverse is equally possible as evidenced both in the case of the affectedly fashionable person and of his shoddier counterpart, the affectedly unkempt. The position of the Eastern imitator, however, is quite different—for such as he the change over to modern dress may easily involve so complete a contradiction of all his mental and physical habits as to result in a sudden violent rending of his personality, to the utter confusion of his sense of discrimination as well as the loss of all taste in its more ordinary sense. Indeed such cases are all too common.

Some people affect to believe that a movement to submerge specific differences reveals a unifying tendency in mankind, but they are suffering under a great delusion in that they mistake for true unity what is only its parody, uniformity. For any individual, the realizing in full of the possibilities inherent in his *svabhava* marks the limit of achievement, after which there is nothing further to be desired. As between two such beings, who are wholly themselves, no bone of contention can exist, since neither can offer to the other anything over and above what he already possesses; while on the supra-individual level their common preoccupation with the principial Truth, the central focus where all ways converge, is the guarantee of a unity which nothing will disturb; one can therefore say that the *maximum of differentiation is the condition most favorable to unity, to human harmony*; an immensely far-reaching conclusion which René Guénon was the first to voice in modern times, one which many may find difficult of acceptance just because of that habit of confusing unity with uniformity that we have just referred to. Against this peace in differentiation, whenever two beings are together subjected to the steamroller of uniformity, not only will both of them be frustrated in respect of some of the elements normally includable in their own personal realization, but they will, besides, be placed in the position of having to compete in the same artificially restricted field; and this can only result in a heightening of oppositions—the greater the degree of uniformity imposed, the more inescapable are the resulting conflicts, a truth which can be seen to apply in every field of human activity, not excepting the political field.

*

*   *

Enough has now been said to enable the reader to appreciate the general principle we have set out to illustrate: if the subject of dress was chosen, that is because it lent itself most easily to such an exposition; but it would have been equally possible to pick on some different factor pertaining to the Active Life, to the *Karma Marga,* such as the furnishing of people's homes, or music and musical instruments or else the art of manners; since each of these is governed by the selfsame law of *svadharma* and it is only a question of effecting an appropriate transposition of the argument to fit each particular case. Behind the widespread defection from traditional dress and customs there undoubtedly lurks a deep-seated loss of spirituality, showing itself on the surface in a corresponding diminution of personal dignity and of that sense of discrimination that everywhere is recognizable as the mark of a character at once strong and noble. In the East, as we have seen, the tendency in question has gone hand in hand with what Henry James described as "a superstitious valuation of European civilization" and this tendency, despite the much lip-service paid to the new-fangled idea of "national culture", is far from having exhausted itself. This is further evidenced by the fact that imitation rarely stops short at those things that appear indispensable to survival in the modern world, but readily extends itself to things that by no stretch could be regarded as imposed under direct compulsion of contingent necessity. The operative cause therefore is to be sought in an overpowering psychological urge, the urge to experience certain possibilities of the being which tradition hitherto had inhibited, possibilities which can only ripen in forgetfulness of God and things divine: traditional dress being a reminder of those things has to be discarded; the modern civilization being the field for realizing those possibilities has to be espoused. Naturally, when one comes to individual cases, all manner of inconsistencies and oscillations will be apparent; the inherited past is not something that can be expunged for the mere wishing. All one can do, in discussing the matter, is to treat it on broad lines, leaving any given case to explain itself.

By way of striking a more cheerful note in an otherwise depressing story, the fact should be mentioned that Indian women, with but few exceptions, continue to wear the *sari*, that most gracious form of feminine dress, both at home and abroad. Their gentle example has actually spread to unexpected quarters; many African women visitors to this country [England. *Ed.*] have appeared clothed in an Indian *sari*, the colors and designs of which were however drawn from the African tradition itself. This adopting of a foreign traditional model instead of the ubiquitous Western one, by adherents of an emergent nationalism, is hitherto quite unprecedented; in its way it is a small and heartening sign, one of which all former subjects of colonialism might well take note. Indeed, sometimes one is tempted to believe that West Africans, in these matters, have tended to show more conscious discrimination than many of their fellows belonging to other continents and this impression has been strengthened by the frequent sight of Nigerian Muslim visitors of commanding stature and of both sexes walking our streets properly clad in their splendid national costume. May this example offered by Africa find many imitators!

To finish, one can but repeat the principle governing all similar cases: one's native attire—or indeed any other formal "support" of that order—is an accessory factor in the spiritual conditioning of a man or woman and this is due both to any associations it may happen to carry and, at a higher level, to its symbolism as expressed in various ways. The assumption of modern Western dress has often been the earliest step in the flight from Tradition: it would be but poetic justice for its divestment to mark the first step on an eventual path of return—too much to hope perhaps, yet the possibility is worth mentioning. In itself such action might seem little enough, for dress is not the man himself, admittedly. Nevertheless, if it be true to say that "clothes do not make the man" yet can it as truly be declared that they do represent a most effective influence in his making—or his unmaking.

Chapter 8

Holy Fools, Sacred Clowns and Demiurgic Tricksters:
On Laughter and the Ambiguity of *Mâyâ*

Patrick Laude

Les hommes sont si nécessairement fous, que ce serait être fou par un autre tour de folie, de n'être pas fou.

—Blaise Pascal

(Men are so necessarily fools that not to be a fool would amount to being one by another twist of folly.)

Der, wer zuletzt lacht, lacht am besten—sagt
Der Volksmund; wohl ein grober Spruch, doch wahr—
Ja voller Weisheit. Denn das letzte Wort
Der Welt ist jenes, das das Erste war:
Nämlich das Schöpfungswort: Es werde Licht—
Und es geschah.
    Und Bessres gibt es nicht.

—Frithjof Schuon

*(He who laughs last, laughs best—says
A popular adage; 'tis a coarse saying, but true—
Yea, even full of wisdom. For the last word
Of the world is the same as the first:
The Word of creation: let there be light!
And it happened.*
    And something better does not exist.)

Some think it so essential that they say: Nor foole, nor Prologue, there can be no Play.[1]

The unconditional metaphysical and spiritual primacy of the Absolute and the adamantine discernment between its Reality and the domain of "illusion" or lesser reality is undoubtedly the cornerstone of integral metaphysics and the foundation of all genuine

---

1. *The Novella*, Brome, 1632, Title page to the first edition of 1653, reprinted by J. Pearson, London, 1873, Vol. I.

spiritual paths. Notwithstanding this cardinal emphasis which is like the unshaking ground of the way, perhaps no reality occupies a position as functionally central in the perennialist exposition of metaphysics and traditional anthropology as that of *Mâyâ* or Universal Relativity. More than any other traditionalist writer, Schuon considers the notion of *Mâyâ*—following that of Beyond-Being and the epistemological preeminence of the Intellect—to be a key element of esoterism as principle and as way, for it truly distinguishes the esoteric standpoint from the exoteric perspective, with respect both to the Principle and to manifestation. In this metaphysical idiom, *Mâyâ in divinis* is none other than the Divine Being envisaged in His relation to the realm of creation.[2] There is a "relativity" of the Absolute that pertains to its "entering" the realm of relation to "otherness."[3] Consequently, relativity *in divinis* allows us to understand the crucial distinction between the Divine Essence as Infinite Possibility and the Divine Person or the Divine Faces turned toward Creation and mankind. Schuon has especially emphasized this distinction in regard to the problem of evil, since the discrimination between Beyond-Being and Being[4] entails a discernment between

2. This is Schuon's fundamental notion of the "relatively absolute."
3. Henry Corbin reminds us that *absolutum* refers primarily to freedom from any binding relationship. Cf. *Le paradoxe du monothéisme* (Paris, 1981).
4. This distinction, that is always present in esoterism in one way or another, seems to replicate *mutatis mutandis* the Chinese distinction between *Wuji* and *Taiji*. The former lies beyond any duality and relation as the great "Void" whereas the latter is the principle of generation. *Taiji* is "needed" as first Ring in the Great Chain of Being, but without *Wuji* the positing of a first principle would amount to a *regressio ad infinitum*. "The Chinese character *'Tai'* means highest, greatest, and remotest. The Chinese character *'Ji'* means the utmost, extreme. The term *Taiji* was found in Book 1, Chapter 11 of the *Great Appendix* (Sung, 1935/1980, p. 299) which was edited by Confucius (550-478 BC) to explain the *Book of Change* (*Yi Jing*) dated back to 3,322 BC. *Taiji*, the grand terminus which produce the two elementary forms of *Yin* and *Yang*. The two elementary forms produce four forms, which produce the eight forms. The eight forms produce the 64 hexagrams. The hexagram is just a six digits binary numbering system, each with a different combination of 6 *Yin* or *Yang*, where *Yang* was represented as a continuous stroke while *Yin* was represented as a broken stroke. The *Book of Change* contains 64 hexagrams and each hexagram is a symbolic representation of a unique event. (. . .)The concept of *Wuji* was developed from the work of Zhou Dun Yi (1017-1073), his *Tai Ji Tu Shuo* (Illustration and Explanation of *Tai Ji*) advocated the concept of *Wuji* and that *Wuji* is before *Taiji*. He differentiates *Wuji* and *Taiji* by motion; *Wuji* is static and *Taiji* is dynamic; it is motion in *Taiji* that generated *Yang*, and generated *Yin* when it slows down to stillness.

the various levels of Divine Will: on one level the Divine manifests itself in virtue of its Infinitude, while on another level God's Will is identified with the promotion of Good within manifestation through Revelation, Law and Judgment.

In the world of Manifestation, the notion of *Mâyâ* accounts for the multiple relative viewpoints and perspectives in which the Absolute is envisaged as it makes us aware of the fundamentally ambiguous character—neither real nor unreal—of the manifested order including our own terrestrial experience. Hindus often associate *Mâyâ* with the creative Divine Play (*lîlâ*)[5] therefore stressing the freedom and spontaneity of the Divine Act, and as such it can also be associated with humor. Schuon himself shows us the way to such an association when he defines the unintelligible nature of *Mâyâ*[6] as an "elusive and almost 'mocking' element."[7] Divine humor reveals itself in the very process of manifestation as *lîlâ* as it involves the humorous play and display of *Mâyâ*, the "play of masks" with which Frithjof Schuon dealt in one of his latest books; but it can also

Therefore, *Taiji* has the opportunity for moving and unmoving or a state of transition between different proportions of *Yin* and *Yang*. (. . .) The concept of *Wuji* was derived from the teaching of *Lao Zi*; his *Dao De Jing* (Book of Ethics) is the most important work in Taoism. The oldest manuscript is written between 206BC and 195BC, more than two thousand years ago. (. . .) The literal meaning of *Wuji* is infinite." Sifu Yueng Yun Choi, "*Taiji*: born of *Wuji*, mother of *Yin Yang*," [http://www.itswa.freeserve.co.uk/taiji.htm].

5. In his *Enneads* (III, 8-30) Plotinus relates two paradoxes: on the one hand all beings without exception are in a state of contemplation, on the other hand it is by virtue of playing or joking that one contemplates. Such an understanding comes very close to the Hindu notion of *lîlâ* since it suggests both the unreality (play or joke) and the reality (contemplation of the archetypes) of the universal manifestation. This ontological and cosmic aspect of play (*Spiel*) is envisaged by Schuon in several of his pieces of poetry: "*Lîlâ, das Spielen/ der Welt, die träumend sich entfalten will/ in tausend Spiegeln. Doch einmal, Herz/ Wird dieses Spiel ums Allerhöchste kreisen/ Kein Hin und Her—Ein Gopi-liebestanz der Guten, Weise.*" *Adastra—Stella Maris*, Band 1 Volume 1 (Sottens, Switzerland, 2001), p.116

6. In monotheistic theological parlance this dimension of immediate unintelligibility is subsumed under divine qualities. The *Qur'ân* may thus speak of God as "*Khayr al-Mâkirin*" that could be translated "the Best of Tricksters."

7. See "Mâyâ" in *Light on the Ancient Worlds* (Bloomington, Indiana, 1984), p.91. As for the doctrine of the "relatively Absolute" which is at the core of our topic, it is presented in most, if not all, of Schuon's books. One may in particular refer to *Survey of Metaphysics and Esoterism* (Bloomington, Indiana, 1986), pp.41-52. The chapter entitled "On the Divine Will" in *Christianity/Islam: Essays on Esoteric Ecumenism* (Bloomington, Indiana, 1985), pp.263-270, is also enlightening in this respect.

be considered as a cause of the unfolding of the manifested universe. As such, it is akin to the "jovial" overflowing of divine joy, happiness and benevolence while pointing at the "not quite serious" nature of relativity as relativity. "You are the Joy, we are the laughter" as Rûmî puts it in one of his poems, thereby identifying creatures with the very vibrations of the Divine Beatitude. At any rate, whether it be considered in its manifesting or manifested dimension, the esoteric understanding of *Mâyâ* is a particularly precious gift to seekers of our day and age. In a world as snarled and fragmented as ours, spiritual men and women have an urgent need to reach an understanding of the webs and mazes of *Mâyâ* as well as of its liberating doors.

*
* *

Humor is commonly defined as "the ability to see or show the funny or amusing side of things;" whereas laughter is nothing other than the most direct manifestation of this ability. This definition already suggests the importance of recognizing that reality or things have multiple sides and it also suggests that rigid "one-sidedness" stands in opposition to humor. Humor involves a keen sensitivity to the moving multiplicity of perspectives; it is incompatible with excessive stiffness because it perceives all positions within the context of their relativity, and it does so without having to fall into relativism or confusing levels of reality.[8] As laughter, but in a more mental and less "existential" mode, humor debunks the ultimate levity of these absolutist pretenses which are not grounded in the Absolute and which remain unmindful, in their zeal, of the ups-and-downs of *Mâyâ*. In a hyperbolic but real sense, only the Absolute cannot be laughed at; if other realities objectively[9] deserve

---

8. Plato's case in relation to humor is highly ambivalent depending on the context in which the matter is approached. Socratic irony is undoubtedly akin to Taoist humor as it constantly mocks conventional assumptions and ignorance; however *The Republic* presents a picture which is much closer to the Aristotelian ethics as it emphasizes the dangers of laughter and sets rigorous rules for its integration. Cf. *Republic,* 388e.

9. This restriction means that there is also a "subjective" need for respect and reverence. Parents may be objectively "laughable" in terms of their limitations but a child must respect his parents for his own good in virtue of his own limitations.

reverence (independently from a subjective need for respect on the part of any human being in virtue of his own limitations) or need to be treated seriously, it is so because they are, in one way or another, vehicles of the Absolute. The "funny side of things" is what reveals both their lack of absoluteness and their pretension to be treated as the Absolute. Humor stems from a subtle sense of the distance separating what appears to be from what actually is. It therefore implies duality: God's humor arises, as it were, from the level of His Relativity—that of the relatively Absolute, to use one of Schuon's key concepts—as it would have no meaning independently from a consideration of it. It could also be said that there is no room for "humor" or "laughter" in the Supreme Non-Duality unless one wishes to consider the All-Possibility as an Infinite Matrix or "Pandora's Box" prefiguring the unfolding of *Mâyâ*.

Be that as it may, God's "humor" may be considered as lying in His apparent negation of Himself in *Mâyâ*. Esoterism is accordingly akin to humor because, by contrast to exoterism, it is supremely aware of the relativity of manifestation as a veil upon Reality or as "unreal reality". For esoterists, the exclusively "serious" treatment of mere terrestrial endeavors—especially on the part of those who wish to "build" a new world independently from the Absolute or who, although they pay lip service to the Absolute, are primarily keen on absolutizing relativity in the name of all kinds of good intentions—always gives away its futility and its absurdity: it lacks a sense of metaphysical proportions, a lack which is the hallmark of its *Weltanschauung*.[10]

It is certainly no coincidence that the religious traditions whose spiritual alchemy emphasizes humor and laughter most—that is, Taoism and Zen Buddhism[11]—are also among those that focus on

10. Let us remember here that according to a *hadîth*, the Anti-Christ resembles Christ with the essential difference that he has only one eye, which amounts to saying that his one-sidedness prevents him from understanding Relativity and therefore the full range of Reality. The lack of a sense of humor and the tragi-comic pretensions which characterize so many modern causes and ideologies stem from the same limitation which is none other than the closing of the eye of the heart or the atrophy of the Intellect. "Hell is paved with good intentions."

11. One may object that Advaita Vedânta, although exclusively centered on the purest definition of the Absolute, does not seem to entail such an emphasis on laughter and humor. Notwithstanding the sovereign humor of a *jivan-mukta* such as Bhagavân Shri Râmana Mahârshi, it is likely that this relative lack of

Reality in its most absolute sense,[12] and therefore show little incli-
nation to treat as real anything that is not the Absolute or the
Essential Void. The eccentric irreverence and asocial pranks of
many Taoist masters, as well as the iconoclastic tendencies of Zen,[13]
rest upon a metaphysical discernment between the absolutely
Absolute and what is not so. One must however mention for the
sake of perfect objectivity that the iconoclastic irreverence of these
spiritual traditions must be situated within the context of an overall
tradition characterized—in traditional Japan for example—by its
"formal" emphasis and perfection, to such an extent that form
becomes as it were essence. Confucianism, Shinto and Bushidô
form the background of Taoism and Zen: the abrupt transcendence
of forms presupposes a kind of formal over-saturation.[14] That is no

emphasis is to explained by two reasons at least: the first intrinsic reason is that
the non-dualistic school of Hinduism does not envisage the Supreme negatively as Void, unlike Taoism and Mahâyâna do, so that the omnipresence of *Âtmâ*
as a Substance does not give rise to the same climate of metaphysical Vacuity
that one may find in the Far-East. Even when considered as "Non-Qualified",
Brahman is more Plenitude than Void. *Mâyâ* itself participates in the "substantiality" of *Âtmâ* on its own level, which is one reason why Coomaraswamy
emphasized "reality" in his translation of *Mâyâ* by the term "art"; the second
reason, of a more extrinsic nature, lies in the fact that by contrast with Taoism
and Zen, Advaita Vedânta does not need to define itself methodically in con-
tradistinction with the exoteric mainstream of its own tradition. Advaitins have
no laughing stock like Confucians since the Hindu tradition is a very diverse
cohabitation of perspectives and schools.

12. In Sufism, it is said that there is a *maqâm* (spiritual station) of laughter.

13. Whether one likes it or not, there is undoubtedly a certain Zen affinity with the
"trivial". Let us remember in this connection that "triviality" has to do with
"crossways" (*trivium, tri-viae*, three ways) that is with the popular and the commonplace as modes of emptiness or receptivity toward the one and only
Greatness.

14. During a private conversation Schuon indicated that, in spite of its apparent
incompatibility with the principles of dignity and logicality that characterize an
integral spiritual perspective, Zen loud laughter and the *koan*'s "illogicality" can
correspond to a moment when a kind of "chemical over-saturation" results in
the "sudden awakening" of *satori*. Schuon remarked that such a modality, albeit
"extreme" in its modalities, is not without analogy with the sudden realization
of a *maqâm* (spiritual station) in Sufism. As Schuon wrote on many occasions,
spiritual dignity stems from a consciousness of the "motionless Center on the
moving periphery", i.e. from a sense of essential continuity between the Self
and the ego, whereas spiritualized laughter stresses the "nothingness" of the latter while mocking its pretensions or limitations, which is no doubt a less essential although quite legitimate way of considering the relationship between the
two aforementioned levels of subjectivity.

doubt one of the major reasons why the most daring Taoist and Zen modalities are in general ill-adapted to Western mentalities, whose flaws rarely contain an excess of respect for forms. Be that as it may, it is in this kind of iconoclastic perspective that humor and laughter may be forged and refined into spiritual weapons for use in a war against the idolatry of forms and the idolatry of the ego. From this vantage point, forms and ego are essentially connected in the comedy of errors of this world. In this connection, the experience of *satori* is often associated with a loss of equilibrium that is akin to burlesque and bursting laughter through its destabilizing directness and "violence." Let us mention for example the *satori* of this Rinzai Master who reached twice the illumination on the occasion of a fall:

> Suddenly the temple bell struck the second hour, time of the first morning service, which we were expected to attend. I tried to get up, but my feet were so numb with cold that I fell to the snow. At that very instant it happened, my *satori*. It was an enrapturing experience, one I could not hope to describe adequately. (. . .) One day on my way back from *sanzen* (presenting one's view of a *koan* to the master) and while descending the temple steps, I tripped and fell. As I fell I had my second *satori*, a consummate one.[15]

Accordingly, such perspectives tend to emphasize the dimension of impermanence of beings and the resulting objective and subjective transmutations or transformations (Chuang Tzu's *wu hua*) at the expense of ontological substantiality, for they also involve a non-substantialist definition of the Ultimate Reality as Void (*shunya*) or Chaos (*hun tun*).

By contrast, more exoteric philosophies and wisdoms represented by figures such as Confucius or Aristotle, although not necessarily lacking in humor, enjoy a much more ambiguous and tense relationship with the world of laughter. Confucius is often derided by Taoists for his seriousness in dealing with the ordering of the world and the conventions of society.[16] It must be stressed however

---

15. Rinzai Zen Master Yasuda-Tenzan-Roshi in Lucien Stryk, *Encounter with Zen* (Chicago/Athens/London, 1981), pp.124-5.
16. "Tsekung hurried in and said: 'How can you sing in the presence of a corpse? Is this good manners?' The two men looked at each other and laughed, saying, 'What should this man know about the meaning of good manners indeed?' Tsekung went back and told Confucius, asking him, 'What manner of men are these? . . . They can sit near a corpse and sing, unmoved . . .' 'These men,'

that, as a genuine sage, he is also depicted by Taoists as one who understands the limitations of his own perspective, since he sacrificially and painstakingly resigns himself to work within its boundaries.[17] As for Aristotle, it is obvious that his priority in dealing with humor and laughter is to draw limits and promote a sense of moderation and propriety which would keep them from transgressing the realm of the law. Joking, as everything else indeed, including contemplation, has to manifest itself within the "middle state" (the *ariston metron*) for otherwise it runs the risk of erupting abusively: indeed for the Stagirite "a joke is a kind of abuse."[18] Society and the Law cannot leave the potentially transgressive nature of laughter unchecked.[19]

*

* *

In one of his most remarkable metaphysical pages, Frithjof Schuon masterfully differenciates between the main ways in which the various traditions have drawn a line between universal realities.[20] This differentiation is highly relevant to the metaphysical understanding of our topic. The first and most adamantine of these ways discriminates (as do Advaita Vêdânta and Mahâyâna Buddhism) between the Divine Essence and Universal Relativity (including Divine Being). The second way (which is basically that of

replied Confucius, 'play about beyond the material things; I play about within them. Consequently, our paths do not meet . . ." Chuang-Tzu (ch.VI) quoted in W. Perry, *A Treasury of Traditional Wisdom*, p.231.

17. In the *Chuang-tse* Confucius himself goes so far as to state that the reason why he respects conventions is because he is "condemned by Heaven" to do so.

18. "Can we then define the man who jokes well as the one who says nothing unbecoming a well-bred man, or as one who does not give pain in his jokes, or even as one who gives delight to his listeners? Or is that definition itself undefinable, since different things are hateful or pleasant to different people? The kind of jokes he will listen to will be the same, for the kind of jokes a person can put up with are also the kind he seems to make. There are, then, jokes he will not make, for a joke is a kind of abuse. There are some kinds of abuse which lawgivers forbid; perhaps they should have forbidden certain kinds of jokes." *Nichomachean Ethics*, Book IV, ch. 8 quoted in John Morreall, *The Philosophy of Laughter and Humor* (New York, 1987), p.15.

19. *Treasures of Buddhism* (Bloomington, Indiana, 1993), p. 193.

20. Cf. *Logic and Transcendence* (New York, 1975), pp. 170-1. The order in which Frithjof Schuon comments upon these five perspectives is the opposite of that which we have been led to use for the sake of our current argument.

Semitic Monotheism) draws a theological line between God (considered both as Beyond-Being and Being) and Creation or the Universal Manifestation (including its supra-formal levels). A third perspective draws the religious boundaries between the Divine domain, including the Spirit or Logos, and the cosmos of which the latter is the Divine Center. A fourth point of view separates the Celestial Realm (including God and the spiritual levels of manifestation) from the psychic and physical domains. Finally, a fifth way of envisaging universal realities, which is characteristic of Shamanism, distinguishes the world of the Spirit (including its immanent terrestrial dimension and its animic extension) from the physical and visible realm.

It is instructive that humor and laughter primarily manifest themselves—although in quite a different way—in their spiritual dimension in the first and fifth of these perspectives, which represent the most exclusive and the most inclusive of metaphysical possibilities. We have already commented upon the affinity between humor and the first of these perspectives as exemplified in Taoism and Zen. As for the perspective of the Shamanistic traditions, it involves humor and laughter while giving to them a different meaning and a cosmological and demiurgic emphasis under the guise of the Trickster, represented by such figures as Iktomi, Coyote or Raven among North American Indians, or Ananse the Spider and Leuk the Hare in West Africa.[21] Let us mention, however, that

---

21. The Spider is a major trickster figure given the very direct symbolism of its web linking the center and the periphery, the spiritual and the material. Other small, cunning or marginal animals play a similar role in a variety of traditions. One may mention the example of insects like the moth and butterfly as spirits of the confusing whirlwind for the Oglala warriors; cf. Joseph Epes Brown's *Animals of the Soul* (Shaftesbury, 1992), pp.45-6. In the same minuscule dimension, Frithjof Schuon has devoted some of his didactic pieces of poetry to the ladybug, an insect that the German language associates with Mary (*Marienkaefer*) and that is related to the Divine (*"la bête à Bon Dieu"*) in French as well. For its part, Zen Buddhism would tend to emphasize the fly as a "trickster" figure. "The 'gadfly' effect that is at work in Kyorai's poetry (. . .) finds a symbolic and revelatory expression in the relatively frequent use of the fly in the contemplative staging of *haiku* (. . .). This insect is small, easily 'annoying' and may even be associated with impressions of dirtiness and disgust. The fly tends to disturb the well ordered, carefully tended and 'perfectly' cleansed ambience that the ego would like to build for and around itself. The persistent fly 'buzzes' in our ears and flies around us as a slightly irritating reminder of relativity; it can upset even the most serious and the most dignified pose."

Taoism seems to provide us with a case where the non-dualistic and Shamanistic perspectives meet, as is evidenced by the Shamanistic origin of major Taoist metaphysical concepts. Be that as it may, shamanistic cosmic humor is related to the play with possibilities, the experimental imagination of the Demiurge. The erratic and chaotic character of the demiurgic tendency is "humorous" insofar as it defies any sense of order and intelligibility. It deals with "contingent possibilities including the most insignificant 'haphazard occurrences.'"[22] As such, it has strong affinities with the absurd, that is with the absence of intelligible foundations or at least our inability to perceive any such foundations.[23] This random and apparent senselessness may enter into the operative modalities of some functions of shamanism. As Eliade has indicated, "even the symbolism of chaos can be deciphered in the 'madness' of future shamans, in their 'psychic chaos': this is a sign that the profane man is in the process of 'dissolving' and that a new personality is in the making."[24] Titus Burckhardt has indicated how the traditional mask makes it possible for the "psychic matter" to undergo a process of alchemical liquefaction;[25] this is also relevant to the clown and to

Patrick Laude, *The Way of Poetry: Essays on Poetics and Contemplative Transformation* (Oneonta, New York, 2002), p.154.

22. Cf. Frithjof Schuon, "Concerning an Onto-Cosmological Ambiguity" in *To Have a Center* (Bloomington, Indiana, 1990), p. 102.

23. What was unintelligible and "unreal" on the ontological level becomes "arbitrary" on the social level. That is the reason why Trickster is constantly involved in a process of unveiling the absurdity and illusoriness of social conventions while defining thereby the social "rules of the game." "Trickster makes the world by playing with cultural categories and highlighting the arbitrary nature of cultural rules and categories and constantly reminding the normative culture that there is much beyond its own perspective and understanding." C.W. Spinks, *Trickster and Ambivalence: The Dance of Differenciation* (Madison, Wisconsin, 2001), p.8.

24. "Même le symbolisme (du chaos) se laisse déchiffrer dans la 'folie' des futures chamans, dans leur 'chaos psychique': c'est le signe que l'homme profane est en train de se 'dissoudre' et qu'une nouvelle personnalité se prepare à naître." "Expérience sensorielle et experience mystique chez les primitives", *Du corps à l'esprit* (Paris, 1989), p.75.

25. "The sacred mask, on the contrary, along with all that its wearing implies as regards gestures and words, suddenly offers one's 'self-consciousness' a much vaster mold and thereby the possibility of realizing the 'liquidity' of this consciousness and its capacity to espouse all forms without being any one of them." Titus Burckhardt, "The Sacred Mask" in *Mirror of the Intellect* (Cambridge, England, 1987).

the trickster who "is" a "mask"—in the sense of a function—and actually often wears a mask,[26] like the Lakota *heyoka*[27] whose identity may remain more or less anonymous under the guise of a comic mask. In the spirit of the monkey as a grotesque and ex-centric figure—which may still be considered from the standpoint of a partial positive symbolism in India and China, this function manifests itself as "random consciousness" or as "a consciousness decentralized and dissipated."[28] That is the reason why the trickster figure, who embodies this tendency in many traditional societies and folklores, nearly always reveals some elements of stupidity[29] side by side with

26. He may also simply "enter" a "clownish" role, which is another way of saying that this "role" enters him spontaneously.

27. The following lines about the *heyoka* phenomenon are among the most informative on the topic: "*Wakiniyan* is a material god whose substance is visible only when He so wills. His properties are *akan* and antinatural. He abides in His lodge on the top of the mountain at the edge of the world where the Sun goes down to the region under the world. He is many, but they are as only one; He is shapeless, but he has wings with four joints each; He has no feet, yet He has huge talons; He has no head, yet has a huge beak with rows of teeth in it, like the teeth of a wolf; His voice is the thunder clap and rolling clouds; He has an eye and its glance is lightning. In a great cedar tree beside His lodge He has His nest made of dry bones, and in it is an enormous egg from which His young issue. He devours His young and they each become one of his many Selves. He had issue by the Rock and it was Iktomi, the oldest son of the Rock. He flies in the domain of the Sky, hidden in a robe of clouds, and if one of mankind sees His substance he is thereby made a *heyoka*, and must ever afterwards speak and act in clownishly and anti-natural manner. Yet, if He so wills, He may appear to mankind in the form of a (. . .) man, and if so, He is then the God, Heyoka. One who looks upon the God, Heyoka, is not thereby made a *heyoka*. The potency of the Winged God cannot be imparted to anything. His functions are to cleanse the world from filth and to fight the Monsters who defile the waters and to cause all increase by growth from the ground. The acceptable manner of addressing Him is by taunt and vilification, the opposite of the intent of the address. He may be visualized as a bird whose wings have four joints. His symbol is a zigzag red line forked at each end. His *akicita* (messengers or police) are the dog, swallow, snowbird, night hawk, lizard, frog, and dragon fly, and if either of these is seen in a vision the one to whom it appears is thereby made a *heyoka.*" J.R. Walker, *Anthropological Papers of the American Museum of Natural History,* 16, pp.83-4, 1917.

28. Cf. F. Schuon, *Perspectives spirituelles et faits humains* (Paris, 1953), p.62.

29. In the Middle Ages, during the Carnival preceding Lent, a *sottie* was a comedy played by fools. The words *fou* and *sot* were virtually synonymous. Stupidity or a certain lack of intelligence can be paradoxically assigned to the trickster as well. This stupidity is not without connection to the awkward naivety that "breaks the ice" of social conventions and brings human ridicule to the fore, thereby liberating us from more or less unconscious pretensions.

gifts of cunning intelligence. He works to the benefit of the cosmos which he contributes to shape, but his way of doing so is either haphazard or awkward, if not downright foolish or scandalous. Obviously, this dimension of cosmic absurdity is not unconnected with the nature of *Mâyâ*, for *Mâyâ* is undoubtedly absurd when considered exclusively on its own level.[30]

Given its functional association with the unfolding of *Mâyâ* it would be a radical mistake to envisage this unintelligible aspect of the demiurgic "tricks" from the standpoint of morality, as it would be misleading, or at least quite useless and for that matter somewhat wanting in a sense of humor, to try to understand or judge the trickster figures by the compass of moral imperatives. It is so, metaphysically speaking, because *Mâyâ* and the Demiurge "work out" the essential and infinite dimension of the Divine Will on the level of accidence, therefore in a domain where the category of a strictly moral intelligibility of things does not apply. There results from this, on the level of *natura naturans*, an ambiguity that "sentimental moralism finds it difficult to understand."[31] Let us specify moreover that the demiurgic tendency to which we refer may manifest itself on a variety of levels—cosmological, spiritual, social and even psychological—which makes it difficult to define as a single reality, and compels us to deal with it in a wide array of phenomena of diverse functional import. It may manifest itself on the divine as well as on the human and animal levels. As for the modalities of its function, they may also differ greatly, both intrinsically and extrinsically. The trickster may be purely chaotic, impulsive and self-seeking as Ananse the Ashanti Spider and the Irish Bricriu "Poisontongue" (hero of the Old Irish story *Fled Bricrenn*), he may even border on what monotheistic religions would apprehend as demonic, or he may be well-meaning, and even charitable and just like the Hui Fool

---

30. It is plausible that such a dimension be most often envisaged in the form of an animal or human mythological personification given the highly problematic nature of its conceptualization. However, the animal or semi-animal character of many tricksters also refer to a state that precedes and initiates differentiation.

31. "*Mâyâ* is beyond good and evil, she expresses both plenitude and privation, the divine and the all too human, and even the titanic and the demonic; sentimental moralism finds it difficult to understand an ambiguity of that order." (*Light on the Ancient Worlds*, p.76).

Kuanzi (in Muslim Chinese culture)[32] and the famous Nasr-al Din Hodja. The first case generally involves a cosmic and demiurgic function—wherefrom its amoral aspect, whereas the second appears to refer to a social, moral or spiritual dimension. However, such a distinction should not be generalized without great care since the "amoral" Trickster is more than often envisaged as a founder, a culture hero and a benefactor of mankind. The Protean aspect of the trickster figure may thus challenge definitions that are all too rigid and stable.

However difficult, if not impossible, it may be to define a phenomenon that stands precisely in opposition to the very notion conveyed by the Latin words *fines* (boundaries) and *definire* (to limit)[33], we would like to propose the following conceptual diagram as a possible approach to the trickster phenomenon. This diagram involves the four-fold relationship between marginality, liminality, connection and transgression in which the four characteristics are tied together by the grotesque or burlesque element. A sixth aspect, concerning the effect or result of the presence and action of the trickster figure, lies in change, whether it be creation, restoration or modification. Our diagram could therefore be sketched as follows:

MARGINALITY
(outcast, lowly, aberrant, discordant)
||

LIMINALITY   =   GROTESQUE   =   CONNECTION
(threshold, initiation)   (trick, parody, mischief, joke)   (communication, encounter)
||

TRANSGRESSION
(gluttony, lust, sacrilege)
V

CATALYST of CHANGE
(demiurgic function, invention, creation, restoration, healing)

The transgressive nature of the trickster figure clearly appears throughout most cultures in the paradox that his character is both sacred and sacrilegeous, hero and villain, initiator and scapegoat.

---

32. Cf. Shujiang Li & Karl W. Luckert, *Mythology and Folklore of the Hui, A Muslim Chinese People* (New York, 1994).
33. The Trickster transgresses limits. He opens up the boundaries of formal relativity, thereby reflecting on his own level and his own mode the liberating infinitude of Reality.

This highest ambiguity necessarily entails an element of transcendence without which it would be utterly incomprehensible, for such an apparent contradiction can only be the consequence of the juxtaposition of two different levels of reality or two hierarchically ordered viewpoints. The demiurgic trickster is sacred with respect to his cosmic function, sacrilegeous with respect to his personal behavior. Let us remember in this connection that the term *sacer* means both sacred and wretched or cursed, this duality being a reflection of the profound sacrificial law associated with the function of the scapegoat.[34] The principle of transformation incarnated by the snake thus partakes of a metaphysical necessity without which the Biblical drama and Redemption itself would have no meaning: that is one of the possible meanings of the Augustinian *felix culpa.*

Although the sacred imposes itself by virtue of its own power and evidence, there is a certain extrinsic and indirect way in which it must be differentiated from the non-sacred on the plane of terrestrial experience. When performed by the grotesque trickster, sacrilege becomes a sort of consecration *a contrario.* The story of Iktomi the Spider and the sacred buffalo skull, narrating the trickster's outlandish curiosity and its negative consequence—his head remains tucked into the skull—is a typical example of this paradoxical phenomenon. In that connection, the trickster is a mere instrument of divine providence, a kind of reverse exemplar. By contrast, the mysterious companion of Moses—often identified with Al-Khidr, in the Surah of the Cavern—acts according to divine and spiritual ruse when he seems to break normative and moral ways of behaving. Unlike Iktomi, he knows what he is doing, notwithstanding that such a distinction is only "relatively absolute," for only God knows in the fullest sense.

One of the most universal aspects of the humorous or burlesque personifications of the demiurgic trickster—which is akin to both his communicative and transgressive functions in our dia-

---

34. Schuon does not hesitate to relate this delicate question to the function of the snake in Paradise. "In Biblical terms, it can be said that there is no terrestrial Paradise without its serpent, and that without the serpent there can be no fall and therefore no human drama, nor any reconciliation with Heaven. The creation being in any case something that stands apart from God, a deifugal tendency must necessarily be inherent in it, so much so that it can be considered under two aspects, the one divine and the other demiurgic or luciferian." *Light on the Ancient Worlds*, p.76.

gram—shows that he is capable of being and doing everything and nothing, as well as borrowing a wide variety of forms and shapes. He is the one who "works out everything," as does Rabelais' Panurge (Pan-Urgos): he speaks all languages, wears all kinds of contrasting hats and garbs, and mingles with people of all walks of life. In his *Pantagruel* (Chapter IX), Rabelais introduces Panurge as an ambiguous young man who both looks like and acts as an aristocrat and a rogue. He tellingly makes his first entry in the book as an enigmatic chatterbox displaying a bewildering ability to speak all kinds of dialects, or rather to imitate them with all the appearances of fluency. Imitation is the hallmark of the trickster figure insofar as his realm is *Mâyâ*, the very kingdom of imitations and Platonic *phantasmata;* relativity is "imitation," and only God does not imitate.This sense of imitation often entails some element of boasting and burlesque grandiosity which leads him into trouble. It also involves a tendency to outdo everybody and everything in good and evil deeds, both as a caricature and a gluttonous trespasser. From another angle, the trickster revels in and thrives at crossroads and market places—places which were devoted to Hermes-Mercury—establishing connections *tous azimuths* in a meddling and often mischievous manner. He is a wanderer, constantly on the go, like Iktomi, the North American trickster, and Ananse, his African counterpart who roams about "more often there than here." He can be a thief or a liar for the sake of men, as Raven when he stole the light. He facilitates connections between the most different levels and the most diverse realities, as he also makes things happen in the most unpredictable[35] and unconventional way, bringing about changes, transformations[36] and some-

---

35. "You never know what they are going to do!" in "Description of contemporary *heyoka* practices by informants," Thomas H. Lewis, *Anthropos* 69, 1974, p.24.
36. Whence his frequent association with the color green. Let us remember in this context that green appears both in a beneficent and maleficent aspect. Green is the color of springly renewal, but it is also—in alchemy—that of putrefaction. These two aspects of the color refer to the two equinoxes of Spring and Fall. Any alchemical modification presupposes a use of "dejections" and "manure" as spiritual "fertilizers." This function is associated with Pluto—and to the sign of Scorpio—as planet of inner regeneration. Jean Biès gave an interesting commentary of this mystery of transmutation in his *Les chemins de la ferveur* (Paris, 1995): "The great secret of all wisdoms is that once this 'evil' has been integrated, the energies that it was stifling or spending do not produce any revolt or despair anymore—for this would be a dilapidation of strength—while

times even upheavals. Paradoxically, he tends to be both a trouble-maker and a mediator: he opens up cracks in the walls of social and cosmic orders through the incongruency of his manners and deeds, but he also allows for new connections and communications through the velocity of his zigzagging impulses.[37]

In order to gain a better understanding of this function—to which Frithjof Schuon deemed worthy a whole chapter entitled "The Demiurge in North American Mythology" in his *Logic and Transcendence*—it is worth noting that the trickster figure is often a divine or semi-divine being or an animal, or both. Demiurgic and trickster-like features thus characterize Hermes-Mercury, Loki and Odin, and maybe even *cum grano salis* the younger Krishna; they also apply *a fortiori* to Iktomi and Ananse the Spiders, Monkey, Coyote, Hare, Turtle, and several creatures of the air such as birds and insects. Even when considered as a human or humanized being, the trickster figure does not belong to the ordinary run of mankind. His characteristics, whether physical or psychological, set him apart from society and from his fellow humans. He may be an Old Man, a young Prankster, even an Old Woman at times. He is often envisioned as the Fool, the Jester or the Madman. In one way or another, his marginality has to do with the ambiguity of his nature, which is both spiritual and physical, lofty and lowly, constructive and destructive and so on. His being and experience defy all categories and norms of ordinary existence and morality. This ambivalence is attuned to the reconciliation of extremes. In that respect, the demiurgic work could therefore be described as follows: to bring out, often quite indirectly and unintentionally, the intelligibility of luminous Spirit in the dark absurdity of matter. In the case of the mythological trickster, this result is clearly achieved as the unintended

being freed to gain access to higher levels, to work toward the unification of contraries." (Cf. pp.64-5) Let us add that the color green is the result of a blend of yellow and blue, the absolute and the infinite. Green is the "transformation" of blue into yellow and conversely. Whence its association with renewal, transmutation, realization and changes. It symbolizes the integration of opposites and is akin to Mercury.

37. The complete lack of independence of the trickster vis-à-vis his impulses is best illustrated by his "submission" to the wheel of becoming in the form of objects of his desire. Popular theater, particularly the Italian *Commedia dell'Arte*, has immortalized this type in characters such as Arlecchino whose sexual desire is immediate toward any passing woman. Harpo Marx has embodied this type, both "innocent" and "concupiscent", in moving pictures.

consequence of an otherwise aberrant behavior. The case of divine trickster-like figures such as Hermes and Odin seems different insofar as these figures function as epiphanies, although the modes of this function may appear ambiguous when considered extrinsically. As for folkloric types of tricksters such as Nasr al-Din Hodja and Ulenspiegel, they tend to act as inventive and liberating channels of manifestation for the "collective wisdom," as a passive reflection of the Logos on the plane of popular culture. In all cases, trickster figures operate as instruments of connection and communication, and thus contribute to the renewed and enlivened conservation and growth of a given sector of reality.

At this juncture, it is important to emphasize that the demiurgic function which is embodied by the trickster undergo a wide variety of manifestations ranging from quasi-demonic figures to messengers of Heaven, from chaotic outcasts without a center to highly ambiguous divine characters such as the Scandinavian Loki. This diversity of symbols and manifestations makes it impossible to restrict the demiurgic function to a single modality. As Frithjof Schuon has indicated, within a given culture the demiurgic function may be "embodied in three or several personifications depending on whether it is passional, tenebrous or on the contrary luminous."[38] Moreover, as we have already suggested, it is often difficult to distinguish the mythological trickster from the mischievous culture hero or the holy fool. Methodically speaking, it may be helpful to consider that a demiurgic or trickster-like figure is divine and luminous in proportion to his active awareness of the Divine Will which he contributes to carry out while being tenebrous to the extent that this mission is all the more passively, unconsciously and indirectly fulfilled. That is, approximately speaking, the wide gap separating Hermes from Ananse the Spider. In other words, the demiurgic process is a participation in the cosmic intelligence because it involves an element of divine ruse; but that ruse may be exercised or carried out by the trickster figure (Hermes' and Odin's cases represent the highest possibility of the kind), whereas in other cases (which involve a definitely buffoonish element) the trickster may be both the instrument and the

38. Cf. *Logic and Transcendence*, pp.152-3, note 1.

victim of that divine ruse, insofar as he tends to follow his own desires and whims.

The cases of a Ulysses and a Nasr al-Din Hodja correspond to two possibilities of a somewhat different nature. They present us with cunning or mischievous heroes who somehow participate in the divine "ruse" or "prudence." Ulysses seems to express a practical, prudential and strategic intelligence which may be ultimately identified with the Intellect, whereas Nasr al-Din Hodja may be interpreted as manifesting holy wisdom in its light and carefree dimension as it debunks the fanatic, conventional or hypocritical facets of religious and social life. It would however be pedantic and futile to try to delineate absolute boundaries between these various possibilities for the type of demiurgic function that we have in mind always implies an element of intrinsic or extrinsic ambiguity in virtue of its dealing with the "substance of incomprehensibility"—to use Frithjof Schuon's expression—of the world.

When considered on the cosmological level, the demiurgic trickster functions as the instrument of the ontological contact between extreme levels of reality. Since nothing can lie outside of the Divine Reality, even that which is apparently the most remote from its Source, there must be a way in which the obscure may "participate" in the Light—aside from its mere aspect of privation. The reality of that indirect participation should in no way obliterate the clear distinction between good and evil, nor should it imply the idea of a need for evil on the part of the good. It simply points to a paradoxical consequence of the unity of Being and, so to speak, to the impossibility of non-being to be or, if one prefers, of Being not to be. The crystallization of this paradox is accomplished by the trickster, insofar as he embraces the lower realms of *Mâyâ*. It is through the fissure opened by the trickster figure that something of the perfume of heaven infiltrates the taverns of worldly stench. This coincidence of extremes analogically reflects the supreme mystical *coincidentia oppositorum*. As everything is "contained" in the Divine Essence, the Divine Presence is "contained" in everything; but diverse are the ways in which this Presence actualizes itself.

*

* *

As Frithjof Schuon taught,[39] we may see God as the very Substance of the world—as revealed in the perception of the miracle of existence—and we may also see Him through terrestrial manifestations of His Qualities and, indirectly, through the privation of these Qualities. Given a beautiful phenomenon, we may or can see God in three ways: as an occurrence of the miracle of existence, as a manifestation of Divine Beauty, and possibly even as a limitation testifying to the Illimitation of the Divine, for it must not be forgotten that, as Schuon wrote on several occasions, a phenomenon, as beautiful as it may be, is also a limitation, if only because it excludes other beauties.

Now, by contrast with this experience of the Divine in its direct and positive symbols, "seeing" God in profanity and even ugliness is an altogether different matter. On the one hand, these phenomena are negations of Being, on the other hand, they affirm Being *a contrario* through and in spite of their lack of Being, or their lack of Beauty, which amounts here to the same. So there seem to be two ways in which profane or ugly phenomena can be reduced or "reassimilated" to the One. First, by considering their manifestation in the context of existence as such, the latter being a symbol of Divine Absoluteness (which does not mean that these phenomena are themselves "symbols" as phenomena, *quod absit*, since they are privative); second, by a kind of subversion of their attempt at negating Divine Being and Divine Beauty, a ruse with the Devil so to speak. This second way leads us to a further spiritual dimension of our topic.

As a projection of the myriad possibilities contained in the Divine Essence, *Mâyâ* can be conceived either as dissolution or else as solidification or segmentation on the one hand, and as condensation on the other. The "tenebrous" *Mâyâ* is fundamentally a condensation of reality, and as such, it has affinities with *tamas*, the last and lowest quality in Hindu cosmology. Most often considered from the standpoint of its dark and descending quality, *tamas* is notwithstanding also, in virtue of the law of reverse analogy, the reflection of Divine Infinitude on the plane of material existence.[40]

---

39. Cf. the chapter "Seeing God Everywhere" in *Gnosis: Divine Wisdom* (London, 1978).
40. On this topic, one must refer to the enlightening article of Martin Lings, "The Seven Deadly Sins" in *Symbol and Archetype* (Cambridge, England, 1991), where

Symbolized by the color black in its negative aspect—as opposed to the positive black of the Night of the Essence—*tamas*, inasmuch as it cannot be ignored or denied, must somehow be converted into positive energy, or at least diverted from its negative function.

From a certain standpoint, we may therefore distinguish between two aspects of *Mâyâ*: a theophanic and elevating one which corresponds to *sattva* (it also corresponds to the color blue which manifests illimitation), while the second is congealing, obscuring and descending, and is akin to *tamas*. The first dimension refers to the liberating and saving *Shakti*—corrresponding to Lakshmî[41]—whereas it is in the second dimension of *Mâyâ* that the Luciferian tendency toward what Schuon calls the illusion of "metaphysical extraterritoriality" dwells. This tamasic tendency of *Mâyâ* calls for a divine reaction in the form of rigor, majesty and even destruction, and that is the role of Kâlî.[42] Kâlî is so to speak the negative aspect of the *Shakti* which reduces the "subversive" extension of time to the instantaneity of space. The age of Kâlî points to an ultimate "change of time into space" (to use René Guénon's phrase) which resolves the raging madness of *Mâyâ*.

It may therefore be legitimate, from a slightly different standpoint, to envisage a third dimension of *Mâyâ*, one that is highly ambiguous or ambivalent and akin to *rajas*, the dynamic and passional quality of the Cosmogonic Substance, which is also the quality predominating in the *kshatriya* caste.[43] This *Shaktic* dimension may be destructive or liberating, depending on the direction in which it is channeled. First among all the terrestrial manifestations of that dimension, the ambiguity of sexuality reflects its ambivalence on the plane of human existence.

The symbolism of the *Taming of the Shrew* may be particularly relevant as a literary illustration of the abovementioned reality. As it plainly appears in Shakespeare's comedy, the negative side of femininity—or the destructive potentiality of the rajasic *Mâyâ*—must be

the author clearly shows how deadly sins constitute the analogic reversal of positive tendencies of the soul toward the Infinite.
41. Cf. Frithjof Schuon, *Roots of the Human Condition* (Bloomington, Indiana, 1991), p.33.
42. Cf. *Roots of the Human Condition*, p.32.
43. Frithjof Schuon has himself sometimes opted for this "three-dimensional" perspective on *Mâyâ*, as in his *Survey of Metaphysics and Esoterism*, p.57.

brought under the yoke of positive masculinity as an expression of the Absolute or its Intellective refraction; in this alchemical process, to bring under the yoke does not mean to destroy, but on the contrary to use, and to direct toward liberating ends.[44] To this end the hardened masculine must also undergo a transmutation that "feminizes" it as it were in the form of a seductive and charming cunningness. In a sense the masculine Sulphur has to become feminine Quicksilver and conversely; or, from another standpoint, the "feminine" unconscious impulses must be brought into the light of intelligence as corporeal Intellect, whereas the "masculine" consciousness must be made "integral" by a kind of "incarnation." This seems to be the deepest meaning of the mythological story of Omphale—Queen of Lydia—and Hercules[45], in which the hero dresses as a woman and trembles before his lover who takes up a masculine stance. Now it is not without relevance to our topic that Petruchio undoubtedly appears as a character akin both to the *kshatriya* caste and to the archetype of the mercurial trickster, in whose ambiguity he revels. Such an association between the trickster figure and the second caste is common in a variety of traditions. The North American Indian tradition presents cases of vocational functions associating a warrior path with eccentric or clown-like deportment. In Japan as well, the cosmogonic trickster Susa-no-o reveals connections and affinities with the explosive turbulence that may characterize warriors.[46] He is the one who brings demiurgic trouble to the empire and readily stands in opposition to the sattvic and brahmanic figure of Amaterasu-Omikami. Notwithstanding, Frithjof Schuon has explicitly indicated that Susa-no-o's "passional element" is necessary in the "cosmic economy," as "productive ener-

---

44. "Psychologically speaking, that which at the beginning of the work appears as a dangerous and disturbing impulse, becomes, with the achievement of mastership, a force carrying the consciousness into higher spheres." Titus Burckhardt, *Alchemy* (Louisville, Kentucky, 1997), p.118-120.

45. As suggested to the author of this article by Giorgio Jannaconne.

46. "(. . .) It is Susa-no-o who fits into the second function. Like Vayu and Starkdr elsewhere, he epitomizes the wild and disruptive aspect of the warrior's calling, even as Takemikazuchi exemplifies its controlled and benign aspect. So it is that Susa-no-o's outrages in heaven can be interpreted as the 'sins' against the first-function cosmic order common to second-function figures everywhere." "A Japanese Mythic Trickster Figure: Susa-no-o", by Robert S. Ellwood, in *Mythical Trickster Figures*, ed. William Hynes and William Doty (Tuscaloosa, Alabama, 1993), p.149

gy," which is why, although "first sinner," Susa-no-o can thrive on earth without losing his "celestial dignity."[47]

An impoverished nobleman of somewhat martial demeanor, Petruchio also appears, in *The Taming of the Shrew*, as an eccentric marginal figure, a blend of nobility and *prima facie* coarseness, who seems to have acquired a wealth of experience in the ups-and-downs of the play of *Mâyâ*. Significantly, at the beginning of the play he acknowledges that he has "thrust" himself into the "maze" of this world (I, ii, 54). Although undoubtedly firm, and even violent at times, he rarely opposes the destructive energy of Kate-Katherine directly. It is rather through a combination of seductive ruse, humor and laughter that he succeeds in channeling his soul-mate's energy toward the Good, symbolized by the harmony and peace of marriage. It could be said that the ability that Petruchio displays in juggling the outbursts of his wife's hot temper and converting the latter into a positive energy participates in an alchemy that shares both in the archetypes of both Hermes-Mercury and Krishna. In this alchemy, Petruchio may be identified with the Spirit as it corrects and informs the soul by negating the latter's centrifugal impulses.

The Krishnaite component of *The Taming of the Shrew* seems to be connected to sexual alchemy in relation to *Shaktic* reality. The possibility of such an alchemical transmutation lies in the essential unicity of *Shaktic* energy as expressed, for example, by the fact that the various Hindu and Buddhist *dâkinî*, as expressions of the nature of feminine energy on the plane of multiplicity, range from the most celestial to the most infernal.[48] In other words, it is not the energy in itself which is tenebrous or destructive, but the direction and modality imparted to it.[49] Moreover, the connection between

---

47. *Treasures of Buddhism* (Bloomington, Indiana, 1993), p.193.
48. The designation *dâkinî* refers to a wide range of celestial and demonic female beings. These "Sky Dancers" may be tutelary deities, or even enlightened initiates, in *Vajrayâna* Buddhism. They may also appear—in Tibet—as wrathful female figures and—in Indian folklore—as witches and female tricksters. The *Bardo Thodol* defines them as "feminine energy principle, associated with knowledge and intelligence, which may be either destructive or creative." Cf. *Roots of the Human Condition*, p.33, note 2.
49. In a sense, Katarina is to be identified to the terrible aspect of Kali; her untamed and tyrannical nature being also the pure *shaktic* substance and energy that ultimately leads to liberation.

the *Shaktic* element—not the Supreme Divine *Shakti* or a given man-ifestation of it, but general cosmic energy—and our central theme plainly appears in the fact that the former may be envisaged—like the Mercurian dimension of Shakespeare's play—in a humorous manner. Let us remember in this connection, that even Krishna's divinity—his divine substance—in no way excludes a mischievous and even naughty side (that is, his masks) either as a playful butter-thief or as a butterfly lover. The esoteric outlook requires that we make sense of these two dimensions without confusing them.

Adding a definitely comical bent to the sprightly character of love, *The Taming of the Shrew* presents us with a somewhat grotesque sexual alchemy that ridicules the feminine in its centrifugal aspect. This peculiar tendency may stem paradoxically from the fact that femininity represents for man the most direct manifestation of the Divine in terrestrial existence. As such however, it is also what may give rise to the most idolatrous behavior, both subjectively and objectively. As object of man's love, and when unaware of her "essential beauty," woman may become an egocentric "goddess" and tyrant, whereas man may become a foolish and passionate slave oblivious of the feminine archetype. The trickster-like behavior of Petruchio and other literary and folkloric figures in relation to woman may well correspond in its way to a symbolic and sometimes preventive war against such a sorry possibility. Other trickster fig-ures like Ulenspiegel or Rabelais' Panurge fulfill the same cathartic function by indulging in ridiculing women, or rather, more specifi-cally, beautiful but proud and arrogant young women. Panurge (lit-erally "the one who works out everything") is particularly nimble and devious in the amorous war that appears as a grotesque parody of the worship of the Lady. There is no doubt that such behavior corresponds to an imbalance grown out of an opposite imbalance, and it is obvious that this possibility takes us far from the normative definition of social congruency. However, the *Troubadours* them-selves, medieval devotees of courtly love, were not always unaware of these unsettling ways, as is shown by the example of Marcabru.[50] If the exaltation of positive *Mâyâ* may be a way of affirming the Real, the playful mockery or defilement of negative *Mâyâ* may be an indi-

50. On the Gascon Marcabru or Marcabrun see Henri-Iréné Marrou's *Les trouba-dours* (Paris, 1971), p.72.

rect way of denying the illusory. In a climate that takes us away from any similar comical intent but which is not without analogy with the realities to which we have just alluded, Odin's and Hermes's wooing and amorous escapades as well as—notwithstanding their higher meaning—Krishna's love games may refer to a sort of "quickening" of the *Shaktic* element which paradoxically neutralizes its subversive potentialities.[51]

As for the mercurial character of Petruchio, it is somehow identified with the cosmic intelligence of the Logos. In Greco-Latin mythology, Hermes-Mercury is characterized as a witty and sometimes deceitful god, with erotic and healing functions. Ruse and laughter are two of his common attributes. These are also Petruchio's main weapons, for they allow him to participate in the function of the Logos in different ways. In the first respect, he ironically treats Kate as if she were already identified with her archetype (Katherine) by referring to the latter in order to ridicule the fallen nature of his wife (Act II, scene 1, verses 185-194). He therefore cunningly reminds her of what she really is and what she will become again at the end of the play.[52] This kind of comical humiliation is a

51. The highest symbolism of Krishna's love games with the *gopis*, representing God's attraction of the many souls, does not exclude a more directly "sexual" interpretation, provided that one keeps in mind that sex is not primarily a physical phenomenon but, in a much more profound sense, a spiritual and psychic reality. On this topic, one may refer to Julius Evola's *Metaphysics of Sex*. Let us mention in this connection that the ithyphallic nature of many trickster figures corresponds to a cosmological reality. The main characteristic of the *Candomblé* statues of Exú is an immense phallus (Paul V. A. Williams, "Exú: the Master and the Slave in Afro-Brazilian Religion" in *The Fool and the Trickster. Studies in Honour of Enid Welsford*, edited by Paul V. A. Williams (Ipswich, England, 1979), p.118). The potentialities of the Logos brought out by the Demiurgic Principle—as expressed through the sexual symbol—are in this case envisaged in their "blind" and grotesque aspect. The North American Indian *Heyoka*'s clown power is also associated with the generative and sexual energy. The *Heyoka* "bomb effect" has to do, on the psycho-spiritual level, with sexuality as the most intense repository of energy and the manifestation of the infinite on the terrestrial level.

52. The aspect of ruse, and even seduction, pertains to the transforming alchemy of the snake in its beneficial character. The Hindu and Buddhist *nâga* is also closely associated with the principle of spiritual fertilization which is obviously not unrelated to the fecundating rain and to the tantric channeling of sexual desire. Amphay Doré thus describes the Buddhist understanding of *nâga* in Laos: "The *nâga* are mythical beings who rule over serpents. Being snakes themselves, they possess, in relation to their subjects, the power of metamorphosis in various forms, particularly in the form of seductive young men in order to court

way to simultaneously espouse and dissolve the inferior *Mâyâ* in order to bring her back to the superior archetype of which she is an inversion. Laughter fulfills an analogous function, although in a different mode, since it proceeds as a kind of explosion that breaks and shatters the coagulation of the dense and rebellious *Mâyâ*. It manifests itself as a symbolic destruction whereby the illusion of reality shatters with the irresistible suddenness of a liberating blessing. Such an understanding of the alchemy of laughter may grant some plausible symbolic meaning to a suggestive definition of the apocatastasis as "God's laughter" insofar as the latter may be understood as a sudden and liberating shattering of the illusory dimension of reality "from within" as it were. Divine laughter is both destructive and apocalyptic as it expresses the instanteneous removal of veils and limitations. As such it also expresses a victory over death and over the fear of death as is most likely indicated by the phenomenon of ritual laughter during the *Hilaria* and the *Lupercalia*[53] in Rome.[54] Analogically, and on the highest spiritual level, the capacity of laughter to provoke the utmost liberation is suggestively expressed by Râmana Mahârshi in its subjective dimension: "A day will dawn

young women. They are generally respectful of Buddhist precepts. Both aquatic and aerial, moving both on earth and in the sky, the *nâga*, as the dragon, provokes rain. As in the West, the snake is in Laotian culture the expression of *libido*. However, because of his celestial character, the *nâga* also expresses sublimation. That is why *nâga* are often used as ornamental figures in the stairs or gutters of monasteries. They signify the passage from one level to another. They are the vehicle of spirituality and at the same time the expression of its level" (translated from *Un après-goût de bonheur* [Vientiane, 1974], p.39).

53. The *Hilaria* were celebrated in honor of Cybele at the vernal equinox whereas the *Lupercalia* were held in honor of Lupercalus in mid-February—Lupercus is identified to Faunus and Pan. The Dionysiac and Panic inspiration is akin to the Lakota *Heyoka* in many of its modalities, including its "subversive", "manic" and sexual powers. Let us remember that Heyoka is first of all a deity, a god who must be addressed "by taunt and vilification, the opposite of the intent of the address" ("The *heyoka* Cult in Historical and Contemporary Oglala Sioux Society", Thomas H. Lewis, *Anthropos* 69, 1974, p.19). Cybele as Goddess of Nature is associated with the triumph of life. She corresponds to the archetype of the zodiacal sign of Taurus.

54. In his articles "Lupercales" and "Rire" (cf. *Dictionnaire critique de l'ésotérisme*, edit. Jean Servier, Paris, 1998), Joël Thomas notes judiciously that the laughter of the young men who were touched by the bloody sacrificial knife during the festival of the month of lustration (February) "reproduced mystically the first victory of the forces of life over those of death" (p.1109). To laugh is in this sense to overcome death through a consciousness of the precariousness of existence.

when you will yourself laugh at your effort (to seek to gain Reality). That which is on the day of laughter is also now."[55]

*
* *

Much like femininity, authority, whether spiritual or temporal, stands among the most direct manifestations of the Divine in terrestrial experience, and may therefore enter, because of the risk of its abuse, into an ambivalent relationship with the principle of humor and its manifestation in the trickster.[56] The figure of the King's Fool has often been mentioned as a revelatory political institution allowing for the open manifestation of unwelcome truth in the guise of a beguiling joke. Here again, laughter functions as a reminder that the relative is not to be confused with the Absolute, that man is only man, and that the highest terrestrial destiny may quite unintentionally mislead those who are richer in faith and obedience than in discernment to treat it as if it were the Supreme. Far from being subversive, laughter and jokes thus reinforce order and hierarchy by preventing the manifestations of potentially fatal abuses. Metaphorically speaking, they crack open a grin in the potentially idolatrous traditional order, thereby preventing it from closing in on itself.[57]

It follows from all the preceding considerations that humor and laughter may be considered as divinely inspired ways of revealing and fighting the solidifying and obscuring tendency of *Mâyâ*. Besides this somewhat combative dimension of laughter and humor, one must acknowledge a more defensive function—a func-

---

55. Swami Rajeswarananda, *Thus Spake Ramana* (Tiruvannamalai), p.111. The Book of Genesis present occurrences of laughter which are akin to such a swift removal of limitations: Abraham's laughter at his hearing God's promise of a son (XVII, 17) should be understood as a sudden understanding of the disproportion between "human impossibility" and "Divine Possibility", so to speak. Such laughter involves an abrupt shift of metaphysical level.

56. Traditional authorities and administrators entertain an ambivalent relationship with clowns and tricksters. Let us mention the typical case of this organizer and announcer at Lakota powwows who, after having explained the mystical meaning of *heyoka*, cannot help concluding his statement with the following: "I don't like a *heyoka* at a powwow and if I had my say about it I would skin their rear out of there. I just don't like them . . ." (T.H. Lewis, op. cit, p. 24).

57. Whence the affinity of tricksters with odd numbers which remain as it were open.

tion of dissimulation. Objectively speaking, the abnormal social and psychological conditions presiding over a secular society place *sapientia* and mysticism in an uncomfortable position since they must, more than ever, protect themselves against incomprehension, mocking profanation and hostility. The latter reactions may manifest the negative aspect of humor and laughter as a defilement of the sacred. Christian unease toward laughter and religious tendencies to associate its manifestations with the diabolic stem from this point of view. In this context, laughter is perceived as the subversive hallmark of the Fall, since it thrives on a duality that results from being separated from God. Baudelaire wrote, in a similar sense, that laughter was unknown in the garden of Eden, for it implies a kind of disassociation in correlation with the Fall, and is therefore incompatible with primordial innocence. It is at this juncture that one may distinguish—schematically, for ambivalence cannot be excluded in this domain—between a godly laughter expressing pure joy, the mirth of gods, and devilish and sarcastic laughter with its resounding shattering of reality.

This duality is also reflected in the ambiguity of the demiurgic principle. In most if not all religious climates, exoteric theology cannot do justice to the latter since religion cannot work with too many shades of meaning without jeopardizing its volitive and sentimental effectiveness, whence its reduction of the demiurge to a diabolical figure, and its definite tendency to associate laughter, and even humor, with the latter. Christian exoterism—or let us say the Christian tradition in its collective and institutional dimension—particularly upholds a gravity and a sense of penance, stemming from an acute and painful sense of sin, against the joking tendency which it cannot but perceive as threatening[58] and dangerous.[59]

---

58. We must add two important qualifications to this statement. First, the Church was sometimes able to integrate laughter into its spiritual economy, particularly through religious plays that emphasize the ridicule of vices "since in the face of God's unquestionable laws they (vices) were bound to fail, and so fit for unlimited laughter, no matter how evil they might appear" (Sandra Billington, "'Suffer Fools Gladly': The Fool in Medieval England and the Play Mankind", in *The Fool and the Trickster*, p.51). Secondly, following Saint Paul, the "fool" can also be a figure of the Christian as perceived by the world. "Nos stulti propter Christum . . ." (I Corinthians, 4, 10).

59. Paradoxically, carnavalesque laughter took up a particularly extreme and subversive character in the Christian world, especially in the Middle Ages with the Festival of Fools.

In point of fact, the semi-diabolic nature which is attributed to many tricksters of folklore seems to confirm this point of view in an often grotesque or burlesque manner. The famous Flemish trickster, Ulenspiegel, is described as having been born with a small black dot on his shoulder—a kind of devilish parody of the miraculous birth-marks of Messengers from Heaven—which the midwife who delivered him interpreted as "the dark mark of the devil's finger."[60] However—in addition to the fact that this is only a small dot and that only the devil's finger was involved—this semi-diabolical nature, common to most if not all tricksters, must be situated within the more encompassing context of the ambivalence of *Mâyâ*. This amounts to saying that the aforementioned duality must be specifically related to the subtle question of demiurgic process which is characterized by a fundamentally dual character. It must even be added that the trickster figure may sometimes become a deceiver of the devil, therefore confirming that his nature is neither good nor evil, or both.[61] The Cuban trickster *El Bizarrón* tricked the devil by pretending that he had sent his donkey to heaven, thus prompting the devil to abandon his search.[62] Dealing with the delicate point of the demiurgic ambiguity, Frithjof Schuon specified that "the lowest point of the demiurgic domain and the highest point of the satanic domain may coincide".[63]

The dual character just highlighted is sometimes mythologized and symbolized by being placed under the symbolism of twin brothers which may ultimately refer to the two sides of a single original demiurge. In this vein, Karl Kérenyi has argued that the two demiurgic brothers of Greek mythology, Prometheus and Epimetheus, might have originally been one single figure characterized both by slyness and stupidity.[64] Such a distinction between two demiurgic brothers, one good and the other evil, is a way to express the dual character of the demiurgic principle while playing down the most disconcerting aspects of its ambiguity. The double character of the

60. Cf. Charles de Coster, *La légende d'Ulenspiegel* (Bruxelles, 1983), p.17.
61. Shamanism does not envisage the Devil as such because it includes negative and deifuge tendencies into the overall realm of the Demirge.
62. Joanna Cole, *Best-loved Folktales of the World* (1983), p.746.
63. *To Have a Center*, p.105.
64. Cf. Karl Kerényi, "The Trickster in relation to Greek Mythology", in Paul Radin, *The Trickster; A Study in American Indian Mythology* (1969), p.181.

astrological sign of Gemini, placed under the rulership of Mercury—the planet of Logic intelligence—refers to a similar duality positively associated by genethliac astrologers with the nimble acumen of the mental faculty as an instrument of good, while negatively entailing a kind of youthful and erratic sense of experimentation which may be combined with a certain inability to consider the consequences of one's actions, thus a kind of evil stupidity.

In the highest sense this enigmatic combination of intelligence with a lack thereof, which often leads trickster figures themselves to be tricked and fooled, must be referred to two levels of the demiurgic function: on the one hand the demiurge brings about the good by unfolding the possibilities included in the All- Possibility, therefore participating more or less passively in the Divine Logos, but on the other hand, the providential and all-encompassing meaning of the process and modalities of this unfolding remain unknown to the stupid and "blind" demiurgic trickster. This amounts to saying that the trickster is "intelligent" or cunning in carrying out a creative and transforming process while being in fact "foolish" and stupid, since he does not understand the real scope of this process. Whence the recurrent theme of a competition between God and the trickster-demiurge in which the latter is always the loser. For example, this theme appears clearly in Western Africa where the Akan's Ananse the Spider is said to have failed in his attempt at competing with God or Nyame by imitating him.[65] The Dogon's mythology also presents Ogo as a rebellious trickster who fights the Supreme Amma, and is ultimately banished from His kingdom.[66] In a sense, the trickster stands for mankind as it awkwardly participates in the unfolding of *Mâyâ*. Like the trickster, man is a "*bricoleur*" who strives to "fix up" the world with highly ambiguous results that oscillate between the "pontifical" *tikkun* of the Kabbalah[67] and the subversive *hybris* of Prometheus.

---

65. Christopher Vecsey, "Ananse the Akan Trickster", in *Mythical Trickster Figures*, p.112.
66. Robert D. Pelton, *The Trickster in West Africa* (1980), p.169.
67. The *Tikkun* refers, in Lurianic Kabbalah, to the spiritual work of man as he strives to remedy, on the level of Creation, the breaking of the Sephirotic vases which were to receive the emanation of Perfection. This symbolic metaphysical statement accounts, in its own suggestive way, for the "incomplete" and imperfect nature of *Mâyâ*.

As a liminal being, the trickster is also akin to adolescence, an intermediary and imbalanced stage between childhood and adulthood. This critical phase stands between a reality left behind and another that is not yet fully reached. This liminality is traditionally associated with initiatory rites which symbolically enact a period of death preceding rebirth and life. Adolescence therefore potentially challenges all boundaries and classifications, it entails both an awareness of the nothingness of existence and an intimation of the Absolute as Infinite Possibility. The awkwardness and pain of this age lie precisely in the inability of most adolescents to integrate their aspiration to totality within the ontological framework of relativity provided by their immediate and limited experience. Now, the "stupid intelligence" or the "intelligent stupidity" of the trickster corresponds analogically to the predicament of this phase of human growth. The demiurge has to bring the All-Possibility into actual being within the constraints of relativity, and he cannot do so without a full measure of imbalance, contradiction and unpredictability. On the most profound level, this imbalance can be understood as characterizing the destiny of a "living death," since it precludes any integration of the normative exteriority that characterizes human life.

The complex question concerning the ambivalence of the demiurgic process leads us back logically to that of the ambiguity of laughter. On account of that very ambiguity, the subversive and desacrating tendency of laughter cannot be better neutralized than by higher—if not louder—laughing.[68] The poison is also the remedy. The key point here is that enlightened laughter undoubtedly implies some transcendence, and consequently an ambivalent feeling of superiority. We laugh at what we transcend and master. The ultimate laughter is that of the Self. This is also why spiritual laughter implies an element of totality: beyond and in spite of some social and cultural conventions and constraints that sometimes limit its manifestations, it expresses, in principle, an intense existential con-

---

68. If one were to doubt that powerful laughter may be a legitimate spiritual expression one may refer to this passage from the autobiography of Zen Master Hakuin (1686-1769): "As for sitting, sitting is something that should include fits of ecstatic laughter—brayings that make you slump to the ground clutching your belly." In *Mystics, Masters, Saints and Sages: Stories of Enlighenment,* Robert Ullmann and Judyth Reichenberg-Ullmann (Edmonds, WA, 2001), p.76.

sciousness that involves our whole being. The Japanese association of the Samurai's thunder-like laughter with the *Hara*, the existential center of consciousness is highly relevant in this respect. Analogically—but on a higher plane—Mâ Ananda Mayî's *attahâsi* (divine laughter) expresses this sense of totality by evoking the power of thunder that embraces, according to Swami Gitananda, all the levels of manifestation and leads him to state that "no human being can laugh like this."[69] On its highest spiritual level, laughter allows us to escape upward, as if we were flying up and through the confining net of *Mâyâ*. In his *Mathnawi*, Rûmî tells the story of a lover who, when asked by his beloved to take his love back to its roots in God, "lay back on the ground laughing, and died laughing; (. . .) that laughter was his freedom and his gift to the Eternal."[70]

By contrast, subversive laughter as a manifestation of the cosmic downward flux toward negation and nothingness must be turned upside down—or rather downside up—by a laughing response. In this way, laughter places wisdom and mysteries out of the reach of the "mockers" of the Bible. Some critics have argued that is the precise way in which Rabelais proceeded in his stories of giants, using laughter and profanity both to veil and to hint at the "*substantifique moelle*" (substantive marrow) of his books.[71] The humorous, and at times unconventionally grotesque, expressions of wisdom in Taoism have a similar meaning: the sage laughs at those who laugh by laughing with them. On the one hand, the Tao would not be the Tao if fools were not laughing at It; on the other hand, the sage

---

69. "These states (Mâ's) often included *attahâsi*, or 'laughing like thunder,' as described by six devotees and mentioned by several others. Swami Gitananda referred to it as 'the laughter that goes on at all eight levels' and said: 'When I saw Mâ, the first thing that struck me was her *attahâsi*. Such joyful laughter reverberates out of all the pores of Mâ's body. The laughter and supreme bliss was coming out of her, radiating unlike any human being. I felt both wonderment and joy. I wondered to see such a person. No human being can laugh like this." Lisa L. Hallstrom, *Mother of Bliss* (New York, 1991), p.111.

70. *Delicious Laughter*, translation of excerpts from Rûmî's *Mathnawi* by Coleman Barks (Athens, Georgia, 1990), p.18.

71. "Rabelais was wearing one of these masks the vulgarity of which protects from the vulgar. To vehicle the spiritual in a gross language may mean first of all that one protects it from the attacks of ignorants, it also means preparing the corporeification of the spirit, 'fixing the volatile'. Wisdom is this mad Mother who knows that one must not despise the world's behind." Translated from Jean Biès, *Les chemins de la ferveur*, p.67.

laughs at the fools while appearing to laugh with them at the Tao. His laughter is a kind of sacrificial gift of himself for the sake of the Tao. It is not without relation to the arcanum while at the same time being a sort of symbolic language of its own for those who have ears to hear. This indirect and ironic language is a way of alluding to the successive inversions that preside over the unfolding of *Mâyâ* on the various levels of the universal ontological hierarchy. In riding the tiger of this ambiguous unfolding, the laughing sage intends to provide concrete evidence that the devil is never the last one to laugh, for *"rira bien qui rira le dernier."* ("He laughs best who laughs last.")

Thus, the sacred itself may thus be expressed in such a way as to guarantee its integrity and be a parry for potential profanation. This is for example the meaning of sacred laughter in Bali, when the parodic performance of the sacred becomes a kind of decoy, taking upon itself the baleful laughter of the enemy. These clown-like performances of myths, inextricably linking the godly and the demonic in a never-ending cosmogonic struggle, constitute the best affirmation and defense of tradition. The "devil" is so to speak integrated into the very drama of the traditional mythology as the dance opposing the good and the bad, Barong and Rangda, reproduces and expresses the cosmic dance of *Mâyâ.*

This parodic integration of the sacred leads us to specify that when the trickster mimics the holy, through a grotesque imitation[72] of the priest or the shaman, he does in fact confirm and foster, in his own way, the very power that he acts out. Acting subjectively as a rebel, he scouts the confines of acceptable—or unacceptable—behavior in such a way that, objectively and ultimately, he brings home the reality and necessity of that with which he plays and wants to transgress. Granted, this desire might be more than imaginary given his propensity to skirt the boundaries of propriety. His running the risk of going too far is part and parcel of his ambiguous and unstable nature, whence what could be called the "sacrificial" dimension of his being.[73] If Nanabozho, the Algonquin Trickster, can be considered by Frithjof Schuon as the first *heyoka,* it is because

---

72. Imitation or mimicry is the prime character of Relativity, including its most extreme degree of "non-being". As Frithjof Schuon pointed out, even "nothingness" tries to "transcend" the world by "aping" the Transcendence of the Supreme Principle, Cf. *To Have a Center,* p.106.
73. *Logic and Transcendence,* p.158.

his "irregularity" sets him apart and makes him "sacred" (*sacrificare=sacer facere*=to make sacred) precisely in virtue of this marginality. His "sacrificial" function is therefore not to be understood in moral terms but in a quasi-ontological sense. It could also be said that the function of the trickster in regard to society, tradition and the cosmos is comparable to that of *Mâyâ* toward *Âtmâ*: affirming through negating, consolidating through destroying, asserting Being through nothingness.

*
* *

Humor and laughter fulfill an important spiritual and psychological function, whether it be in a profane world *de facto* negating all transcendence or in an esoterically stifling ambience reducing spiritual realities to confessional formulas and sentiments. Henry Corbin has been one of the few students of spirituality to shed some light on this subjective aspect of the matter.[74] In a world in which esoterism and mysticism are considered as "foolishness" or "madness," the esoterist and the mystic must be able to trick out their deadly serious purpose with the playful colors of humor and laughter. Subjectively speaking, this path may also help them to avoid the dangers inherent in their inner tension vis-à-vis the Divine. Since they have reached a higher degree of familiarity with a dimension of reality that is commonly denied or ignored by most of their fellow humans, mystics must protect themselves by displaying a certain distance toward the expression of their knowledge or experience. In this way, they will not be taken too seriously by others, nor will they take themselves too seriously. The world and the ego are kept at a safe distance. Humor and laughter may be useful cards in this game.

This possibility may, however, raise a subtle question, since the mystic cannot normally act as a joker or as a fool without running the risk of jeopardizing, in the eyes of some qualified seekers, the impact of the Reality he protects in his heart. Granted, one may assume that those qualified for a spiritual path must have a suffi-

---

74. On this subjective dimension, we are indebted to Henry Corbin's interesting article entitled "Mystique et humor chez Sohravardî, shaykh al-Ishrâq" in *Collected Papers on Islamic Philosophy and Mysticism* (Teheran, 1971), pp.13-38.

cient discernment to be receptive to humor, as well as some intuition of the spiritual meaning of laughter, if not some intimation of the serious side of trickster-like fooleries. Notwithstanding this assumption, such modalities will require a sense of proportions, as well as some discernment as to the context and the dosage of the therapeutic foolery; and such modalities obviously entail a very peculiar, and in a way slippery, vocation.

Moreover, the meaning of this type of behavior may well vary, depending on whether the mystic lives within a traditional context or within a modern society. In the first case, humor and laughter will often function as an implicit denunciation of "pharisaic" attitudes, and they will also provide the mystic with a safety zone against possible threats from exoteric authority. Omar Khayyam's unconventional humor evidently falls into this category: it is at times much safer not to be taken seriously. It must be added that in the latter context, the spiritual dimension of humor, laughter, jokers and fools is always more or less acknowledged—albeit more often *in abstracto* than in the flesh[75]—as an odd,[76] marginal but ultimately profound and necessary "safety valve" which provides relief from the collective and individual tensions necessarily involved in a traditional structure. The Roman Saturnalia—as well as the various popular carnivals which were known thoughout the world—fulfilled this liberating function. It is significant that the association of the stern Saturn, god of the paternal and rigorous "narrow gate", with upside-down, grotesque, and obscene festivities is a paradox of a rich symbolism. The extreme condensation represented by Saturn calls for an extreme release in the form of festive excesses of all kinds.

On a higher level, traditional people also understood, if only intuitively, that such "joking" possibilities subtly point toward a transcending of horizontal and worldly affairs, therefore conveying some sense of otherworldliness, or even wisdom, in virtue of the principle that "the last will be the first" and "the inferior man among men is superior in Heaven" (Chuang-tse). Traditional peo-

---

75. The clown is shocking, disturbing and even terrible or he is not. The negative reactions that his behavior may arise in the soul of other men are more often than not accurate symptoms of their own animic disharmonies and knots.
76. Oddity has to do with "unevenness" but also—and therefore—with a return to Unity. There is nothing more incapable of self-transcendence than a "perfect" evenness that shuts the door off to any "oddity."

ple know, to some extent at least, that this world is, after all, in many respects, an inversion of the next. Still, one may well question the utility or legitimacy of fooling ways in the modern world, since the latter is already based, by definition, on a rejection or a subversion of any sense of an ontologically grounded hierarchical order. We have provided the first element of an answer to this question when dealing with the disproportionate "seriousness" that characterizes the various modern ideological enterprises. It should be added that laughter may provide the contemplative with a welcome shield in the often straining alchemy of his relationship with the modern world. In other words, it may no doubt ease the process of "sincerely playing one's part", to use F. Schuon's phrase. In a sense, this predicament is exemplified by Hamlet's status in the Kingdom of Denmark. His "madness" is both a catharsis and a mask. The "rottenness"[77] of the Kingdom of Denmark and Claudius' usurpation of the throne are images of the *Mâyâ* aspect of subversion and inversion. As the only witness to Justice and Truth Hamlet takes this inversion upon himself through the appearance of a madness that is in fact supremely "sane." His "imbalance" fulfills a cathartic function inasmuch as it expresses and "acts out" an "inversion of the inversion." The recourse to theater (III, ii) as a means of "telling the truth" in a world in which it cannot be uttered amounts to an analogous process. Like Christ who takes upon himself the sins of world through the folly of the cross, Hamlet must be sacrificed so that the Father's Kingdom may be restored while his death testifies at the same time to the separation between the celestial and terrestrial kingdoms. Let us mention in passing that the famous lines between Hamlet and Polonius ("for you yourself, sir, shall grow old as I am, if, like a crab, you could go backward," [I, ii, 194-203]) points to this same aspect of inversion, and is actually akin to the *heyoka* contrary behavior.[78] Hamlet is sad when others rejoice, he is madly joyful

---

77. Hamlet: Something is rotten in the state of Denmark. Horatio: Heaven will direct it. (I, iv, 90).

78. "Slanders, sir: for the satirical rogue says here that old men have gray beards, that their faces are wrinkled, their eyes purging thick amber and plum-tree gum and that they have a plentiful lack of wit, together with most weak hams: all which, sir, though I most powerfully and potently believe, yet I hold it not honesty to have it thus set down, for yourself, sir, should be old as I am, if like a crab you could go backward." One could not better express the way of the clown for, as Schuon has written, "in this world of theatrical artificiality which

when others are saddened or shocked. Black Elk explains that "the truth comes into this world with two faces. One is sad with suffering, and the other laughs; but it is the same face, laughing or weeping. When people are already in despair, maybe the laughing face is better for them; and when they feel too good and are too sure of being safe, maybe the weeping face is better for them. And so I think that is what the *heyoka* ceremony is for."[79] This type of behavior is connected to a function of psychic and collective equilibration that is also highly sacrificial. In this respect the clown is like a lightning-rod, taking upon himself the psychic effects of the disharmonies and tensions of the ambience.[80]

The preceding considerations suggest that humor, laughter and tricks may paradoxically involve a higher degree of inner solitude. Spiritual humor and laughter are in a sense the symptoms of a spiritual exile. They are ways of restoring a sense of Reality, either through the liberation of pure joy or through the derisive negation of the illusory. As for the trickster figure, his solitude is that of the exception; it is also that of the erratic and restless instrument of the gods who cannot but be condemned to his own immediate absurdity. As an exception that confirms the rule and as a puzzling cozener, he cannot stop spinning the wheel of *Mâyâ* to make the world be what it is. In fact, he has no choice but to incarnate and give way to the deifuge tendency of cosmic unfolding.[81] Like the mystic who is constrained by God's will, trickster is constrained by his eccentric function as orchestrator of the dance of *Mâyâ*. When considered simply as a laughing fool, his solitude is no less real, even though his antics do require the eyes and ears of fellow humans. His solitude is

is society, the pure and simple truth is madness." *Light on the Ancient Worlds*, p.25, note 4.

79. *Black Elk Speaks*, edit. John Neihardt (Lincoln, Nebraska, 1979), p.189.
80. A fact that is not without significance when related to the connection of *heyoka* with lightning. The psychic oversaturation and tension that the clown "dispels" is analogous to the equilibration and pacification that is the outcome of the storm.
81. "Trickster is at one and the same time creator and destroyer, giver and negator, he who dupes others and is always duped himself. He wills nothing consciously. At all times he is constrained to behave as he does from impulses over which he has no control." Paul Radin. Quoted in Spinks, *Trickster and Ambivalence*, p.13.

actually deepened by the veil of incongruity that he weaves around him through his pranks. Some of the Sufi *malâmatiyyah* draw an ascetic path out of such consciously cultivated inappropriateness. According to Ibn Arabî, the *malâmiyya* "hide from creatures (. . .) by creatures. (. . .) God has hidden them among His creatures by submitting them to the form that is demanded by the moment . . . They have no authority in this world." One must also emphasize that some *malâmiyyah* do not distinguish themselves in anything from the common faithful in their outer practices. The blame that they seek is rather that of the elite than that of the common folk with whom they relate as if they were part of them. This is akin to the idea of "popular mask" mentioned by René Guénon concerning some esoteric modalities of Sufism and Taoism: "(. . .) They hide their spiritual degree and disappear in the mass of the faithful, exposing themselves, as common men, to the blame of the elite, that is to say both *fuqahâ* and Sufis."[82] As for the holy clowns, God's fools, Russian *urodevoi*, or even *heyoka*, who systematically behave in an apparently absurd manner, they do so—dementedly attracted by God's inward pull or consciously conforming to a celestial call—because they are witnesses to—or simply instruments of—a higher reality that their surroundings can neither accept nor conceive.

Black and white[83] like the checkered mantle of the Balinese Shiva,[84] destroyer and builder like Loki, the clown of the *Ragnarök* whose return is expected at the end of the cycle, the demiurge is ambivalent like *Mâyâ* and the *Shaktic* energy that presides over her deployment. The ambiguity is both objective and subjective. Frithjof Schuon has clearly expressed this delicate but inescapable point when describing one of its central manifestations, which is sexuality where "the ambiguity is not only in the experience, but also in the

---

82. Translated from "Les Malâmiyya dans la doctrine d'Ibn Arabî", Michel Chodkiewicz, in *Melâmis-Bayrâmis: études sur trios mouvements mystiques musulmans*, edit. Nathalie Clayer, Alexandre Popovic and Thierry Zarcone, Istanbul, pp.18-20.

83. He can also be "gray" like the Apache clown who plays a major part in "spinning the wheel of transformation" in the central rite of the "Changing Woman."

84. Frithjof Schuon has underlined the ambiguous character of the "non-Supreme" Shiva in whom the "demoniac initiative" and the "principial necessity" are not always easy to distinguish. Cf. *To Have a Center*, p.104.

subject as well as in the object."[85] That ambiguity is ultimately
grounded in the nature of *Mâyâ* as universal unfolding or manifestation which cannot but involve an illusory negation or subversion
of the essential Goodness of the One. However, one should not lose
sight of the fact that this ambiguity is not contradictory—from a
more discontinuous standpoint—with the objective distinction
between a higher and a lower *Mâyâ*, nor should the essential unity
of Being (*wahdat al-wujûd*) preclude a discrimination between hierarchical levels of reality. Indeed good in itself does not need evil to
be what it is, but the Infinity of the Supreme Good "needs" the "possibility of impossibility" that evil is, as a negation of Reality and
Goodness.The distinction between divine and benevolent demi-
urges and semi-diabolical tricksters, inasmuch as it can be drawn, is
parallel to the distinction between a positive and a negative *Mâyâ*.[86]
The Indian differentiation between Right-hand *Shaktism* (dealing
with the higher and benevolent Divine *Shakti*) and Left-hand
Shaktism (making use of otherwise forbidden or dangerous realities) presents a similar duality on a spiritual level.

*
* *

85. *Christianity/Islam*, p.113.
86. However, Tantrism as a path of integration of the *shaktic* ambiguity is not situated in a perspective of discrimination but in one of methodical use of the
immanent energetic unity. "Those who do not perceive the truth think in terms
of Samsara and Nirvana, but those who perceive the truth think neither of
Samsara nor of Nirvana. Discriminating thought is then the great demon that
produces the ocean of Samsara. But being free of this discriminating thought,
the great ones are freed from the bonds of existence. Ordinary folk are afflict-
ed with the poison of fear as though with poison itself, but he who has identified himself with compassion should uproot it completely and go his way. Just
as crystal, which is clear, becomes colored from the color of another object, so
likewise the jewel of the mind becomes colored with the color of mental con-
ceits. Like a jewel the mind is naturally free from the color of these mental con-
ceits; it is pure from the beginning, unproduced, immaculate and without any
self-nature. So one has to do with all one's might those very things that fools
condemn, remaining in union with one's chosen divinity and with purity of
mind as one's motive. Just as water that has entered the ear may be removed by
water and just as a thorn may be removed by a thorn, so those who know how,
remove passion by means of passion itself. Just as a washerman removes the
grime from a garment by means of grime, so the wise man renders himself free
of impurity by means of impurity itself." *Cittavishuddhiprakarana*, vv. 24-94, 37-

Given the indefinite plurality of its aspects, *Mâyâ* may be all things to all people, both objectively and subjectively. The trickster and the fool are agents or manipulators of her display. "Free from all," they are also "slave of all".[87] Their utter freedom is perfect service. The Afro-Brazilian *Candomblé* trickster Exú "may be described as *o chefe* (the chief) but he is also referred to, paradoxically, as *escravo* (slave)."[88] The trickster and the fool serve a necessary function within reality by being the "cosmic institutor of good and evil,"[89] or simply by helping release unresolved tensions.[90] Mediator and go-between, hermeneutic puzzler, apotropaic jester, sacrilegeous trouble-maker, the trickster is the necessary enigma of a world that cannot exclude absurdity since it is not "necessary" in its phenomenal literality. As for the holy fool and the cunning practical joker, they also reveal in their own ways the folly of a world which claims to stand on its own feet when its feet—to use a Kabbalistic image—stand on the Abyss.

The essential messages of humor, laughter, and the various types of fools who manifest them in an often ambiguous manner, converge on spiritual liberation. Like a distance expressing a sense of proportions, like an outburst of sudden understanding, or a buffoonish dismemberment of apparent reality, they show us the way to overcome the limitations of a fragmented vision. Therefore, they may play the role of an unexpected *upaguru*. To a certain extent, they even echo the nature and function of the Spiritual Master: first, as does humor, by crystallizing a de-identification from the ego, its illusions and its "serious" passions; secondly, as does laughter, by shattering the layer of our ego to help us unveil our true nature; thirdly, as do the fool and the trickster, by presenting us with the paradox of a sort of *koan*. For the latter is also a manner of joke,

---

38, in *Buddhist Texts through the Ages*, edit. Edward Conze (New York, 1964), p. 221.

87. *"Omnibus omnia factus sum, ut omnes facerem salvos"* ("I have become all things to all so as to save all") (I Corinthians 9, 22).

88. Paul V. A. Williams, "Exú: the Master and the Slave," p.115.

89. *Logic and Transcendence*, p.158.

90. "Where someone's sense of honorable behavior has left him unable to act, trickster will appear to suggest an amoral action, something right/wrong that will get life going again. " Lewis-Hyde, *Trickster Makes this World, Mischief, Myth and Art* (New York, 1998), p.7.

whose seeming absurdity cannot be reduced on its own level. Such is sometimes the liberating enigma, indeed the living *koan*, which the Master embodies and proposes to the disciple's discernment: that of the manifestation of Illimitation in human limitations. The resulting ambiguity is no doubt extrinsic in the case of the Sage and the Master, while it is intrinsic in that of the demiurgic trickster. In a sense the cycle that opens with the chaotic and exteriorizing infra-formal mystery of the demiurge closes with the concentrated and interiorizing supra-formal mystery of the Sage.[91] In both cases, but in an inverse way, the enigma results from the confrontation of two levels of reality: that of Necessary Infinitude and accidental finitude; the Absolute as such and the individual as such. As Frithjof Schuon expressed it: "This confrontation is both impossible and unavoidable; it obliges us in any case to combine extremes in some way."[92]

It appears that the realities we have discussed, in spite of their apparent "ex-centricity," reveal a profound affinity with the esoteric principle and gnostic perspective. This principle enjoins us not to shun any ambiguous reality on the pretext of opportuneness, and prompts us to put each thing on its proper level and in its right place. The spiritual dimension of humor, laughter, fools and tricksters is an expression of the discerning distance from oneself and the world that is the hallmark of the intellective way. Accordingly, it involves a keen sense[93] for the swift and sharp integration of the

---

91. This explains why both are not identified with their body, one from above and the other from below. A Hindu sage such as Mâ Ananda Mayî may constantly emphasize that she is not "this body," for she identifies with the Self and the Divine Will is her will. On the opposite side of the spectrum, the Winnebago Trickster burns his anus and eats his intestines, and he also tells his penis "that is always happening to me," but he does so because he has no will of his own, being as it were a pure instrument of *Mâyâ*. (see Radin, p.136).

92. The trickster figure is undoubtedly one the most disconcerting of these extremes, since it gives all the appearances of the good to evil or all the appearances of evil to the good.

93. As a cultural expression of some of the dimensions of *Mâyâ* and the Trickster principle, the Andalusian and Spanish notion of *duende* constitutes another telling and interesting symbol of the ambiguity of *Mâyâ*. The several concrete meanings of *duende*, that of elf, goblin, or glazed silk refer to the same ability to play with this ambiguity through a kind of grace that has nothing to do with moral merits. According to James Michener in his *Iberia* (1968), *duende* can

myriad of shifting viewpoints that are so many refractions of the Self on the broken mirror of *Mâyâ*.

never be the result of a deliberate effort, it is rather a kind of gratuitous gift which "rises from some deep reserve within him (that is, the person who 'has' *duende*)", p. 69. The mercurial character of *duende* is expressed through its relationship with subtle creatures of the air—the mutable and transforming element—whereas its affinity with *Mâyâ* is clearly indicated by the visual qualities of glazed silk, a symbol that Frithjof Schuon has used to explain *Mâyâ*. See for example "Mâyâ" in *Light on the Ancient Worlds*, (p. 89) where Schuon refers to the "shimmering ambiguity" of the "fabric" of *Mâyâ* (translation mine).

Chapter 9

Work and the Sacred

Brian Keeble

Man is a slave in so far as alien *wills* intervene between his action and its result, between his effort and the task to which it is applied.

This is the case in our day both for the slave *and* for the master. Man never directly confronts the conditions of his own activity. Society makes a screen between nature and man.

—Simone Weil

Work, whether as a topic of discussion, a fact of daily experience, or merely as a mental preoccupation, touches the lives of all of us. We argue endlessly over who should do what and how much; about what are the appropriate conditions for the performance of work; and above all what is the just reward for its accomplishments. We live in a society that has for some time now devoted a considerable effort to the eradication of work—at least as physical toil—only suddenly and paradoxically to discover, at a time of unemployment, that we need the dignity of work. Certainly we are heirs to the problems that work poses, even to the point of wondering whether it has a future at all. But in the midst of all the activity and preoccupation it engenders we seldom pause to reflect upon the essential nature of work.

Towards the end of her book *The Need For Roots* Simone Weil observes of modern civilization that "it is sick. It is sick because it doesn't know exactly what place to give to physical labor and to those engaged in physical labor". This may seem at first hearing a somewhat unusual diagnosis of the malaise and alienation common to our age. But remember the phrase "physical labor". It is physical labor—merely quantified human effort, unrelieved by any qualitative satisfaction to transform it—that to Simone Weil is the essence of our sickness. She goes on:

Physical labor is a daily death.

To labor is to place one's own being, body and soul, in the circuit of inert matter, turn it into an intermediary between one state and another of a fragment of matter, make of it an instrument. The laborer turns his body and soul into an appendix of the tool which he handles. The movements of the body and the concentration of the mind are a function of the requirements of the tool, which itself is adapted to the matter being worked upon.

She ends her book with the following two sentences: "It is not difficult to define the place that physical labor should occupy in a well-ordered social life. It should be its spiritual core".

This seems an audacious claim until we recall that meaningless work and soulless work are one and the same thing. Work imposed upon our lives so as to be meaningless we feel to be a burden that is contrary to our inmost nature—in some sense a denial of our very being. Yet work is man's very signature. It is said that by his fruits we might know a man. So the question we have to ask is not "What does a man get *for* his work?" so much as "What does he get *by* working?"

To speak of there being a "spiritual core" to work is not only to invoke a certain image of man, it is also to hint at the existence of a subtle thread that joins the sacred to whatever demands are made upon man in order that he sustain his physical existence. It is to presuppose, in some way or other, that the spiritual forms the implicit context of our lives and that our being is not fully real without this hidden context. If this is not so then we would have to face an awkward question: how it ever came about that, in order to sustain his earthly existence, man should be obliged to follow a course of physical action that seems a direct denial of his deepest nature, as if by some ghastly mistake of his Creator it is man's destiny to follow a direction that leads him away from the very thing it is his nature to be? If we are to avoid such a dilemma, we must conclude that in some way work is, or should be, profoundly natural and not something that must be avoided or banished as being beneath our dignity. So, we are here concerned to enquire whether, in what ways and under what conditions, work possesses a contemplative dimension.

If we are to fully understand this dimension of work, we must lay bare its essence; what it is *before* it is conditioned by any social, moral or economic prescription. We must apprehend it as an inner experience prior to any productive outcome it may have. We must isolate it from all the modes it assumes as a consequence of our presence in the world and which result in the obligations society imposes on us; obligations we discharge by working. These obligations can make such totalitarian claims upon us that we tend to lose sight of the immaterial significance that lies at the very heart of work.

The modern habit of equating work with time-consuming toil makes us prone to forget that it is *man* who is the instrument and the agent of work. Only man works. A horse may toil, as may a beaver. But only man can be liberated or uplifted by working. Only man can be demoralized by work. And herein lies the danger of the work ethic of mechanized industry; that it makes an ethical absolute of our social and economic necessity to make and do things. In having no real and effective use for the intangible and pre-productive impulse that is at the core of work, modern industry loses the spiritual function of work. And in its tendency to push man to the periphery of the productive process it effectively loses man as well. In an environment in which man is subordinated to mechanical techniques it is all but impossible to experience the physical effort of work as the natural and inevitable medium through which body and soul effect the transformation of matter.

The problems and paradoxes of work that are all too evident in our society will only be resolved if and when we are willing to return to a spiritual anthropology, when we are willing to acknowledge our theomorphic self-image and restore our traditional constitution as beings that possess an integral threefold structure of spirit, soul and body.

In our threefold constitution all three states of the human microcosm are thought of as receiving their life and illumination ultimately from that which is uncreated and therefore "above" that process of continual change and development that is manifest life. At the highest level the spiritual faculties of the soul act as a mirror reflecting the archetypal realities of the Divine Intellect. It is in the light of this level of reality that we contemplate the mystery of our subjectivity and discover it to be finally irreducible as an identity within the Divine itself. In the middle realm the faculties of the soul are bipolar; they act like a window that in one direction looks above, or inwardly, onto what is beyond our subjectivity as such. In the opposite direction they look "below", or outwardly, onto our sensory experience in order to localize or "clothe" and give continuity to our psychological life. By means of these two directional impulses of the soul we map out the intelligible value of all our experience.

Finally, even though the substance of the body, as the living, organic sheath of our individual life, is renewed by physical matter, it nonetheless gathers the reasons of its purposes from the soul. Itself unilluminated, the body is the sustaining instrument of material transformation. But its bodily nature is only in harmony with the material world it inhabits when it is empowered to relate its actions and its appetites directly to the higher levels of being which give them meaning.

Work is the chief means by which the focal point of consciousness is concentrated "outside" the individual's subjectivity. The effort of work is an act of transformation in which the worker has the possibility of rising to the level of those values and meanings that transcend the operations of physical life. It is this potentiality for transmutation that we should at all times keep in view in any consideration of what constitutes the essence of work. Whenever this potentiality is not present in the effort of work then our physical engagement with the world of matter becomes no more than a burden, and we become merely brute instruments in the manipulation of material substances. If this were not the case we could not even conceive of, much less experience, joyless, soul-destroying work. And such an experience is no less possible in the most mechanized and hygienic industrial workplace as it is in the most unremitting physical drudgery. However much we increase the effort, and however much we elaborate the mechanical means of shaping matter in the pursuit of production, we cannot escape the paradox that at its most meaningful and its most accomplished, work can provide us with an *inner* harmony and balance when those means are kept relatively simple and direct.

This paradox poses an important question in relation to the fact that the manipulation of matter exacts its price in the expenditure of both material and bodily energy. (The Latin *homo,* for man, incidentally, is closely linked with *humus*—of the earth—from which we derive our words *humble* and *humility.*) Should we not see, then, in this expenditure of energy, an in-built correlation between the finite material resources of the world and the physical limitations of the human body? Should not this consumption of bodily energy awaken in us a recognition of and a humility towards our physical limitations, thereby setting a limit to our exploitation of the living body of the earth? In other words, ought we to consider whether there is a natural, integral correlation between the limitations of our bodily energy and the degree to which we should consume material resources in order to sustain ourselves, a correlation that should not be betrayed by any means of production that does not take account of the *inner* meaningfulness of work?

One of the most pernicious ideas that prevents us from realizing the intimate relationship that should exist between work and our spiritual nature is an idea that has seemed almost impregnable to attack in western thought over the last three centuries, and even now shows little sign of exhausting the springs of absurdity it constantly draws on. It is the idea that art and work are and must be separate categories of activity. We have got into the habit of thinking of art as a separate category of aesthetic *feeling*, and so have also got into the habit of acting as if art were a separate category of *making* that is not directly related to the immediate demands of our physical life. We have forced an artificial division between the outer and the inner man which amounts to sustaining a pretence that human kind constitutes two races: that of man as artist and that of man as workman—as non-artist.

This is to fly in the face of common sense. Neither can it be said that the work of the workman—that is the work of utility—that it is necessarily non-beautiful in contrast to the work of the artist. Nor can it be said of art—that is works of refined sensibility—that it serves no human need. If we admit that man is a spiritual being then it is clear that he has needs and requirements beyond and in addition to his bodily needs. It is also clear that the integral wholeness of his being demands that he should not be divided within himself so as to serve his spiritual needs with one sort of activity and his physical needs with another. For the work of utility rightly done may result in a type of beauty that is informed by a refinement of sensibility, just as art inevitably involves some form of making and utility such as is characteristic of practical work. Just as there is no art without work, so there should be no work without art, so that all who are actively involved in work should be in some sense artists. All artists are workmen. At least to the extent that each seeks to achieve some mastery over his material, to effect its transformation, and to the extent that such transformation, properly accomplished, will involve mastery over oneself. If we are to save ourselves from any division between our making and our thinking, in which our houses, the fixtures and fittings in them, our everyday utensils, our clothes and all the things we use daily are one part of life (produced industrially with the minimum of human agency), while we have a few "art" objects (that are the expression of nothing more than the sensibility of the person who made them) to "transform" another part, we must see such a state of affairs as profoundly unnatural and demoralizing. Can we really believe that a visit to an art gallery, in our "spare" time, is sufficient to compensate us for the meaninglessness of a humdrum experience of work unrelieved by any personal satisfaction?

If we are to recover the "spiritual core" of work we should not only remember that to accept a division between art and work is to falsify our true nature, we should also remember that it is with man himself that any reform must begin, for man is greater than what he creates. In Philo's words, "Even a witless infant knows that the craftsman is superior to the product of his craft both in time, since he is older than what he makes and in a sense its father, and in value, since the efficient element is held in higher esteem than the passive effect." In reminding ourselves in this way of the anteriority of man's being to his work we also catch a pre-echo, as it were, of the relationship between the human context of work and the archetypal nature it mirrors. As Plotinus wrote: "All that comes to be, work of nature or of craft, some wisdom has made: everywhere a wisdom presides at a making".

Once we have recovered the idea that there is no unbridgeable gulf between art and work we can go on to consider the ways in which man is linked by his spiritual nature to the work of his livelihood. For if the sacred is not present in things at hand it is unlikely to be present at all. It does not function only in exclusive categories of thought and spirituality. The numinous, sacred essence of things is nearer to us than is our jugular vein—to borrow a phrase from the Koran. How can this be? Let us examine some of the words we habitually use when we discuss the relation of work to life. Wisdom so often works in words like a preconscious. directive energy.

It is still just possible to speak of the workman as having a trade, or as following a vocation. The etymology of the word *trade* is uncertain but its root is possibly *tread*. What we tread is a path—a walk towards some goal. A trade, then, is a form of work or craft, an occupation conceived as a walk in life. From this we can see that the idea of a manual trade contains the sense of a vocation, and as such possesses the possibility of some form of realization, by way of conforming a set of external circumstances to an inner imperative, an inner voice.

A vocation is, of course, a calling, and functions by virtue of an inner summons (and, incidentally, raises the question of *who* is summoned by whom?). The etymology of the word *work* implies the expenditure of energy on something well or finely made—made with skill. As such it points towards a kind of perfection of attainment in the human artificer. So, hidden in the word *work* we come again upon the idea of realizing or attaining something above or beyond the mere expenditure of physical energy. Moreover, this attainment implies not only the rejection of certain possibilities and the adoption of others, it also implies (as Plotinus suggests) an inherent wisdom to make the choice that will permit the effective realization of whatever is to be attained. Now, since strictly speaking there is no perfection in the created order of things, this perfection towards which skill inclines must belong to another order, a supranatural order of things; precisely that towards which man is called.

The abstract Greek noun *techne* gives us, in its Latin equivalent, *ars*, meaning, in one of its general senses, a way of being. From the Latin *ars* we derive our word *art*. The Indo-European root of *art* means to fit together. *Techne* has the same root as the word carpenter (in old English a skilled worker is especially one who works in wood). The carpenter is one who fits things together. *Techne* means a visible skill in craftsmanship. But in Homer it is used in the sense of something in the mind of the artist—what later comes to be called imagination. And this sense of art as being a mental predisposition that stays in the artist was deeply embedded in our language until the seventeenth century, when it began to be applied to a select category of things made. So, permeating all the meanings that accrue to the language of work and art we have the sense of one who fits things together: one who fits the domain of manual necessity to the order of a higher imperative. Certainly the symbolism and the mythology of the various sacred traditions, as they are connected with the arts and crafts, indicate that such is the case.

To stress the idea of art as an effective reasoning of the person who makes things, rather than applying it to an exclusive category of aesthetic objects, is not to suggest that there is no difference between say, the art of cathedral building and the art of the potter. (The difference is one of degree rather than one of kind.) That is not the point: which is that in all cases (and who would care to decide which was the most important art between say cathedral building, motherhood and agriculture), human making is a wisdom. In each an art is involved, and in so far as this involves the expenditure of effort, both mental and physical, it is a sacrifice— and one of the meanings of sacrifice is "making holy", to perform a sacred ceremony.

The primordial meaning of human work, then, is to be found in the fact that it is not only a skill about doing but that it also embraces a supra-human wisdom about being. Or, to put it another way, the act of making has a contemplative foundation at the heart of our being. And when we turn to the sacred traditions, whose expression in human artifacts is a constant source of wonder for their beauty and skill, we find that the workman or craftsman or artist does not receive his vocation from the material circumstances of his life but that his calling is from the highest source.

In the Indian tradition the source and origin of the craftsman's calling is derived ultimately from the Divine skill of Visvakarma as being revealed by him. The name for any art is *silpa,* a word that is not adequately translated by our words *artist,* or *artisan,* or *craftsman* since it refers to an act of making and doing that has magical powers. In the context of the Indian tradition works of art imitate Divine forms and the craftsman recapitulates the cosmogonic act of creation as the artifact itself recapitulates the rhythms of its Divine source. By his action of making, and in conjunction with his practice of yoga, the craftsman as it were reconstitutes himself, and thereby goes beyond the level of his ego-bound personality.

In the craft tradition of Islam certain pre-Islamic prototypes were preserved and came to be connected with parables in the Koran and with certain sayings of the Prophet. Speaking of his ascent to heaven the Prophet describes an immense dome resting on four pillars on which were written the four parts of the Koranic formula—In the name—of God—the Compassionate—the Merciful. As Titus Burckhardt has pointed out, this parable represents the spiritual model of every building with a dome. The mosque in Islam is the symbol *par excellence* of the Divine Unity, the presiding principle of Islam itself. The mosque thus acts as the center towards which the arts and crafts of Islam are orientated in virtue of its involving so many of them. From the construction of the mosque the crafts, as it were, flow, since architecture, along with calligraphy, is the supreme art of the Islamic revelation.

In Islam the crafts were organized around guilds which were themselves closely connected with Sufism, the esoteric dimension of the Islamic faith. Similarly, the guilds of medieval Christendom employed a symbolism and a knowledge of a cosmological and hermetic nature. The symbolism of the crafts in the Christian tradition take as their starting point the person of the Christ who was himself a carpenter. (The Christ of the trades appears as a carving in many English Parish Churches.) It may be argued that the highest sacred art of Christianity is the icon—the re-presentation of the Divine image. But alongside this is the craft tradition, pre-Christian in origin, which is above all cosmological in its symbolism, beginning with physical space as the symbol of spiritual space, and the figure of Christ as Alpha and Omega, the beginning and the end, the timeless center whose cross rules the entire cosmos.

Such symbolism is innate to the arts and crafts—which is to say, the livelihood—of past civilizations, and has a ubiquitous presence in the physical artifacts of people's lives. All crafts and trades, from ploughing to weaving, carpentry to masonry, metal work to poetry and music, are traditionally interwoven with their transcendent principle. Here is one such witness to the fact, from K.R.T. Hadjonagoro's *Batik, Fabled Cloth of Java*:

> [Batik] was a vehicle for meditation, a process which gives birth to an uncommonly elevated sublimity in man. Truly realized beings in the social fabric of Javanese community all made batik—from Queens to commoners. . . . It is almost inconceivable that in those days batik had any commercial objective.
>
> People batiked for family and ceremonial purposes, in devotion to God Almighty, each man's endeavor to know God and draw near his spirit.

According to Genesis, work is the result of original sin. Nonetheless, for the Christian there is always the exemplar of God "who made the world and saw that it was good." Against this there is the counterpoint of a recognition that His Kingdom is not of this world, so that man, who has some remembrance of the Divine Paradise of his origin, retains the possibility in his work of traveling the path back to God, for "there is no faith without works" (James 2: 26).

Between these two perspectives the earthly destiny of man takes place. What proceeds from the Divine Principle is good; the archetype of perfection is the unmanifest reality of the Divine Principle: "Every perfect gift is from above, and cometh down from the father of lights" (James 1:17). The following passage from H.J. Massingham's *The Wisdom of the Fields* (1945), indicates something of the remarkable longevity of this idea:

> The most eloquent example I know of this inborn and indwelling principle comes from Droitwich where lives a cabinet maker named Fowkes. For in him it has become conscious and part of his philosophy of life. He made a small oval hand-mirror in mahogany scrap-wood for the wife of a friend of mine. When my friend called for it, he disclosed his belief that the crafts were originally divinely bestowed and the gifts had ever since been passed on from father to son. In support of this hereditary theory he told my friend that his grandfather on the mother's side was renowned in his day as being one of the finest workers in veneer and inlay in England. He himself had known nothing about veneer work. One day he "felt the itch" to do it and immediately and with ease, so he said, accomplished it. Having discovered that no trial and error nor self-teaching were necessary he derived his proficiency from his grandfather.

In all human work the archetype is a prior knowledge or wisdom in which resides the Divine prototype or perfect model of any particular act of making.

The vision of the Divine prototype as a wisdom inherent in the actual tools of trade is beautifully evoked in Exodus (Book 25), where, after describing in some detail the making of a sanctuary, Moses is urged that it be done, "According to all I shew thee, after the pattern of the Tabernacle, and the pattern of the instruments thereof, even so shall ye make it." But on the indefinite number of possibilities capable of being realized it is the burden of work to place a limitation, since all work involves a pre-conception or image that is subsequently shaped to a determined end. Without this pre-conception and its subsequent determination there would be no distinction of means from ends. Work would be sufficient unto itself. But as Aquinas points out, "As God who made all things did not rest in those things ... but rested *in* himself *from* the created works . . . so we too should learn not to regard the work as the goal, but to rest from the works of God himself, in whom our felicity lies." Work is the imposition of order on matter, matter transformed by human intention and will. The true workman does not work merely to perfect the operations of work itself, but according to an inner order that is his perfect nature. That is why the worker must be free to become the very thing he makes. As Eckhart says,

> The work that is "with," "outside," and "above," the artist must become the work that is "in" him, taking form within him, in other words, to the end that he may produce a work of art in accordance with the verse "The Holy Spirit shall come upon thee" (Luke 1:35), that is, so that the "above" may become "in".[1]

It follows that if the artist or the workman is to achieve perfection in his making he must let nothing come between his conception of what is to be done and its execution. And this conformity of his being to the final realization of the work is the primordial model of human workmanship. It implies that work is, in essence, for the sake of contemplation, just as much as it implies that the perfection of work is achieved only at the expense of self-consciousness. As the Japanese potter Hamada puts it: "You have to work when you are not aware of self." In work perfectly realized there is no thought of reward, no love of procedure, no seeking after good, no clinging to goals, whether of attainment or of God himself.

Eckhart, in a sermon on justice, gives a further clue as to how our work and our being are interwoven; how, essentially, our work is to *be* and our being *is* our work:

> The just man does not seek for anything with his works, for those who seek something with their works are servants and hirelings, or those who work for a Why or a Wherefore. Therefore, if you would be conformed and transformed into justice do not aim at anything with your works and intend nothing in your mind in time or in eternity, neither reward nor blessedness, neither this nor that; for such works are all really dead. Indeed I say that if you make God your aim, whatever works you do for this reason are all dead and you will spoil good works. . . . Therefore, if you want . . . your works to live, you must be dead to all things and you must have become nothing. It is characteristic of the creatures that they

---

1. *Treatises and Sermons of Meister Eckhart*, trans. by James M. Clark and John V. Skinner, (1958), p. 251.

make something out of something, but it is characteristic of God that He makes something out of nothing. Therefore, if God is to make anything in you or with you, you must beforehand have become nothing. Therefore go into your own ground and work there, and the works that you work there will all be living.[2]

As if to expand and annotate this passage from Eckhart we find at the end of Plotinus's Fourth Ennead the following:

> All that has self-consciousness and self-intellection is derivative; it observes itself in order, by that activity to become master of its Being: and if it studies itself this can mean only that ignorance inheres in it and that it is of its own nature lacking and to be made perfect by intellection.
>
> All thinking and knowing must, here, be eliminated: the addition introduces deprivation and deficiency.

None of this is in any way meant to deny that our acting upon a material substance is conditioned by that substance proceeding through our senses. But at the very core of the act the senses are not consciously involved and there is an immediate and unconditioned intuition in the soul of the timeless source of action: something that is not part of the act of making as the dead center of a hub does not take part in the rotation of the wheel. And no degree of perfection in work is attained that does not touch upon this stasis of Perfection itself. That is the spiritual function of skill. No perfection is embodied in that which is unprepared or insufficient, for like is known by like, and skill in the execution of work is first of all a skill residing in the workman. The skilled maker intuitively knows that the perfection of his work rests upon his own being and is not determined by external circumstances. It is the worker's own lack of self-discipline that prevents the perfect realization of his task. It is just this interior perfection of being that the crafts, with their tools as an extension of the physical body, serve and which the machine destroys. The tool nurtures the integral relationship that lies at the heart of all work; the total freedom of potentiality in physical effort corresponding with the necessary determination inherent in perfectly realized workmanship. Such is the "spiritual core" of work. H.J. Massingham recorded the living process in his

---

2. Clark and Skinner, op. cit., pp. 53-4.

Shepherd's Country (1938); watching a craftsman who was making a traditional Cotswold, five-barred gate or "hurdle", he wrote:

> The intrinsic contact with his material must and does human-ize him and unseal the flow of the spirits. He seemed to be talking to his wood as well as to me, and sometimes he forgot I was there.... It would be meaningless to say that such a man as Howells loved his work: he lived in it.

We mentioned earlier that the word *homo* (man) is connected with *humus,* and has important ecological implications. Man is quite literally "of the soil", his life is sustained hourly and daily by what the soil provides. All traditional cultures have been sustained by the crafts, especially agriculture. By virtue of their being intimately root-ed in a specific geographic place, and so to the specific set of social, material and ecological circumstances that provide the formal occa-sion and substance of the means of livelihood, the crafts conserve the natural environment. This is so because the crafts are in turn tool-based. The tool is a conservative instrument of manufacture precisely because of its intimate relationship with the bond that unites hand, eye and the intuitive sources of skill.

Skill is to some extent cumulative. It is born of circumstances that are relatively stable and it flourishes in the context of tried and tested ways of doing things. We can only measure skill against a given set of conventional procedures and a pre-determined end. We cannot determine whether a totally new procedure is skilful since the novelty of the method required for its accomplishment will be outside any convention and will be unique to the occasion. The worker cannot test himself against a set of circumstances that are unknown to him. For which reason the constant search for novelty and innovation in work demoralizes the worker (as indeed it has demoralized the artist in our time). Constant innovation must even-tually undermine the conventions and social occasions that unite the worker and his patron—not forgetting that all workman are also patrons.

There are profound reasons why the crafts tend not to elaborate the means of production away from the elementary procedures of hand-tool skills. To do so has the effect of diverting the operation of the worker's skill away from the perfecting of his inner resources, and diverting it towards the external, instrumental circumstances of the means of production. When this happens, as we see today in the almost total uniformity of the machine-made infrastructure that surrounds us, the natural world that sustains us is eventually reduced to no more than so much raw material, to be plundered regardless of any ultimate outcome. We should not be surprised that such an amoral and indiscriminate view of the material context of work has slowly lead us to poisoning the environment. The crafts, on the other hand, are far more likely to be materially sustainable. They tend not to work against the interests of man and nature but integrate the rhythms and substance of both while at the same time opening a door internally upon states of mind and of beauty that transcend the necessarily physical conditions by which life proceeds.

The fact that in the mechanized, industrial milieu men confuse *needs* with egotistical appetites and have great difficulty in imposing any restraint upon them is itself a demonstration of that same milieu's amoral irresponsibility in seeking infinite expansion of consumption in a world of finite resources. When we speak about our needs we have to remember that they are determined not by our appetites but by our nature as spiritual beings. It is in virtue of the intuition of our spiritual nature that we understand who we are. Which is to say we understand that we are not, as creatures, sufficient unto ourselves but are beings who are called to perfect ourselves. That we are able to regard our appetites, our passions, our desires, objectively as *part* of our nature proves the possibility of our being raised to a level above them. And this obliges us to recognize that whatever is required to bring about our human perfectibility constitutes our needs. As Plotinus says: "In the matter of the arts and crafts, all that can be traced to the needs of human nature are laid up in the perfect man." To labor is to pray. When work is truly for the sake of contemplation it carries the same import as a passage of scripture. The work of Gothic cathedral builders speaks with the same voice as Gothic spirituality. There is as much a message of non-attachment to the ego in a Sung vase as there is in a Zen text.

To make something by hand is a relatively slow process, it requires commitment, patience, aptitude and skill such as is usually gained over a period of gradual mastery, during which the character of the worker is also formed. The tool draws upon the unwritten and accumulated wisdom of past usage. The hand, and its extension, the tool, challenge the inner resources of the workman in a direct way. His mastery of the working situation must operate so that there is a vital accord between mental concentration, physical exertion and the material properties of the substance worked to the degree, as we have seen, that the workman lives *in* his work. What he produces is vibrant with a life and a human signature that is missing from the uniform products of the machine. Why else should we feel nostalgia at the artifacts of the past but for the fact that they have been invested with a quality of human involvement that is so evidently absent from the mass-produced products that surround us? We feel in such artifacts something of the pulse that is common to the pulse of our own being.

By contrast, the mark of the machine product is its uniformity. To the rhythms of life and the rhythms of nature the machine is indifferent, if not disruptive. Although the development of the machine is based upon a cumulative, technical knowledge, for the machine operator there is no wisdom of past methods of production. The machine has no "history" since it is continually updated by technical innovation, so that it cannot be an instrument of human continuity. The organic link that binds one generation to another in mutual interdependency is thus severed by a quantitative mechanization that responds only to the economic imperative. The continual technical development of the machine projects forward to an uncertain future and is disruptive of those natural rhythms of renewal and consumption that tend to be conserved by the tool. In a craft culture, which is in a sense a flowering of nature that addresses itself to heaven, production fosters the primary human qualities of resourcefulness, self-reliance and moral integrity in the context of man's obligation and responsibility to his natural environment. What in the tool is the possibility of a reciprocal rhythm of exertion and contemplation open to the spiritual dimension, becomes with the machine a sort of diabolic ingenuity and contrivance that stifles the soul through an inimical, mechanical pace. In other words, and by way of summary, the tool produces *according* to human needs, the machine *regardless* of human needs.

Nothing is easier than to point to the many ways in which life has been made easier by the machine. But are these benefits such that we may have full confidence in the direction and final goal towards which the machine blindly forces us? There is little point in arguing that life is now more comfortable and convenient for the mass of men and women (which is far from being incontrovertible in any case) than it has ever been before if we do not consider at the same time the ultimate price of this achievement. Our progress is towards a future that no one can accurately envisage, let alone claim to determine. Are we to accept unquestioningly this blind enterprise?

In looking back to the craft cultures; in recognizing the essentially spiritual character of the arts and crafts of the sacred traditions; in studying tool-made artifacts as a repository of wisdom through the means of symbolism and initiative practices, there is no need to deceive ourselves that such things can be re-instituted by our simply wishing it to happen. We know that this cannot be the case. Our world has not yet finished with its self-mutilation. But in so far as we are human and able to recognize for that very reason that we are made for that which is greater than our own productions, so we must address ourselves to the truths above and beyond the fact of our historical circumstances. By that much we may avoid falling victim to historical fatalism.

If we are to seek some ultimate cure for the sickness Simone Weil spoke of then surely we must first establish the nature of the disease. The very least we might achieve in taking stock of past cultures of people for whom work and the sacred were an organic unity is to have, in a positive sense, some measure of what we have fallen from. Rather this, surely, than to conclude negatively that we are merely the victims of events we have neither the power to control nor the will to understand. The dominant forces at work in our society would have us believe that the next step in our technological development will rid us of our work altogether. That such a utopian dream should go hand in hand with the possible destruction of man himself is no coincidence. It is certainly the projection of a false image of our nature. If we are to offer any effective resistance to this dream it can only be on the basis of our understanding of how the "spiritual core" that is the heart of workmanship both fosters and safeguards the inter-relationship between man and the sacred.

Chapter 10

The Role of Culture in Education

William Stoddart

The spiritual life has been described as the "interiorization of the outward" (*khalwah*) and the "exteriorization of the inward" (*jalwah*)[1]. Education is an aspect of the latter process; the very etymology of the word (*e-ducare*, "to lead out") is an indication of this. As a "leading-out", education is a rendering explicit of the immanent Intellect (*Intellectus* or *Nous*), the seat of which, symbolically speaking, is the heart. As Frithjof Schuon has said more than once: "The Intellect can know everything that is knowable". This is because "heart-knowledge" (*gnosis*) is innate, and thus already fully present within us, in a state of virtuality. This virtuality[2] has to be realized, and this realization is education. This corresponds to the Platonic doctrine of "recollection" (*anamnesis*), which in the last analysis is the "remembrance of God" (*memoria Dei*). "The Kingdom of Heaven is within you."

Man is constituted by the ternary: Spirit, soul and body (*Spiritus, anima, corpus*); only the last two are exclusively individual or human, the first being supra-individual or universal. The Intellect (*Intellectus*) is identifiable with the Spirit: Intellect and Spirit are but two sides of the same coin, the former pertaining to the theoretical or doctrinal and the latter to the practical or realization. They pertain respectively to the objective (or discriminatory) and the subjective (or unitive) modes of knowing.

It is easy to see how education, both etymologically and philosophically, is an "exteriorization of the inward". But it is also an

---

1. These "alchemical" definitions come from Frithjof Schuon. In Arabic, *khalwah* means "spiritual retreat" and *jalwah* means "spiritual radiance", the former being logically prior to the latter. The two processes are symbolized respectively by the colors black and gold.
2. Examples (immediately apparent, and built into the human substance) of this innate and objective knowledge are our sense of logic, our capacity for arithmetic, our sense of justice, and our sense of right and wrong.

"interiorization of the outward", for an important function of education is precisely to ensure that the myriad of impressions coming from the outside be "inwardly digested" and reduced to unity. Thus education is both "exteriorization of the inward" (intellectuality) and "interiorization of the outward" (spirituality). It is both *jalwah* and *khalwah*.

The following summary of terminology may be useful:

English	Latin	Greek	Arabic
Spirit	*Spiritus*	*Pneuma*	*Rûh*
(Intellect)	*(Intellectus)*	*(Nous)*	*('Aql)*
soul	*anima*	*psyche*	*nafs*
body	*corpus*	*soma*	*jism*

In modern parlance, "intellectual" is often wrongly taken as a synonym of "mental" or "rational". In fact, unlike the Intellect, which is "above" the soul, the mind or the reason is a content of the soul, as are the other human faculties: will, affect or sentiment, imagination, and memory. The spiritual or intellectual faculty, on the other hand—because of its higher level—can be categorized as "angelic". The operation of the Intellect is referred to as "intellectual intuition" or "intellection".

Let it be said right away that there is no impenetrable barrier between Intellect and mind: the relationship of the former to the latter is like the relationship of the pinnacle of a cone to its circumferential base. Metaphorically speaking, the majority of philosophers, since the end of the Middle Ages, have concerned themselves solely with the circumferential base, with little or no transcendent content in their thought. Henceforth the transcendent (previously known to be accessible either through revelation or intellection) has been regarded as mere "dogma", "superstition", or arbitrary imagining. The result has been the tumultuous *dégringolade,* from Descartes to the present day, known as the "history of philosophy"! One miraculous exception to this cascading downwards were the Cambridge Platonists of the 17th century. The words of Virgil were never more applicable: *Facilis descensus Averni; sed revocare gradum, hic labor est!*

In the light of the foregoing, we are also able to see that the error, in a nutshell, of psychologists such as Jung, is completely to confuse Spirit and soul and so, in the last analysis, entirely to "abolish" Spirit (the only truly supra-individual, "archetypal", or "objective" element). It is not difficult to see the chaos—and the damage—that results from this fatal and anti-Platonic act of blindness.

The linking of education with spirituality may cause some surprise; but the parable of the talents applies to the mind as well as to every other faculty. "Thou shalt love the Lord thy God with all thy heart and with all thy soul . . . and *with all thy mind.* "It is at our peril that we neglect the need for "a well-stocked mind"; for it is surely obvious that, from a purely spiritual point of view, the mind cannot be allowed to lie fallow. This would allow it to become a playground for the devil, and *si monumentum requiris, circumspice.*

Use of the phrase "a well-stocked mind" makes it necessary immediately to specify (and never more so than in the "reign of quantity" that is the present age) that, as far as true education is concerned, it is nevertheless a question, not of quantity (however intoxicating), but of quality; not of shadows (however beguiling), but of substance; not of trivia (however intriguing), but of essentials. In the present age, more than in all previous ages, the grasping of a true and permanent principle is infinitely more precious than the piling up of a hundred undigested and un-understood contingencies. In addition, there is no greater joy.

Since education, by definition, is a thing of the *mind,* we can do no better than cite here the injunction of St. Paul:

> Whatsoever things are true, whatsoever things are honest, whatsoever things are just, whatsoever things are pure, whatsoever things are lovely, whatsoever things are of good report; if there be any virtue, and if there be any praise, *think* on these things.
>
> (*Philippians,* 4, 8.)

One might say: whatsoever things are true, good, and beautiful; or whatsoever things manifest or reflect the absolute, the infinite, and the perfect.

*

*   *

All civilizations—for example, the Chinese, Hindu, Greco-Roman, Christian, and Islamic—manifest the central or cardinal role of learning, at least for those classes or individuals capable of it. In this connection, it might be objected that the North American Indians—who possessed a daunting spiritual tradition if ever there was one—were not educated. In the light of the considerations expressed above, however, it is clear that the Red Indians too, in their own fashion, were "educated". To regard the Indians as uneducated because they were un-lettered, would be like regarding the Buddhists as atheistic, because they envisage Ultimate Reality as a supreme State *(Nirvâna* or *Bodhi)* rather than as a supreme Being. Just as the Buddhists are manifestly different from the superficial and arrogant atheists of modern times, so the Indians are manifestly different from the technologically-trained but culturally-uneducated and mentally-immature people of modern times. The Indians' Book is Nature herself, and none have ever known this book better.

Education has many forms and, in any case, has in view only those classes and individuals who are capable of receiving it. Indeed the type of literacy resulting from the non-discriminating "universal" education of the last hundred years may even be inimical to culture, as Ananda Coomaraswamy has so trenchantly pointed out in his important work "The Bugbear of Literacy". Coomaraswamy demonstrates beyond any dispute how the new-found capacity of the immature mind to read modern printed material—now always at hand in such staggering quantity[3]—has killed the rich traditional culture (largely oral for the mass of the people) in many societies, including European ones. This is the opposite of true education, which is depth, subtlety, and finally, wisdom.

The European tradition consists of two currents: the Greek and the Christian, or the Classical and the Medieval. The Greek current is evoked by such names as Homer, Pythagoras and Plato; the Christian current is evoked not only by such figures as St. Gregory Palamas and Meister Eckhart ("apophatic" and "gnostic" metaphysicians respectively), but also by St. Augustine and St. Thomas Aquinas (whose viewpoints represent two important strands, amongst others, of Western Christian thought). Christianity is also epitomized by that "second Christ", St. Francis of Assisi, and by the great epic poet of Christendom, Dante Alighieri. In practical terms, education in Europe has obviously to take account of both the Classical and the Medieval currents.

---

3. As Lord Northbourne has said (referring to the industrialized countries): "We live in an age of plenty; but what use is plenty of rubbish?" *(Look to the Land* [London, Dent, 1940]).

In English-speaking countries, a good education must start with the Christian catechism and attendance at Divine Worship, as well as the study of the Bible and the most celebrated Christian authors, such as the great names just mentioned. It must include the study of Greek and Latin, coupled with some Homer, Plato, Virgil, Cicero and other ancient authors. The "history of philosophy" (an understanding of the relative "stability" of Ancient and Medieval philosophy as contrasted with the innovative nature and "instability" of Modern philosophy) is obviously necessary. Likewise, some notion of the "philosophy of science"—especially as regards the differing conceptions of science on the part of Ancient and Medieval times on the one hand and Modern times on the other—is also desirable. In present circumstances, some "comparative religion" is no doubt essential, but this must be of high quality and taught from a conservative and believing point of view, which is not lethal to the student's faith in his own religion.

Also essential are subjects such as English and European (and perhaps world) history and literature—within the limits of the reasonable and the possible. It should be stressed that this proviso applies throughout, as does also the frequently forgotten principle that formal or "scholastic" education is only intended for those fit to profit by it. The need for the study of modern languages, above all French and German, is apparent. A study of these two languages, coupled with the study of Greek and Latin, has the additional merit of facilitating access to other modern European languages, such as Italian and Spanish. Obviously all aspects of mathematics must be available, and the essentials taught to all.

In the modern situation, modern science and technology are inescapable, since, in some branch or other, they will be indispensable for most, from the point of view of earning a livelihood. Modern science and technology, however, are alien to culture and consequently do not pertain to education as defined in this paper.

Chapter 11

Every Branch in Me

Kurt Almqvist

One of the most important themes in religion—*the* most important—is the confrontation between the two "selves" in man: the inner, which partakes of God's unconditional, infinite nature and is identical with his "kingdom", and the outer self, or human personality with a certain name. It is the intersection of these two dimensions that comprises the religious life. One sees man horizontally from the earthly side; the other vertically as a vehicle of divinity. The crossing point may be multiplicated both horizontally and vertically, making a cosmic web formed in one direction of layered worlds or conditions and, in the other, of the beings embodied in them—horizontal and vertical, woof and warp.

The warp or vertical dimension consists of invisible threads that unite all beings with their common source, while the woof is made up of the horizontal threads that cross them and are supported by the warp, thus symbolizing the substances of worlds. Each knot or crossing represents an entity, for instance, a human being. René Guénon elaborates on this theme in his book *The Symbolism of the Cross*.

If we look at our world from the weft or woof point of view, horizontally, it appears to be simply the sum of its parts, of all beings and things. Because there is no truly cohesive principle within this type of world, they are seen as little worlds irrevocably separate from one another, and symbolized in our image by the seemingly discrete crossing points in the web. Nothing prevents each little world from believing itself to be the only one in existence and behaving as if it were. This we call self-assertion, selfishness, egoism; and how could it lead to anything but chaos?

From the other, the warp or vertical viewpoint—the religious view—the world is seen, above all, as divine creation. Every being and thing is then regarded not primarily in its relationship to oth-

203

ers but as something which, by grace of the warp threads, derives its very existence from God, and its real significance from its oneness with divinity: the Being in all beings. All are united with one another through this common origin, the "love of God" preceding and containing within it the "love of neighbor". The love of one's neighbor, in this metaphysical sense, comes from the true qualitative "alikeness" among all entities, whereas the merely quantitative, outward uniformity in present-day organizations is in fact a distortion of this transcendent "identity", or oneness in God. "The letter killeth, but the spirit giveth life".

The organ with which man apprehends and realizes this oneness is his spirit, the transcendent, direct-seeing intelligence, whereas the multiplicities of the world are perceived by means of his fragmented human intelligence, the mind. Spirit is transcendent and immediate by nature, being a direct reflection of the Holy Spirit. God "hath also sealed us, and given the earnest of the Spirit in our hearts" says Paul (2 Cor. 1:22), and the apostle also explains (Eph. 1:14) that this is the earnest of our inheritance, the redemption (from that which divides us from the divine unity).

Having our reality in God implies that we actually are that part of our being which is his image: the spiritual part. Only therein is man wholly himself. As in the Hindu concept of the Self (*âtman*), the word "self" here has a different connotation from that given it above, for with this perspective the protection and furthering of Self are diametrically opposed to the usual idea of selfishness. Instead of emphasizing one entity at the expense of others—divisiveness at the expense of harmony and unity—this type of "self-sense" which is unaffected by multiplicity stresses the divine indivisibility (Sanskrit *advaita*—non-duality) wherein the human being participates through the spirit.

The important thing is to make a clear distinction between our two selves or egos, so that we love and respect the right one. Much is being spoken and written about seeking one's identity, but this presupposes a subject and an object as two separate elements. What, then, is this object or goal with which we seek to identify if not the Self, which is more essential and autonomous than our ordinary, empirical self? What other meaning could self-identification have? What would it, in fact, be? To be "beside oneself" or, contrariwise, to "be oneself", implies the loss, or gain, respectively, of that essential self-identity which is constant, and independent of outer circumstances. The outer or empirical self is that which is seeking its identity.

All that applies to the idea of identity applies also to self-realization Both actually denote different aspects of the same thing—one static, the other dynamic. If one looks only from the "horizontal" plane, there is but one self—the outer, the points of crossing or knot in the weave—so that the same ego is both the seeker and the sought, which is an absurdity.

A third commonly used word is "integrity". It comes from the Latin *integritas* and is related to *intact,* which means "untouched" and, in a secondary sense, "whole, possessing all its (original) parts". From this we see that it must refer to the inner, vertical self, though in current worldly usage, it is applied to the outer, fragmented ego, and then in the sense of "inviolable": the inviolability of the personality. However, the only inviolable element in man is that inmost secret relationship with Deity which should be the deciding factor throughout his existence and all his activity on the "horizontal" plane.

It follows that the ego holds a median position between the true, enduring, innermost Self which is one with the kingdom of God, and the surrounding world, similar to the central position where woof crosses warp. To the extent that the ego remains subject to the kingdom within as prescribed in *Revelation*—in other words, to the degree that it holds itself to be a servant of this kingdom—it will serve the inner world in the outer environment. Throughout all its struggles and efforts it never ceases to be permeated with the flow from within: to be the branch which "abides in the vine" (John 15:4). This is self-forgetfulness or self-sacrifice in a more than moral sense.

It is quite misleading, however, to speak of self-effacement or self-annihilation without some further explanation. Even if the metacosmic sphere is the only absolute reality, the world of the senses is by no means completely unreal. It has reality insofar as it reflects the supersensuous and is illusory insofar as it asserts independence apart from its source This means that in man his reality flows directly from the spiritual Self like a ray from the Sun. This may then be said to be man's only real Self, though the outward mortal self has reality to the degree that it reflects and manifests the inner, immortal Self. In the final analysis only the divine Self *(Âtman)* is real; but, as the Hindus say, all is *Âtman.*

Chapter 12

On Being Human

Joseph Brown

One component that is frequently and paradoxically lost sight of is the individual human being; that is, a man or a woman bearing within himself or herself the totality of the richness we usually know best in the outer expressions of those academic disciplines we have come to call by that useful term, the humanities. The ultimate bearer of culture is a person who is religiously human within the context of a traditional heritage.

Many Native American peoples today retain, even though often in fragmented manner, elements of a heritage of ancient primordial origins. Present within all the dimensions, forms, and expressions of this heritage, or rather of these multiple heritages, is a pervasive sense for the sacred. In one manner or another all life is seen to participate in the sacred, all cultural forms express the sacred, so that inevitably within this context the lives of those peoples who live close to their sacred traditions may be called religious, and they are thus beings who are religiously human. Religion pervades all of life and life's activities leading a native person once to remark, "We do not believe our religion, we dance it!"

What then does it mean to be a human person within these native American cultures? What are the supportive elements, or traditional means of being and seeing, that contribute to this way of being human in a sacred manner?

Webster's Unabridged Dictionary gives this definition for the word *human*: "Man or his attributes, in distinction from the lower animal world; or, relating to man as distinguished from the superhuman, . . . from the divine. . . , belonging to finite intelligence and power."

On both scores these Western definitions are in direct opposition to the Native American sense of being human. For in the Native American worlds, one does not generally find such quasi-absolute dichotomies between humans and what we call animals, nor on the other hand is humankind by definition considered to be absolutely distinct, separated from divine or sacred power or powers. How then do Native American traditions express such an alternate point of view in their beliefs and lives?

In the multiple expressions of Native American lore, in myths and folktales, in rites, ceremonies, art forms, music, and dances, there is the constant implication of, indeed direct references to, the understanding that animal beings are not lower, that is, inferior to humans, but rather, because they were here first in the order of creation, and with the respect always due to age in these cultures, the animal beings are looked to as guides and teachers of human beings—indeed, in a sense their superiors.

According to a Pawnee account, a great council of all the animals *(Nahurac)* meets in perpetual session in a cave under a round mountain *(Pahok)* (actually located, it is believed, near the Missouri River). These animals monitor the affairs of humans wherever they may be on earth, and if a man or a woman is in need or in trouble and seeks aid in humility, perhaps through the vision quest, the council will choose one of its appropriate members—whether winged, four-legged, or crawling—who will then appear to the man or woman and give something of its own power, or present advice that should thereafter guide the person's life.

Beliefs concerning the nature, authority, and meaning of the animals in these traditions may perhaps be summed up in a general manner. In the people's intense and frequent contact with the powers and qualities of the animals including birds and eventually all forms of life, humankind is awakened to, and thus may realize, all that an individual potentially is as a human person. Human completion, wholeness, or religious awakening depends on this receptive opening up to the potentialities and sacred mysteries in the immediate natural environment. Especially in the nomadic hunting cultures, the oneness of essence underlying the visual differences between humans and animals is stressed; on occasion humans and animals may even be interchangeable.

The theme of reciprocal interrelationship between humans and animals, or more generally between humans and all the forms and forces of nature, is translated onto other levels. There appear specific types of theism, for instance, that contrast markedly with certain quasi-absolute Western dichotomies of human/God, nature/

supernatural, matter/spirit. One such example is found in the diverse versions of the widespread Algonquin Earth-Diver myth of creation. What is often overlooked, however, is that in diving down through the primordial waters for that little bit of earth, the original aquatic beings were cooperating with First Man, Earth Maker, the All-Spirit, or Maheo, who created four things out of the void: water, light, sky-air, and the peoples of the water, but not yet of the earth. Thus water people were co-participants in the actual creative process itself. This reinforces respect for the aquatic beings, for the earth and humanity's very being is due to their sacrifice. The myth also suggests that the creative principle itself is not locked into some separate time-space orientation; creation is an eternal, ongoing process of the here and now, in which what is created continues to participate. It is eminently important to this perspective that the account has the water beings say of Maheo, "I know," or, "I see, you must be everywhere."[1]

The full import and impact of oral traditions upon those who live by them, whether myth, folktale, song, or everyday language itself, may only be sensed when the meaning and power of words and names in Native American languages is understood. The majority of Native American names, both personal and sacred, refer to animals, or their qualities, and also to other forms of forces of nature. Further, a person's sacred name, which is never used in everyday speech, was normally obtained through prayer and sacrifice in the vision quest. In everyday Native American languages, words and names have sacred power; one uses them carefully, for their power affects both speaker and hearer.

In his seminal essay "Verbal Art," Dennis Tedlock reminds us that it is the breath that, universally identified with the essence of life itself, and proceeding from the center of a person's being nearest the heart, bears and fashions the word.[2] Interpersonal verbal communication involves the intermingling of the beings' most sacred element, thus establishing through breath made audible the bond of sacred relationship not only between people, but with all phenomena throughout the cosmos.

1. Alice Marriott & Carol K. Rachlin, *American Indian Mythology* (New York: Mentor Books, 1968), p. 39.
2. Chapter 50, *Handbook of North American Indians*, vol. 1, ed. by William C. Sturtevant.

Not of the order of the myth perhaps, but still critical in the humanizing of individuals at least on the not-unimportant moral or behavioral level, are those rich traditions of tales involving trick-ster/hero beings and animals—Coyote, Nanabozo the hare, Iktomi the spider. At appropriate times and places the narrator of these tales, through rich and dramatic means, brings to life before the hearer these beings who, in their devious and exciting ventures, define for young and old the perimeters of acceptable behavior. The less-than-human qualities of greed, avarice, selfishness, uncontrolled passions, and sneaky, deceitful, and unaesthetic behavior are graphically and eloquently spelled out. Children and adults get the point and remember in a manner that lecturing and moralizing never accomplish.

As children grow up within the context of their native traditions, they are constantly exposed to forms and actions and ever-widening types of relationships appropriate to the process of becoming a religiously human person. This process commences when the child is in the mother's womb, for especially in this fragile state the being is especially sensitive, it is felt, to all surrounding influences. Barre Toelken tells of a Navajo family close to starvation. The father would not hunt even though there were many deer about, for it was *inappropriate* to take life when a new life was being expected.

The child's first home, the cradle-board of buckskin and specially selected sacred wood (lightning-struck, among the Navajo), provides security and protection for the child not just in its material form but in the sacred powers latent in the wood and the hide, which was once the clothing of the deer itself. A psychological advantage of the cradle-board is that it allows the eyes of the child always to be on the same level as the grown person, the infant never having to look upwards toward the adult. Among the Lakota a young child, especially a girl, is placed in a spider-web type hammock strung out between four trees. In this manner the infant will receive the qualitatively differentiated powers of the four directions of space, and like the spider she may grow up to be an industrious person.

Periods of change or crisis in the life of a boy or girl are recognized as sacred moments of transition. Through rites, ceremonies, and initiations (often traumatic as with the Hopi), the child is enabled to enter into adulthood in a manner that integrates or transforms all that the person had been into what he or she now is. In contrast, Western adults have been taught or forced to eliminate from their being the states of the child, so that too often they live only fragments of what they might and should be.

The so-called arts and crafts of a people, found in such imaginative diversity and aesthetic elegance among Native American peoples, are not just utilitarian, as they are usually treated by art historians, but represent external projections of a people's inner vision of reality. (The Museum of Northern Arizona bears above its main portal a statement to this effect: "Herein Are Exhibited Ideas, Not Things.") It is through both creating and living with such ideas, values, sacred powers made tangible, that people are led to realize who they are in their fullest and deepest potentialities, as beings religiously human. So it is with the forms and presences of the sacred *Kachina* beings, whether as so-called dolls, or masked gods, or of the *Yei* who grace the drypaintings with the healing Power of their presence. To wear the mask is to become that being; to depict the *Yei* is to compel its sacred presence which is transferred to the patient.

Among the peoples of the Plains there is a tradition of two types of paintings on bison hides. One style, painted on the hide of a bison cow and known to art historians as the box and border design, appropriately may be worn only by women, for there is depicted on the hide in highly stylized, abstract manner a kind of vision penetrating into all those inner vital and generative life forces of the cow, manifesting all that is most sacred to womanhood. To wear such a robe is to participate actively in that sacred vision, and thus to be sacred in the fullness of being human as a woman. As a counterpart, the robe worn by a man is made from the hide of a bison bull upon which is painted a dynamic solar device, the sun-burst motif. By wearing such a robe a man participates in the solar power of both the bison bull and the painted sun, reinforcing the essence of all it is to be a man. In the shield paintings of the Plains peoples the protective power is similarly understood to be really present in the depicted form originally received through a vision experience. As with the power that is one with the spoken audible word, so also in the visual and dramatic forms of art; the power of sacredness is really present in the form, whether painted, quilled, sculptured, or danced.

Traditional Native American ways of seeing and living, of being human religiously, have things to tell us about ourselves today. Some of the examples may seem remote from the hard problems of contemporary reality for both Native and non-Native Americans. But I am reminded of a statement written by the late John Collier in 1947 (under the chapter heading "The American Indian and the Long Hope").

> They had and have this power for living which our modern world has lost—as world-view and self-view, as tradition and institution, as practical philosophy dominating their societies and as an art supreme among all the arts.

> They had what the world has lost. They have it now. What the world has lost, the world must have again, lest it die. Not many years are left to have or have not, to recapture the lost ingredient.[3]

---

3. John Collier, *Indians of the Americas* (New York: Mentor Books, 1948), p. 7.

Chapter 13

The Vocation of Man
According to the Koran

Jean-Louis Michon

Introduction

Today we often hear questions such as "Where do we come from?" or "What, if any, is the meaning of life?" Questioning of this kind is typical of Western Man, by which I mean people of modern Western societies, because Medieval Man, the Christians of the Middle Ages, did not ask themselves such things—any more than do contemporary believers, whether they be Christians, Jews, Muslims or, to go farther afield, Hindus, Buddhists or even animists.

All religions have, in fact, answered these fundamental questions in a peremptory way. Their responses have differed so greatly, some people would argue, that they have given rise to wars of religion. Moreover, under these conditions, how can we know what the truth is, or who is right?

This dilemma has not held any ambiguity for me for a very long time, ever since I grasped and tasted, beyond any difference in form and ritual, that which the present-day philosopher Frithjof Schuon has so justly called "the transcendent unity of religions."[1] In this paper, however, without taking a position on the subject, I will content myself with presenting, as clearly, accurately and objectively as possible, the point of view of Islam on the meaning of our destiny.

The following exposition will be based on facts drawn from the Koran and sometimes completed by quotations—*hadîth*—from the prophet Muhammad. This is to say that it will never reflect person-

---

1. Title of a work by Frithjof Schuon, *The Transcendent Unity of Religions*, Gallimard, Paris, 1946, Collection "Tradition". It was subsequently republished several times, both in the original French and in English translation.

al opinions, but rather the doctrine of Islamic scholars and legal experts, as well as the belief of the ordinary faithful, both of which are founded on adherence to two certainties: that the Koran is the Book of God, and that Muhammad is the Messenger who was chosen to spread the Book's truth.

The Koran

It was in the year 610 of the Christian Era (the Era of the Hegira would not begin until twelve years later), that Muhammad at age forty—the age of prophecy—received the first revelations of the Book of God, *Kitâb Allâh,* which is the most excellent reading and recitation: *al-Qur'ân.*

Here, then, is the account of this important event that was the first descent of the Koran, a narration that was compiled from the earliest and most authentic sources by the British scholar Martin Lings, whose biography of Muhammad I had the privilege of translating into French, and which was published at the beginning of 1986.

It must be remembered that Muhammad, predisposed since childhood to an intense contemplative life, often withdrew to solitary places to pray and call upon the one true God (contrary to the great majority of Arabs of the time, who had little by little deviated from the cult of Abraham toward idolatry). One of his favorite places of meditation was the cave of Hirâ, situated on the side of a mountain that juts out over Mecca. Here, then, is the account:

> Ramadan was the month that was traditionally set aside as a time of retreat, and it was one night at the end of the month, during his fortieth year, when Muhammad was alone in the cave, that an Angel came to him in the form of a man. "Read!" the Angel commanded him; to which he replied, "I cannot read!" Whereupon, as he himself related, "The Angel seized me and grasped me tightly in his arms until I was unable to endure it any longer. Then he loosed his embrace and told me 'Read!' 'I cannot read,' I answered again, and he grasped me once more until I could endure it no longer; thereupon he let go of me and said a third time, 'Read!' and I repeated my answer, 'I cannot read!' Once again he clasped me as before and then freed me and said:

> 'Read: In the name of thy Lord who createth,
> Createth man from a clot.
> Read: And thy Lord is the Most Bounteous,

214

Who teacheth by the pen,
Teacheth man that which he knew not'."
(XCVI, 1-5)[2]

The Angel left immediately, and Muhammad recited the same words after he had gone. "It was as if these words had been written on my heart," he would later say; but he was afraid that what had taken place meant that he had to go back to the valley. When he was half-way down the slope he heard a voice above him that said, "Oh Muhammad, you are the Messenger of God, and I am Gabriel." Lifting his eyes to the sky, he recognized his visitor, whose angelic nature at that moment manifested itself with unmistakable clarity, filling the horizon. The Angel again said, "Oh Muhammad, you are the Messenger of God, and I am Gabriel." The Prophet watched the Angel without moving; then he turned away, but in whichever direction he looked, whether to the north, south, east or west, the Angel was there, blocking the horizon. Finally the Angel disappeared, and the Prophet descended the mountain and returned home.[3]

And it was thus that, little by little, over a period of twenty-two years—twelve of which were spent in Mecca and ten in Medina—from the year 1 of the Hegira (622 AD.) until the death of the Prophet (632 A.D.), the entire Book was revealed to Muhammad through Gabriel as intermediary, and was retained in the memory of men, transcribed at first on bones and skins in order later to be transmitted practically *ne varietur* in its original language, Arabic, across more than thirteen centuries.

The Creation

Read: In the name of thy Lord who createth,
Createth man from a clot. (XCVI, 1-2)

These two verses, which were the first ones revealed in the Koran, set the tone of the Sacred Book. They immediately evoke the

2. All Koranic quotations are from *The Meaning of the Glorious Koran: An Explanatory Translation*, trans. Marmaduke Pickthall, George Allen & Unwin, London, 1948, 2nd edn.
3. M. Lings, *Le Prophète Muhammad*, Seuil, Paris, 1986, pp. 57-58. Originally published as *Muhammad, His Life Based on the Earliest Sources*, Islamic Texts Society Allen & Unwin, London, 1983.

directing will of the Lord, creator of the world and man, who descends bringing a new message to his human creation.

But how is creation itself to be explained? Does it have a reason for being or a finality? These questions are answered in the Koran and in the prophetic tradition.

One verse of the Koran is particularly explicit. It says:

> I created the jinn and humankind only that they might worship me. (LI, 56)

Hadîth are quotations from the Prophet that consist mostly of simple statements, words of advice, or narratives directly related by Muhammad. However, the *hadîth qudsî* are veritable inspirations in which God Himself speaks through the tongue of his Prophet. One of the *hadîth qudsî*, which is very often quoted, particularly in mystical treatises, says:

> I was a hidden treasure, I wanted to be known and I created the creatures.

The will to be worshiped, to be known: these two "desires" of God are at the center of our research at present, at the center of an interaction between God and man, and man and God, that explains and justifies our presence on earth, and, as we shall see, sheds light on many aspects of the human condition that at first seem obscure.

Let us return, then, to the previously cited verse on the creation, which says that God created jinn and men only that they might worship him. The last verb, "to worship", is formed from the triliteral root *'a-b-d,* as are the derivations *'ibâda* ("worship") and especially *'abd* ("servant"), and *'âbid* ("slave"); all are key words and are among the most frequently found in the Koran. Who, moreover, does not know the word *'abd,* which figures among such compound first names as Abdallah, Abdelkarim, Abdelkader, and so on. Abdallah is the most common of these names; it means "the worshiper", "the servant" or even "the slave of God"; all of these meanings are equally valid. In the other compounds such as Abdelkader, Abdelkarim, etc. the name Allâh, that of the unqualified Divinity Himself, is replaced by one of His more than one hundred other names, which are those of His attributes, such as Severity or Forgiveness, Beauty or Majesty, attributes that deserve to be glorified and venerated by all creatures. It must be emphasized that the first name Abdallah, which is so widespread, is not only that of the Prophet Muhammad himself, but is also that of each prophet. In the Koran, for example, the young Jesus, when speaking to the men who surround Mary, cries out, "Lo! I am the slave of Allâh (*'abd-Allâh*). He hath given me the Scripture and hath appointed me a Prophet" (XIX, 30).

Abdallah is, in fact, the true name of each human being. Thus the preacher who addresses the faithful from high up in his pulpit, before prayers every Friday, begins his sermon with the words, "Oh servants of God! (*Yâ 'ibâd-Allâh)*" (*'ibâd* is the plural of *'abd*).

What then is meant or implied by the condition of being the servant of God, of having the status of servitude? There are two modes of servitude to be considered. On the one hand, there is a passive means, a state of existential worship that is submitted to, a total and absolute constraint that is exerted on all creatures; in this sense, the rocks themselves, the trees, and the animals are the servants and slaves of God. On the other hand, there is also an active means of servitude: it is conscious adoration, worship that is voluntarily offered by the being that recognizes its place in the universe and renders thanks to the Supreme Artisan. Only man is capable of this active mode of worship, and he is obligated to it by the very nature of his unique and privileged position.

Another notion that is very close to that of *'abd* is when a man is described as being *faqîr,* or "poor". This Koranic idea is expressed, *inter alia,* in the verse that declares "Allâh is the Rich, and ye are the Poor" (XLVII, 38). Like the condition of servitude, the state of poverty, i.e. of extreme dependence on the Dispenser of all good, can either be passively submitted to or actively recognized and accepted, in which case man returns what he has to God and strips himself of all pretension to self-sufficiency. This attitude, according to the teachings of the Koran, is the supreme act of worship, which makes a man a true believer (*mu'min*) and a true Muslim (*muslim*): "They are the (true) believers whose hearts feel fear when Allâh is mentioned, and when the revelations of Allâh are recited unto them they increase their faith, and who trust in their Lord" (VIII, 2).

Why is only man called to this conscious and active form of worship? One answer is that it is because he is the culmination, the completion of the creative work, because it is to him that the principle of *noblesse oblige* applies in its full right. "Surely we have created man of the best stature," says a verse of the Koran (XCV, 4), and another adds: "Allâh it is Who . . . fashioned you and perfected your shapes" (XL, 64). Finally, in the words of the Prophet, man has been created "in the image of God" *('alâ sûrati-Allâh)*. Let us now turn our attention to this form that is so beautiful that it resembles the Divine.

Externally, man is endowed with five senses that give him the ability to:

see the blessings of God, His signs, and His reflection "on the horizons" (according to a Koranic expression, XLI, 53);

hear the song of creation, for "All that is in the heavens and the earth glorifieth Him" (LIX, 24 *et passim*);

smell the scent of flowers, symbol of the invisible presence of the Creator within his work;

taste the fruits of His generosity: the dates, pomegranates, figs and grapes that, even after the Fall, have retained the taste of Paradise;

touch, so that he may know her whom God has given him as a companion.

Man is also endowed with inner faculties, which permit him to enter into contact not only with visible things and beings, but also with the Invisible, with the hidden face of things. They are the memory, the imagination, the will, the reasoning mind and, above all, the spirit *(rûh)*, which God has breathed into him. Spirit is also intellect *('aql)*, direct and intuitive intelligence that is able to grasp the deeper nature of things and beings without passing through the reasoning process.

Finally, man is endowed with the faculty of speech, which makes him fundamentally different from all other beings in the animal kingdom.

The exceptional nature of man, which is destined to be the very mirror of the Divine, also explains the marked anthropocentrism of the Koranic message:

He it is who created for you all that is on the earth. (II, 29)

He it is who hath appointed for you the night that ye should rest therein and the day giving sight. (X, 68)

And after that [after the creation of the vault of heaven, *samk*] He spread the earth And produced therefrom the water thereof and the pasture thereof, And He made fast the hills, A provision for you and for your cattle. (LXXIX, 30-33)

218

Plants—grapevines, vegetables, olive and palm trees, gardens and various fruits—have been put on earth so that man can take his sustenance and create remedies from them (II, 2).

God has made subject to man:

• the animals, so that he may drink their milk, ride them, use them for transporting his goods, make his clothes from them, eat them for his nourishment, and admire them in the morning when they go out to their pasture, or in the evening, when they come back from it (XVI, 6);

• the stars, that he may use their paths to find direction at night and to measure time (VI, 97);

• the earth, that it may be a stable dwelling-place *(qarâr)* (XL, 64) and a restful bed *(firâch)* for him (II, 22);

• the sea, "that ye eat fresh meat from thence, and bring forth from thence ornaments which ye wear" (XVI, 14);

• ships, so that man may voyage on the sea (XIV, 32).

Man the Caliph

Placed at the center of creation, man has been designated by God to be his lieutenant, his "caliph *(khalîfa)* on earth," in the terms of the Koran (II, 30). The office is a distinguished one, to the point of giving man a status superior to that of the angels, whose bodies are pure light and whose sole mission is to glorify the Lord by revolving around the divine throne. In order that he might exercise his earthly magistracy, God taught man the names of all things, names which man then passed on to the angels; afterwards He ordered the angels to prostrate themselves before Adam.

Was this primordial man going to remain faithful to the mission that had been entrusted to him? Alas, no: "Everyone that is thereon [on earth] will pass away" (LV, 26). And since perfection only belongs to God, even an image of God can become tarnished.

It must be admitted that a certain risk of estrangement existed between the creature and its Originator, due to the fact that man had been made of water, clay, semen and blood, and that spirit had been breathed into coarse matter. From that moment on, a composite form existed, its hybrid nature (not yet beast and angel, as

Pascal would say, but at least earth and angel) containing the potentiality for both destabilization and corruption.

This is why the Koran contains warnings such as: "Man is made of haste" (XXI, 37); or again, that he has been created as "weak" (IV, 28), "anxious" (LXX, 19), "in affliction" (XC, 4), and "ever thankless (*kâfura*)" (XVII, 67).

There are, therefore, imperfections in the painting, and in spite of his deiform nature, man has degenerated. This is what is known as the Fall in biblical terms, and it is an event that is related in several passages of the Koran; for example:

> And when thy Lord said unto the angels: Lo! I am about to place a viceroy in the earth, they said: Wilt Thou place therein one who will do harm therein and will shed blood, while we, we hymn Thy praise and sanctify Thee? He said: Surely I know that which ye know not.

> And he taught Adam all the names then showed them to the angels, saying: Inform me of the names of these, if ye are truthful.

> They said: Be glorified! We have no knowledge saving that which Thou has taught us. Lo! Thou, only thou, art the Knower, the Wise.

> He said: O Adam! Inform them of their names, and when he had informed them of their names, He said: Did I not tell you that I know the secret of the heavens and the earth? And I know that which ye disclose and which ye hide.

> And when We said unto the angels: Prostrate yourselves before Adam, they fell prostrate, all save Iblîs. He demurred through pride, and so became a disbeliever.

> And We said: O Adam! Dwell thou and thy wife in the Garden, and eat ye freely (of the fruits) thereof where ye will; but come not nigh this tree lest ye become wrongdoers.

> But Satan caused them to deflect therefrom and expelled them from the (happy) state in which they were; and We said: Fall down, one of you a foe unto the other! There shall be for you on earth a habitation and provision for a time.

> Then Adam received from his Lord words (of revelation), and He relented toward him. Lo! He is the Relenting, the Merciful.

> We said: Go down, all of you, from hence; but verily there cometh unto you from Me a guidance; and whoso followeth My

guidance, there shall no fear come upon them neither shall they grieve. (II, 30-38)

It will be noticed in this passage that Eve is not shown as having induced Adam into temptation; Satan, however, caused both of them to "deflect". The same thing occurs in another chapter of the Koran, in which the same event is related in a slightly different way and, in particular, the nature of the temptation is made more explicit:

> And verily We made a covenant of old with Adam, but he forgot, and We found no constancy in him.
>
> And when We said unto the angels: Fall prostrate before Adam, they fell prostrate (all) save Iblîs; he refused.
>
> Therefore We said: O Adam! This is an enemy unto thee and thy wife, so let him not drive you both out of the Garden so that thou come to toil.
>
> It is (vouchsafed) unto thee that thou hungerest not therein nor art naked.
>
> And that thou thirsteth not therein nor art exposed to the sun's heat.
>
> But the devil whispered to him, saying: O Adam! Shall I show thee the tree of immortality and power that wasteth not away?
>
> Then they twain ate thereof, so that their shame became apparent unto them, and they began to hide by heaping on themselves some of the leaves of the Garden. And Adam disobeyed his Lord, so went astray.
>
> Then his Lord chose him, and relented toward him, and guided him. (XX, 115-122)

What is particularly important in this account is the existence of a pact *('ahd)* that God had made with Adam and that the latter had forgotten.

Such a pact was in fact concluded with all men even before they came into existence. It was the "primordial" pact or Covenant that was made in pre-eternity when all souls were, as the Koran says, "within the loins of Adam." At that time God had asked them: "Am I not your Lord?" They said: "Yea, verily. We testify" (VII, 172).

In the primordial state, that is to say in conditions of existence like those in the Garden of Eden, man stayed faithful to his pact and worshiped without fault, overwhelmed with and grateful for the blessings of his Lord, whom he praised unceasingly. Various traditions call this time the Golden Age.

However, Adam's sin broke apart this primary state, and from that point on he was to be exposed to the constant seduction of evil: in other words, of his own soul, which whispers to him to devote himself to the illusory and ephemeral goods of the world as if they were destined to endure, and which wants him to give up what he already has in order to obtain uncertain benefits.

But God, who created man to be his regent on earth, pardoned and "came back to" Adam and gave him "a guidance," capable of abolishing fear and sadness for those who would follow it, for him to use among the greater hardships of his new earthly existence. From that time on, as humankind increased in number, spread over the earth's surface and split up into different races and tribes, God would send guides and messengers—angels, prophets, and saints— through whom he would renew His original pact with man. In the words of the Koran, "And when We exacted a covenant from the Prophets, and from thee (O Muhammad) and from Noah and Abraham and Moses and Jesus son of Mary. We took from them a solemn covenant (*mithâgan ghaliza*)" (XXXIII, 7).

In many passages the Koran reminds us that in the course of human history there is not a single nation that has not received its alliance and its messenger. With the coming of the latest of these messages—the Koran—the earlier religions, especially those of the "people of the Book" (Jews and Christians) were confirmed as being expressions of the one Truth, while at the same time a new union was proposed to mankind: Islam.

What makes a Man a *Muslim?*

He must believe in one God, who is all-powerful and is the creator of everything. This is the monotheistic credo, the doctrine of divine unity, the *tawhîd*. He must also believe in the truth of the Koranic message brought by Muhammad. These two articles of Muslim faith are summed up in the formula with which one bears witness to God *(shahâda):* "There is no God but Allâh, and Muhammad is his Messenger."

Said with sincerity, the above formula re-establishes union with the divine and restores to fallen man his primordial status. It is the equivalent of baptism for the Christian. Thus, spoken at the moment of death, it erases previous sins and opens the doors of Paradise. Being at the same time an adherence of the spirit to the dogma of divine unity and a recognition of the authenticity of Muhammad's mission, the *shahâda* implies a commitment to abide by the law proclaimed in the Koran. It is therefore considered to be the first pillar of Islam. The four other pillars are canonical prayer, said five times each day; the fast of Ramadân that requires each believer to go without food from sunrise to sunset for one month every year; the law of alms-giving, by which each well-to-do Muslim must give a sum to the public treasury in order to take care of the needy; and lastly, the pilgrimage which each Muslim must make to Mecca at least once in his life if he can afford it. These are the individual obligations that make up the fundamentals of the religion and that each Muslim must practice if he wishes to be right with the Lord. Beyond that, there is the set of rules of behavior and social conventions that makes up the code of personal morality and social ethics: measures governing marriage, inheritance, commercial transactions, the penal code, etc. Indeed, Islam, like Judaism and Christianity before it, although in a different form, bases itself strongly on community life in order to assure the individual salvation of the faithful.

The Muslim community, according to the Koran, was founded by God: "We have appointed you a middle nation" (II, 143). This community has brought harmony to the hearts of its members: "And hold fast, all of you together, to the cable of Allâh, and do not separate. And remember Allâh's favor unto you: how ye were enemies and He made friendship between your hearts so that ye became as brothers by His grace . . ." (III, 103). "Ye are the best community that hath been raised up for mankind. Ye enjoin right conduct and forbid indecency; and ye believe in Allâh" (III, 110).

Islam distrusts the recluse; it considers him to be overly exposed to the temptations of the devil and too weak to defend himself. While it is true that the Koran lauds the Christian anchorites, the monks of the desert, for their piety, it does not put forward their way of life as an example. "No monasticism in Islam (*Lâ rahbâniyya-ta fî al-Islâm*)," advised Muhammad. Indeed, marriage and the founding of the family are the norm, to the point that the Prophet also states that "marriage is half of *dîn* (religion)."

Let us return, however, to the community, the *umma,* and to its merits, not the least of which is to have received, in the words of a Koranic verse cited above, the gift of the "middle nation" (II, 143). It forms an organic whole of interdependent elements. In a *hadîth* that is often cited—without much of a lasting effect, unfortunately, judging by the dissensions within the Muslim world today—the Prophet said that, "The believer is to another believer as are the parts of a building that give each other mutual support." He also stated: "You will see Muslims in their kindness, their affections, and their reciprocal feelings, form a body which, when one of its members suffers, sees all the other parts share its sleeplessness and fever in emulation." Finally, Muhammad gave assurance that "My community will never agree together on an error": a statement that was to have considerable repercussions in the formation of law through the principle of the consensus of the believers *(ijmâ').* This solidarity, in Muslim law, was expressed by a statute of collective obligation called the duty of sufficiency *(fard kifâya),* which frees the individual believer from a compulsory prescription whenever a sufficient number of the faithful join together to fulfill it. This obligation applies, for example, to prayers for the dead, holy war *(jihâd),* and to the carrying out of duties that require a detailed knowledge of religious science.

It goes without saying that man, through his conduct, commits only himself, and that it is he alone who will appear before the Supreme Judge to answer for his actions. However, his ties with the social body are so strong that, in order to find his salvation, he depends in large measure upon those around him and upon whether or not his surroundings provide conditions that are favorable for the fulfillment of the Revealed Law. As the Koran says: "Lo! man is in a state of loss, save those who believe and do good works, and exhort one another to truth and exhort one another to endurance" (CIII, 2-3). These verses underline the importance of mutual encouragement for the fundamental virtues. The goal that is assigned to the community, to the Islamic Holy City, is to achieve the most complete harmony possible between, on the one hand, the search for individual salvation and, on the other, the functioning of the social body that is the guardian of the Divine Message, of institutional wisdom, and of the example of the just.

It is a question then, as has recently written Professor S.H. Nasr, author of numerous works on Islamic spirituality and science, of an "egalitarian theocracy" or, to use another expression, of a "normocracy" (the latter term emphasizes the sovereign domination of the Revealed Law).[4]

Let us examine the principal functions incumbent upon the community of believers.

First of all, there is the *executive power.* In the image of the community that Muhammad founded in Medina and that was ordered to "obey Allâh and His messenger" (VIII, 1), for "Whoso obeyeth the messenger obeyeth Allâh" (IV, 80), the supreme head of the Muslim nation is the caliph, or "commander of the believers," who is the successor to the Prophet and who unites all the duties associated with spiritual authority and temporal power.

The main concern of the Umayyad Caliphate, quite soon after the death of the Prophet, was to strengthen its political power, and the later Abbasid Caliphs transformed the caliphate into a royal autocracy. Thus a split arose between political and administrative duties on the one hand, and juridical and religious ones on the other; this split has become more accentuated with the division of the Muslim world into a multitude of autonomous entities. It was not, however, until the formation of nation-states along the Western model and the abolition of the Ottoman Caliphate in 1924 that the break between the executive and the religious functions became complete in most of *dâr al-islâm,* the Muslim world.

It seems understandably surprising that today, in what is called the Muslim world, so many peoples are subjected to governments that are quite obviously not impelled by any concerns of a religious nature.

Without entering here into a discussion that would necessitate large numbers of examples, it could nevertheless be stated that if there exists a certain passivity or resignation towards the lack of government interest in religion, it is because the Muslim conscience is thoroughly impregnated with the idea, expressed in the Koran, that "Allâh's is the whole command" (XIII, 31). God therefore can carry

---

4. Seyyed Hossein Nasr, *Ideals and Realities of Islam,* Allen & Unwin, London, 1966, Chapter IV. Published in France as *Islam—perspectives et réalités,* Buchet/Chastel, Paris, 1975.

out his government as and through whomever he wishes. He commands the faithful to "Obey Allâh, and obey the messenger and those of you who are in authority" (IV, 59), so that they must recognize constituted authority, at least as long as those in power do not overtly contravene the precepts of the Revealed Law.

The second function of the Holy City of Islam is to provide justice. The idea of justice is fundamental to Islam, for the Islamic world itself, *dâr al-islâm,* is also called the world of justice, *dâr al-'adl,* since the Law that prevails over it is that of God, the Just (*al 'adl*). All the obligations and prohibitions stipulated in the *sharî'a,* the body of Koranic law, as well as the virtues that are for the believer the corollary and consequence of his submission to the Will and Wisdom of the Divine Legislator, have the same end result: "Give the right to each who has the right," or, more explicitly, "Respect the rights of God and the rights of men."

Thus, all the functions of the Holy City are organized around contractual relations. The first of these relations is the original pact through which God suggested that man be his lieutenant on earth and to which man subscribed by his acceptance. Next, there is for those in authority the duty of protection, and its inverse, that of obedience for those who are ruled over. Finally, there are the contracts that regulate the acts of social life and private law by which men pledge themselves to each other without ever losing sight of the sovereign prerogatives of Him who, before any human intervention, had already fixed the order of all things.

The affinity between the above conception and the Platonic vision of a just society is immediately evident. Moreover, when Farabi, in the tenth century AD., described an ideal of the city of virtue *(madina fâdila),* it was both as a Muslim and as a disciple of Platonism that he specified the ends and the means: "To make men enjoy as much as possible, during this life and on this earth, the happiness and delights of the life to come by making use of community institutions based on justice and solidarity."

On the level of the Holy City, the exercise of judicial power is left to the judge, the *qâdî,* who receives his office from the caliph or head of the executive branch of government. Enthroned in the mosque where he will often be called to preach the Friday sermon, his domain is that of the law, the *sharî'a,* and includes all the Koranic prohibitions, which he ensures are applied to specific cases.

He pronounces marriages and divorces, attends to the execution of wills, cares for the upbringing of orphans and the handicapped, and, in particular, decides the disputes that are submitted to him and, in the case of a public or private transgression, applies the penalties provided for by the Koran.

The *teaching of religion* must also, of course, occupy an important position in the Community.

Government legal officials are of necessity chosen from among the *ulemâ'*, or Doctors of Law, and the important role that is assigned to them explains why the formation of the *ulemâ'* was established as one of the Community's "duties of sufficiency". Indeed, there is no higher distinction for the Muslim than that which is conferred by learning *(al-'ilm)*, that is, knowledge of the Revealed Law. "He to whom God wishes well," said the Prophet, "is made learned in matters of religion." He also stated that, "One single Doctor of Law has more strength against Satan than a thousand men who devote themselves to worship." This does not mean that the learned man can dispense with worship, but that religious practices, when combined with the intelligent knowledge of their significance, acquire an almost invincible power against temptation, error, and excesses of passion.

The duty of calling the believers to their religion and of preaching good conduct does not belong solely to the learned judges or imams of the Community. The upholding of high moral standards and the encouragement to do good are duties that are incumbent upon each citizen. "And there may spring from you a nation who invite to goodness, and enjoin right conduct and forbid indecency," declares the Koran (III, 104). Thus, each Muslim is expected (within the conditions defined by jurisprudence, and which, except for circumstances beyond one's control, exclude the shedding of blood) to criticize and denounce public or private acts which are contrary to the "limits" *(hudûd)* set by God. If it is within his power, he is also expected to reform the transgressors, so that order may be reestablished in the Community, which suffers as does a body when one of its members becomes diseased, and the wholeness of which is an almost indispensable condition for the salvation of its constituents.

Not even a detailed enumeration of the precepts and rules of religious law would be able to exhaust the contents of Muslim life.

Jean-Louis Michon

Transformations and syntheses take place inside of the institutional framework within which the believers live; they constitute a veritable spiritual alchemy that, although entirely inspired by the Koranic message, nevertheless transcends its normative aspects.

The Mystical Path

The Revealed Message has two dimensions or faces: one is external and superficial; the other is internal and profound. The first is the Law of which we have just spoken: it is imposed upon all responsible men, must be accepted in terms of reason, and governs their faculties of sensation and action. Followed to the letter, it institutes and assures a sacred order that aims to restore created beings to their original status, and to make them able to attain the promised happiness of the Hereafter. The second dimension is that of the truth (*haqîqa*): it is concerned with the essential realities hidden behind appearances and is only perceived by "the eye of the heart" that is open to contemplation. It is a kind of advance vision that God grants to those close to Him in this world. Access to this interior vision, of opening the eye of the heart to the penetration of the divine light, is by the mystical way (*tarîqa*), which is like a tree that rises toward the sky while its roots thrust down into the common way, the *sharî'a*.

I spoke at length several years ago of the mystical way and of the practices that are associated with it. I will not, therefore, repeat myself, but will simply bring to mind again its essential element: the *dhikr*, the remembrance or recollection of God.

The word *dhikr* can be interpreted on various levels because it in fact refers to every act and every thought that brings one closer to God. Thus the whole Koran is *dhikr-Allâh*, or "remembrance of God," and its verses are *ayat*, "signs", that recall the existence of the Creator. *Dhikr-Allâh* is also one of the over 200 names of the Prophet Muhammad, which are used in the litanies and praises that the faithful address to him. "Remind them, for thou art but a remembrancer," Muhammad is told in the Koran (LXXXVIII, 21), and in fact for all believers, the imitation of the customs of the Prophet (*sunna*) is the means of remembering God.

The *dhikr*, in the language of the Muslim mystics known as the Sufis, refers in particular to the mention of the Divine Name, or of

228

one of the ninety-nine ritual Names of the Divinity, such as the Beneficent, the Merciful, the Generous, etc. Its repetition, under conditions and in forms that can vary from one school of mystics to another, is always and everywhere the supreme sacrament. Many verses of the Koran recommend the practice of the *dhikr*. Here are several of them:

> Cry unto Allâh, or cry unto the Beneficent *(al-Rahmân),* unto whichsoever ye cry (it is the same). His are the most beautiful names. (XVII, 110)

> Therefore remember Me, I will remember you. (II, 152)

> O ye who believe! Remember Allâh with much remembrance. And glorify Him early and late. He it is who blesseth you, and His angels (bless you), that He may bring you forth from darkness unto light. (XXXIII, 41-43)

> (This lamp is found) in houses which Allâh hath allowed to be exalted and that His name shall be remembered therein. Therein do offer praise to Him at morn and evening men whom neither merchandise nor sale beguileth from remembrance of Allâh and constancy in prayer and paying their due. (XXIV, 36-37)

> Verily in the messenger of Allâh ye have a good example for him who looketh unto Allâh and the Last Day, and remembereth Allâh much. (XXXIII, 21)

The spiritual advice given by Muhammad to his disciples is in the same vein:

> Men never gather to call upon Allâh without being surrounded by angels and covered with Divine Favor, without peace *(sakina)* descending upon them and Allâh remembering them.

> There is but one means of polishing all things, that removes rust; and that which polishes the heart is the invocation of God.

> "Shall I point out to you the best of your acts? The purest in intent toward your King, that which raises you the highest in degree, the accomplishment of which is more beneficial than distributing gold and silver (as alms)? Or than meeting your enemy and hitting him on the back of the neck, or being hit upon the back of the neck?" His companions said, "Tell us what it is." The Prophet replied, "It is the invocation of God Most High."

Among the most commonly used formulas for the *dhikr,* there is the repetition of the first part of the testimony of faith: *La ilâha il-Allâh.* The special effectiveness of this formula comes from its evocation of two phases of spiritual realization: a first phase of negation of all "divinity", that is, of all secondary "reality", of that which does not have sufficient reason in itself; and a second phase that is the affirmation of the sole reality of the Absolute Being. In other words, it represents phases of the obliteration of the created being and of the return to the Creator; or the annihilation of separative consciousness, followed by reunification in God.

However, the highest invocation is that of the name *Allâh*, the name of the Unqualified Divinity, "the Supreme Name," "the Unique Name," "the Name of Majesty." Within its two syllables and four letters, the symbolism of which has been often commented on, this name concentrates all of the redemptive effectiveness of the divine word. "God is present in His Name," say the Sufis. Indeed, through the conjunction of this Presence and serious concentration on the part of he who invokes Him, the worshiper finds himself practically obliterated, reabsorbed into the Invoked, the *dhikr* becoming that of God alone, in which the invocation, the invoked, and the invoker are one with the One that has no second.

Doubtlessly this state of perfect concentration is not attained automatically by practicing the *dhikr*. The initiate needs a master to instruct and educate him; he must learn to know himself, For, according to one of the sayings of Muhammad, "Whoever knows himself, knows his Lord." In short, the initiate must travel over a difficult itinerary, the steps of which have often been described by mystics of diverse traditions, sometimes in symbolic form, sometimes with great psychological realism. In Islam in particular, there exists a tradition of examining the conscience which was specifically illustrated by a Sufi who lived in Baghdad in the third century of the Hegira (ninth century AD.), and who was given, while he was living, the title *Muhâsibî*, that is, "Master of Introspection."

In order to describe the way of the Sufis, I will make use of a teaching that, in its written form, dates back to another great master, a contemporary of Muhâsibî, and who, like him, lived in Baghdad, where he was buried. His name was Junayd, "the Master of the Circle (*shaykh al-tâ'ifa*)," a name that he received because the first mystical fraternities, the *turûq* (plural of *tarîqa*, "the way"), were formed around him. Moreover, this particular teaching has been handed down without interruption ever since that time, and I personally found it in a treatise written at the beginning of the last century by the Moroccan Sufi Ahmed Ibn'Ajiba, who died in 1809.

The mystical journey, Junayd explains, consists of three stages. The first is the realization of the *unity of actions (tawhîd al-ad'al)*, which is the understanding that none of our actions belongs to us, but that God is actually the only Agent. This is what God, speaking through the Prophet, expressed in the famous *hadîth qudsî* that says:

> My servant never ceases to approach me through pious devotions until I become the mouth through which he speaks, the eye through which he sees, the ear through which he hears, the hand with which he grasps, and the foot with which he walks.

The second stage is that of the *unity of qualities (tawhîd al-sifât)*. This unity, for the human being, lies in the realization that his own attributes, powers, gifts and abilities come from the Lord of the Worlds, are only reflections of divine qualities, and do not in any way belong to him. "The most beautiful names are of God; call Him by them!" the Koran often advises; and the recitation of the Divine Names is one of the means used to attain this second stage of the mystical way, in which the *faqîr il-Allâh*, the "poor man within God," having renounced granting himself some merit or qualification, sees his own deficiencies replaced by the riches of the Most Generous.

The last level of the way is the *unity of the Essence (tawhîd adh-dhât)*. At this point, the human subject completely dissolves into the Infinite Being; the drop enters the ocean. Subject and object become one, and even if he remains among his fellows, without any apparent change, the person who has extinguished himself within the Divine Essence, who is one with it, is no longer the same. Having achieved the way of return through its final stage, the subject from that time on enters the category of the "intimates of God" *(awlîya' Allâh)*, those saints of whom the Koran repeatedly says that "they will not know either fear, nor affliction" (X, 62ff.).

Such is, finally, the vocation of man, for, again according to the Koran, "Lo! we are Allâh's, and lo! unto Him we are returning" (II, 156).

Chapter 14

The Forbidden Door

Mark Perry

Fostered by sacrifice, the gods will grant the enjoyments thou desirest. He who enjoys these gifts without giving to them in return verily is a thief.

—Bhagavad-Gita 3:12

There is a curtain before the Holy Ark of the Covenant, a veil, in the Temple of Jerusalem, before the Holy of Holies and another one separating the vestibule itself of the Holy. One finds, in medieval churches, a rood screen and, in Eastern Orthodox churches, an iconostasis set between the nave and the sanctuary.[1] These veils or screens are placed between the Divine and man— "And it was not vouchsafed to any mortal that God should speak to him unless it be . . . from behind a veil" (Quran 42:51)—for who can behold the countenance of the Lord and live? The deadly holiness of God requires shrouding—"Lo, I come unto thee in a thick cloud" (Exod. 19:9)[2]—lest mortal man, glimpsing the Supreme, be

---

1. In the Eastern Orthodox Church, which protects the holy mysteries better than the Roman Catholic does, only the priest is allowed to enter through that screen, through what are aptly called the "Royal Doors" in the center of the iconostasis. However, it is traditional for the priest to bring a newborn child into the Holy of Holies and to carry it around the altar, which makes sense if one understands that the soul of an infant is still not tainted by the world. Students of history will observe that these screens are later additions; but this does not detract from their meaning, all the more as the rood screen could be considered to be no less than a reversion to the veil of the Ark of the Covenant. One could also retort that, in the case of the church, the intense piety of the faithful who, in ancient times as in all sacred civilizations, knew how to abase themselves before the Supreme, rendered such partitions superfluous for their humility presupposed a natural veil. Moreover, it is also true that the veneration of the host, confined in a sacred urn, is a rather late development, occurring only in the latter Middle Ages—thus, obviating the immediate need for a partition.

2. In Islam, reference is made both to the Night of Revelation, *Laylatul Qadr*, and to the Night of Ascension, *Laylatul Mi'raj*—the encounter between man and the Divine occurring in the blessedness of darkness.

burnt to cinder. Various legends allude to this reality, at different levels, for instance the telling of the arrival of the White Buffalo Maiden among the Sioux Indians: two men behold her but one of them, who had impure thoughts, is struck dead and out of his corpse snakes appear. And there is the legend of the hunter Actaeon who was turned into a stag when he chanced on the virgin goddess Artemis as she bathed in her unclad beauty. The legend recounts how he was then assaulted and killed by his own hounds which symbolize the animal passions that can rend the soul.[3] The paradox of these veils is that the Divine, which is essentially mercy, goodness, and beneficence, requires shrouding lest its mercy slay, if such an ellipsis is permitted. Now, it is clearly not beneficence-as-beneficence that is lethal but the contrast between light and darkness that can have a shattering effect, all the more so when darkness is inveterate and repulsive of light. On another level, the manifestation of the center or of the One can have an annihilating effect on the peripheral or on the many, whence the necessity for transitional hypostases without which the appearance of the Divine would signal instant and pulverizing resorption into the singleness of its inviolable aseity. In other words, without these veils, manifestation could never pass from principial potentiality to the manifested state. Thus, in Islam, it is said that the countenance of God is veiled by seventy thousand curtains of light and darkness without which everything His gaze fell on would be consumed.

The brilliance and majesty of the Divine principle is such that even its perfect creation, man—or man as the *avatâra*, as *atmas-varupa* (created in the image of God)—cannot be beheld directly by the angels. Thus, even the cherubim are said to avert their gaze

---

3. In the Odyssey, Ulysses meets the enchantress Circe who turns all men into beasts but, falling in love with the wandering hero, spares him a similar fate. In esoteric terms, Ulysses is in fact immune to the spell of Circe's magic because as central man he dominates his soul. And this is why, also, Circe cannot but fall in love with him just as the soul, when it is all that it ought to be, cannot elude the riveting attraction of the Spirit. Concerning the tale of Actaeon, there is another interpretation that links him to the cult of the sacred stag whose dismemberment hearkens back to the sacrifice of a Purusha or an Osiris. There is no direct need to reconcile the divergence in meanings since our basic point about the *terribilitas* aspect of the divinity still holds, not to mention the inevitable polyvalence of symbolism which accounts for reality synthetically and not analytically, in the way rationalism does. Hence, the possibility of contradictory levels of meaning within the same unit of symbols.

when in front of Christ[4] which they do partly out of fear and partly out of respect which are really the two faces of the same attitude. Conversely, Moses, after entering in communion with the Lord, veils the radiance of his face before addressing the Hebrews.[5]

The symbolism of the lifting of the veil, that of Isis, as that of the bride, can only be operated after the taking of the initiatic or the marriage vow, both of which provide the spiritual basis or moral qualification for the gift of the nakedness of the spirit granted either in the form of knowledge of the Divine, in the case of the initiatic vow or, for marriage, that of the maidenly splendor of woman disrobed. That the kindred symbolism of these two gifts is actually the same is seen in the idea of the *Shekinah*, the divine essence—or wisdom—manifested as feminine beauty. The necessity of the preliminary vow is founded on the fact that before wedding the Absolute, man must commit his immortal soul sacrificially and absolutely, for such an oath is the only one to accord with the essential nature of the gift—which, in its essence, is no less than the gift of divine immortality and eternal bliss.[6] Anything less is inherently sacrilegious, and the petitioner becomes no better than a common thief now open to the dread retribution of the law. But, for the man who is worthy—or who makes a worthy profession of faith, thus declaring sufficient rightness of intention—what he is bound to find ultimately, upon the lifting of the veil, is none other than his immortal self for in beholding the Self he is thereby restored to himself.[7]

---

4. By way of example, a reference to this can be found in *Romanos Melodes Hymnes*, an early medieval collection of hymns for the laity gathered around the turn of the fifth and sixth centuries. The cherubim's discretion is, by cosmic analogy, a recognition of their lower order of reality. This humility probably does not apply in the same way to the seraphim, the highest order of angels, although all the angels are said to have had to prosternate themselves before Adam.

5. The taking of the veil by nuns in the convent symbolizes not only the withdrawal from the world but also, and more essentially, the protection of the intimacy of their relationship with Christ from profane interference—which recalls in its own way these words from the Song of Songs: "I am black but beautiful."

6. Thus Isis is made to say: "I am all that has been, and is, and shall be, and my veil no mortal man has yet lifted." No "mortal" man refers, implicitly, to the need for man to die first through the sacrificial consecration attendant upon his solemn oath to honor and serve the Lord.

7. Novalis speaks of this mystery in his *Lehrlinge zu Sais*: "A man succeeded in lifting the veil of Sais [Isis]. But what did he behold? He beheld—oh, miracle of miracles—himself."

The veiled nakedness of the bride conceals the mystery of love and of the heart, the love—*amor* is *a-mors*, "without death"—that rescues from death, yes, but also that slays the false self: the Valkyrie's kiss brings death for it is also the kiss of life immortal.

*

*   *

Much of what has been said about the symbolism of the veil or the screen applies naturally to that of the door. However, the idea of the door presupposes a passageway that can be crossed in two directions—entering the one or exiting the other, which echoes the image of the *Janua coeli* or celestial gate and the *Janua inferni* or infernal gate found, among other places, in the cosmology of the zodiac.[8] Where the veil both conceals and reveals, the door's threshold indicates the possibility of two opposite destinations. More generally, however, the idea is that the same threshold marks the isthmus between a sacred interior and a profane exterior and, as a result, the door, in the lore of tradition, is defended by fierce guardians that forbid ingress to the impure. One does not cross the threshold without appropriate obeisance as seen in the customs of prosternation, of removing one's shoes, of kissing the threshold or an amulet, and other similar marks of respect that are everywhere to be found in sacred civilizations.

The image of the Forbidden Door is a common motif found in fairy-tales and in traditional tales. In its essential symbolism, it narrates, in the popular style of the folk cultures where it appears, the loss of Eden and of primordial innocence—the main character committing the unforgivable error, or sin, of opening the one door forbidden in an Elysian realm (which is really an earthly Paradise or a realm of innocence) where he is heir to every pleasure and delight he can dream of. There are two main ideas at stake here: the first is that man cannot pretend to a knowledge that is only safe for God to have because this knowledge, being that of duality, can engender fatal division. The second idea, which is essentially the

---

8. They are depicted as separate doors; however their symbolism can apply to the two directions implicit in one door and this symbolism is seen notably in the approach to the feminine sex which can be either consecrated or profaned, which proves that the spatial symbolism of outward or inward location defers to the superior importance of the symbol itself.

reverse of the first, is that man cannot approach the Divine without suitable preparation; in other words, he cannot approach the Divine on the basis of duality which means that he is not prepared to meet God so long as he is the dupe of egocentric separation.[9] Just as the sun—central symbol of the divine in the natural order—cannot be viewed directly without dire injury, likewise, the approach to the Divine requires both a ritual and a moral preparation in which the aspirant learns to "die" spiritually, for only the immortal is meet for the Immortal. This is as much as to say that self-naughting constitutes the preliminary basis for any sincere spiritual quest. In the motif of the Forbidden Door, the hero must vow not to open this door; in so doing, he must die to his curiosity and find contentment in the treasures and pleasures granted him in reward for his pledge—treasures and pleasures that surpass anything mortal man knows, but which lose their allurement or magical essence when curiosity and its step-sister, discontent, take over the soul.

It should not be difficult to understand why, in all religious traditions, the performance of rites is considered the indispensable preliminary in any quest for knowledge just as it constitutes the guarantee for such a journey. In Hinduism, for instance, *Uttara-Mimamsa*, or the Vedanta as it is generally known, presupposes the *Purva-Mimamsa* which deals elaborately with correct ritual sacrifice and cleansing.[10] The rites not only serve to correct and mold the soul, but provide the "narrow gate" through which the ego can only

9. This seems to be the meaning to the version of the tale mentioned below although, inevitably, this central motif of what is the Fall, has been modified by the fancy of folk retelling or by the superimposition of moral scruples—Christianization or Islamicization, for instance—until it may stray rather considerably from the original idea, acquiring in the process some meanings or teachings that, on the surface, are logically ridiculous. For example, in the Brothers Grimm's version, the heroine is punished for beholding the Holy Trinity—which at first sight seems absurd. However, if one can make allowance for the intensely moral climate in which the tale was transmitted, then it is possible to understand that God cannot be approached through curiosity. That sin is of more didactic import, in such a zealous climate, than the fact that the heroine chances on the Trinity, the vision of which presupposes sanctity, at least of substance.

10. Dispensing with these is not impossible given that there are men, very few indeed, who are born already initiated in the Spirit, and who thus are immune from the scar of original sin. They have virtually direct knowledge of the Divine owing to their naturally ascensional substance; by definition, they are inherently incorruptible.

pass once it surrenders its individualism, or once it dies to itself. The objective nature of the rites—indeed, they are Divine Law—ensures that the riotously subjective propensities of the ego are collected, concentrated, and channeled God-wards and not world-wards— theocentrically and no longer theofugally: "If thou give to thy soul her desires, she will make thee a joy to thy enemies" (Eccl. 18:31). The goal of the spiritual life is not to experience bliss—though this, in the divine order of things, can be its coveted reward—but to achieve a permanent change of character. Virtue is happiness, as Schuon has frequently remarked. Man can offer God nothing except his self.

The essence of the mystical experience could be summed up as the meeting between grace and faith: God's grace, free and uncon-strainable, coming to meet man's faith, also free[11] and unconstrain-able. This is as much as to say that the subjective foundation of all spiritual endeavor is intention—not techniques of concentration, not sensational trance-inducing manipulations of the soul, not drug-induced defenestrations of the soul's physical mold. And, to repeat, to the pillar of intention must be adjoined the pillar of ritu-al, namely of correct method. In other words, mysticism, to be spir-itually operative and blessed, depends on both a subjective guarantee,[12] intention, or *niyah* in Sufism, and an objective guaran-tee, the Heaven-bestowed means. The second of the two terms, method of prayer—including liturgy—validates the first, intention. In other words, the sincere aspirant understands that he cannot approach God without availing himself of the divine means Heaven places at his disposal. Humility forbids any alternative. This proviso is what distinguishes true mysticism from pseudo-spirituality.

---

11. "Also" but not "equally" free since man's freedom is loaned from God.
12. The term "subjective guarantee" may strike some as being a contradiction in terms. But by "subjectivity" we mean, not what is arbitrary, but the pole "being" which is meant to apprehend the truth—the bride and groom of all alchemical marriage. What is more, this "intention", when correct, is far more than just a personal frame of mind. The Cambridge Platonist, William Law, admonishes: "Above all things beware of taking this desire for repentance to be the effect of thy own natural sense and reason, for in so doing thou losest the key of all the heavenly treasure that is in thee, thou shuttest the door against God . . ." (quot-ed in Whitall N. Perry's *Treasury of Traditional Wisdom,* George Allen and Unwin, London, 1971, p. 486).

Counterfeit spirituality, instead, will place emphasis on impressionistic experience, on the subjective pole of mystical endeavor, practically to the near-total or even total exclusion of the objective pole, and derives its motive force—and abusively personal justification—in heightened emotionalism or vagrant intuitionism, or even in altered states of consciousness. And by its emphasis on developing its own subjective experience of consciousness—as opposed to consciousness of the Real—it depreciates or dismisses the petitionary or supplicative premise of traditional prayer which operates on the assumption of the believer's nothingness in front of God and hence of his readiness to endure obscurity and emptiness, if necessary, before any heavenly consolation is forthcoming, to say nothing of illumination. In other words, illumination is never seen as something that can be engineered, so to speak, but either (or both) as a reflux of intelligence back to its primal ground in Truth or as the meeting of a long-lost love won through the tribulations of time and loss. In both instances, this return depends on forces that transcend the mechanisms of effort or, indeed, of anything the seeker is able to undertake purely on his own skill and merit.[13] For the sake of the love of God, the sincere spiritual postulant accepts the possibility of a life of obscurity, of poverty, even of psychic deprivation. At the very least, he closes the door to the world to retreat to the oratory of the virginal heart;[14] *clauso ostia.* This is spiritual poverty and this is humility. He accepts this extinction (*fana* in Sufism or the *imitatio crucis* in Christianity) first out of principle, because the divine nature of the object—God and the Truth—which, being unconditional or absolutely precious or alone absolutely real, allows of no conditions to be set upon It; and, secondly, it is understood that only a virginal soul is meet substance for the reception of the Holy Ghost. In the Catholic Church, this is the meaning, formerly, of fasting before receiving communion.[15] Finally, he accepts it as both a

13. Shankara, in one of his commentaries on the Bhagavad Gita, explains that *Moksha* (spiritual liberation or illumination) too, being no effect of an act, no action will be any avail to a *mumukshu*, a seeker of *Moksha* (Introduction to the 3rd Chapter).
14. The heart is "virginal" because, as Plato might have explained, "it is self-existent" and thus incorruptible.
15. Modern man has almost no idea of how seriously Medieval Christians took this preparation to heart, consenting to astonishing asceticism in view of receiving the holy sacrament, or even not taking it from utter dread of unworthiness.

proof and test of his sincerity.[16] Or, he accepts it out of his healthy fear of God, whose majesty and might commands self-annihilation, as well as out of his ardent and undiscourageable love of God, whose goodness, bounty, and beauty he trusts and longs for. He would never assume, as pseudo-spiritualists do with an impunity that betrays their presumption, that he could effect by his own means a spiritual experience or gain access to the divine essence by a mere technique of concentration.

Now, even if prayer, be it ritual or jaculatory (the invocation of a sacred word or formula), obviously must meet certain technical standards in the form of a systematic method, without which the ego would have no objective mold or bridge, such "techniques" are in no way sufficient unto themselves, as we have seen, to guarantee a charismatic result. What matters here is to understand that if the Divine is above all a conscious entity, then It is not susceptible to being manipulated or impudently conjured[17] as if it were merely an inert, or even an energetic, substance, *quod absit.* In other words, if God is love or intelligence, then this love and this intelligence will

16. In the Christian framework, this acceptance of suffering as a pre-condition for approaching the Divine is even more radical given the fact that God in the person of Christ consented to die on the cross for the sins of man. Thus, to believe in Christ entails, for the devout Christian, a heroic willingness to share in his redemptive sufferings. To suffer for God is, in fact, to taste the joy of proximity to Christ: in the agony lies the ecstasy. Thus the Dutch mystic Hadewijch could write that to suffer hunger was to find replenishment: "To die of hunger for her [the love of God] is to feed and taste; / Her despair is assurance / Her sorest wounding is all curing" ("The Paradoxes of Love" in *Hadewijch: Works*).
17. The question of "impudence" before the Divine is not as easy to seize as might appear. Some devotees will assume an exquisitely dignified attitude with a perfection of dress and manners in a place consecrated with incense and flowers—all of which, in itself, is perfect. However, such trappings must defer in importance to the question of attitude; and this attitude is often not immune from the expectation of wanting to obtain a result, thereby of setting certain conditions on the Divine. And this expectation of a result corrupts the perfection of the setting because then the attitude is not disinterested. To love God means to love Him unconditionally and to trust perfectly that He will do what is for our best in His own way and in His own time, whether we are made aware of it or not on this earth. The great and heroic merit of faith is this veil of darkness—or this door, which God alone can open—separating it from the Divine. And in its utterness of commitment, which no trial can unsaddle, there is a certitude which, in its essence, is intellective for it is, even though veiled, a knowledge—or a pre-knowledge—already of the Real.

only respond to what, *mutatis mutandis,* in man, corresponds to Its own numinous nature.

Put differently, as we feel constrained to repeat, the Divine is not just an energy that can be actualized by the virtuosity of some means or another—techniques such as breath retention or circulation (*pranayama,* or *pranagnihotra*—if one emphasizes the idea of the sacrifice through the breath), extreme asceticism, hypnotic one-pointedness of concentration, or via the use of psycho-chemical adjuncts.

By way of example, one could mention the frequent misuse, by Westerners, of Zen techniques of the void or of the Hinayana Buddhist technique of *vipassana* meditation. In the latter case, the approach consists in objectifying all impressions, mental as well as psychic and physiological, until, through a kind of exfoliation of the ego, the heart is laid bare and restored to its pre-mundane or divine essence. The difficulty, for Westerners, who usually practice such a method outside of an integrally sacred culture, lies in attempting to achieve perfect contemplation without reverence or without a sense of devotion and adoration: communion with the Divine is more than an experience, it is a sacrament. In the case of a Râmana Mahârshi, who commented on the similarity of his "method" with that of *vipassana,* we have the example of a natural contemplative, what Schuon terms a "pneumatic" or someone who ascends to Heaven effortlessly by virtue of the purity of his substance, and therefore who cannot fall. Adoration of the divine was innate to the Maharshi's being, which can hardly be said about the majority of Westerners embarking on such a path who have everything to learn about this and cannot do so by examining their mental phenomena. In fact, the artificiality of such a technique leads to ludicrous results, if not far worse.

Be it mentioned in passing, much has also been made, in pseudo-esoteric circles, of awakening the *kundalini* or the "serpent energy" lying coiled at the base of the spine, of lifting the ego-consciousness through the ladder-rungs of the energy centers—or *chakras*—so as to achieve a "transcendental vision" of the cosmos by penetrating into the supra-sensual realms. Now, having said this, one must grant the fact that man has a godlike intelligence and imagination that enables him to gain insights no other creature can have. And who is then to say that man cannot take advantage of his gifts? Does not the very availability of such gifts qualify him, at least implicitly, to avail himself of the full means at his disposal? And is he not in fact obliged to exploit his talents on pains of living beneath himself or of missing out on the fullness of his divine possibility? In this respect, to condemn such attempts will be seen—wrongly—as the province of a narrow moralism, ever solicitous of keeping the soul on the "straight and narrow" and fearful of unleashing energies or powers it dreads because it does not understand them or because they threaten to upset the banal security offered by a conventional life. One solution to this dilemma is to understand that these powers can be either the direct result of these techniques, in other words, something sought for its own sake, or they can occur as indirect results of a spiritual practice, in the natural course of things because to be a human being is potentially to be god-like. It is obvious that, from a certain point of view, man cannot help being other than what he is: if he is gifted, he cannot abjure these gifts, be it in the name of an over-zealous humility. The question then becomes, how will he use—or misuse—them? And, more importantly, will he become attached to them to the point of forgetting Who the loaner of these gifts is and that, therefore, he has no permanent—or personal—claim to them? In Hinduism, *siddhis*, or special gifts—supra-normal powers of sight, hearing, or ethereal flight—are well-known by-products of *tapas*, extreme ascesis, whereby a mortal can acquire god-like powers. However, by their very nature, they can not only become a major distraction, intoxicating the recipient with a false self-sufficiency if not a potentially monstrous self-assurance, but they in fact guarantee nothing spiritually—namely, in favoring sanctification—because they belong to the lower order of phenomenalism;[18] in other words, they are not properly of the Spirit though they perforce derive their qualities from attributes belonging to the Spirit. Even at their height, none of these powers—not even supposedly omniscient or telepathic insights, be it of former lives or of the future—have either true intelligence or true love which are the interchangeable marks of the Spirit. Thus, among many others, a Patanjali or, in our epoch, a Râmana Mahârshi radically disavowed them and therefore made

---

18. They are essentially of the order of *Prakriti*, deriving their energy from the cosmic genius of the three *gunas*, for example powers like the capacity to become as heavy as a mountain or as transparent as light—both of which occur, we suppose, within the framework of the fleshly body; in other words, the body does not just melt into thin air when the soul becomes transparent.

no use of them. In the last analysis, such confusions arise from a difficulty in properly distinguishing the spiritual from the psychic.

One example of this, among so many, is the bizarre interest lavished on the mystical potential of epileptic seizures and other such anomalies, not least the simulacrum between a hysteroid tendency and the heightened sensitivity of spiritual emotionalism, for example the "gift of tears". All that needs to be said, here, is that the divergence between this world and the next entails the possibility of imbalance, and in this domain it is not always possible to draw clean lines of demarcation between the abnormal and supranormal. A soul touched by God can lose its equilibrium, though rarely permanently so,[19] just as a disequilibrium of temperament can produce a fissure in the soul which may, with the right substance, be a catalyst for a mystical opening. But taken in itself, a psychic fissure means nothing spiritually, otherwise lunatics would be mystics.

*
* *

The principal difficulty for the soul embarking on the spiritual journey lies in reaching the isthmus of conversion (*metanoia*): before man can know anything about the divine he must replace his subjective sense of self with an objective sense of Self. The Truth must replace the illusion of his importance as a person. He does not yet know, from spiritual experience, that the Truth by which he is now to guide his life is actually what corresponds perfectly, vitally, and totally to his real self—beatifically so. When at the Narrow Gate, the spiritual path may appear as a desert, a barren land where the

---

19. In connection with this, one has the possibility of what, in Islam, is known as *majnun* or of souls who are "touched by jinn" (if one follows the literal translation of the Arabic term), but are more generally open to psychic possibilities that are usually considered to be spiritual. Every traditional world displays instances of such human beings who are spiritually unbalanced while not being crazy and who, as a result, cannot adjust to the stereotypical behavior of collective man. In the best of cases, their awareness of the *baraqah* (spiritual influence) prevents them from being sober. Mention should be made also of the spiritually perilous possibility of inducing hysteria or a kind of madness so as to break the soul's worldly moorings. From the frenzied Dionysian bacchantes to the Holy Rollers, or the love intoxicated devotees of Chaitanya, or the example of a Beatrice of Nazareth who sought to live Christ's agony to its bitterest end, we have instances where rationality is methodically eliminated in favor of a derangement of feelings and sensations in which the soul is meant to be "abyssed" in God.

soul is doomed to die because compelled to sacrifice its previous inclinations, opinions, and habits. In alchemical terms, the substance of the soul is taken out of the world to be enclosed in the vessel (athanor or retort of the alchemists) which is hermetically sealed and then committed to darkness and the heat of fire. It longs and struggles wildly to escape, but cannot do so; its former substance must be "cooked" and the vapors of its residue purified and transmuted. If it escapes the vial, the transubstantiation fails; in physical terms this means that if there is a leak, the pressure cannot abolish itself—the image of the dragon biting its tails or of the entwined snakes comes to mind here. Without the *nigrido*, no *albedo*: the final whitening issues from the initial blackening.

But there is not only the negative aspect of mortification, there is a positive one as well, and it consists in this: when the soul does encounter[20] the Divine, or gleans a taste of Heaven, the sheer wonder of the Object compels extinction.[21] There is—at that moment—no sense of one's importance, no ambition, no desire, utterly none.[22] These considerations should enable one to understand how it is not only illegitimate or foolhardy, but actually impossible—according to the law of spiritual "physics" to seek to experience the Divine on terms not set by the Divine Itself: the very nature of ambition precludes divine grace. And without grace, no salvation and, *a fortiori*, no spiritual realization.

A return to God entails, first, a return to the center away from the periphery—or the peripheral being—the ego represents. And this return depends basically on three elements: first, extinction and, along with it, self-effacement, humility, and the slaying of the *moi haïssable*—the despicable self: "He that humbleth himself shall

---

20. And these processes do not follow necessarily in this order: the sequence can be reversed to begin with a positive grace, in which case it serves as a prelude for the spiritual death to come, provided, of course, that the soul has the good sense to follow through and not to arrogate the nature of the grace to itself. How many have fallen supposing that for one divine grace granted them they were magically superior to other men?
21. In the alchemy of love, an immediately accessible symbol of the blissful meeting with the Divine, the soul is emptied of itself: it is stripped, cleansed, and laid bare before the wonder of the beloved who, to it, possesses all riches.
22. As Shaykh Ahmad al-Alawi expressed it, "He who knows God is disinterested in the gifts of God, and he who is negligent of God is insatiable for the gifts of God."

be exalted" (Lu. 18:14).[23] Secondly, it depends on entering the mold of perfect man, such as is found in the imitation of Christ or that of the Buddha—the living personification of the Divine Center. And, thirdly, and on the basis of the second step, it entails self-transcendence. In other words, one cannot approach God except through the model and mold of the perfect man or *avatâra*; and, likewise, one cannot approach the perfect man before one has given up one's trivial or accidental self. The possibility of immanence, wherein the Divine wells from the depths of one's innermost heart is premised on at least the initial adoption of these three steps without which spiritual life is mere pretension or even a lethal illusion. Rapturous ecstasy—which may or may not be a grace—is not the formal criterion by which one can measure one's progress towards perfect objectivity and, as such, it offers no spiritual guarantees, all the more as it can be no more than a species of euphoria which, if not arrested, can be a prelude to insanity. Some souls are more naturally permeable to the Divine, but this does not mean that the battle is won; far from it! The problem, if one must address this, is that graces received passively, can be passively lost. What matters is to become wholly active with reference to the soul, to dominate it and not let it dominate us. Otherwise man is not prepared to receive a grace without risk of deviation. Finding one's center and learning to live within it means not to desire anything that can lead one astray, that is to say, away from oneself—a self modeled on the One Self. It means that desire becomes not appropriative but transfigurative for in the appropriation there is a risk of corruption and of being led astray, whereas the fierceness of one's sense of veridical certainty—St. Bernard's *vehemente cogitatio*—and the fierceness of one's singleness of divine commitment compels the world to serve us, or rather one's God-centered desire, and not to have it seduce and shipwreck us in the *Samsara*'s endless sea of becoming and disappearing. The soul thus becomes like a blazing funeral pyre where everything that the world feeds it feeds the flames of its sacrificial fire. And, rather than dampening its spiritual ardor, actually serves

---

23. Which Nietzsche, in a cynical perversion of that supreme maxim recasts as: "He that humbleth himself wants to be exalted." (We quote from memory.) Such hypocrisy, perhaps, could apply to the ambitious or the profane but, taken in itself, it is self-defeating and therefore absurd and will fool only the irrational or the megalomaniacs.

to rekindle its all-consuming intensity; and where every contrivance of desire is smelted in a roaring furnace of love[24] which, at the same time, through the grace of detachment—what St. Francis calls purity of heart—is as serene as a lighted oil lamp in a prayer niche. Thus for the God-centered man, solicitations, either from the soul or the external environment, are no longer like whirlpools that threaten to drown the soul in subjective musings and longings, but are turned into fountains that celebrate God. And this is why St. Augustine can say, "Love God and do what thou will". *Omnia munda mundis*: for the pure, everything is pure.

*

* *

The most dangerous thing in the spiritual life is the cult of singularity. And the next most dangerous thing? Sheep like conformity. Dwelling on one's individual uniqueness, or what distinguishes us from others or makes one special, is also to emphasize what usually is the most accidental, fragmentary, or unreal. The paradox, for the ego, is that in effacing itself, it actually finds itself for in effacing itself before the Real, the sole Unique—or the uniquely Unique. And the less conspicuously individualistic one becomes, the more inspiredly real. Uniqueness is not bestowed by dint of our mere existence. Rather, it grows in proportion to one's awareness of the Unique, whence the irreplaceable value of the imitation of a divine model—the "singular nature" (*al-fardaniyah*) which is the supreme exemplar.[25] What characterizes a normal traditional civilization is the same prophetic stamp imprinting the countenance and attitude of a majority of its members; this seal derives first from a central divine figure of the stature of the major prophets and secondly from the great saints who reflect and re-echo across generations the nature of that seminal figure.[26] Ancestor worship is also based on

24. Cf. for instance Richard Rolle's *Incendium amoris*.
25. Strictly speaking, Sufism reserves the idea of *fardaniyah* to God alone—an equivalent to the *kaivalya* of Vedanta—and quite understandably so given Islam's insistence on the Unicity of the Divine Principle. However, one finds an Ibn al-Arabi speaking, in his *Futuhat al-Makkiyah*, of the "*fardaniyah* of our Lord Jesus".
26. And it is re-echoed by the priests—as well as by pious parishioners—for instance, today still, the Christ-like features and bearing found among so many of the Eastern Church's priests.

the idea of such a divine paternity. To assume the contrary, namely that an individual—and his or her experience—is important *tal quale*, that is in their unreformed state, is a cosmological impossibility because even if, in a normal civilization, there is vibrant diversity it always occurs within an underlying unity which prevents the whole social web from unraveling. An image of this principle of variety within unity is perfectly expressed in all the great civilizations' sacred arts whose canons always impose a set of rules which, far from stifling creativity, actually guarantee it just as the stalk helps the vine. In reverse, when singularity—as seen, notably in modern arts which makes an ultimately suicidal cult of the individual—overrules conformity,[27] one has the formula for a breakdown, a disintegration or, in medical terms, a kariolysis: the social body cannot survive the dismemberment the cult of singularity entails when carried to its logical extreme of chaos, to say nothing of the nature of the aberration itself because if, in art, out of a crazy need to be original, one wants to revolt against the canon of the human body—to take but one example of the kind of madness at stake here—the only avenue open is to disfigure it.[28] Otherwise, one is not considered to be truly creative. What is forgotten is that it is far easier to destroy than to build[29]—not forgetting that only the Creator can grant life.

27. This word, "conformity," has acquired an unjustifiably negative connotation in modern culture, and not surprisingly so given the points made above. However, one might want to make a distinction between the idea of conformity—which need not entail dull uniformity—and a flat conventionalism. Nonetheless, even the latter has its place in a society because if not enough members behave in a predictably consistent manner, this society cannot function, and this quite apart from the question of the qualitative merits of such a uniformity that, under normal conditions, follows a cosmic norm; this is what iconoclasts refuse to understand.
28. The yearning for singularity can take on many guises, even spiritual. Thus, committing oneself to some ascecis, outside the guidance of a competent spiritual advisor or in arrant disregard of a proper context—such as adopting a vow of silence while still engaged in the world—is, finally, only a way of cultivating a sense of singularity, a way of self power. God, even though nominally invoked, is essentially left out of the equation or, worse, perversely made to serve as a prop to serve one's covert ambition. Now, adopting a vow of silence where everyone else is submitting to the same rule, such as in older orders of Trappist monks, this is truly ascetic and thus truly sacrificial, a living death daily consented to.
29. One finds the same counterculture prejudice in the theater (which includes cinematography) in that an actor considers that to play the role of an ambigu-

*

* *

Now, when considering the nature of mystical experience, one has to concede at the outset that there are, in the nature of things, innumerable possible modes whose content varies considerably according to the nature of the individual soul—which does not mean, however, that it can be anything one pleases; that would be a parody.[30] And even the richest imagination cannot give a fair account of these modes for the mystical experience as such is finally something that can only be lived and not thought—or *just* thought, a crucial distinguo! It may seem strange, then, to affirm when speaking of mystical experience that, all things considered, experience, no matter how rapturous, is not the proper goal of spirituality and, therefore, neither is it, when taken alone, a criterion of spirituality. In fact, to embark on the spiritual path with the hope of finding special mystical experiences is an axiomatic disqualification for the spiritual path and a tell-tale sign of individualism—the supreme pitfall on the sacred journey. At the risk again of repeating ourselves, we will say that to seek God is first to seek His will as it is expressed fundamentally in His Law. Heeding His Law—"I delight in thy law," King David says (Ps. 119:70)—is the touchstone of one's sincerity and respect, as well as one's sense of proportions about the divine wager at stake. Also, and this is another paradox ensuing from the necessity for renunciation, the sincerity of a soul's resolve may hinge on its willingness to endure the absence of the Divine Presence; in fact, this is the operative foundation of all apophatic mysticism. At this juncture, right intention is everything;[31] the whole perspective of heroic merit hinges on such faith.

Does all of this mean that the principle of "experience" is to be discarded as useless, as something purely subjective and therefore

---

ous or of an evil person is far more challenging or even prestigious than to play the role of a good person, when in fact it is far easier for man to be a devil than it is to be a saint. Such is the ransom of cosmic gravity.

30. The Quran warns repeatedly against those who would just follow their impulses or desires (for instance, 20:16).

31. Schuon, in one of his unpublished texts explains this as follows: "The right intention excludes the personal expectation of sensible results, be it graces or spiritual degrees, or even powers or other purely profane advantages. And 'one must not tempt Heaven.'" (# 930)

to be distrusted or rejected? It has been alleged that a religion cannot long outlive the loss of experience. And this is true to the measure that any creed must involve the heart and not just the mind. But this notion of experience must be carefully separated from that of sensationalism; we keep harping on this. In other words, one will want to distinguish between subjective experience, which is inherently unstable and arbitrary, and objective experience—which may sound like a contradiction in terms until one understands that the soul is made to partake of the Real through the magic of perfect adequation, its reverence, awe, and love then becoming a form of the soul's knowledge of What is and where, correspondingly, not to love the True, the Beautiful, and the Noble is a major form of ignorance. In Vedantic Hinduism, emphasis is placed on the concept of *anubhava*, the certitude occurring from experience, whether ontological or merely occasional. And, indeed, until knowledge descends into the heart, there can be no effective certitude. At the same time, there is a certitude of the spirit, reflected in the mind as Truth, which serves as the necessary prelude to actualize the certitude of the heart.[32] And for this intellectual certitude to become fully operative—existentially and morally—it needs to free itself from the entanglement of subjective experience; hence the necessity of spiritual death, of dying to oneself, of cleansing the soul thoroughly of its profane otherness, of making a *tabula rasa*[33] of all psychic presuppositions about reality. Only then is the mirror made spotless or the vessel transparent enough for the self to experience the Self.

32. Once again, Schuon, in *The Transfiguration of Man*, the chapter "Axioms of the Sophia Perennis" speaks of "truths which present themselves as axioms because they fall within the realm of the five senses and that, as a result, can be proven *ab extra* (from the outside); and there are others that are axiomatic owing to the fact that they are to be found in the very substance of intelligence and therefore, by that fact, can only be seized as evidence *ab intra* (from the inside)."

33. This image of the *tabula rasa* is not to be confused in the slightest with David Hume's idea, by the same name, wherein he posits that the soul—or whatever his shallow materialism allows him to understand of this term—is a blank slate with no innate principles. Already a Leibnitz—and even a Kant—objected to this idea that there are no innate principles in human nature. Kant's version of this, expounded as the transcendental unity of consciousness, was later distorted by Jung when he posited the idea of a collective unconscious which, in fallen man, is really a bric-à-brac of shattered archetypes, a bad dream of reality now become outlandishly fragmented and chaotic, and verging on insanity.

However this term, "experience of the Self", is something of a misnomer for inasmuch as it is the Self alone that can in fact know Itself, the human subject has no part in this as an operatively separate individual. Thus, it turns out, the "experience" is no longer an experience, in the crude sense of the term, but something at once so transparent and so infinite that to describe it in baser sense categories amounts to a falsification and a betrayal. This does not mean, however, that the soul can have no part in a communion where, intrinsically, it is really the Essence repossessing Itself acausally without "a thine or a mine". Indeed, at this stage, the soul is ascensionally reclaimed by God through the experience of grace. And the particular coloring or aroma of that experience, insofar as it cannot not have some incidence on the psychic plane, is no longer separative or ego enhancing but simultaneously resolving and restorative—akin to the *liquefactio* of the alchemists in which a formerly base substance is transfigured back into its eternal essence according to the formula that the soul must become disembodied so that the Spirit can become embodied; "*verbum caro factum est*" (John 1:14). Be that as it may, in all considerations of graces experienced, what matters is not what the soul feels but what it does—operatively, concretely, objectively; and this belongs to the realm of character, not of experience.[34] As a matter of fact, some of the greatest changes in a soul often take place beneath the threshold of consciousness, somewhat in the fashion of a solution becoming progressively and invisibly saturated until, at the fulcrum point, it undergoes instant crystallization. Many men have become saints wholly unawares, which proves the poisonous irrelevance of the cult of consciousness extolled in "new age" spirituality.

*

* *

The emphasis on the subjective pole of existence, in our present-day (dis)culture is part of backlash against a tradition deemed

---

34. Once again, Schuon: ". . . instead of being governed by phenomena and following inspirations," one should "submit to principles and accomplish actions." For "what counts in the eyes of God is not what we experience, but what we do. Doubtless we may feel graces, but we may not base ourselves upon them. God will not ask us what we have experienced, but He will ask us what we have done." (Unpublished Text # 982)

outworn and even tyrannical. Specifically, it is a revolt against the Judeo-Christian idea of a patriarchal tradition in which the concept of regal authority, and of its objective law-giving instance, or father figure, is seen as repressive and stunting to the full development of the individual. Like all revolts, there is a basis for this groundswell because collective reactions are never eccentric. One of the origins for this can be found in the advent of the machine age whose mortally cold, brutal pragmatism, and the ruthless science of numbers connected to it, and its application in unnatural social regulations, could not but provoke a counter reaction from a life force—the primal *eros*, for one, but also, *affectus*, the feeling or affective soul—that cannot fit the crippling strictures of pure rationalism, namely of an overly mental culture that misprizes instinct as primitivism and of a metrically Cartesian mind that not only outlaws supra-rational intuition, but misunderstands the body both as a form of intelligence as well as a receptor of consciousness in its own right.[35] In parallel, and this is a problem that far predates the so-called Age of Reason, the cult of virility can degenerate all too readily into a physical ethos that exploits brute force at the expense of the feminine genius—the essence of which is the sense of beauty. Chivalry's idea of the *Coeur gentil*, the gentle heart,[36] and its cult of the lady, could compensate such excesses within the limits possible in the dark, terminal age of the Kali Yuga. But dread the fury of woman—and of nature—spurned. By stooping to barbarity, as well as seeking to overcome it by the sterile unmanliness of humanistic reasonableness,[37] man has

---

35. Citadine man is mostly dead to the sense awareness that the body of a nature dweller has, who understands through all of his senses and not just his mind alone. The Cartesian legacy, of which modern or allopathic medicine is a prime example, understands the body as no more than a machine with replaceable parts or as an inherently gross substance susceptible mainly to external manipulation. In other words, the body, divorced from soul, is treated as a virtually inert material mass though mysteriously electrified.

36. The idea of the "gentleman" is a rather pallid, enervated vestige of this noblest of ideals. Despite its handsome gallantry, when it attains to its best potential, it is in fact too weak and too civilized to tame and sublimate nature's magnificent fury and is therefore closer to effeminacy than to heroic or patrician self-control and courtesy.

37. The cult of reasonableness, which the "Enlightenment" philosophers so prized and which our modern culture promotes as the summit of civilization, is actually a complete and contemptible capitulation of man to a bourgeois horizontality. More fundamentally, it is the loss of a vertically heroic sense of grandeur, premised on self-transcendence, and, with it, the loss of the apocalyptic sense

forfeited his cosmological role and incited woman, in a reversion of roles, to supplant him. In so doing, she must, in turn, forfeit her own cosmological function and compete on forever unequal terms by perversely virilizing herself.[38] Thus does civilization invert its poles and proceed to destruction—while imagining, in the process, that it is promoting fairness, freedom, and happiness.

There is no question but that a secular civilization, premised on mercantilism and industrialism, operated and directed by material science—whose distant roots are detectable in the Greco-Roman cult of reason—has produced a monstrous hypertrophy of the mind, a type of human being who is excessively cerebral and who lives mummified in a sterile cocoon of plastified, metallic, and chemical substances whose molecular inflexibility are alien to the natural rhythms of the soul because they do not "breathe"[39] and thus are immune to the influx of the Spirit. To descry this, however, does not grant one license to castigate reason itself, but only an excessive rationalism divorced from an affective sense of beauty. Reason, in itself, is a divine faculty whose justification lies in *recta ratio*, namely in a sense of logic premised on an impartial sense of the truth. In man, the most direct expression of this is to be found in character— namely, in truthfulness, rectitude, and incorruptibility.

of good and evil. In traditional Christian terms, it is the virtue of prudence that has been misappropriated and caricatured.

38. Woman's liberation and the cult of the sacred feminine mystery are as vertical opposites as can be.

39. A scientist might object that even artificial substances have some kind of porosity and therefore are not absolutely stable. This may be true, but only up to a certain point because one of the characteristics of an unnatural substance is the fact that it is not organically dissolvable except at temperatures that exceed the normal—and therefore normative—parameters of our biosphere. Traditional metallurgy (whether of the gold-casters, wheel and rim makers, or the sword-smiths) probably constitutes the outer boundary of this normal realm. Moreover, one must also mention that even a natural substance such as wood is now (when not literally pulverized and re-compressed) processed and trimmed according to the symmetries of the most mathematically mental of angles— bent or twisted to conform to the unnaturally acute angles or mercilessly recti-linear planes—and finished off with sterilizing seals or paints that kill what is left of the wood's "soul". In contrast, one remembers entering homes in Morocco where the scent of cedar still exuded fragrantly from the wood panels and beams or posts, the latter of which, the craftsmen claim, are still not fin-ished growing as if by organic, or rather spiritual, echo. This is what Shintoists know as "*ke*", the "mysterious force of nature," a supreme architectural example of which is the Grand Shrine at Ise.

To be born a man is to be endowed with the divine gifts of will, love, and intelligence. And these attributes, if they are to be properly developed, *Deo juvante*, find their fulfillment respectively, as expressed by the Neoplatonists, in the good, the beautiful, and the true. Practically speaking, this means—to paraphrase Schuon—that man is meant to will the good, to love the beautiful, and to know the truth.[40] The pursuit of happiness is inconceivable without a proper understanding and integration of these elements whose absence opens up onto the subhuman. And what characterizes traditional man and, by extension, a whole traditional civilization whose architectural summit is a Chartres, the Temple of Heaven, a Taj Mahal, or the Dome of the Rock, is the crystallization of these tripartite faculties into modes of dress, behavior, and art that surrounds man in both a protective and liberating mold which prevents him from either forgetting or escaping the Divine.[41]

If one can look back at ancient man and avoid the twin pitfalls either of a pretentious depreciation or that of an overly sentimental romanticism, one will note that the value—and valor—of the individual can be summarized essentially by one central attribute: character. Even in a civilization such as Rome, which is in many ways a precursor of our own modern (or secular) world, the stoic virtues of *pietas, gravitas,* and *simplicitas* were the measure of a man or a woman. And this merit of character prevailed until the age of the novel or of psychology when it was gradually replaced by the cult of subjectivity and then of its bastard offspring, idiosyncrasy. After which, the sense of objectivity receded until it became, in practical terms, something abstract or difficult to understand, and even less to agree upon.[42] In simplest terms, in a sacred civilization, objectiv-

40. In this delineation, we are following a trinity whose leitmotif is found in all of the great traditions, most notably in the Vedanta, Neo-Platonism (including its ramifications in Christian gnosis), and Sufism, and, recently, magisterially expounded and crystallized anew in the works of Frithjof Schuon.

41. For a full development of this perspective, which is as far from the arbitrary as one can imagine, see Frithjof Schuon's *Light on the Ancient Worlds* or Titus Burckhardt's *Sacred Art East and West.* Both works explain the inherently intellective nature which constitutes the basis of a sacred civilization. The celebrated historian Arnold Toynbee, on a far more discursive level, himself recognizes that the genesis of the main civilizations originates each in a divine revelation.

42. However, the sense of objectivity still prevails—in its most pragmatic form—in the army, in sports, and in the business world which, for efficiency's sake, depends on results and not on opinions or states of soul. What is forgotten is

ity, both of attitude and especially of behavior, was all that mattered. Either an individual conformed to the law and acted honorably or he exposed himself to sanctions; the personal reasons for his deviation from the norm were almost irrelevant. Doubtlessly, if someone stole food to fend off starvation, this might provide sufficient attenuating circumstances to blunt the penalty attendant on theft. However, the cause would be assessed as an objective fact, in other words something obvious to any man of common sense; it would never occur to a magistrate, in such a civilization, to investigate the emotional state of the defendant in view of exculpating him, nor would it occur to the defendant to blame "an unhappy childhood" or "a poor choice of friends" for his behavior.[43] The objective reality of right and wrong were simply too obvious to be skirted, and mattered immeasurably more than an individual's flawed perception of them. Indeed, the correctness of that perception is what mattered and that could be assessed by the individual's practical ability to live in accordance with the laws and measures of value of his world. His sentiments would be, on that score, meaningless.

The starkness of such alternatives may strike present-day people as almost barbarically insensitive—as if "sensitivity" were here a relevant factor[44]—all the more as their sense of the absolute has been fatally eroded by the cult of relativism which, among other things,

---

that a realm, such as that of the arts, responded formerly to rigorously objective norms; in other words, each civilization promulgated rules that could not be deviated from either in painting, music, or poetry. The foundation for these rules was premised on the idea that the arts were merely instruments to apprehend the Real and therefore not means that carried their end in themselves and even less a trick for expressing arbitrary states of soul with which an individual could virally inflict his psychic derangement on a whole community or even a culture.

43. The confusion between the objective and subjective components of behavior has so muddled modern-day jurisprudence that it has become difficult to differentiate properly between the criminal and the victim, so much so that often, by way of ultimate reversal, it is the victim who is blamed, be it only implicitly, for the crime, in the sense that an inordinate amount of effort may be expended by the defense in attempting to discredit him. Some will claim that this is the only way to attain an unimpeachable verdict whereas, too often, the victim is victimized anew and justice becomes injustice. Indeed, inversion, whether moral, sexual, or intellectual, is a mark of the terminal phase of a society; no sector of mankind is immune from it.

44. It is not that sensitivity, so fervently advocated by humanism, has no place in the reckoning of reality, but that "feeling" must not replace intelligence, or that subjectivity must not be substituted for objectivity, because then it subverts the

allows for a virtually infinite spectrum of possible alternatives and a fathomless indulgence of that bottomless sinkhole called subjectivity. Doubtlessly, it would be easy, from the deceiving vantage point of our "age of information", to catalog the defects found in any traditional civilization, to single out the collective passions and superstitions of the masses and, especially, to berate them for their ignorance of other cultures or for their frequent intolerance of strangers or alien customs. We, today, know better—it is averred—than our ancestors about other people and hence have grown in tolerance and in understanding, not least with the "sinners" in our own midst who would formerly have been sanctioned.[45] What passes undetected, however, is that this modern sense of tolerance, disguised as charity or empathy, ultimately conspires with the dissolution of a cycle, of a morality, and thus of an entire society—because a society is built on morality or it ceases to exist. The godlike virtue of forgiveness presupposes a sound context whereas undiscriminating tolerance is, in reality, an avowal of a lack of conviction—or none at all—that, in turn, stems from a subhuman lack of profound values. This is the whole drama of modern nihilism and the true cause of man's individual sense of alienation. Far from causing repression, sacred values are the cure for all complexes.[46] It is only man in revolt who thinks otherwise.

natural order of the soul. In other words, intelligence, in the natural order of things, rules feeling which then serves as an extension of intelligence, otherwise one has the blind leading the blind.

45. In a typical inversion of logic, modern man assumes that the prosecution—vilified by moderns as persecution—of immorality in a traditional civilization created a cruelly repressive social climate when, in fact, the reverse is true: the priestly and royal models, and the saints available, along with clear-cut boundaries for model behavior in a normally functioning traditional civilization—we are not considering degenerate traditional civilizations—nipped the problem in the bud so that the necessity for so-called "persecution" did not arise except in the inevitable instances of abuse inherited from the Fall. In other words, sentimental tolerance, like a deficient immune system, allows moral "bacteria" to multiply and thrive when, in fact, the social body, like a healthy organism, is designed to throw off disease. Moreover, the refusal to understand that a parallel can be drawn between organic and social or moral disease, proves liberal humanism's lack of good faith: while everyone agrees about the fact of germs, few understand that the same laws of nature are transposable to the plane of the soul.

46. Provided, of course, they are not misapplied by over-zealous confessors or moral tyrants who appropriate an authority that, ultimately, belongs to God alone. But then it is not the values that stunt, but the abusers.

*
* *

Extremes conjure extremes: understanding that modern man, especially Western man, is, in many decisive respects, a hypertrophied brain, a counter-cult has arisen celebrating the spontaneous impulse of primal feeling, of pure spontaneity, or of an animal-like naturalness and the like. This counter swing of the pendulum comes with a whole vocabulary or nomenclature[47] which is not worth detailing since it is essentially artificial insofar as it pins labels on problems or attitudes that either should not exist or are illegitimate when considered with respect to man's true or theomorphic nature. And, in an inevitable reflex compensation, modern man reverts to primitive cultures to recover a wisdom that has been lost. All would be well if this reflex did not entail a parallel revolt against reason whereby intelligence is jettisoned in favor of pure intuitionism or is treated as the obstacle that segregates man's soul from communion with the primal cosmos—the *sahaja-samadhi* Râmana Mahârshi referred to as being his state, namely the "natural state" of consciousness, untrammeled by mental constructs and ego-desires. In a sense, this is poetic justice. Unfortunately, too often the sought after "cure" actually perpetuates the alienation or destruction begun with the excess of mentalism just described since instead of attempting to rise above himself man too easily confuses the supra-rational with the subhuman and therefore, in a misguided if not perverted lunge for freedom, seeks to reject all strictures, moral or otherwise, as being repres-

---

47. Thus one finds artificial expressions such as freeing oneself from the thralldom of the "persona", or the social mask imposed on us by society, of "finding oneself", "of realizing oneself", of overcoming "inferiority complexes", or simply the detailing of "complexes". It is not that such "complexes" do not exist, or that something like the "persona" is a pure figment, but that by focusing on such abnormalities one grants them a *de facto* status that, at some point, becomes self-fulfilling. Such concepts, as well as the problems linked with them, would literally evaporate in a social milieu that was normal. But, instead, one analyzes them to death, thus granting them an inveteracy of fact that makes it virtually impossible to talk about a human being in a truly intelligent way. In a normal society, God is the pole of focus, not man; and man is so to the measure that he conforms to a divine archetype—whence the reverence accorded elders which were not doddering old fools desperate to imitate youngsters or congealed in the bitterness of youth forever lost.

sive. A cult of sensation, of feeling, of intuition and of personality or of individualism is meant to replace—or avenge—the previously mind-centered burden of an education ignorant of the supernatural.

To take one specific example, the blight of industrialism has provoked a flight to animistic or shamanistic practices. One speaks of recovering the primal soul or *"nagual"* which is trapped underneath the so-called *"tonal"*[48] soul (the equivalent of the persona). This *"nagual"* entity is able to experience the plenitude of existence whose free flow the *"tonal"*, by its mental superimpositions of artificial classifications and categories, blocks. What is forgotten, in this uncritical wooing of the chthonic energies of the unconscious, is that man must learn to channel the force of instinct even if, in the process, he hobbles it. In other words, the nature force that is the all-powerful ally of the man of self-control and self-mastery, is the enemy of the unreformed man; the Chinese alchemists refer to this as riding the tiger, the corollary being not to arouse him lest one is well prepared to handle the raw fury of elements unleashed. At the same time, this so-called *"tonal"* soul—really the reasoning soul[49]—is condemned as a usurper when, in fact, and when it is all that it is meant to be, it is the delegate faculty of no less than the Spirit itself.[50] This antagonism, in essential form, can be reduced to the ancient dichotomy between Dionysus and Apollo, or the forces of nature and the forces of light, the polarization between being and consciousness, or being and truth, of music and mathematics—neither of which can be intimately divorced from the other. And what is forgotten, in this attempt to return to visionary being, is that man cannot but be a hypocrite with regard to his full self so long as he has not overcome and, especially, transcended himself spiritually. In other words, he is bound to live to some degree or another as a "house divided" until

48. This terminology is borrowed from Toltec cosmology whose shamanistic heritage is perpetuated, in hybrid forms, in the Mezzo-American tradition of the *brujos* or sorcerers and has acquired a hypnotizing currency in so-called New Age mysticism. We refer to it out of reluctant expediency (not by way of endorsement) given the reading public we intend to address.
49. It is not incorrect to speak of a "reasoning soul" since one cannot divorce reason from the subject; one could just as well say the "thinking subject".
50. The Spirit Itself, in man, is the intellect or the luminous cardiac center of consciousness with respect to which reason plays the role of a moon to the sun.

his conversion to the Spirit is completed. Thus, he must behave as he aspires to be—or should be—even if this may feel artificial and foreign with respect to what his instinctual self craves. In order to become virtuous, he may first have to pretend virtue, whence a forgivable, and in fact inevitable, type of hypocrisy which it would be suicidal to reject in the name of a false naturalness because naturalness, for man, is not synonymous with animalism or unbridled emotionalism. It is through the imitation of a normative model that the magic of real being may be actualized, the pattern of noble behavior conjuring, as it were, a reminiscence of true being from out of the depths of one's individual being which, however buried, is never dead. This is the basis of traditional iconography which, when it is all that it is meant to be, works by sympathetic magic with a divine archetype.

Now, in this headlong flight away from civilization, it is proposed that primitive man held a special communion with the animals who, traditional lore affirms, have a unique wisdom,[51] and that this ability to share an animistic relationship corresponds to a distinct superiority over civilized man. While it is true that nomadism is, originally, synonymous with primordiality and that the nomad's existence in intemporal space grants him—*de jure* but not necessarily *de facto*—a cosmological superiority with reference to civilizations which are inevitably temporal and thus condemned to degeneration, it is also true that civilization, in its turn, corresponds to an archetype—for instance, that of the Celestial Jerusalem—which completes the total possibility of man that nomadism alone cannot account for. Thus, if the loss of communion with animal spirits perpetuates, in certain decisive respects, the banishment from Eden, it is not true that this loss is as absolute as it may appear since the animals, as delegate faculties of the universal spirit (*mahat* in the Vedanta), are manifestations of a cosmic intelligence that is not limited to expressing itself merely in animal form. This means that there are other ways of recovering or of benefiting from the bond with that same universal intelligence which, before it actualizes as

---

51. This wisdom corresponds to the fact that they existed on earth before man and thus have a special knowledge of the universe which man, it is said, had to learn from them. The theory of evolution is a caricature of this because, precisely, it denies animals that wisdom, which is static or principial and not transformational.

nature in its multiple modes,[52] is pure Spirit. The figurative art of Christianity, both in its form as icons or in its statuary—incorporated in shrines and temples without, of course, discounting the towering figurehead of Christ himself translated in icons and crucifixes—is meant to give man a pictorial example of attitudes of humility, piety, dignity which will make him a worthy interlocutor with God. The same can be said for the art of Hinduism and Buddhism which incorporate a transfigurative understanding of the human form into their sacred art. In Islam, where the emphasis is not on man but on God and, by extension, on the divine genius of His creation, the didactic method of the art is geometric, abstract, and decorative and therefore does not offer an example in the way the figurative arts mentioned do.[53] However, what this art does is to convert the chaotic centrifugality of nature back into a unifying order in which the Oneness of the divine principle is multiplied star-like everywhere a thousandfold thus creating a salvific architectural net in which man cannot escape the Divine and is everywhere redemptively reminded of Him, each strand of his existence leading him back to the ubiquitous Center. The impersonal simplicity and uniformity of this art creates an attitude of soul that is both poor and rich at the same time, or a richness in poverty and a poverty in richness in which self-effacement becomes synonymous with radiance since the Light can only shine through an empty vessel.

And both forms of sacred art, the figurative and the geometric, produce an attitude of humility in the beholder. And it is this humility which is the *sine qua non*, the indispensable elixir for communion with God. True nomadic shamanism entails the same result in that the vision seeker or lamenter must consent to mortification before receiving a "message" from the divine, usually in an animal form. In other words, the animal—or animal spirit—will not "tell" the seeker anything unless his sincerity and faith have been thoroughly tested. The difference between shamanism and the world of the great religious civilizations does not lie in the difference of basic

52. The temple of idols housed in the Kaaba, which the prophet of Islam had destroyed, corresponds partly to a degenerate survivance of such animal or nature spirits worship.
53. Of course, there are always exceptions which confirm the rule. Thus one finds the depiction of human forms in the paintings of the Safavids who, in fact, are not Semites, which may account for the providence of the exemption.

attitude, since man's moral constitution is the same everywhere, but in the means employed. For the shamanist nomad, nature is the book of God and it speaks to him insofar as he learns to respect it. To cross the divide between awareness of the Divine and profane unawareness, between earthly and heavenly consciousness, between egocentrism and theocentrism is as impossible, whether for this nomad[54] or for civilized man, without virtue as it is to fly without wings. And this affirmation requires a rather lengthy exposition because it is often—and surprisingly—assumed that man can open the Forbidden Door separating the two realms simply by attempting to do so, by using the right technique.

*
* *

The suggestive and possibly over-quaint use of the term Forbidden Door may be taken by some to belong to a type of childish folklore. Or, it may be taken as the type of mythic tale, such as the image of the Forbidden Fruit, to induce man to keep to "the straight and the narrow" while binding him in a crippling moralism that forbids him to use his intelligence and imagination.[55] It may be dismissed as a type of lame grandmother's tale favored by people unwilling to stand on their own two feet. What such cynicism conveniently forgets, however, is that man in front of the Divine, is always a child. Without that preliminary understanding, his kingly or prophetic essence cannot be fostered. Thus, in Christianity, one finds the formerly prevalent worship of Christ the child in which devotees take care of him, much like in Hinduism the cult of Gopala or Krishna as child, and this form of devotion becomes, reflexively, a manner of learning oneself to be a child.[56] The nega-

---

54. There are many legends among the Indians and other nomads of presumptuous individuals who sought to steal divine secrets or powers on their own abilities and who, invariably, meet with disaster when not death.

55. One of the more heinous accusations against priests, whether in Ancient Egypt or in Christianity, is to exploit the pretext of the great mysteries of the unfathomable divine to cloak their alleged humbuggery—as if there were no objective basis for such legitimate secrecy—while "scaring" the faithful. But the fact of abuse, however deplorable, cannot be grounds for a wholesale indictment of the divine which is what freethinkers, who sling the accusations so recklessly, actually want.

56. Among the countless examples of this form of worship, one can mention that of the Rhenish mystic, Henry Suso who, in imagery that bespeaks the com-

tive corollary of "being a child" is to accept that the ego has a propensity to waywardness that can only be addressed with the medicine of salutary fear.

To be born a man is to be born captive of the lock of the five senses which both prevent and protect a human being from experiencing the possibility of a near endless[57] and terrifying scale of alternative states ranging from the angelic to the demonic.[58] Only a fool, lacking both in the fear of God and in gratitude for his God-given gifts, might be tempted to seek to experience these "other" states with an impunity that tempts the Devil himself.[59] Again, it must reaffirmed: to attempt to pierce the envelope of the merciful womb of the five senses presupposes forfeiting the very basis of what constitutes the nature of the human state and thus entails a dangerous, if not criminal ignorance of this state's *raison d'être*. To understand

---

pleteness of his mystical sincerity, repeatedly described himself as a nursing baby: "When he enjoyed the familiar of Eternal Wisdom he felt like a smiling babe held securely on its mother's lap, hungrily nuzzling its head against her breast" (*The Exemplar: Life and Writings of Blessed Henry Suso*, trans. M. Ann Edward). Similarly, St Bernard's *lactatio* communion is well known. Most recently, one has the example of Frithjof Schuon's own childlike relationship with the Holy Virgin which he represented in numerous icons.

57. Practically, or experientially, endless by virtue of the infinity of divine All-Possibility, but not absolutely endless by virtue of the Absolute which circumscribes everything, otherwise endlessness would unravel into nothingness.

58. For a child born in a traditional world, all is well: he is subjected from birth to a normative mold that, even if it imposes limitations on intelligence—or rather on intelligence in its total possibility—serves the formative purpose of enabling the maturation of a moral personality which, in fact, is the foundation of character in the sense that "fear of the Lord is the beginning of wisdom." Gifted individuals are never limited by such providential limitations and, conversely, less gifted individuals cannot benefit from the freedom granted by the removal of such limitations; quite to the contrary. In the modern world, however, the problem of cultural limitations can prove disastrous since a child is molded in a deforming set of mostly expeditious habits that are, at best, either superficially normative or, worse, destroy the sense of beauty and innocence while inculcating false ideas and reflexes about reality. Moreover, the stain of ugliness can wreak incalculable havoc in the soul's immanent sense of paradise for sanctity is beauty, which allows one to say: only the beautiful can enter Heaven.

59. Of course, the Devil, no longer exists or so would allegedly "intelligent" or "mature" people have us believe. The flatness of such a cosmos, eviscerated of all meaningful verticality, cannot be described—to say nothing of the lack of imagination of those who propound it. If evil does not exist, then neither does the good and the universe might as well have never been, or it would be a mere rock floating through incomprehensible space.

that man as such—not fallen man[60]—corresponds to a norm is to understand that our waking consciousness, and the manner in which all men apprehend the universe through the five senses, also corresponds to a norm. To seek to modify, manipulate, or violate this mode of perception is to play with fire because attempting to do so is, implicitly, to discredit the validity of this state. What measure of presumption or folly these urges are culled from can only be guessed at. "Moralistic prudery", some will conclude, while tripping over the little Vedanta they think they know, preferring to speak in terms of exotic notions such as the *chakras*, or the energy centers of the subtle body, or of the *koshas*, namely the doctrine of the sheaths enveloping the *âtman* or individual soul. These sheathes, they believe, must be discarded to reach the great cosmic mind or *Mahat*. The utter falsehood of this viewpoint lies less in the theoretical conception but in its practical realization. In other words, it is impossible to approach the Divine except through the Logos—in Buddhist terms, through the *nirmanakaya* or radiant Buddha-body manifested by Shakyamuni; and this entails reverence. Without homage of the Divine in its manifestation as the Logos, there is no rebirth in blessed immortality.[61] Moreover, even having mastered meditation or the *kundalini*, or having developed all kinds of tremendous psychic powers, it is possible to go straight to Hell. To understand this is to understand not only the gross vulgarity of attempting to manip-

60. Such a difference is absolutely crucial to grasp because the supposition that men as they happen to be in our times constitute a norm is so deeply entrenched as to suppress the last remaining vestiges of what man as *imago Dei* corresponds to. To take collective man as a norm is akin to grading students on a sliding scale: instead of using an absolute or ideal standard of knowledge, one grades according to a lesser measure of ignorance. This is the story of modern civilization in a nutshell, at least with regard to culture, philosophy, and politics.

61. Even in Islam, whose religious emphasis radically minimizes the human, the imitation of the Prophet constitutes the indispensable basis on which man approaches God. There is simply no religious tradition in which veneration is not an essential alchemical feature because man cannot return to the Absolute by bypassing man who is, after all, the quintessential creation of God. Even the worship of God Himself presupposes some human adequation in the "personality" of God otherwise worship would not only be meaningless, it would be impossible. What we are saying is that one cannot love an abstract principle: one loves God because He—to use a *personal* pronoun—is lovable, supremely so, in virtue of the fact that He is a being and not just an axiom or some ethereally blank luminescence.

ulate what is inherently a divine energy, whether one calls it the *kundalini* or otherwise, but to understand that one cannot experiment with the Divine as if it were an exotic pastime. The intention to do so is always a species of glorified egocentrism that is as far removed from *ad majorem Dei gloriam* as can be imagined, no matter the protestations of humility and of universal love such trespassers[62] into the Mysteries claim. What we are saying is that to achieve a state of serene dispassion, through some meditational technique, while a good in itself, guarantees nothing with regard to one's ultimate salvation. Bluntly stated, God will far prefer some cranky bungler, who stumbles along, stepping on every toe he finds but who fears Him reverentially, than a conceited "samadhist" who smiles benignly at the world's folly but who has no fear of Him.

To repeat, the commonality of perception of the universe shared by all men corresponds to a God-ordained norm, or *dharma*, which is inseparable from the earthly destiny of man. To disrupt this—on one's own gratuitous initiative—is to disrupt the normative ratios upon which the human state depends and, by extension, on which man's soteriological course depends. The dynamic ratio the five senses represent is built on universal laws of order and harmony that correspond to the nature of the realm to which physical man is heir while on earth. If it is objected that our bodily consciousness is an inferior mode of being—"For now we see through a glass, darkly" (I Cor. 13:12)—with which the heavenly state of the blessed is as the difference between sight and blindness, one will concede that this is so more because of the contents of consciousness than because of the mode. In other words, consciousness, to be divine, need not be visionary in the sensationalistic or empirical sense of the term, but simply noble. That is enough—for man—while on earth, otherwise God would have created a human being with operatively supra-mundane faculties. But then, this man would be elsewhere than on earth. At which point, creation would lose its point

---

62. Obviously, one has to take into consideration the fact that not all seekers of oriental wisdom are cut from the same cloth. It becomes difficult in a climate in which a hodgepodge of oriental doctrines, esoteric and otherwise, have become part of the vocabulary of "New Age" spirituality, to distinguish between "ego-trippers" and sincere travelers—*salikun*, in Sufism. And then there are those who simply have an esthetic or personal affinity with such possibilities and, therefore, integrate them into their lives as naturally as possible, spreading the good and the beautiful in virtue of their own inherent grace of soul.

for being—and so on and so forth in a kind of reductionism *ad absurdum.* Now to say that earth-bound consciousness corresponds to a norm is not to say that it is ideal. Although one cannot describe in empirical terms what the heavenly vision of the blessed is, one can assume, metaphysically, that all phenomena in Heaven are transparent in the sense that the divine unity is never eclipsed by the possibility of antagonistic duality the way it is on earth. The difference between the mystic's perception and that of profane awareness is really more an issue of depth than of surrealistic difference. And this dimension of depth results essentially from the aspirant's sincerity which perceives archetypal meaning in creation's attributes.

In order to properly situate creation and, specifically, the formal world of material forms—*nama rupa* (name and form)[63]—corresponds to a terminal point in the creative arc that extends first out from a divine cause to an effect (the process of *pravrtti marga* or "path of unfolding") and, having reached this terminal point of crystallization provokes a counter motion (*nivrtti marga* or "path of extinction") wherein the gross effect is reabsorbed back into its sublime cause.[64] In the first phase the effect testifies to the cause but, in so doing, reaches a point of denial because the duality entailed presupposes a negative modality of absolute difference which, however, can never be fulfilled. And this negative modality of separation is the basis for all the efforts of transcendence. However, no less equal in importance is the aspect of immanence whereby the effect is as the crystallization of both a divine quality and a divine desire, which proceeds out of it as the perfume and color of a flower or as radiance and joy.[65] To admit this is to grant that creation carries within itself a divine justification as crystallized in its forms, or at

63. The term is also synonymous with that of the *skandhas,* which are the aggregate of sensation, feeling, and consciousness that constitute the existence of a creature on earth and that, therefore, are to be mortified to death, if one follows an ascetic form of extinction. This, however, is an altogether different issue.
64. One signature of this dual process in creatures is the image of the heartbeat and the breath which, in Yoga, is considered to be a permanent process of offering oblations—certainly so in primordial man—when human consciousness is fully awake to what it is meant to be.
65. To the objection that the Spirit is beyond desire, or has no desire since It carries its fulfillment within Itself and is Self-enjoying, one will counter that inasmuch as creating corresponds to a need for the Self to enjoy Its totality, one is

least in its noblest forms, and certainly in its totality. And this justification, for man, entails what might awkwardly be termed a perfection of limitation which, of course, its purpose once fulfilled, must be dissolved with time. This "perfection of limitation"—which seems like a contradiction in terms[66]—means that the Divine creative urge consents to specify Itself in a limited form which crystallizes, like the sparks of a fire, a multitude of possibilities in which It mirrors Itself. Man is, of course, the supreme form of the Divine, in which God has chosen to limit Himself so as to radiate out to the periphery of His cosmic vastness. And, for man, it is through this form that he is meant to realize the perfection of formlessness. This perfection, however, is not consummated except, *mudra*-like, through the perfection of form and substance: attitude (or behavior) and consciousness, dignity and God-awareness—that, by extension, is also awareness of the trace of the Divine in creation wherever It manifests Itself. Thus, the *skandhas* or aggregates of consciousness referred to previously are not meant to be dissolved—that is sublimistic nonsense!—but actually purified and transfigured: sensation, feeling, memory, intelligence, operating within the confines of the five senses, are truly meant to experience the Divine as theophany and therefore become limitations only when, out of inertia, the soul becomes their slave instead of the lord it is meant to be.

False spiritualists dream of transcending, not themselves—that would defeat the purpose—but states of consciousness, namely, as mentioned above, to pierce through the envelope layers (*koshas*) enclosing consciousness from the immortal spirit within. There is

allowed to speak of the Self—on the level of Brahma *saguna* or God with "attributes"—intending and, thus, desiring, all the more as "desire" is a dimension of Its Self-enjoyment without which It would not be complete. In like manner, one can speak of the Self desiring to save and this notion entails the possibility, albeit on a relative level, of a want requiring satisfaction. This "want," however, is not a lack in the sense of penury, but an internal dimension of divine gracefulness and abundance wherein God is seeking Himself, so to speak, in a wonderful game—*lila* or divine play—of love and knowledge. An eloquent illustration of this is found in the stories of Radha and Krishna.

66. In fact, this is merely a paraphrasing of Aristotle's doctrine of teleology or the perfection of formal fulfillment every created form strives to achieve.

an assumption that this can be done at will, without first "seeking permission from the gods", for example, as alluded to above, by taking psychogenic substances. And it has been assumed that ingesting such substances was a normal mode of relationship between man and the Divine prior to religious moralism, as if moralism created the notion of sin and was not in fact responding to a pre-existing issue. And it is even supposed that the supreme state of absolute consciousness (*turiya* in the Vedanta) can be accessed by such psychogenic substances or, at least, that they can open the way. At the risk of repeating ourselves, we must say that two major things are overlooked in this extravagant and ultimately Luciferian presuppositon: the first is that our waking state (*vaishvanara*) is, as stated earlier, a necessary or divinely willed state of existence. Thus, it will take revenge on those who wantonly misprize it.[67] The second thing that is overlooked is that the waking state, at its level—unlike the dream state (*taijasa*)—is analogically, if not intimately, connected to the supreme state (*turiya*).[68] This waking state's main capacity is that of objectivity, even if it is an objectivity calibrated to the material world as well as to the phenomena, both inner and outer, which are part of *Maya*'s weaving. It is thus, *mutatis mutandis*, a witness in its own right, in the outward world, of the manifested forms of the Divine Self; no less. Thus, learning to live in the "here and now", as

67. This could be in the form of a disease or in the form of a gradual crippling or shriveling, the atrophied backlash of a faculty or vital dimension spurned. In this respect, asceticism does not qualify as an abuse, unless, of course, the intention is not virtuous.
68. In the Mandukya-Upanishad, this final state of consciousness, *turiya*, is defined as "neither subjective nor objective experience," (sometimes translated as "neither consciousness nor unconsciousness") which does not mean that it is neither subjective nor objective but, on the contrary, that it is both subjective and objective at once, together, but neither alone. In other words, it is both awareness and non-awareness in the sense that deeper awareness beholds reality in its non-differentiated substance before it differentiates. To repeat, the difference between the profane waking state and that of the holy man's is not that each beholds an altogether different reality but that what the former perceives is a flat picture of creation in which he divines none of the symbolism whereas the holy man beholds everything in depth and sees that it is vibrant with spiritual presence and meaning. Frithjof Schuon has this to say about these two modes of consciousness: ". . . the difference between ordinary vision and that enjoyed by the sage or the gnostic is quite clearly not of the sensorial order. The sage sees things in their total context, therefore in their relativity, and at the same time in their metaphysical transparency." (*Light on the Ancient Worlds*, Ch. "Man in the Universe", Perennial Books, 1965, p. 116)

opposed to some dream state of subjective musings and longings, corresponds to a real victory over the ever-shifting and treacherous realm of the psyche that, when left to shift for itself, acts as a solvent seeking to weaken or to emasculate the Spirit. To formulate the issue in different terms, one could say that man's sin or limitation is not the fact of his existence, which, to repeat, is necessary and willed by God, but in existing outside of God, or in wishing to do so. While it is true that, from the point of view of the Fall, fleshly existence entails a stigma, this scourge has less to do with the possibility of flesh as such than with man's will, otherwise one would not encounter the possibility of some saints whose bodies were exhumed incorrupt, nor *a fortiori* the possibility of the Assumption.

Because of his outwardness, man idolatrously divorces the effect from its divine cause: "They know only an outward appearance of this lower life" (Quran 30:7). Fallen man is a fragmented man and therefore not only fragments what he sees but is then prone to absolutize or idolize the fragments. Thus, through the "waking state", he superimposes—Shankara terms this *adhyasa*—his own limited awareness, desires, and fears on a universe that, for the contemplative, presents itself in its essential mode as a unified tapestry of inspiring beauty and grandeur, and as a formal liturgy of truth. Or, the subjective man, insofar as he can objectively enjoy beauty, vampirizes phenomena: instead of seeing things as signs of the Divine, he takes their animic force to feed his own boredom, egoic needs, or fantasma. He is really a thief because he takes the gifts of creation without due sacrifice. He assumes, inasmuch as he has access to it, that he can just plunder beauty and pleasure at will, take a woman or seduce a man, or enjoy a savory meal unaware of the transfigurative possibility of divine communion hidden in the seemingly exclusively sensual pleasure. Not surprisingly, if offered the means to enjoy ecstatic experience, a blessing normally reserved for only the most graced of mystics, he will do so without the slightest scruple about the price, assuming that if something is there for the taking, take it. And, in so doing, he may dull his soul to Heaven, or, to paraphrase St. Paul, eat his own damnation because, in exchange for His gifts, God requires our soul.

The above comments bring us back to the important issue of experiencing divine states through means other than grace. Our assumption, throughout this article, has been that truly mystical states are not obtainable without the intervention of divine grace (namely of a state operated only *ex beneficio*) that, in turn, presupposes the right virtuous predisposition. If such is the case, what is one to make of claims by people using psychogenic substances, be it through natural means such as mescal mushrooms (appropriately called "flesh of the gods")[69] and other plants, *ayahuasca* ("vine of the soul") for instance, or through artificial chemicals, who maintain that ingestion of such substances has led them to a beatific vision of Reality? The first thing one will want to consider is that joy itself, even ecstasy, is not synonymous with spirituality per se and that is why the Church has always treated all purportedly mystical rapture and various transmundane states with extreme circumspection until the agent—or cosmic agency—of that rapture is properly identified. In other words, the cause of the rapture could be angelic or satanic or anything in between, which proves the relative nature of ecstasy when taken in the absence of other more reliable criteria, the main one being a permanent change of character for the better.[70] Thus, it is not enough by half to claim a mystical insight after having experienced, as a result of ingesting a hallucinogenic

---

69. In every realm of creation, there are specific creatures or substances—an archetypal one being soma, "the King of Plants", said to have been grown in Indra's heaven—that can embody or symbolize the divine. Thus, in the vegetal realm, one finds psychogenic substances, also known as "entheogens" (*en-theo-gen* or "putting the god within"), which open onto the supra-formal realm and which, in principle and in the "right hands", can serve as catalysts towards the divine. Furthermore, in the case of psychogenic mushrooms, it should be noted that they are fungi which feed and grow on the decomposition of life; this feature gives them a kind of "gatekeeper" role in the natural order between life and death, or between life and the supernatural and, as such, can only be manipulated with the greatest of caution because they can precipitate the user into realms which, as alluded to over and over in these pages, he is not prepared to handle. The case of these "fungi" illustrates, at their level, the saying *corruptio optimi pessima*—which is exactly their effect in the unprepared or unqualified soul.

70. Of course, the reverse is not necessarily true: if a mystical experience does not change a person's character, this does not necessarily prove its falseness, because a person may not live up to a grace received. Indeed, the issue is not simple to adjudicate. Other criteria consist in the quality of the experience, that is to say not only the beauty of the experience but the absence of trivial or ugly elements; also, the homogeneity of the experience, as well as its objectivity—admittedly, this latter factor not being easy either to ascertain or to explain. However, a garbled account of a purportedly true mystical experience should raise suspicion as to its authenticity, because in the case of a true or Heaven-

substance, intense universal love in which the ego is extinguished into an ineffably beautiful communion with all creatures, especially if, after having returned to sobriety, the individual remembers only the vividness of the feeling but is unable to maintain the genius of the experience itself. The same applies to beholding the universe transfigured into an apparently celestial light, hearing ethereal choruses, and the like.[71] From the point of view of practical spirituality, the only one that concerns man concretely, these experiences are not only totally beside the point,[72] they may actually prove fatally misleading, inducing a false sense either of confidence or goodness, thereby relaxing the soul's impetus towards God or the urgency towards salvation, or just softening the soul up until it becomes tearfully loving in the most indiscriminatingly besotted of fashions or pathologically meek.

That said, it is entirely possible that a psychogenic substance, by producing a disruption of the normally fixed parameters of consciousness, can dislocate an individual's understanding of reality and open the imagination to a much vaster frame of reference. Of course, this can also fissure the psyche, perhaps permanently, in a diabolic delirium of cascading horrors, or even lead to madness.[73]

---

sent experience, the recipient's subjective state is as extinguished before the wonder of the divine object, leaving a distinctly clear impression in the memory afterwards because it is unmixed, in its distinctive features with that person's defective individuality. Much, if not all, of these criteria should be obvious to common sense.

71. Even though this should be apparent to an intelligent person, it is far from understood by everyone. And this obliges us to belabor the point a bit: if a drunk derives a sense of omnipotence, or of superiority, from a fermented brew, does that mean that he is actually stronger or better than before? And does the sudden omnipotence or sense of superiority bear any resemblance to the divine power coursing through the universe, or is it a pure delusion? It is a delusion insofar as the individual has an accidental experience of strength, but the experience of strength is that of strength itself even if it is morally meaningless for that person. This comparison, when transposed to the claim of mystical states, may help to situate the nature of the confusion above.

72. Once again, Schuon: "There is in metaphysics no empiricism: principial knowledge cannot derive from any experience, though," he continues, "experiences—scientific or otherwise—can be the occasional causes for intuitions of the intellect . . ." (*Roots of the Human Condition*, "Preface").

73. To look at things from another point of view, we can quote the Swiss astrologer, Charles Vouga, who mentions the traditional assimilation of the planet Saturn with the function of St. Peter, "guardian of the gates of Heaven, who forbids entry to those who have not fulfilled the requirements that he alone knows"

It is easier to open the Forbidden Door than, once opened, to close it.[74] However, if in the best of cases, in which the experience can loosen the grip of material illusion holding the soul prisoner in a suffocatingly small cocoon, to free it for flight in an immense universe undreamt of previously in which objects that once seemed disconnected share intelligent relationships formerly unsuspected, the individual will be courting the devil. Once again, intention may make the difference between success and disaster, without forgetting the concomitant of a particular individual's intelligence and innate predisposition for Heaven. This last factor can account for the fact that an experience which for one individual could be ruinously dissipating could be ascentionally unifying for another. But let none presume of who they are in this respect, for presumption shares a close kinship with folly. *In vino veritas*: wine brings out the truth of a soul. Thus, wine and intoxication, which are central symbols of the divine and of mystical union, in vulgar people, serve only to make them grosser: "I have trodden the winepress alone; and of the people there was none with me. . . . And I will tread down the people in mine anger, and make them drunk in my fury, and I will bring down their strength to the earth." (Is. 63:3-6)

One might counter that there are cultures, the Amazonian Indian tribes notably, in which ritualized drug use is a normal mode of communion with the divine. However, this fact calls for two comments that should apply to similar cultures. First, because of destiny, the psychic homogeneity of such peoples combined with the con-

---

(*Une astrologie pour l'ère du verseau*, Ch. "Saturn"). To quote him further: "He [Saturn] ensures that we have the necessary solidity, that we are changed into marble or, to be more exact, into a diamond. . . . One finds many experiences of ecstasy which are made while ignoring the order Saturn represents, and these are those produced by drugs. Out of ignorance for the Laws, one wishes to force one's way through and there are terrible repercussions in the individual. One must not go into the 'Transfinite' without Saturn having said: 'Now you are ready . . .' (*ibid.*)." And this readiness is the stern formation of character Saturn provides in the planetary economy of an individual horoscope.

74. In an Arabian version of the tale, the hero, young Shaykh Hakim, after opening the door out of greed and curiosity, having lost everything he loved, is condemned to a life of poverty. However, this fate can be reversed as in the Faustian bargain: a man can have his best wish granted on earth but at the cost of eternity. Thus one reads in the Quran (42:20): "Whoso desireth the harvest of the Hereafter, We give him increase in its harvest. And whoso desireth the harvest of the world, We give him thereof, and he hath no portion in the Hereafter." Everything has its price.

sistency of their shamanic cosmology, cannot be compared with the porous psychic heterogeneity of Westerners. Thus, if under the guidance of a shaman, an Amazonian Indian can enter into communion in a predictably consistent manner with a spirit animal which will act as a teacher and a guide, the same result cannot be necessarily expected for a Westerner intent on duplicating the experience. Secondly, the prevalence of such ritualized psychism obviously, in the light of all that has been developed in this chapter, does not constitute a superiority per se. In fact, there is reason to believe that much, not all, but much of this culture constitutes more of a degeneracy[75] when compared with the possibility of what one will call golden age spirituality where a man was his own priest and carried Heaven's Law directly and naturally within himself and had access, through his intellect, to divine and earthly wisdom. Immanence of divine wisdom is the human norm. Once lost, man depends on priestly intermediaries and on outward agents. To assume that ancient or primordial man communed with Heaven through psychogenic plants[76] is to misunderstand the nature of the

75. Mircea Eliade has been wrongfullly derided as an academic ignoramus for alleging a similar thing in his book, *Shamanism*, where he mentions that drug-induced ecstasy is a degenerate practice and therefore a latter-day phenomenon. Karl Kérenyi, in his book, *Dionysos*, avers the same. To understand this is to understand the epidemic nature of magic, sorcery, and spiritism where things are not done in "God's Name" but for the sake of harnessing powers. Similarly, one cannot fully endorse a "spiritual" practice such as the Peyote cult of the so-called Native American Indian Church, which, even if it rescues drunks and promotes some social good, cannot compare to the centrality and fullness of the Sun Dance religion, the qualification for which is rooted in a good character or, namely, what is universally understood by all religions to be the assimilation and development of virtues. One is reminded here, of the story of the Shoshone medicine man, John Trehero, whose vision of two trails, one that stopped after a short distance near the hills and one that went over the hills "into the horizon," going on and on without end. Seven Arrows, his spirit helper, explains that the first one is the way of Peyote and the second that of the Sun Dance religion. (*Yellowtail, Crow Medicine Man and Sun Dance Chief,* "as told to Michael Oren Fitzgerald," University of Oklahoma Press, 1991)

76. It has been proposed that the heart of the Eleusynian mysteries involved the use of drugs which is properly monstrous because this hypothesis destroys the premise of the intellect which is self-sufficient by its very nature. It is also to ignore the countless examples of sanctity, notably in the Medieval Christian West where mystics communed with Christ directly through the sacrament of the host to the degree that the material world lost its hold on them. Many of them, in defiance of all scientific laws of nourishment, subsisted on the host alone, their bodies exuding fragrant oils while they carried the taste of honey

heart-intellect which is prophetic by its very nature and therefore independent of any physiological catalysts.[77]

*

* *

The sin of curiosity, which prompts one to open the "door", comes with the loss of wonderment. And this loss is also that of innocence. If man could take pleasure in life's beauties, as God intended him to, no restless urge would goad him to pierce the veil of the five senses to seek out extra-human states. He would find contentment in the plenitude of his spiritual possibility here on earth. It may seem simplistic—or boring—to affirm that one of the goals of the spiritual life is to rediscover a state of perfect simplicity attendant on a sense of gratitude wherein man would find blissful sufficiency in the blessings of the day vouchsafed by a beneficent Creator mindful of granting him the love of kith and kin, the shelter of a beautiful home and garden, victual bounties, and a measure of wealth whereby to enjoy them.

And, more profoundly, man must understand that his relationship with the Divine is determined by faith—and its extension as *ratio fidei*, St. Anselm's "understanding, or intelligence, of faith"— because, on earth, the Divine is necessarily hidden. Thus: blessed are those who have not seen yet believe. It is faith, the degree of one's personal faith, that makes this earth both bearable and enjoyable—bearable with regard to its trials and enjoyable with regard to its benefits.[78] And faith entails gratitude, hence a King David can declare, "I will wash mine hands in innocency, that I may publish with the voice of thanksgiving, and tell of all thy wondrous works." (Ps. 26:6-7)

in their mouths in keeping with the sweetness of their heart. Thus, it is the body which translates the effect of a divine cause and not the other way round as the above hypothesis implies, betraying thus its materialistic intent.

77. The fact that modern science has discovered that there are "pleasure" centers in the cerebral cortex that can be stimulated by electrodes to emulate states of mystical bliss and love proves not that the soul is reducible to matter, as one might want to suppose, but that the body, being an expression of the soul, is composed of physiological correlates of the soul's attributes.

78. It may seem strange to link faith to enjoyment, but less so when one understands that it is faith that grants one an in-depth appreciation of earth's gifts.

It is piety that opens the gates of Heaven. The soul which has not rippled in awe or whose heart has not leapt for joy at the mention of the Name of God is unfit to meet the Lord. What we want to say is that God does not just want our mind, or our awareness—even if non-mental.[79] He wants our hearts so that we can say, echoing Hannah's canticle: "My heart rejoiceth in the Lord" (1 Sam. 2 : 1). And deeper still, and fuller, He wants our divine likeness born of sanctifying virtue so that, to quote from William of Thierry's *Golden Letter* (*Epistola aurea*), we can declare: "O Lord, our God, who created us to your image and likeness, that is, to contemplate you and to enjoy you whom no one contemplates to the level of enjoyment save insofar as he is made like you".[80] It is then on this holy basis, to rejoin our opening theme, that the soul can aspire to the "face-to-face meeting" with the Divine.

When the heart melts in love, then the mind, like the full moon rising, reflects the solar truth and beauty of the Lord and it is all that it is meant to be, not just a cold, impersonal, meditative witness but a luminous mirror of the radiant Intellect.

79. This cautionary qualification is meant as a cuff to all those who expend—with prolix verbal virtuosity!—a great amount of intellectual energy to prove that language is a shackle to intelligence and that it must be somehow surmounted or discarded before illumination can be attained. What is forgotten is that creation is issued from Divine Speech, as the Upanishads teach, and that man's capacity for language, which reflects it, is a god-like gift enabling intelligence to seize Reality.

80. *Exposition on the Song of Songs* 1 (Sources chrétiennes, Paris, Cerf 1940).

Chapter 15

Even at Night, the Sun is There

Gray Henry

"In the name of Allâh, the most gracious, the most merciful"

A few years ago I was living in an English village outside Cambridge while researching my doctorate and working with the Islamic Texts Society, an academic organization which publishes important works from the Islamic heritage after having had them translated into English.

One evening as I reached to switch off the bedside lamp, I noticed my arm would not stretch out to do so. In fact, I found I was not able to pull the blankets up about me except by using my teeth; neither arm seemed to function. When I tried to take a deep breath it seemed as though my lungs were incapable of expansion. At the approach of a cough or sneeze, I held my arms closely around my chest for fear the sudden and painful enlargement of my breast would rip me apart. When I arose the next morning, the only way to get out of bed was to hang my knees over the edge and slide off since my upper torso had become powerless. I couldn't even raise my arms to brush my hair. Turning the bathroom faucet was an excruciating affair. By holding the bottom of the steering wheel in my fingertips, I was able to drive to the village clinic. The doctor concluded I had some type of virus for which there was no treatment other than time.

A day or so later, my husband and I were to fly to Boston for the annual congress of the Middle East Studies Association. I viewed my affliction as an inconvenience which would ultimately pass and decided to ignore my condition. I noticed, however, that on the day we were to leave England I began to have trouble walking, and getting upstairs was extremely difficult. By the time we reached the hotel room in Boston, more and more of my system seemed to be shutting down. I could no longer write or hold a teacup, bite anything as formidable as an apple, dress myself, or even get out of a chair unless assisted. Everything ached. I could not move my head in the direction of the people I was speaking to—I looked straight ahead, perhaps seeing them from the corner of my eye.

Friends gave all kinds of advice that I simply shrugged off. The worst part was lying in bed at night. It was impossible to roll onto either side, and my whole body felt on fire with pain. It was terrible to have to lie flat, unable to make any shift whatsoever all night long. I thought to myself, "If only I could scratch my cheek when it itched, if only my eyes were not dry but cool, if only I could swallow without it feeling like a ping-pong sized ball of pain, if only I could reach for a glass of water when thirsty during the long night."

*

* *

As we traveled on for work in New York, I continued to make light of my infirmity and to ignore suggestions that I seek help. On the plane, however, when it was necessary to ask the stewardess to tear open the paper sugar packet, I suddenly realized—"I can't even tear a piece of paper!" I requested that a wheelchair await me in New York and that I be transferred to a flight home to my parents in Louisville, Kentucky. Since my husband was obliged to stay in New York, a kind soldier returning to Fort Knox helped me during that leg of the trip. I felt like a wounded fox that wanted nothing more than to return to, and curl up alone in, the nest of its childhood. My father met me, and the next day took me for every test imaginable. Nothing was conclusively established—was this rheumatoid arthritis, or lupus? I was brought to my parents' house and at last put in my childhood bed with a supply of painkillers, which I was not inclined to take. Since I found I could tolerate great pain, I wanted to observe the situation and know where I stood. I started seeing my body as an object separate from me and my mind which witnessed its ever-declining condition. When my legs finally "went," with knees swollen like grapefruits and feet incapable of bearing me up, I mused with a kind of detached interest, "Oh, there go the legs!" The body seemed to be mine, but it was not *me*.[1] Later that night *it* hap-

---

1. "Islamic physicians saw the body of man as but an extension of his soul and closely related to both the spirit and the soul . . . They envisaged the subject of medicine, namely man, to be related both inwardly through the soul and the

pened. As I lay gazing out my bedroom door and noticed the carpet in the quiet hall, I thought, "Thank God I'm not in a hospital and the hall is not linoleum and that I am not subjected to the clatter of ice machines and the chatter of nurses. I know I'm in trouble and I do need help, but *that* would be too great a cost for my soul."

A few moments later I became aware that I seemed to be solidifying, my body had stiffened and seemed to be very much like a log—I was totally paralyzed. Then, I seemed to separate from my body and lift a distance above it. I glanced back and saw my head on the pillow and thought, "This is remarkable—I've read about this kind of thing . . . I am thinking and my brain is down there in my head! I must be *dead*." I considered what to do. At the moment of death in Islam, the dying person repeats the *shahada* "There is no divinity except God."

As I thought the phrase, *"La ilâha il-Allâh,"* I noticed that I seemed to be pulled back towards my heart—as if by a thread of light. But then there I was—quite all right, but utterly rigid and still. The light of the moon comforted me as it passed through the leafless November branches making patterns on the blankets. I thought, "Even at night, the Sun is there. Even in darkness and death, the Light is present." The season seemed to parallel my state.

I then began to imagine my future. I have friends who are paralyzed who have always been placed along the sidelines for various events. Had I now joined them? Was I now out of the normal life of others? I began to see myself like a hunchback or a dwarf. I had always been known for my inexhaustible energy and activities. I could always, somehow, get to my feet and do one more thing. This was now over. I would no longer be able to do anything. I thought of people in this world who have impressed me most—the Mother Teresas of our world. I realized that what was exemplary in these people was not what they *did*, but what they *were*; the state of *being* which determined their movement was what actually inspired others. And so I set upon a plan of inward action: The best thing I could

spirit, and 'outwardly' through the grades of the macrocosmic hierarchy to the principle of cosmic manifestation itself. . . . whatever may have been the historical origins of Islamic Medicine, its principles cannot be understood save in the light of Islamic metaphysical and cosmological sciences." From S. H. Nasr, *Islamic Science* (London: World of Islam Festival Publishing Co. Ltd., 1976), p. 159.

do for others would be to sanctify my soul, to let my state of being become radiant. Having concluded this, I felt things were in order.

In the morning I was found, fixed in place; I was given eggnog—chewing was over. My husband came from New York and I recall marveling when I observed him. He could, without considering the matter in depth, shift his position in a chair, scratch his forehead, or lean over to pick up a dropped pencil—all painlessly! Imagine—reflex action! Occasionally if I really wanted to move, for example, my fingers, I would think to myself, "All right, now, I-am-going-to-try-to-move-my-fingers," and I would concentrate my entire attention on the task. With *incredible* pain and focus, I could at most shift a few millimeters. It struck me profoundly that when someone is able to move in this world without pain—that is, in health—that he *resides in paradise on earth* without ever being aware of it. Everything after that is *extra.*

Ultimately, it was decided that I should be given a week's course of cortisone so I could return to my children and the British specialist who might be able to figure out what I had. The cortisone was miraculous and frightening—I could actually walk and pick up things—yet I knew that I couldn't.

*
* *

On the return to Cambridge, it was decided that I should be removed overnight from the cortisone. I then discovered what withdrawal symptoms are—a level of pain that seems to consume one alive with fire. But the pain was nothing compared to the frightening mental confusion I experienced: I could not grasp proper thinking, or even normal reality. What I needed was not only a doctor, but a kind of scholar/saint who could describe to me the hierarchy of meaning so that I would not be so painfully lost. I suppose true doctors are a combination of all three.

The Islamic physician/philosopher was called a *hakim* (a word which refers to wisdom). I grasped some rosaries and clung to them like lifelines thrown to a drowning man, and I made it to the light of dawn on the invocation of God's Name, my sanity intact.

The English specialist could not make a conclusive diagnosis. Our Vietnamese acupuncturist suggested toxins had built up in the entire muscle system and prescribed massage during steam baths to release them. It sounded definitely worth doing. At the same time, I had come to that point that the very ill come to, where, though they take advice with gratitude, inside of them something has dimmed and they no longer wish to make any effort. Pleasantly, I had reached a great calm within. Each day I was brought downstairs where I directed the preparation of meals and worried the children who saw I could no longer sew on a button or sign a check. I was resigned to never moving again. I had never experienced such peace. It was touching that people prayed for me and it was lovely that so many asked after my condition. I felt like an upright pole stuck in the middle of a moving stream.

In the spring, my husband had work in Arabia and suggested that as he would be traveling by private plane I could as easily sit in a dry climate as I could in cold, damp Cambridge. I agreed to go. On my arrival a dear friend managed to get me to Mecca, because she thought that prayers in the mosque there would help. But when I found myself before the Kaa'ba, I felt it would be wrong to pray for my affliction to be lifted, as its good had come to outweigh its bad, in terms of my heart and soul.

*
* *

A few days later I was asked to give a talk in Jeddah. I declined, explaining that I was unable to research and prepare a topic properly. Friends said they would be delighted to do this, if I could come up with a subject. I answered, "All right, why does *this* happen to someone, in the view of Islam?" The passages they wrote down and translated to English from both the Koran and *hadîth*, the sayings and recorded deeds of the Prophet Muhammad—all seemed to say the *same* thing. In Islam, illness is understood to be a great blessing because it is an opportunity, if borne with patience free of complaint, to purify oneself of past sins—to burn away wrong thoughts and deeds.

As I delivered my talk, it began to dawn upon me why Muslims always reply with *Al hamdulilah* (the same as *Alleluia*) whenever anyone inquires as to their health. I had always wondered why one could ask someone who suffered from an obviously terrible physical or emotional pain or loss, "How are you," and all one could get out of him was, "All praise belongs to God." I kept wanting them to talk about their pain with me, to share their suffering, and I wondered why they would not. *Suddenly I realized that they were praising God for their state of being.* The suffering they endured, no matter how great or small, was an opportunity to be purified, which is the very aim of human existence. In an instant, my own illness was seen in a new light. I no longer patiently tolerated it—*I loved it, I flowed with it.* I saw how blessed I was to have been given, not something small, but something as total as paralysis.

As I loved my illness, my fingers suddenly began to regain movement. Bit by bit the movement in my hands returned, until at last in late spring, I was restored. What had been the most painful and difficult time in my life turned out to be the best thing that ever happened to me. I had gained a deepened perspective, a sense of proportion and freedom. God had blessed me with near total dependence on others, a symbol reminding me of my utter dependency on Him. And even when I had not been able to move one inch, I was able to be in touch with His Divine Presence.

> O God, to Thee belongs praise for the good health of my body which lets me move about, and to Thee belongs praise, for the ailments which Thou causes to arise in my flesh!
>
> For I know not, my God, which of the two states deserves more my thanking Thee and which of the two times is more worthy for my praise of Thee: the time of health, within which Thou makest me delight in the agreeable things of Thy provision, through which Thou givest me the joy to seek the means to Thy good pleasure and bounty, and by which Thou strengthenest me for the acts of obedience which Thou hast given me to accomplish; or the time of illness through which Thou puttest me to the test and bestowest upon me favors: lightening of the offenses that weigh down my back, purification of the evil deeds into which I have plunged, incitement to reach for repentance, reminder of the erasure of misdeeds through ancient favor; and, through all that, what the two writers[2] write for me.
> —Imam Zayn al Abidin Ali ibn al Husayn, Al Sahifat
>   Al Kamilat Al Sajjadiyya (William Chittick, tr.)

(The illness described above was later diagnosed as Guillain-Barré Syndrome.)

---

2. According to Islamic belief there is an angel on either shoulder who records one's good and bad deeds.

Chapter 16

Outline of a Spiritual Anthropology

Frithjof Schuon

At the summit of the ontological pyramid—or rather beyond all hierarchy—we conceive the Absolute, which comprises by definition both Infinitude and Perfection: Infinitude which radiates intrinsically and extrinsically, that is, which on the one hand contains the potentialities of the Absolute, and on the other hand projects them; and Perfection which is identified with these potentialities and which, by the effect of projection into Relativity, gives rise to all possible qualities: in the divine Being, in the world and in ourselves. If the Absolute is pure Reality, the Infinite will be Possibility, whereas Perfection or the Good will be the totality of the contents of the Infinite.

Now the contents or modes of the divine Perfection pertain essentially to the orders of Knowledge, Love and Power, which evoke the human faculties of intelligence, sentiment and will. The substance of the divine Perfection is the divine Subject inasmuch as It knows and It loves, and in knowing and loving, It wills; on the one hand, Knowledge and Love cannot represent an irreducible duality, they cannot but be two modes of the same Subject, and on the other hand, both Love and Knowledge are prolonged by a single "energy," that is, precisely, Power or Will. For Will is not an end in itself: one cannot will except by virtue either of a knowledge or of a love.

In God, Knowledge, Love and Power are absolute; but they are equally infinite and perfect, since God is Absoluteness, Infinitude and Perfection. Thus this ternary, which is only differentiated subsequent to ontological projection, is necessarily and supereminently found in the Absolute Itself, hence in the divine Essence, but in an undifferentiated manner, so much so that it can be affirmed that the Essence is Knowledge, or Love, or Power, but not that it contains these realities in distinctive mode as is the case on the level of ontological/cosmological projection.

*

* *

All "anthropology" depends on a "theology" in the sense that every science of man must prolong a science of God, for: "Let us make man in Our image, in likeness to Us."[1] To speak of a "spiritual anthropology" is already a pleonasm—to say man is to say spirit—but it is justified in a world which, having forgotten the divine, no longer can know what is human.

God is "pure Spirit": which is to say, implicitly, that He is at once Knowledge, Love and Power. Power—or "Will"—is a function either of Knowledge or of Love; each of these two "Energies" or "Hypostases" is prolonged by a Power proper to it, then by an Activity deriving from this Power.

Similarly for man: being made of spirit, he is made of knowledge and love—or of intelligence and sentiment—then of will, the latter necessarily drawing its inspiration from one or the other of these two faculties. Knowledge and love proceed from the spirit as light and heat proceed from the sun; in the latter, these two energies or functions remain in a quasi-undifferentiated state, which is to say that they are indistinguishable in practice from the very substance of the sun.

In other words: there is in man—as in God, his Prototype—a single spirit, and this spirit is knowledge and love; and there is a will which prolongs each of these and which in turn is polarized into intention and activity, according to whether it is intrinsic and latent, or on the contrary extrinsic and efficient.

The reality of God and that of our final ends determine at one and the same time: our conviction; our happiness; our activity; our virtue. Conviction pertains to intelligence; happiness, to sentiment; activity, to the will inasmuch as it prolongs intelligence; virtue, to the will inasmuch as it prolongs sentiment. Intelligence, in discerning the real, establishes conviction or certitude; sentiment, in loving

---

1. "Image"—taken in the sense of something "relatively absolute"—denotes that man, on account of his deiformity, can in no way be a relative degree of animality; "likeness," on the contrary, means that in another respect the analogy between God and man can only be relative, otherwise precisely, God would not be the Absolute. It behooves us to add here that there are animal species which in their way are nobler than given human individuals, which is perfectly evident.

the good in all its forms, enjoys happiness; and the will, in their train, brings about both spiritual activity and virtue, or contemplative concentration and moral conformity. Which is to say that the reality of God and of our final ends determine all that we are.

*

* *

We have said that man is knowledge and love and that each of these elements is prolonged by the power that is adjoined to it; in other words, man is intelligence and sentiment and each of these elements determines a third element, the will. If in this perspective intelligence-knowledge has as its complement sentiment-love, it is because this complementarity is in their nature; it is the polarity of the masculine and the feminine. According to another perspective, equally possible, what has precedence is not contrasting complementarity, but, on the contrary, affinity: we would say then that man is made of intelligence and will—the latter being the immediate secondary mode of the former—and that it is sentiment or the feeling soul, in short, the affective faculty, which prolongs both will and intelligence.

But one could equally place intelligence alone at the summit, and consider will and sentiment as its subordinate prolongations, the will appearing then as masculine, and sensibility as feminine; together they constitute our character, which in fact combines what we will and what we love; this is the domain of the virtues. This way of looking at things—inasmuch as it places intelligence at the summit—pertains, as does the preceding one, to the intellective perspective; in both cases, the driving force of the way is Truth, Idea, Intellection, and not some threat or seduction.[2]

The perspective of love, on the contrary, places love at the summit and views intelligence and will solely as functions in service of love; love participates in the divine Love and is called upon to melt in it; whence the sensualist epistemology proper to this perspective. Moreover, this perspective readily makes love coincide with will:

2. Starting from the axiom that integral spirituality comprises by definition a doctrine and a method, we would say that the first is linked, to some degree or other, to discriminative and contemplative intelligence—active and passive, if one will—whereas the second comprises operative will and stimulating and interiorizing sensibility. The initiatic qualification combines all these elements.

where there is "loving," there is "willing"; intelligence or "knowing" being more or less reduced to dogmatic speculation and to apologetic activity, or even simply to pious registering of the dogmas.

*

* *

Man, we have said, is made of intelligence, sentiment and will; now the notion of "sentiment" is no doubt ambiguous due to the fact that there is a pejorative prejudice attached to it: one generally distinguishes between reason and sentiment, attributing to the second a character of unrealistic subjectivity, hence of arbitrariness and passion, whereas reason is supposedly objective; and in so doing, one loses sight of the fact, on the one hand, that reason is objective only on condition of basing itself on exact data and of proceeding correctly, and on the other hand, that sentiment lacks objectivity only when it is excessive or misplaced, hence erroneous, not when it is justified by its object and is, by this fact, a kind of adequation; love of holy or noble things, even to the extent that it is only sentimental, is in conformity with reality, which is not at all the case with skeptical, agnostic or atheistic rationalism.

"God is Love": divine Love is not identical with human sentiment, but the latter is analogous to the Divine Love. Human sentiment reflects, in its essential function which is the faculty of loving, a hypostatic quality, and consequently it cannot have a merely privative character and be opposed in practice to the intelligence.

Intelligence, sentiment, will; or truth, virtue, freedom.

*

* *

In our heart, the elements knowledge, love and power—or intelligence, sentiment and will—are combined as so many dimensions of one and the same deiform subjectivity. Outside our heart, these faculties become dissociated in the sense that intelligence seems to reside in the brain or the mind, and sentiment or affectivity in the soul, the *psyche*; the will, and with it the capacity to act, is then combined with each of these regions—for we have need of will in order to think as well as to practice the virtues—but at the same time, its seat is the heart, which in this case assumes a particular, extrinsic role, independently of the heart's intrinsic character of synthesis and root. In other words: although the substantial dimensions of the heart-intellect are knowledge, love and power—intelligence, sentiment, will—we can consider the heart as the region of the will alone as soon as we attribute intelligence to the mind and sentiment to the soul, in which case our perspective is more exterior; and we can do so with all the more reason given that, in a certain respect, the will is identified with the subject, with the individual who "wills"; who "wills" because he "loves."

However: as the heart is in itself the seat or the organ both of sentiment and intelligence, as well as of will, it must be said that a sentiment comes from the heart to the extent that it is profound, exactly as is the case with knowledge.[3] Indeed, thought pertains to the brain or to the mind, but intuitive knowledge, which is not the fruit of reasoning, pertains to the heart; similarly, ordinary senti-ment, determined entirely by phenomena, comes from the soul or from the sensibility, but profound sentiment, which is nourished *ab intra* by the very essence of love—while most often having outward perceptions as its occasional cause—comes from the heart and not from the animic sensibility alone; for the heart by its nature is love as well as knowledge and power. It is therefore rootedness in the heart which characterizes, not the mere phenomenon of love to be sure, but the greatness of this sentiment; such is clearly the case with mystical love, which is inspired only secondarily or incidentally by external factors; but such is also the case with natural love to the extent that it is profound, or in other words, to the degree that its quality, in its depths, rejoins love as such.

From the heart-intellect come knowledge and love, but it is not with the heart that we are able to think and feel; by contrast, it is with the heart—with pure subjectivity—that we are able to concen-trate our spirit, and that is why we say that the will in general and concentration in particular pertain to the heart, even though in its depths, it is not limited to this function and possesses equally and *a priori* knowledge and love. The mind receives its light from the heart, and its power is to comprehend, to discern, to think; and in so doing it opens the way to Intellection, which, however, it cannot

3. Thus, common opinion is far from being mistaken when it equates the heart with love; as for the intellective character of the heart, it goes without saying that ordinary language cannot adequately express it.

produce. As for the soul, it can love the good, or things that are good; and loving them, it must practice them, otherwise it excludes itself from the happiness which good things confer; love in itself comprises beauty, goodness and beatitude. In a word: if the mind permits comprehension, and the heart in its turn concentration, the soul has the power of being virtuous, and consequently of being happy through its very nature.

There is no valid virtue without piety, and there is no authentic piety without virtue; which means that these two coincide, and also that the accent is on piety inasmuch as piety relates more directly to God. We could also say in consequence, that if intelligence brings about discernment, and will concentration, sentiment brings about piety, devotion, the sense of the sacred, then gratitude and generosity; these attitudes being linked to the qualities, both divine and cosmic, of Beauty, Goodness and Happiness.

*
* *

There are two ways of viewing the modes of human subjectivity: either we consider them in respect of their functions, in which case we distinguish intelligence, sentiment and will; or else we consider them as regions, in which case we distinguish between the world of the heart and that of the brain, the three faculties acting in both sectors or at both levels.

Normally and primordially, human intelligence realizes a perfect equilibrium between the intelligence of the brain and that of the heart: the first is the rational capacity with the diverse abilities attached thereto; the second is intellectual or spiritual intuition, or in other words, it is that eschatological realism which permits one to choose the saving truth even apart from any mental speculation. Cardiac intelligence, even when reduced to its minimum, is always right; it is from this that faith is derived whenever it is profound and unshakeable, and such is the intelligence of a great number of saints. Nevertheless, the absolute norm or the ideal is the plenitude—and not the sufficient minimum—of cardiac intelligence and the perfect expansion of dialectical intelligence.

The treasures of inner science must in fact be able to establish and communicate themselves: to establish themselves, for mental formulation contributes to the actualization and assimilation of the immanent lights of the heart, and there, moreover, lies the role of meditation; to communicate themselves, for cardiac intuition must be able to radiate as do all good things. On the one hand, the essential certitudes are everything; but on the other hand, man needs to exteriorize himself the better to be able to interiorize himself; synthesis requires analysis; man, who is as if suspended between two dimensions, cannot do without language. Without the heart, there would be neither message nor doctrine; yet the well-formulated idea is necessary for the awakening of immanent knowledge. To say that mental intelligence—when it is what it ought to be—is inspired by that of the heart-intellect, is another way of saying that the intelligence of the heart manifests itself in and by that of the mind.

The mind is the moon, and the heart is the sun: even though the brightness of the moon is nothing other than light, this light belongs to the sun and to no other source. In the heart, knowledge coincides with love; the heart delegates truth to the mind and virtue to the soul. This is to say that intelligence is pious to the extent that it is total.

The fact that spiritual realism, or faith, pertains to the intelligence of the heart and not to that of the mind, permits one to understand that in spirituality, the moral qualification outweighs the intellectual qualification, and by far.

The refusal to understand a transcendent truth lies moreover less in the intelligence than in the temperament, the imagination, the will; which means that the obstacle lies, either simply in attachment to the world and to the ego, or on the contrary in an innocent and honorable limitation of the heart-intellect, but not necessarily of the heart-love; otherwise there would be no narrow-minded saints. In any case, familiarity with transcendent concepts is far from being a guarantee of realizatory capacity; moreover, spiritual realization can content itself with key notions, not very demanding intellectually but nonetheless anchored in the science of the heart and centered on a virtuality of Intellection.

The most extensive metaphysical science is subjectively superficial and can go astray if it is purely bookish, and similarly, the most efficacious social virtues are worth nothing from the spiritual point of view if they are not linked to the spirit of devotion and the sense of the sacred. As piety is "supernaturally natural" to man, a virtue without piety is tainted with pride, and for that reason loses all its value; and similarly, as Intellection also springs from our "natural supranature," an idea which we grasp only from without and as a mental form is not a "knowledge" to which we can lay claim, although we have a certain right to it in proportion to our sincerity and also our piety, precisely. Everyone is compelled to truth, no one is compelled to gnosis.

There is nothing more contradictory than a cerebral intelligence opposing itself to cardiac intelligence, whether it be to deny the possibility of knowledge or to deny the ultimate Knower: how can one not feel instinctively, "viscerally," existentially, that one cannot be intelligent, even very relatively so, without an Intelligence "in itself" and which is both transcendent and immanent, and not grasp that subjectivity by itself is an immediate and quasi-fulgurating proof of the Omniscient, a proof almost too blindingly evident to be able to be formulated in words?

The intelligence of the heart is *a priori* the one which, outside any mental workings, possesses the sense of the real, and thereby the sense of proportions as well; now to have the sense of the real, is also, and even essentially, to have the sense of the sacred.

The intelligence comprises four functions: objectivity, subjectivity, activity, passivity; in the mind, these are reason, intuition, imagination and memory. By "objectivity" we mean that knowledge is inspired by data which are exterior to it, and this is so in the case of reason; by "subjectivity" on the contrary, it must be understood that the knowledge in question operates through existential analogy, this is to say that it is inspired by data which the subject bears within himself: thus, we have no need of reasoning in order to observe the natural mechanism of another subjectivity, and this is the faculty of intuition. In "activity," the intelligence relives, recreates or combines the possibilities which are known to it, and this is the imagination; in "passivity," the intelligence registers and preserves the data which present themselves to it. Since these four functions pertain to intelligence in itself—independently of the mental faculties which we have enumerated—the intelligence communicates these functions to its so to speak feminine complement, sentiment, and to the will which prolongs both sentiment and intelligence.

In the macrocosm, "reason" is the order of things, whereas "intuition" is their symbolism and their providential entanglement; "imagination" is then the inexhaustible diversity of forms and destinies, and "memory," the persistence of possibilities throughout the vicissitudes of time and space.

It might be well at this point, by way of parenthesis, to take into consideration the fundamental human phenomenon which is the hierarchy of mental types: the contemplative or sacerdotal, the combative or princely, the practical or industrious, the obedient or loyal;[4] these qualities or predispositions, while rigorously distinguishable, can always combine, and they do so even necessarily, in indefinitely varied proportions. In each of these models, or within each of their combinations, are additionally situated the four temperaments and the twelve astrological types;[5] but all this is of a much more contingent order than the fundamental constitution of man—that of man as such—which opens out onto the divine order and has no meaning outside of it.

*
* *

The spirit, we have said, is polarized into knowledge, love and power, which permits the following question to be asked: what is the spirit in itself? The answer is given by the very elements of this polarization: the spirit—or the subject—is knowledge, not inasmuch as it looks "outward" and perceives "objects," but inasmuch as, bearing within itself its unique and total object, it looks "towards the Inward" and "extinguishes itself"—or on the contrary "realizes itself"—in the consciousness of its own one and indivisible substance. If we start from the idea that the object of knowledge is Truth or Reality; that the object of love is Beauty; and that the

---

4. This last definition clearly means, not that the superior types would be devoid of loyalty, but that the fourth type—scarcely capable of governing himself—has *grosso modo* this one quality only, which as it were constitutes his way; and this of course to the extent that the individual is limited to this typological possibility.

5. In summary, men are differentiated by sex, age, temperament, zodiacal type, caste and race.

object of the will is the Good; then, starting from this idea or this datum, we could affirm that the spirit or the subject, which by definition knows, loves and wills, is in its essence Truth, Beauty and the Good.

The Absolute "radiates" by virtue of its intrinsic "dimension" of Infinitude, which brings about the "springing forth" of *Mâyâ*, the latter both containing and producing reflections, world, beings: it is thus that one must distinguish a fundamental separation within the human subject, namely the complementarity spirit and soul; the first element belonging to the universal order, and the second constituting the individuality, hence the *Mâyâ* of the microcosm.

It has been said, quite paradoxically, but not without reason, that the great mystery for the human spirit is Relativity rather than the Absolute; or *Mâyâ* rather than *Âtmâ*. But one could also say, and more profoundly, that the mystery of mysteries is the internal Radiation of the Absolute; ungraspable Cause of the first Cause, and Cause without entering into any causal chain.

Chapter 17

The Prodigal Returns

Lilian Staveley

Extracts from the book of that title, written by Lilian Staveley, who also wrote *The Golden Fountain.*

To a woman atheism is intolerable pain: her very nature, loving, tender, sensitive, clinging, demands belief in God. The high moral standard demanded of her is impossible of fulfillment for mere reasons of race-welfare. The personal reason, the Personal God—these are essential to high virtue. Young as I was, I realized this.

*
* *

I entered a stagnant state of *mere* resignation, whereas accompanying the resignation there should have been a forward-piercing endeavor to reach out and attain a higher spiritual level through Jesus Christ: a persistent effort to light my lamp at the Spiritual Flame to which each must *bring his own lamp,* for it is not lit for him by the mere outward ceremony of Baptism—that ceremony is but the Invitation to come to the Light: for each one individually, in *full consciousness of desire,* that lighting must be obtained from the Savior. I had not obtained this light. I did not comprehend that it was necessary. I understood nothing; I was a spiritual savage. Vague, miserable thoughts, gloomy self-introspections, merely fatigue the vitality without assisting the soul. What is required is a persistent endeavor to establish an inwardly felt relationship first to the Man Jesus. His Personality, His Characteristics are to be drawn into the secret places of the heart by means of the natural sympathy which plays between two hearts that both know love and suffering, and hope and dejection. Sympathy established—love will soon follow. Later, an iron energy to overcome will be required. The supreme necessity of the soul before being filled with love is to maintain the will of the whole spiritual being in conformity with the Will of God. In the

achievement of this she is under incessant assistance: in fact everything in the spiritual life is a gift—as in the physical: for who can
produce his own sight or his own growth? In the physical these are
automatic—in the spiritual they are accomplished only, as it were,
"by request," and this request a deep all-pervading desire. We cannot of our own will climb the spiritual heights, neither can we climb
them without using our will. It is Will flowing towards will which carries us by the power of Jesus Christ to the Goal.

*
* *

Slowly I learnt to differentiate degrees of Contemplation, but to
my own finding there are two principal forms—Passive and Active
(or High) Contemplation.

In meditation is little or no activity, but a sweet quiet thinking
and talking with Jesus Christ. In Passive Contemplation is the beginning of real activity; mind and soul without effort (though in a
secret state of great love-activity) raise themselves, focusing themselves upon the all-unseen Godhead: now there is no longer any
possible picture in the mind, of anyone nor anything, not even of
the gracious figure or of the ways of Christ: here, because of love,
must begin the sheer straight drive of will and heart, mind and soul,
to the Godhead, and here we may be said first to commence to
breathe the air of heaven.

There is no prayer, no beseeching, and no asking—there are no
words and no thoughts save those that intrude and flash unwanted
over the mind, but a great undivided attention and waiting upon
God: God near, yet never touching. This state is no ecstasy, but
smooth, silent, high living in which we learn heavenly manners.
This is Passive or Quiet Contemplation.

High Contemplation ends in Contact with God, in ecstasy and
rapture. In it the activity of the soul (though entirely without effort
on her part) is immensely increased. It is not to be sought for, and
we cannot reach it for ourselves; but it is to be enjoyed when God
calls, when He assists the soul, when He energizes her.

And then our cry is no more, "Oh, that I had wings!" but, "Oh,
that I might fold my wings and stay!"

292

*

* *

God says to the aspiring soul: "Come, taste of paradise and taste of heaven, and then return thou to the earth and wait, but not in idleness, and suffer many things till thou become perfect."

*

* *

Since Contemplation is so necessary for Union with God and for the soul's *enjoyment* of God—is it a capacity common to all persons? Yes, though, like all other capacities, in varying degrees; but few will give themselves up to the difficulties of developing the capacity; and it is easy to know why, for our "natural" state is that we work for that which brings the easiest, most immediate, and most substantially visible reward.

Those who could most easily develop their powers of contemplation are those to whom Beauty speaks, or those who are delicately sensitive to some ideal, nameless, elusive, that draws and then retreats, but in retreating still draws. The poet, the artist, the dreamer *that harnesses his mind*—all can contemplate.

The Thinker, *thinking straight through,* the proficient business man with his powers of concentration, the first-rate organizer, the scientist, the inventor—all these men are contemplatives who do not drive to God, but to the world or to ambition. Taking God as their goal, they could ascend to great heights of happiness; though first they must give up ("sacrifice") all that is unsavory in thought and in living: yet such is the vast, the boundless Attraction of God that having once (if only for a few moments) retouched this lost Attraction of His, we afterwards are possessed with no other desire so powerful as the desire to retouch Him again, and "sacrifice" becomes no sacrifice.

Truly, having once known God, we find life without Him to be meaningless and as unbeautiful as a broken stem without its flower: pitiful, naked, and helpless as the body of a butterfly without his wings.

*

* *

Sins are all imperfections, thickenings of the soul from self-will: pure soul is necessary for the *happy* reception of this celestial activity, and because impurities are automatically dissipated by this activity, and the dissipation or dispersion of them *is the most awful agony conceivable* when too suddenly done, what is bliss to the saint is the extremity of torture to the sinner. Now we come very fearfully and dreadfully to understand something more of the meanings, the happenings, of the Judgment Day. Christ will inflict no direct willful punishment on any soul; but when He presents Himself before all souls and they behold His Face, immediately they will receive the terrible might of the activity of celestial joy. The regenerated will endure and rejoice; the unrepentant sinner will agonize, and he must flee from before the Face of Christ, because the agony that he feels is the dispersal of his imperfect soul; and where shall the sinner flee, where shall he go to find happiness? For saint and sinner alike desire happiness, and there is in Spirit-life only one happiness—the Bliss of God. So then let us be careful to prepare ourselves to be able to receive and endure this happiness, even if it can at first be only in a small degree, so that we shall not be condemned *by our own pain* to leave the Presence of God altogether and consequently lose Celestial Pleasures; let us at least prepare ourselves to remain near enough to know something of this tremendous living.

The more we experience God, the more we are forced to comprehend that we have in us an especial organ in this spirit with which we can communicate with God and by which we can receive Him without the mind or body being destroyed. For when God takes up His abode with a man He will communicate Himself to this loving Spirit-Will or Intelligence in ecstasies. And through His Son He will communicate Himself in another manner, to the heart and mind, so graciously, with such a tender care, that without the stress of ecstasy we are kept in a delicate and most blessed Awareness of God. In these ways we can know, even in flesh, the beginnings of the true love-stage, the beginnings of the angelic state, which is this same love-state brought to completion by Beholding God.

Although this blessed condition of Awareness of God is a gift, and at first the mind and soul are maintained in it without effort on their part, it being accomplished for them solely by the power of the Grace of God, yet later—and somewhat to their dismay after receiving such favors—they discover that it must be worked for in order to be maintained. The heart must give, the mind must give, the soul must give: when they neither work nor give they may find themselves receiving nothing: God ceases to be present to them. Generosity on our part is required. It works out in experience to be always the same thing that is needed for our perfect health and happiness—reciprocity. Without us maintaining this reciprocity we shall experience *extraordinary disappointment.*

*

* *

We hope for much from "education"; but what education is it that will be of enduring value to us? Is it the education which teaches us the grammars of foreign languages, scientific facts, the dates when wars were won, when kings ascended their thrones, princes died, artists painted their masterpieces, that will bring us to our finest opportunities of success? To the soul there is little greater or less chance of success offered by the degree of "polish" in the education we have the money to procure: the peasant who cannot read or write may achieve the purpose of life before the savant: we know it without caring to acknowledge it to ourselves: the education that we really require is the education of daily conduct, the education of character, the education by which we say to Self-Will, to Pride, and to Lusts, "Lie down!"—and they do it!

When a soul knows herself, has repented and become redeemed, she knows all other souls, good or bad: there are no longer any secrets for her, no one can hide himself from her: she sees all these open and living books, reads them, and avoids judging and bitterness in spite of the selfishness, stupidity, and frailty revealed on every page: she finds the same faults in herself; selfishness, stupidity, and weakness are engraved upon herself; the redeemed and enlightened soul with tears perpetually corrects these faults: the unenlightened soul does not—this is the difference between them.

Like knows like: it does not "know" its opposite, but is drawn towards its opposite before and without "knowing" it: here we have the cause of the condescension of the Good towards the imperfect, and of the aspiration of the imperfect to the perfect long before it can "know" the perfect. Without this attraction of like to opposite the imperfect could not become the perfect (we desire, are drawn to God, long before we are able to know Him). The imperfect is able to become the perfect by continually aspiring to it: it gradually becomes "like". There are no barriers in spirit-living, therefore there is nothing to prevent the soul becoming perfect, save its own will-failure. The barrier existing between material- or physical-living and spirit-living can only be overcome in and by a man's own soul: in the soul these two forms of living can meet and become known by the one individual, who can live alternately in the two modes, but it is necessary that the will and preference shall be continually given and bent towards spiritual-living, physical-living being accepted patiently and as a cross. Then flesh ceases to be a barrier to spiritual-living. This is the work of Christ and of the Holy Ghost. Because the soul has recaptured the knowledge of this rapturous living we are not to suppose that it is possible to continually enjoy it here or introduce its glories into social and worldly living: it is between the soul and God only; but earth-life can and should by this knowledge be entirely readjusted.

*
*   *

We have a Critical Faculty. It is above Reason, because it sifts and judges the findings of Reason, throwing out or retaining what Reason has deduced. This is a Higher-Soul faculty: it concerns itself solely with knowing Perfection. Reason is not occupied with knowing Perfection, but in analyzing and digesting all alike that is brought to it.

It is to the Critical Faculty that art, poetry, and music appeals, and make their thought-suggestions. We do not enjoy music because of the noise, but because of the thoughts suggested by it— we float upon these motion-thoughts (we may float low, we may float high, and do not know to where; but it is somewhere where we cannot get without the music), so we say we love the music; but it is the emotion-thoughts we love. The sound and the thoughts suggested by it appeal to the Critical Faculty of the Soul, and, if it is perfect enough to be accepted by this faculty, we may pass, for the time being, into soul-living, not only very delicately, tentatively, and nothing to be compared to the soul-living, produced by the Touch of God. When God communicates Himself to the soul, she lives in a manner never previously conceived of, reaching an experience of

296

living in which every perfection is present to her as Being there in such unlimited abundance that the soul is overwhelmed by it and must fall back to less, because of insupportable excess of Perfections.

Chapter 18

Hope, Yes; Progress, No

Huston Smith

I no longer desired a better world, because I was thinking of creation as a whole: and in the light of this more balanced discernment, I had come to see that higher things are better than the lower, but that the sum of all creation is better than the higher things alone.

—St. Augustine, *Confessions,* VII, xiii, 19

I only pass on to others what [has been] passed on to me. If there is any lack of learning in my writing, any obscurity of expression or superficial treatment, you may feel sure that it is in such places that I am most original.

—St. Bellarmine

Hope is indispensable to human health—to psychological health most immediately, but because man is a psychosomatic whole, to physical health as well. Situated as we are in the Middle (hence middling) World, vicissitudes are a part of the human lot: external vicissitudes (hard times), and internal vicissitudes—the "gravitational collapse" of the psyche that sucks us into depression as if it were a black hole. Against such vicissitudes hope is our prime recourse. Ascending a sheer-faced cliff, a mountaineer can lodge his pick in an overhead crevice and, chinning himself on it, advance. Hope is the psyche's pick.

In the primordial outlook hope is vertical, or at least transhistorical. "Vertical" here means that the fundamental change that is hoped for is an ascent of the individual soul through a medium— the world—which does not itself change substantially but provides stable rungs on which the soul can climb. Or in cases where the prospect is viewed collectively and in worldly terms—as in the Kingdom of God that is to come "on earth," the coming age of the Maitreya Buddha, or Islam's Day of Resurrection—it is assumed that this Kingdom will differ in kind from the history that preceded it and will be inaugurated by God's direct if not apocalyptic intervention. In neither its individual nor its collective version is progress in the traditional sense envisioned as sociopolitical, the gradual amelioration of man's corporate lot through his collective efforts and ingenuity.

By contrast, the modern version of hope is emphatically historical. And its imagery is horizontal, for its eye is on an earthly future instead of the heavens. In one sense all hope is future-oriented, but that of modernity is doubly so—for mankind as a whole as well as for the individual. In fact, hope for individuals is for the most part tied to hope for history; it is on the hope that human life as a whole can be improved that hope for the individual primarily relies. If the traditional view rested its case on the fact that in boiling water bubbles rise, the modern view hopes to escalate the water itself.

What effected this Copernican revolution in the way hope—or progress; the same thing—is conceived? Three agents.

The first was science. Around the seventeenth century the scientific method began garnering information at an exponential rate. True, its findings pertained to physical nature only, but even so, the vista was breath-taking. Moreover, by virtue of improvements that occurred in methods of experimentation, the new understanding of nature could be *proved* to be true. It seemed evident, therefore, that in this one respect at least, corporate progress was being effected. Never again would mankind be as naïve as it has been regarding its habitat.

On the heels of this progress in pure understanding came science's utilitarian spin-off, technology. It multiplied goods, relieved drudgery, and counteracted disease. Since these are not inconsiderable benefactions and, like the findings of pure science, can be dispensed—bestowed on people, unlike character, say, which each individual must acquire for himself—it again looked as if mankind as a whole was advancing. History was getting somewhere.

These two causes for the rise of the vision of historical progress are well known. The third reason has been less noticed because it is privative; it involved not the appearing but the vanishing of something. Science and technology would not have changed man's outlook a fraction as much as they did had they not been reinforced by scientism. Its epistemological assumption that only the scientific method gives "news about the universe" produced the ontological conclusion that corporeal reality is the only concrete and self-sufficient reality there is. In a single stroke the mansion of being was reduced to its ground floor. The consequence for hope was obvious: if being has no upper stories, hope has no vertical prospect. If it is to go anywhere—and hope by definition implies a going of some sort—henceforth that "where" could only be forward or horizontal. The extent to which the modern doctrine of progress is the child, not of evidence as it would like to believe, but of hope's élan—the fact that being indispensable it *does* spring eternal in the human breast and, in the modern world view, has no direction to flow save forward—is among the undernoted facts of intellectual history. If the ratio between evidence and hope in the idea of historical progress were to be laid squarely before us, we would be humbled in our estimate of ourselves as rational creatures.

As things stand, we do not see that picture clearly and historical progress remains the kingpin of the modern outlook. Seeping and soaking, permeating, probing, it diffuses like mist, discovering every corner, saturating every cell. In biology we have Darwinism and evolution, in cosmology an evolving universe. In history we have *The Idea of Progress* (J. B. Bury) and Marx's escalator that rises from slavery and serfdom through capitalism to the coming classless society. In philosophy we have Henri Bergson's early-century *Creative Evolution* and Ernst Bloch's mid-century *Das Prinzip Hoffnung,* and in theology Jürgen Moltmann's Protestant *Theology of Hope* and the Catholic writings of Johannes Metz. Cutting across the lot, as if to pull the vision together, is the work of the scientist, poet, and mystic Teilhard de Chardin, as focused in *The Phenomenon of Man.*

Somewhere in his ponderous *All and Everything* Gurdjieff says in effect, "Now I am going to tell you something people are not going to believe." The statement galvanized our attention, for it seemed to us that the author had been trafficking in notions of this genre for some pages. With an interest the book had not up to then aroused, we raced to discover what this truly incredible truth was to be. It appeared that it would have to do with the reason for wars, and this looked promising; it would be very good, we thought, to know why human beings decimate their kind. We were not prepared for the answer. The reason for wars, it turns out, is that the moon feeds on human beings. Periodically its fare grows slim and a war is needed to beef it up. We thought: the man is right—absolutely, completely, unequivocally right. This people won't believe.

We relate this incident because we sense that it may be about to be reenacted with its roles reversed. Readers who feel that the notions of the last several chapters have already pressed credulity to the limit—notions like the survival of bodily death, incorporeal realms that are more real than physical ones, or infinite beatitude as the human possibility—may find the point we are about to make, the last major one of this work, excessive; *de trop,* as the French would say: too much. In traditional China a gentleman might be found protesting that a friend's modesty "exceeds the permitted limits." Readers may feel that what we are about to say likewise exceeds limits; the limits of credulity most obviously, but possibly of propriety as well. For we are going to say that progress is an illusion; not only future progress but past progress as well. The last part of that statement will have to be qualified, but in essence it will stand. Utopia is a dream, evolution a myth.

To refer to the illusion in its total sweep, we coin the word "prevolution." Phonetically the word joins *pro*gress to *evolution,* showing the two to be faces, prospective and retrospective, of a single, Janus-like deity. In addition the word suggests the current *prev*alence of the cult of this god. The impounding of these ideas in a single word gives us a running start into our theme.

If Western man were to see that this god is a false one—or to put it the other way, that prevolution is a fiction; it *has* not happened and *will* not happen—the modern age would be over, for the notion is so much its cornerstone that were it to crumble, a new edifice would have to be built. By the same token, the case against the notion is going to be difficult to make, for it is not easy to dislodge a notion that undergirds an entire epoch. We shall take it in segments. Working our way backward, we shall look successively at the long-range future, the short-range future, the short-range past, and the long-range past.

The long-range prospects for our universe are not encouraging. Whether it ends by collapsing into a widening black hole[1] or winds

---

1. "The black hole of today is more than a black hole. It is a symbol 'experimental model,' and provider of lessons for the collapse Einstein predicted in far later days for the universe itself." John Wheeler, in Jagdish Mehra (ed.), *The*

down to an entropic deep freeze four degrees above absolute zero does not much matter; be the finale a bang or a whimper, its human import is the same: our universe will not support life indefinitely.[2] Given the rate at which the sun is spending its energy, our particular solar system will die long before our universe does, of course. In 5 billion years it will have thinned out to 250 times its present diameter and swallowed our planet.

Such prospects caused a former dean of Canterbury Cathedral to cry, "Short views, for God's sake, short views." But with the ecological crisis, energy depletion, the population explosion, and the

Physicist's Conception of Nature (Dordrecht-Holland/ Boston—U.S.A.: D. Reidel Publishing Company, 1973), p. 215.

2. I insert a footnote which is at least interesting; whether it is more than that the reader may decide for himself. When in 1961 I had my first audience with His Holiness the Dalai Lama, I resolved in advance not to take much of his valuable time and after about ten minutes arose to take my leave. He stood up with me, and though we had been conversing through an interpreter I heard him say to himself in English. "I must decide what is important." There was a moment's pause, then a smile broke over his face and with the words "Please be seated," he gestured to the divan. When I next arose an hour and three-quarters had elapsed for the most remarkable morning of my life. What secured for me this gift was not, it turned out, good karma but rather a ruse. In Asia calling cards are useful, and the one I had sent ahead in requesting the audience carried in its lower left-hand corner the words "Massachusetts Institute of Technology." It proved to be a magic name, for along with his sanctity and erudition, His Holiness has a lively scientific interest and a mechanical bent: he strips down Austin Healeys and dismantles watches to reassemble them. My card had misled him into thinking that he had a flesh-and-blood scientist in his living room, and he had decided not to pass up the opportunity this afforded.

Specifically, he wanted to check two scientific reports that had recently come his way. One of these concerned DNA; he wanted to know if it bore at all on the doctrine of reincarnation. The other concerned cosmogonies. He had heard of Hoyle's steady-state theory in which a continuing influx of hydrogen (from who knows where) compensates for the thinning out of matter through the world's expansion, and also of the so-called big-bang theory which posits that at its start our universe consisted of a superdense kernel that exploded and has been expanding ever since. To these I was able to add a third, which Harlow Shapley called the bang-bang-bang theory: the theory that the present expanding phase of our universe will be followed by one of collapse, with no reason why the cycle should not repeat itself, accordion fashion, indefinitely. His Holiness nodded, saying that of the three this last was the most nearly right. It has been interesting to note that in the decade since he registered that opinion the steady-state theory has been retired from the running. One waits with interest to see which of the other two receives the astronomers' imprimatur.

To insert brackets within parentheses, I cannot refrain from adding another point which strictly speaking has nothing to do with the topic under discus-

proliferation of nuclear weapons, to say nothing of the interlocking, depersonalized bureaucratization of life,[3] the short-range future, too, looks bleak. Systems analysts, synthesizing their computer data, tell us we are on a collision course with disaster; Robert Heilbroner's *The Human Prospect* is not pleasant reading. Poets and philosophers had anticipated their warning. The century in which politicians have preyed on hope unprecedentedly, promising "The Century of the Common Man," "The War to End All Wars," "The War to Make the World Safe for Democracy," "The Four Freedoms," "The Great Society"—this century of maniacally inflated expectations has seen utopian writing come to a dead stop.[4] "Hope," Kazantzakis concluded, "is a rotten-thighed whore." Even Bergson, who moved Darwin into philosophy, came at the end to the view that man was "being crushed by the immense progress" he has made. Sartre is not profound, but he is a shrewd phenomenologist, and on the existential level where he works he advises that "we must learn to live without hope." The morning newspaper lists a film that is showing at a local cinema. Titled *I Have Seen the Future and It Doesn't Work,* it is billed for "mature" audiences.

sion but which mention of the Dalai Lama invariably brings to mind. No one I know who has been in his presence has failed to be impressed, least of all myself. But the way he impressed me was almost the reverse of my expectations, insofar as I recall having had any. For it was not as if he wore a halo or exuded some sort of numinous glow. Almost the opposite: from the moment he clasped my hand with a firmness that made it feel in comparison to his like a flabby fish, it was his directness, his utter unpretentiousness, his total objectivity, that astonished. I do not believe that before or since I have been in the presence of someone who was as completely himself. Because I have traveled considerably in "the mystical East" I am frequently asked if I have ever encountered the siddhis, the supernatural powers that are believed to accrue in the course of yogic training and advance. My answer is no, not directly. I have heard innumerable accounts from persons who claimed to have been firsthand witnesses, but always the displays have stopped one step short of my door. Since meeting the Dalai Lama, however, I sometimes add an appendage to that answer. How anyone could have been raised as that man was, like a queen bee, really, surrounded from the age of four by no one save persons who assumed as a matter of course that he was God-incarnate for Tibet—how, to repeat, a mortal could have survived this kind of upbringing and escaped the slightest trace of a big head is, I am inclined to think, as close to a miracle as I need come.

3. Ninety percent of the gainfully employed in the United States now work in organizations. Seventy years ago 90 percent were self-employed.

4. *Walden Two* is no exception to this statement. Its unconvincingness, stemming from its lack of insight more than its lack of artistry, debars it from serious consideration.

But if the future will not work, surely the past has. Is not progress up to the present—life beginning in slime and ending in intelligence—a matter of record?

Let us see.

We begin with the short-range past, the career of *Homo sapiens* himself. To the prevolutionist, its career replicates the incline plane of the grand design: the species begins with ape men and moves through primitive savages to culminate in the intelligent creatures we have now become. The view is so taken for granted that when we hear the director of a leading museum observe, "From Stone Age to the present—what a decline," we suspect him either of quipping or of fronting for a museum's vested interest in the past. Perhaps the discovery that the Neanderthal's brain was larger than ours will help us to take the judgment more seriously.[5] Or the assessment of Lévi-Strauss; in terms of man-nature equilibrium, which in the long run must be the ruling consideration, he places the Golden Age of humanity somewhere around the Neolithic.[6] If we shift from ecological to intellectual criteria, he again sees no clear advance; in a way the burden of his entire work has been to make clear that "the

---

5. See Phillip V. Tobias, *The Brain in Hominid Evolution* (New York: Columbia University Press, 1971), pp. 96, 100-103. I am indebted to Gary Snyder, who is an anthropologist as well as a poet, for this point as well as the one in the next footnote.

6. Marshall Sahlins places it even earlier, in the Paleolithic; the view that the transition from hunting and gathering to agriculture constitutes a Great Leap Forward, he discounts as nothing but a "neolithic prejudice." Countering the entrenched theoretical position today, wherein the question "How did the primitives manage to live?" is topped only by the question of whether their existence deserves to be called living at all, he argues in his *Stone Age Economics* (Chicago and New York: Aldine-Atherton, Inc., 1972) that theirs was, as the title of his opening chapter puts it, "The Original Affluent Society." Affluence being a ratio between means and ends, by keeping their ends modest—want not, lack not—their means were more adequate to them than is the case with us. It is we who sentence ourselves to life at hard labor; the primitive is in business for his health. Hunters keep banking hours: "reports on hunters and gatherers... suggest a mean of three to five hours per adult worker per day in food production" (p. 34). The rest of their time is reserved for gossiping, entertaining, dancing and other arts, and daytime sleep. "Savage ... days are nothing but a pastime," a seventeenth-century explorer reported (p. 29). Passing to the question of what our industry has got *us*, Sahlins answers: *"This* is the era of hunger unprecedented. Now, in the time of the greatest technical power, is starvation an institution. Reverse another venerable formula: the amount of hunger increases relatively and absolutely with the evolution of culture" (p. 26).

savage mind" is fully as complex and rational as our own. And if we go with him a final step, looking beyond rationality to the motives that determine its use, Lévi-Strauss sees decline. Is it that analytic thought (the kind man has fallen into) has unseen violence built into it? he asks; or that man is possessed by an obscure fury against the Eden he dimly remembers and unconsciously realizes that he has lost?

Whatever the reason, whenever man now comes on landscapes or communities that resemble his image of a lost innocence, he lashes out and lays waste. Colonizers, rapacious white men and their technology, are the conspicuous culprits, but Lévi-Strauss does not exempt himself and his own discipline. The Western hunt for knowledge, analytic and objective to its core, has violence built into it. For to know analytically is to reduce the object of knowledge, however vital, however complex, to precisely this: an object. This being so, the Western hunt for knowledge, anthropology not excepted, is in a tragic sense the final exploitation and, as George Steiner has observed, *Tristes Tropiques* the first classic of our current ecological anguish.

> It looks forward with haughty melancholy to the image of the globe—cooling, emptied of man, cleansed of his garbage—that appears in the coda of *Mythologiques.* "Anthropology," says Lévi-Strauss in concluding *Tristes Tropiques,* can now be seen as "entropology": the study of man has become the study of disinte-gration and certain extinction. There is no darker pun in modern literature.[7]

Extending our retrospective look past man to the story of life as a whole, we come to evolution in its classic, Darwinian sense. This is the key domain, for it is on biological evolution that prevolution finally builds; this is its bedrock and prime foundation. As biologist Lewis Thomas puts it, "Evolution is our most powerful story, equiv-alent in its way to a universal myth."

In his *Personal Knowledge*—a book once commended to us by Noam Chomsky as the best on the philosophy of science that has been written—Michael Polanyi opens his critique of Neo-Darwinism with this arresting remark: "Only a prejudice backed by genius can have obscured such elementary facts (contradicting this

7. *The New Yorker,* June 4, 1974, pp. 107–108.

school) as I propose to state."[8] There is not space here to reproduce
the details of his argument; we must be content to summarize it.
The history of nature shows "a cumulative trend of changes tending
towards higher levels of organization, among which the deepening
of sentience and the rise of thought are the most conspicuous" (p.
384). "At each successive stage of this epic process we see arising
some novel operations not specifiable in terms of the preceding
level" (p. 389); for example, "while quantum mechanics can explain
in principle all chemical reactions, it cannot replace, even in principle, our knowledge of chemistry" (p. 384). The same holds, of
course, for the relation of biology to chemistry, psychology to biology, and so on. Moreover,

> the consecutive steps of a long-range evolutionary progress—like
> the rise of consciousness—cannot be determined *merely by their
> adaptive advantage,* since these advantages can form part of such
> progress only in so far as they prove adaptive in a *peculiar way, name-
> ly on the lines of continuous ascending evolutionary achievement.* The
> action of the ordering principle underlying such a persistent cre-
> ative trend is necessarily overlooked or denied by the theory of nat-
> ural selection. . . . Recognition [of this ordering principle]
> would. . . . reduce mutation and selection to their proper status of
> merely *releasing and sustaining the action of evolutionary principles* by
> which all major evolutionary achievements are defined. [p. 385]

> The rise of man can be accounted for only by other principles
> than those known today to physics and chemistry. If this be vital-
> ism, then vitalism is mere common sense, which can be ignored
> only by a truculently bigotted mechanistic outlook. And so long as
> we can form no idea of the way a material system may become a
> conscious, responsible person, it is an empty pretense to suggest
> that we have an explanation for the descent of man. Darwinism
> has diverted attention for a century from the descent of man by
> investigating the *conditions* of evolution and overlooking its *action.*
> Evolution can be understood only as a feat of emergence. [p. 390]

This last word, "emergence," epitomizes Polanyi's alternative to
Darwinism and links him to the precursors he acknowledges, Lloyd
Morgan and Samuel Alexander. The entire thrust of Polanyi's philosophical work is against reductionism, the attempt to explain the
higher in terms of the lower, the whole in terms of its parts. In this,

8. Chicago: University of Chicago Press, 1958, p. 382. Page references in the following paragraphs are to this work.

its negative polemic, it is on sure ground; the question concerns his alternative. Emergence is well and good, but where from? From whence do the "ordering innovative principles" he insists on (p. 387, *passim*) derive? If simpler, antecedent principles cannot account for them, is "nothing"—thin air—a more plausible source? For respecting sources, "nothing" and "thin air" are what emergence comes to. "All we can say is that at one moment there is nothing and at the next something," said Hoyle in answer to the question of where the hydrogen in his steady-state theory derived from. As etiology, emergence says no more than this.

Can anything come from nothing? Can a stream rise higher than its source? We are back to the enduring imponderables. On issues this fundamental, this close to ontological sensibility at its root and essence, no argument can deliver verdicts, so we shall enter none. Instead, we shall describe; we shall state. If emergence denies that a stream can rise higher than its source in the sense of simpler ordering principles accounting for ones that are more complex, the primordial outlook agrees with this denial and adds that something cannot come from nothing. *Ex nihilo nihil fit.*

What does this portend for evolution? It does not counter the fact that in the temporal order simple precedes complex. First virus-like specks of living matter; then bacilli with physiological functions that serve survival; then protozoa that can move about of their own accord and effect purposive activities; then multicellular organisms with sexual reproduction, nervous systems of increasing complexity, and sense organs that extend contact deeper into the surrounding space. We do not know when consciousness entered the sequence, but thought proper seems to come with the language that is confined to man. There is no need to deny anything in the sequence that carbon dating tells us transpired. Genesis had already announced the principle, as had other sacred texts and commentaries on them, "Man," said Gregory Palamas,

> this greater world contained in a lesser, the concentration into one whole of all that is, the recapitulation of all things created by God. Therefore he was produced last of all, just as we also (in our turn) round off what we have to say with a conclusion.[9]

9. *The Ascetic and Theological Teaching of Gregory Palamas,* trans. by Father Basil Krivosheine; reprint from *The Eastern Churches Quarterly,* No. 4, 1938, p. 3.

Far from denying life's progression, tradition provides a reason for it (in its own order of explanation, of course). Microcosm mirrors macrocosm, earth mirrors heaven. But mirrors, as we have noted, invert. The consequence here is that that which is first in the ontological order appears last in the temporal order. Not that the higher appears after the lower but that it is produced by the lower— this is what tradition denies. In doing so it counters the dominant mood of our time. Order from revolution (Marx), ego from id (Freud), life from the primal ooze (Darwin); everywhere the reflexive impulse is to derive the more from the less. Tradition proceeds otherwise.

What difference does it make which way we proceed—whether we look up or down for our explanations? We feel enjoined to raise this question explicitly, for we fear the reader may at this point be experiencing a letdown. Taking off from Gurdjieff's "this they won't believe," we had more than intimated that on the question of life's origin we proposed to say something startling. The exotic expectations this introit may have conjured in the reader's mind can only be surmised. That man arrived from another planet? That he was molded directly from dust? And after this buildup the promised surprise turns out to be scarcely one at all. The evolutionary sequence is not denied: amoebas did come first; life does advance. The only difference attaches to what would seem to be a secondary issue: the means by which the advance is effected. In all other respects the prevailing view is ratified and what was billed as a shock wave turns out to be a ripple. Life does evolve.

No, it does not. The point at stake is not a detail or in any way secondary. For evolution does not present itself as mere chronicle, a timetable, so to speak, with curators lining up fossil remains in the sequences in which they appeared. Evolution proposes to be an explanatory theory. It is the claim that everything about man, his complete complement of faculties and potentials, can be accounted for by a process, natural selection, that works mechanically on chance variations. Let its most distinguished recent spokesman phrase the wording. "Evolution . . . the product of an enormous lottery presided over by natural selection, blindly picking the rare winners from among numbers drawn at utter random. . . . This conception alone is compatible with the facts. The miracle stands 'explained.'"[10]

The quotation marks around that last word are interesting, standing as they do as an acknowledgment that Monod himself recognizes that he is using the word "explained" atypically. He does not tell us the deviant sense he has in mind, but by our lights his departure from normal usage is major. For to someone not already predisposed in evolution's favor, Monod's "explanation" is not such at all.[11] One reads his book, takes a sounding of the evolutionary corpus, and the miracle remains.

Let us take our bearings. Why in a chapter on hope are we devoting so much space to evolution?

Because it bears decisively on the chapter's theme. We have saved hope for this last substantive chapter of the book, not only because of its importance to human well-being but because we see it as the topic on which current thought is most confused and mistaken. The mistake lies in founding hope on a collective future, a future that will upgrade the quality of life by the mere fact that lives are born into it. Of the two factors that gave rise to this error, the first—a blend of science and technology—we are on our way to seeing through. There remains its other prop: evolution. We have called it the kingpin of the modern mind because from the standpoint of that mind so much has come to rest on it—nothing less than hope itself—that modernity is more invested in this doctrine than in any other. This in itself should put us on alert respecting it, given what we know about the way desire vectors evidence in favor of its wishes.

To speak plainly, as long as we can believe that there is a principle operative in nature—natural selection—that works to produce the higher from the lower, we can take courage. God is reinstated; a different god to be sure, but akin to the earlier one in that "he" too will see to it that things turn out all right. He does not preclude false starts any more than his predecessor did, but in the long run the victory is assured. We are in good hands.

10. Jacques Monod, *Chance and Necessity* (New York: Vintage Books, 1972), p. 138.
11. See William Pollard's telling critique of it in *Soundings*, LVI, 4 (Winter 1973). Also John Lewis (ed.), *Beyond Chance and Necessity* (Atlantic Highlands, N.J.: Humanities Press, 1974).

As a matter of fact that last sentence happens to be true—the title of this chapter implies as much. But the hands in question are not those of natural selection. Fortunately, considering the latter's brittleness.

This is not the place to enter into a full-scale critique of the theory of evolution. Those who wish to pursue the subject will find the main points summarized in Section IV of Titus Burckhardt's remarkable essay "Cosmology and Modern Science"[12] and spelled out in considerable detail in Douglas Dewar's *The Transformist Illusion*[13] and Evan Shute's *Flaws in the Theory of Evolution.*[14]

12. In Jacob Needleman, ed., *The Sword of Gnosis* (Baltimore: Penguin Books, 1974).
13. Murfreesboro, Tenn.: De Hoff Publications, 1957. It shows, among other things, that the so-called missing links are still missing. The most commonly cited example in favor of the evolutionary hypothesis is the supposed genealogy of the equine animals, which Charles Deperet criticizes as follows: "Geological observation establishes in a formal manner that no gradual passage existed between these genera; the last *Palaeotherium* was extinct long since, without transforming itself, when the first *Architherium* appeared, and the latter had disappeared in its turn, without modification, before being suddenly replaced by the invasion of *Hipparion*.... The supposed pedigree of the *Equidae* is a deceitful delusion, which simply gives us the general process by which the tridactyl hoof of an Ungulate can transform itself, in various groups, into a monodactyl hoof, in view of an adaptation for speed; but in no way enlightens us on the palaeontological origin of the horse." *Le Transformations du Monde Animal*, pp. 107, 105; cited by Burckhardt on p. 144 and Dewar on p. 92. Because the names of these authors are not household words, we add a summary statement by Loren Eiseley, whose name will be recognized: "How the primeval human creature evolved into *Homo sapiens*, what forces precipitated the enormous expansion of the human brain—these problems ironically still baffle the creature who has learned to weigh stars and to tamper with the very fabric of the universe." "Fossil Man," in *Scientific American*, CLXXXIX (Dec. 1953), 65. A final verdict in this list that could go on for pages comes from a former colleague at the Massachusetts Institute of Technology, Murray Eden: "Neo-Darwinian evolutionary theory ... has been modified to the point that virtually every formulation of the principles of evolution is a tautology." "Inadequacies of Neo-Darwinian Evolution as a Scientific Theory," in Paul Moorhead and Martin Kaplan, eds., *Mathematical Challenges to the Neo-Darwinian Interpretation of Evolution* (Philadelphia: The Wistar Institute Press, 1967), p. 109. "Natural selection" has proved to be a key that can be twisted to fit almost any lock.
14. Nutley, N.J.: Craig Press, 1961. The contribution of this book lies in the clear distinction it draws between "micro-evolution" (evolution on a small scale and within narrow limits), which no one contests, and "mega-evolution" (the theory that the class of birds, for example, evolved from the class of reptiles), which is "really a philosophy dating from the days of biological ignorance; it was a philosophical synthesis built up in a biological kindergarten."

Regarding the empirical evidence we shall content ourselves with three things: our own summary assessment, the assessment of a biologist, and a prediction.

Our personal assessment is that on no other scientific theory does the modern mind rest so much confidence on so little proportional evidence; on evidence, that is to say, which, in ratio to the amount that would be needed to establish the theory in the absence of the will to believe, is so meager. In its standard form the evolutionary hypothesis lies too close to accepted belief for today's Westerner to see how much it rides the will to believe, but when the hypothesis is enlarged—blown up, as it were, like a photographic print—the "will" shows up in clear outline. Teilhard de Chardin provides the obvious instance. To him, *The Phenomenon of Man* was science, a clean print-out—"pure and simple" are his words—of the conclusions the facts of nature point to. P. B. Medawar is as schooled in those facts as Teilhard was, but since he does not approach them by way of Teilhard's pseudo-Christian assumptions, he does not find them pointing to the Omega Point at all. The greater part of Teilhard's argument, Medawar writes,

> is nonsense, tricked out by a variety of tedious metaphysical conceits, and its author can be excused of dishonesty only on the grounds that before deceiving others he has taken great pains to deceive himself. *The Phenomenon of Man* cannot be read without a feeling of suffocation, a gasping and flailing around for sense. There is an argument in it, to be sure—a feeble argument, abominably expressed—but . . . it is the style that creates the illusion of content, and which is in some part the cause as well as merely the symptom of Teilhard's alarming apocalyptic seizures.[15]

Touché! And *pari passu!* Our point is that if biologists were to approach the paleontological record as innocent of evolutionary biases as Medawar is unencumbered by Teilhardian ones, their frustration in the face of the claimed scientific status of the evolutionary theory would rival Medawar's frustration on reading the assertion with which *The Phenomenon of Man* opens and on which the book turns; the assertion that "this book . . . must be read not as a work on metaphysics, still less as a sort of theological essay, but purely and simply as a scientific treatise."

15. *Mind*, LXX, 277 (Jan. 1961), 99.

As our judgment here is open to the double charge that not only is it that of a layman but of one who obviously has his own will to believe, we follow it with the judgment of a biologist whose heart is in the opposite, evolutionary camp. "I firmly believe," writes Jean Rostand,

> that mammals have come from lizards, and lizards from fish, but when I think such a thing, I try not to avoid seeing its indigestible enormity and I prefer to leave vague the origin of these scandalous metamorphoses rather than add to their improbability that of a ludicrous interpretation.[16]

Though this judgment has the merit of being that of a professional, it too is vulnerable. Rostand is but one biologist among many; for what proportion of his guild does he speak? So we round off the matter with a prediction: In the next hundred years, possibly less,[17] the fate of the evolutionary hypothesis will constitute the most interesting exemplification of the thesis Thomas Kuhn sets forth in *The Structure of Scientific Revolutions*; the thesis that scientists' need to make sense of their data causes them to continue to pour it into the prevailing mold (explanatory paradigm) until an alternative mold is fashioned that can accommodate the data more comfortably. When the change does occur, it does so quite suddenly. The picture "does a flip," as when one visual gestalt replaces another.

With this prediction we leave the empirical side of the evolutionary question; the data that would have to be sifted is, as we say, too vast to go into here. On the formal side, however, another point can be registered. If it is not entirely (or even primarily) evidence that gives the evolutionary hypothesis its seeming strength, from whence does that semblance derive? We have already mentioned

---

16. *Le Figaro Littéraire*, April 20, 1957. Quoted in Burckhardt, "Cosmology and Modern Science," p. 143.
17. In the several weeks that have elapsed since those words were written, there have been signs that the time span in question may be closer to a decade than a century. Most interesting has been the appearance of Tom Bethell's "Darwin's Mistake" in the February 1976 issue of *Harper's Magazine* (pp. 72, 75). His conclusion is as follows: "Darwin's theory, I believe, is on the verge of collapse. . . . He is in the process of being discarded, but perhaps in deference to the venerable old gentleman, resting comfortably in Westminster Abbey next to Sir Isaac Newton, it is being done as discreetly and gently as possible, with a minimum of publicity."

man's need for hope as one explanation. To this we must now add a second that relates to the scientific enterprise itself.

A Cambridge University professor points to it. In reviewing a book on natural selection around mid-century, Sir James Gray wrote: "No amount of argument or clever epigram can disguise the inherent improbability [of the orthodox evolutionary theory], but most biologists think that it is better to think in terms of improbable events than not to think at all."[18] It being axiomatic in science that one of the best ways "not to think" is by begging the question— that is, by assuming within an explanation that which it purports to explain—the first test a scientific explanation of the origin of life forms must pass is that the operative forces it invokes must not themselves possess life properties. This initial test Darwinism passes brilliantly: neither "chance" nor "the survival of those best suited to survive" presuppose the slightest intentionality or tropism. And because natural selection is the only hypothesis about life's origin that does pass this qualifying examination, it can fail right and left on subsequent tests (How much positive evidence supports it? Can it account for countervailing instances?) without losing its place as king of the mountain. For biologists are not different from other people; as Sir James says, they would rather shoulder improbabilities than not think (in their terms, by their criteria) at all.

In a brilliant paper prepared for the founding meeting of the Society for the Philosophy of Psychology (Massachusetts Institute of Technology, October 26, 1974), D. C. Dennett lays all this out clearly. Titled "Why the Law of Effect Will Not Go Away," the paper focuses on cognitive psychology but is relevant here by virtue of the explicit way it relates the Law of Effect to Darwinism. In the general terms in which Thorndike introduced that law, it holds that actions followed by reward are repeated. It is not a particularly good law; as Dennett says, its history has been "the history of ever more sophisticated failures to get [it] to *do enough work.*"[19] Despite this, its tenacity exceeds that of old generals; it refuses not only to retire but to fade away. Periodically it is given a new title—the Law of Primary Reinforcement (Hull), the Principle of Operant Conditioning

---

18. *Nature,* CLXXIII, 4397 (Feb. 6. 1954), 227.
19. *Journal of the Theory of Social Behaviour,* V, 2 (1976), 172. Subsequent page references in the text are to this article.

(Skinner)—but rather than improving its performance these hon-
orifics merely kick it upstairs, so to speak. Whence, then, its extraordinary lien on life? "It is not just mulishness or proprietary pride,"
says Dennett, "that has kept behaviorists from . . . look[ing] for
another fundamental principle of more power . . . but rather something like the conviction that the Law of Effect is not just a good
idea, but the only possible good idea for this job" of explaining
intelligence (p. 172). "There is something right in this conviction,"
Dennett continues, that something being that it is the only idea that
has been proposed that does not beg the question. But there is also
something wrong with the idea. And

> what is wrong in it has had an ironic result: allegiance to the Law
> of Effect in its behavioristic or peripheralistic versions has forced
> psychologists to beg small questions left and right in order to keep
> from begging the big question. One "saves" the Law of Effect from
> persistent counterinstances by the *ad hoc* postulation of reinforcers
> and stimulus histories for which one has not the slightest grounds
> except the demands of the theory. [p. 173]

The reason for this cross-reference to psychology is, to repeat,
that "the Law of Effect is closely analogous to the principle of natural selection," having been, indeed, consciously modeled after it.
From a "population" of stimulus-response pairs, born of random
responses to a given stimulus, the nervous system reinforces pairs
that are adaptive. This "selects" them by increasing the probability
that they will recur "while their maladaptive or merely neutral
brethren suffer 'extinction,' not by being *killed* (all particular stimulus-response pairs come to swift ends), but by *failing to reproduce.*
The analogy [to Darwinism] is very strong, very satisfying, and very
familiar." It is equally strong in the so-called dry, as opposed to biological or wet, approach to the study of learning and intelligence,
the science of Artificial Intelligence which works with "thinking
machines." Problem-solving computer programs are designed to
generate and test. At a given point or points, the program sets up
generating and testing units. The generating unit invents candi-
dates for the problem's solution and transmits them to the testing
unit, which accepts or rejects them on the basis of stored criteria.
This again is like natural selection, as Herbert Simon points out.[20]

20. *The Sciences of the Artificial* (Cambridge: M.I.T. Press, 1969), pp. 95–98.

Artificial Intelligence and cognitive psychology work from opposite ends of the scale. Artificial Intelligence begins with mechanisms that obviously lack intelligence—magnetic tapes whose segments do or do not conduct electrical currents—and tries to construct intelligence from these, whereas cognitive psychology begins with creatures that obviously have intelligence and tries to work back to neuron firings, nerve reflexes, and selector mechanisms that are as mechanical as computer operations. But forward or backward, the object is the same: to derive intelligence from things that do not possess it in the least. For

> psychology must not of course be question-begging. It must not explain intelligence in terms of intelligence, for instance by assigning responsibility for the existence of intelligence in creatures to the munificence of an intelligent Creator, or by putting clever homunculi at the control panels of the nervous system. If that were the best psychology could do, then psychology could not do the job assigned it. [p. 171]

The same holds for biology. The attraction of natural selection is that it seeks to

> provide clearly non-question-begging accounts. Darwin explains a world of final causes and teleological laws with a principle that is utterly independent of "meaning" or "purpose." It assumes a world that is *absurd* in the existentialist's sense of the term: not ludicrous but pointless, and this assumption is a necessary condition of any non-question-begging account of *purpose*. [pp. 171–72]

In sentences that are remarkable for the light they throw on the life sciences as enterprises—how they proceed, and how their procedures affect their findings by stipulating the kind of findings that will be accepted—Dennett sums up the matter as follows:

> Whether we can imagine a non-mechanistic but also non-question-begging principle for explaining design in the biological world is doubtful; it is tempting to see the commitment to non-question-begging accounts here as tantamount to a commitment to mechanistic materialism, but the priority of these commitments is clear. It is not that one's prior prejudice in favor of materialism gives one reason to accept Darwin's principle because it is materialistic, but rather that one's prior acknowledgment of the constraint against begging the question gives one *reason to adopt materialism* once one sees that Darwin's non-question-begging account of design or purpose in nature is materialistic. One argues: Darwin's materialistic theory may not be the

only non-question-begging theory of these matters, but it is one such theory, and the only one we have found, which is quite a good reason for espousing materialism. [p. 172]

To what degree this entire approach is likely to succeed—life out of nonlife, intelligence out of its absence, explanation out of that which in no way contains that which is to be explained—cannot, of course, be simply adjudicated. The question is fundamental; in a way the whole swing from tradition to modernity turns on it, and the point of this book is to help tip the lever back to its earlier, more natural, we contend, position. Charges of begging the question can settle nothing here, for the *petitio* is not a fallacy in the *form* of an argument; to invoke it, therefore, when the question concerns the truth-status of an argument's material premises or unvoiced assumptions is to commit the very fallacy that is being charged. Apart from material considerations, it is doubtful that the fallacy can even be clearly stated. An inquiry to a colleague in logic requesting a definition of the fallacy of begging the question brings word that the subject is in dispute and references to three current journal articles. Hoping to avoid this detour which looks as though it could lead into a bog, we ask what he would say if a student were to ask him straightforwardly what that fallacy *is*. He answers: "I would tell him no clear formulation of it exists."

We were trying to account for the inflated status of the evolutionary hypothesis and have found thus far, beyond the way it buttresses hope, a methodological reason: the fact that it is the only candidate that meets the formal requirements for being scientific lets it get by with less supporting data than would otherwise be required. A corresponding ontological reason is that in the world with which science works, there is nowhere else to *look* for life's origin. Paraphrasing Sir James of a few pages back, we can say that if scientists prefer to think improbably than not to think at all, they would likewise rather pull rabbits out of hats than out of thin air, literally *ex nihilo*. From this second, ontological angle, we can join Burckhardt in ascribing part of evolutionism's force to "an incapacity—pecular to modern science—to conceive 'dimensions' of reality other than those of purely physical sequences; to understand the 'vertical' genesis of species."[21]

21. "Cosmology and Modern Science," p. 147.

What is this vertical genesis of species? If we were to answer "God" this would not be incorrect, but the doctrine of "special creation" has become so weighted down with anthropomorphic imagery that we do better here to use its less personalized variant. The nonanthropomorphic counterpart of special creation is emanation. In the celestial realm the species are never absent; their essential forms or archetypes reside there from an endless beginning. As earth ripens to receive them, each in its turn drops[22] to the terrestrial plane and, donning the world's fabric, gives rise to a new life form. The origin of species is metaphysical.

First a viable habitat must be devised, hence the inorganic universe is matured to the point where life can be sustained. And when living beings do arrive, they do so in a vaguely ascending order that passes from relatively undifferentiated organisms—though not simple ones; the electron microscope shows unicellular organisms to be astonishingly complicated—to ones that are more complex. But there is no need to force the fossil record to show a univocal and continuous line. If the movement proceeds in jumps with whole categories of plants and animals bursting out at once without discernible predecessors, this presents no problem. There is no need to multiply hypotheses by positing a thread that unites the various classes of life, such as insect, fish, reptile, bird, and mammal. We need not strain to see in the fins by which certain fishes flap their ways on shore rudiments of the articulation that arms and paws require but which fins show no beginnings of. Nor exaggerate the resemblance of birds to reptiles in an effort to prove that one derived from the other, an exercise that must proceed in the face of glaring differences in skeletal structure and the fact that the hearing apparatuses in the two orders are modeled on altogether different plans. If the tortoise turns up all at once in fossil remains or the spider appears simultaneously with its prey and with its faculty of weaving fully developed, such facts can be welcomed with smiles instead of puzzled brows.

As for the variant forms which Darwinists must use to construct their largely hypothetical bridges between species, from the metaphysical perspective these appear as variations which the species in

---

22. After Chapter 2 on "The Symbolism of Space," we use words like this trusting that the reader will not impute false literalisms to them.

question allow. It is as if nature, always more prolific and life-loving than we had supposed, first staked out distinct species and then decided to ring changes on these by having each reflect the forms of the others insofar as it could do so without transgressing its own essential limits. Seen in this light, variations are not generative links between species—it has yet to be shown what the dolphin, say, is a link to or from. They are, rather, mimics; they show species imitating the ways and forms of species that in essence are foreign to them. Not solely for utilitarian reasons of adaptation and survival, we may add; in part—larger part—for *lila*, the divine play: sheer protean exuberance. *Esse qua esse* so *bonum est* (being as being is so good) that God cannot resist any of its possibilities. Wishing with part of herself to be a mother, a child dons apron and suckles her doll. Dolphins and whales are the archetypal mammal wondering what it would be like to be a fish; armadillos the result of its thinking, "Wouldn't it be interesting to dress up in scales and play reptile?"[23] Pressing the image a bit, we might say that hummingbirds in their mode of feeding and flight and their iridescent coloring are birds fancying themselves as butterflies. It is like Indra's Net, each jewel reflecting the others and being reflected in them.

Admitting that, to revert to an earlier image, we are performing here like the generating unit of a computer and not its testing unit, we push on to venture that the skeletons that evolutionists take to be protohuman may in fact be posthuman. They may be the deposits of degenerate epigones, tail ends of earlier human cycles *(yugas)* that were drawing to their close. After all, myths recount devolution more than evolution, and we know for a fact that later human forms are not necessarily more advanced: Steinheim man preceded Neanderthal but was more "evolved." If it be asked, "Where, then, are the remains of these 'giants who walked the earth in those days'?" it might be answered that in his beginnings, when he stood close to provenient spirit, man was ethereal to the point of leaving less in the way of ossified remains.

If this seems altogether too fantastic, we can at least take satisfaction in the fact that at last we have delivered on the promise with

23. We are speaking in the mode of Platonic myth, one consequence of which is that the reader will not be able to determine how literally we intend such statements because we are not sure ourselves. All we feel confident of is that they contain more truth than the alternatives they intend to counter.

which we introduced this subject of human origins, the promise that we would say something faintly scandalous. In defense we say but this. Though we have not been unserious in anything we have postulated, the point we are most convinced of is the following: Whatever the utility of contemporary biological models for discovering useful specifics like antibiotics, for the *understanding* of life these models are largely useless. Moreover, they mislead.[24] The first shall be last and the last first, we are told. We have seen how in the microcosm/macrocosm mirror inversion, this decrees that man, who is first in the order of worth on the terrestrial plane, will be last in the order of his appearance. Now the converse: the last shall be first. Among the sciences, physics is ontologically the lowliest: it treats of matter in its most elementary arrangements. Concomitantly it is the first of the empirical sciences to "see through" its subject to a glimmering beyond. It *knows* the derivative character of space and time; the unimageable, transcendent character of the real. Even assuming that in specifics and details what we have ourselves postulated in these pages may be quite mistaken, we feel certain of this: if modern science continues, the current working premises in biology, Darwinism included, will in time (possibly quite a short time) show themselves to have been as inadequate as were Newton's. The life sciences will crash through them as through a sound barrier. On that glad day biologists will begin to talk like physicists. Like Richard Feynman, say: "We have to find a new view of the world." Or Freeman Dyson: "For any speculation which does not at first look crazy, there is no hope."

At last we have completed our excursus on evolution. As it has monopolized the better part of this chapter on hope, we trust that its object has not been lost from view. With the buckling of science and technology as props for the idea of progress, evolution has become its principal support. (This accounts for the emotional investment in Teilhard de Chardin. We know of no other twentieth-century thinker who has an entire journal devoted to the propagation of his theses.) Part of us feels bad about disturbing this prop, for in an age that has sealed over other outlets for hope, to under-

---

24. "Though modern scientific knowledge reveals much that was previously unknown, . . . it hides or supplants much more." Lord Northbourne, *Looking Back on Progress* (London: Perennial Books, 1970), p. 116. The present chapter is deeply indebted to this lucid little book.

mine *evolution*, the last remaining prop for *progress*, which in the modern world has become the last remaining refuge for *hope*, is to undermine hope itself, and hope is indispensable to human well-being; this was this chapter's opening premise. But truth or consequences—when one must choose between them, jnana yogins at least, those whose approach to God (Reality) is by way of knowledge (gnosis), will understand that choice must favor the former. If within this vast universe a thread of life were to angle always upward, leaving a trail that hooked from a distance like the jet stream of an ascending plane, such a never-circling life force would be a freak. For everywhere else—name one exception—nature favors the curves that space itself conforms to; the yin-yang rhythms of turning gyres and waves that crest and fall. O my people! can you not see how it is hope, not fact, that powers this dream of onward and upward toward the dawning light? If human life is truly natural—and this, surely, the evolutionists would want us to believe—it is seasonal. Fall and winter are its lot as assuredly as summer and spring. Half the art of living is a talent for dying.

Its other half, of course, is its talent for living, and this requires above all else an inward eye. Body dies, but the soul and spirit that animate it live on. At death man is ushered into the unimaginable expanse of a reality no longer fragmentary but total. Its all-revealing light shows up his earthly career for what it truly was, and the revelation comes at first as judgment. The pretenses, rationalizations, and delusions that structured and warped his days are now glaringly evident. And because the self is now identified with its Mind or vital center rather than its Body, Mind's larger norms, to which the embodied ego paid little more than lip service, now hold the balance. It is thus that in hell man condemns himself; in the Koran it is his own members that rise up to accuse him. Once the self is extracted from the realm of lies, the falsities by which it armored itself within that realm become like flames and the life it there led like a shirt of Nessus.[25] When the flames have consumed these falsi-

25. "The experience of death resembles that of a man who has lived all his life in a dark room and suddenly finds himself transported to a mountain top; there his gaze would embrace all the wide landscape; the works of men would seem insignificant to him. It is thus that the soul torn from the earth and from the body perceives the inexhaustible diversity of things and the incommensurable abysses of the worlds which contain them; for the first time it sees itself in its

ties—or to use other language, when truth has set the distortions of terrestrial existence in perspective—the balance is restored and the distortions, too, are seen to have had their place. This is forgiveness. With it, the Mind recedes as the Body earlier did at death, and the self, which is to say attention and identification, passes to the Soul's immortal center, which is now freed for the beatific vision. Lost in continual adoration and wonder, it abides in the direct presence of the Living God who is Being Itself. Beyond this, where the film that separates knower from known is itself removed and the self sinks into the Spirit that *is* the Infinite. . . . Ah, but we can say no more. We have reached the Cloud of Unknowing, where the rest is Silence.

If this sounds "old-fashioned," we trust that those who make this charge are not blind to the fact that it is the tacit progress-premise underlying that word that has turned it into a pejorative. We need not romanticize the past. If the most primitive people now living on the earth are also its sweetest and gentlest,[26] there are other primitives who are sadists. And as for history, it shows grotesque aberrations as well as magnificent achievements; we do not have to be reminded of tyrannies of altar and throne, the rigidities of imperial legalisms, or the closedness of respectable mores and the sectarian spirit. It is only in cosmic outlook that we see the past as superior to ourselves and qualified to be our teacher; there may be other ways, but we have not tried to sift the record. That there have been in this world, and are today in lingering pockets, metaphysical doctrines that are complete along with means for their realization—this is a notion that for moderns is barely conceivable, but it has emerged as the thesis of this book. In this day of neophilia and reflective embrace of the new, when "What's new?" has become standard salutation and quipsters tell us they want even their antiques to be of the latest variety; in this time when clergy themselves have grown "trendy" in worship of their God who is "not yet" (Moltmann); this

universal context, in an inexorable concatenation and in a network of multitudinous and unsuspected relationships, and takes account of the fact that life had been but an 'instant', but a 'play'. Projected into the absolute 'nature of things' man is inescapably aware of what he is in reality; he knows himself ontologically and without deforming perspective in the light of the normative 'proportions' of the Universe." F. Schuon, *Understanding Islam* (Baltimore: Penguin Books, 1972), p. 85.

26. John Nance, *The Gentle Tasaday* (New York: Harcourt Brace Jovanovich, 1975).

age of flourishing futurists when almost the only way to get attention is to claim to be privy to some new discovery, it gives us the most exceptional pleasure, the most piquant delight, to announce what in today's climate of opinion may be the most novel, original, and unexpected prediction imaginable. The wave of the future will be a return to the past. "There is only the fight to recover what has been lost / And found and lost again and again."[27] "I sing the songs of olden times with adoration."[28]

27. T. S. Eliot, "Four Quartets: East Coker," *The Complete Poems and Plays, 1909–1950* (New York: Harcourt, Brace & World, 1952), p. 128.
28. Svetasvatara Upanishad, 11.5.

Chapter 19

The Survival of Civilization

Lord Northbourne

Suddenly anxiety about the survival of civilization and even of the human race as such, has obtruded itself to complicate and confuse the intensive planning for progress that has attained the proportions of an obsession in modern civilization and continues unabated today. "Suddenly" is the right word, for how surprised the early architects of the industrial framework would be to find that the issue of survival had so soon raised its ugly head to confuse their original intention of wealth and leisure for all.

It is not the purpose of the observations that follow to study the reasons for that anxiety in detail, and still less to propose specific remedies or palliatives. It is rather to try to find a point of view from which the situation as a whole may become more understandable, for people are not only anxious but also disappointed and puzzled. By way of preliminary it seems desirable to summarize as briefly as possible the most prominent immediate causes of the anxieties in question. They can conveniently be divided into three main groups, according to their nature, and not according to any view of their relative importance. Firstly, the availability of the hydrogen bomb, together with the continuing development of other scientific weapons, chemical, biological and even psychological, which could be at least as destructive. Secondly, the anticipation of a continuing exponential growth in the population of the world. Thirdly, the anticipation of an early exhaustion of some of the natural resources on which modern civilization depends, not only of fossil fuels and certain metals, but also of biological resources endangered by a pollution of the environment which can also directly affect human health.

Any one of these groups considered separately could afford reasonable grounds for anxiety; taken together their effect is rather overwhelming, especially as the time-scale for the attainment of an acute stage in several of the anticipated crises must be calculated in decades and not in centuries. One may reasonably ask: why has this aspect of our situation come into prominence so suddenly, and what have the scientists and planners in whom we have so far put our faith been thinking about all this time? True, there are scientists and others who maintain that talk such as this is mere panic; that the applications of scientific knowledge have been eminently successful so far, and that therefore science can be trusted to deal with the situation, and moreover that science alone can deal with it, provided of course that it is given ample facilities for research and that people will act upon its findings. There are also people, even scientists, who are prepared to dismiss the whole business on the grounds that no doubt we shall go bumbling along in the future as we have in the past. It is difficult to accept either of these views. The case is too strong and the time is too short. The anxiety exists and is accompanied by a growing disorder, political, social, moral, philosophical and religious. Meanwhile, however, every sectional interest in the field of production and distribution (and that includes most people whether in receipt of salaries or wages) is driving as hard as it can for more and more, while the organized stimulation of desire has itself become an industry and is pursued relentlessly and scientifically.

It is less difficult to accept the view that humanity, and especially its wealthier components, will probably have to postpone, at least for a time, the realization of many current ideals of progress, and may even have to accept something that can, from the point of view of those ideals, only be regarded as a regress, in the form of a lowering of standards of living, a sacrifice of past attainments, and even, if the worst fears are realized, something like a partial return to savagery. All this however applies only to the slowing down of a progress measured solely in terms of material wealth. It is sometimes suggested that something that can be called "culture" ought to be the true measure of wealth, and that a cultural progress need not be impeded by a material regress. Everything depends of course on what the word "culture" means, what it includes and what it does not. It is by no means impossible that a culture should be marked by an excess, a luxury and a futility no less harmful than an excessive material luxury and no less seductive. How does our contemporary culture stand up to examination in the light of that possibility?

The culture of today—using the word inclusively, as one must in this connection, and not limiting it to the more specialized or exclusive branches of the arts—is marked chiefly by a search for the sensational, amounting to little less than an enslavement to sensation; this search justifies experiment in any direction whatsoever. Sensation is not enduring, it cannot satisfy for long; it demands constant renewal and, being satiating rather than satisfying, it demands both intensification and variety. The arts are not exempt; but in that connection we often prefer the word "aesthetic" to the word "sensational", though they mean much the same thing. The result is chaotic, for a true culture is above all disciplined, restrained, selective and intellectual (in the sense of being concerned primarily with the understanding and only secondarily with the emotions). A true culture does not scorn sensation, far from it; its purpose is precisely to canalize sensation in the direction of the edification and purification of the soul. Our culture being what it is, perhaps we ought not therefore to be surprised at the development of "sub-cultures" founded on drugs, on sexual license, on quasi-religious fantasies, or even on violence, usually in the name of a so-called "freedom" which is in reality nothing else but the very same enslavement to sensation as that which marks our culture. All this is fostered and encouraged by a deafening flood of propaganda and distraction poured out almost without pause by press and radio, diluted with miscellaneous information on almost every conceivable subject. The sheer weight of the whole is overwhelming; its coordination and direction is beyond the power of most mortals. It contradicts everything that is simple, calm, gentle, enduring or profound. Moreover, since our outlook is predominantly scientific, and our outlook is reflected in our culture, it may be permissible to suggest that science itself is suffering from a comparable plethora in its own field, a huge and rapidly swelling mass of information, more and more specialized and indigestible; while at the same time the main preoccupation of science is to increase the mass as quickly as possible by more research, as if such research did not in fact usually raise more problems than it solves. The full answer is always as it were round the corner; a "further advance" is always necessary if complete success is to be achieved. Our science and our culture are alike both in their experimental approach and in their lack of finality. This fact is not without significance.

Surely we are suffering in the cultural field from a quantitative over-development and a qualitative deterioration—that is to say a pollution—parallel to those occurring in the material field, and demanding at least as comprehensive a reversal of trends as does the latter. One can at least assert that a culture which could be regarded as a hopeful source of compensations for material losses can hardly be expected to arise out of our contemporary culture.

All these phenomena, whatever the category in which they may be placed, are in fact aspects of a single phenomenon, simply because a civilization, if it means anything, is a single whole; it has an economic aspect and a cultural aspect which cannot be dissociated, any more than body and soul can be dissociated in the human beings who constitute it. These two aspects, which could equally well be called the corporeal and the psychic respectively, are not however the whole of a man or of a society. In both there is something that has usually been called "spirit", and we have no better word for it, despite the many senses in which the word is commonly used. If indeed, as so often seems to be assumed today, there is no reality outside the corporeal and the psychic domains, then the conception of spirit is really superfluous, because the word represents no more than a conventional expression covering phenomena confined to one or the other domain, or to both. The word is used here in a very different sense. It represents that which transcends both the corporeal and the psychic, and is principial with respect to both. It is the divine *afflatus,* the "wind" that "bloweth where it listeth", animating all changeable forms, and manifested through them without itself undergoing change. It is therefore essentially mysterious, and cannot be defined unequivocally or exhaustively; yet we try to ignore it at our peril, since its ubiquity renders it inescapable. By its very nature it demands an approach totally different from the scientific approach, since the latter is undertaken exclusively by way of the observation of the apparent and by deduction from that observation; the scientific approach is always indirect, whereas the spiritual as such can only be approached directly, it can only be so to speak "seen" or "not seen" as the case may be.

The approach of religion to the realities and problems of human life differs in principle from the approach of science because the special and indispensable function of religion is to cultivate and to preserve a conscious apprehension or "vision" of the spiritual and to communicate it to the people in a form adapted to their various needs and capacities. Religion constitutes in principle the visible spiritual center of a civilization: the spiritual is nevertheless manifested in everything, and not least in virgin Nature, either positively or negatively, by way of a relative affirmation or denial, a relative conformity or non-conformity to its all-embracing essentiality. Nothing is independent of it; the possibility of a conscious apprehension of it is however peculiar to man alone; that human apprehension would not be conscious in the absence of the possibility of its contrary in the form of a rejection of the spiritual. This last possibility is therefore also peculiar to man. It is these two contrary possibilities that together constitute the essential distinction between man and the whole nonhuman world; all other distinctions are accidental, they are distinctions of degree or of kind rather than of essentiality. We shall return to this point which is crucial. Meanwhile we can legitimately treat the spiritual as a third "aspect" of civilization, provided that we recognize that it and the material and the cultural aspects are so interlocked as to be in principle inseparable. Since a distinction between them is possible, a relative priority can in practice be accorded to any one of them in thought and action. Some degree of priority is in fact normally accorded to one or the other; not only by specialists—for example by technologists, psychologists or theologists—but by most people in their daily lives. Moreover it seems that the emphasis accorded to each varies in different periods of history. It is at least impossible to deny the predominance of the economic aspect, the subservience of the cultural and the obscuration of the spiritual in the present age; always remembering however that the spiritual "as it is in itself" is not an "aspect", it is unaffected by anything and is present in everything; it is only the human consciousness of its presence that can be obscured. It seems often to be assumed that the cultural as such is inherently "more spiritual" than is the economic; in fact it may be or it may not; everything depends on the quality of the human consciousness that animates it. This truth is very relevant to the pretensions of certain protagonists of culture today, and more generally to the situation of the arts in our civilization. Correspondingly, and perhaps surprisingly to some people, the material domain as well as the cultural can be a medium for the manifestation or obscuration of the spiritual. Let us therefore not be afraid to return for a moment to the material aspect of things.

We have seen that some of the repercussions of the "gospel of getting on" have begun to give cause for alarm, sufficiently at least to persuade many responsible people, including many scientists, that the situation demands close examination—in other words, more research—and that some modification of the economic framework may need to be undertaken rather urgently, perhaps even before the results of that research are sufficiently well established. The driving force behind any action that may be taken will be mainly the powerful but unconstructive impulse of fear, the fear of a loss of advantages gained; being what it is, that impulse is likely to lead to uncoordinated and ill-directed action. The means available will be precisely those that have brought about the present situation and are likely to show a strong resistance to modification. Well, it will be said, the people must be educated so that they can think clearly and vote wisely in all these matters. The question then is—by whom are they to be educated and in what sense? And even more urgently—is there time even to try to educate the people? Whatever expedient we adopt, we are in grave danger of being overtaken by events, if indeed that is not exactly what is happening now.

So let us move a little further back in order to look at an assumption that seems to be fundamental to the philosophy of industrialism. It is to the effect that an all-round increase in material wealth will automatically generate the virtues on which the harmony and stability of a civilization depend. If ever an assumption has been conclusively proved by experience to be false, surely it is this one; yet it remains implicit in most of what we plan and do, and in most public statements related to economics or politics, as well as in many that claim a religious origin. We cannot examine this assumption without considering what virtues must be taken into account. We need not expect to find anything new, nor must we be afraid of taking into account virtues which have in the past been regarded as important for the preservation of human society in its more stable and coherent forms. It may be worthwhile to try to enumerate some that seem to be particularly relevant to the present discussion, and at the same time to glance at some of the vices with which they are incompatible.

Humility is one of them. It consists in a consciousness of the limitations inherent in the human state as such as well as in one's own individuality, manifested first in the relationship of man to God, and then of man to man and man to Nature. Humility is the reverse of self-assertion in all its forms, including ambition, the cult of "personality" and all notions that imply what has been called a "conquest" of Nature. Closely related to humility is the renunciation of worldly superfluities and the acceptance of one's situation in life and of life's accidents with equanimity and patience, while performing the tasks that fall to one's lot to the best of one's abilities, with the excellence of the product in view rather than the material reward the work may bring. Also related to humility is simplicity, the child-like virtue, gentle, free from pretence, trustful and whole-hearted; and it is perhaps relevant to present considerations to recall that the reward of the "meek" is specifically and rather surprisingly that they will "inherit the earth". Then there are the dynamic or "noble" virtues, with all the obligations nobility implies: generosity and self-sacrifice, courage and devotion, together with dignity, not of rank but of soul, unmoved either by calumny or by praise, free from both arrogance and false humility, knowing its place and seeking no other. And one cannot omit, as a foundation for all, faith and fear: faith in an all-wise Creator, and fear of a just Judge, not of loss nor of suffering nor of death.

Among the vices incompatible with these and other virtues it seems appropriate to mention particularly the following: lust, currently accepted and encouraged in most of its many forms; envy, which appears often to be taught as a virtue or as a duty in the name of equality; avarice, stimulated by the advertising industry with its scientific psychological backing designed to make people want what they did not know they wanted, as well as by such things as the stock market and the pools; and, most comprehensive and fatal of all, pride: the presumption that makes man the measure of all things, the disposer of all things and the being to whom all service is due, the arrogance that sets itself up against God himself, while all other vices seek to hide themselves from Him.

It is of course beyond question that very many individuals practice virtues and shun vices such as these, but there is plenty of justification for the view that they are doing so in the face of an increasing pressure which assails them from all sides, and is gener-

ated in the first instance by the motives that govern our technolog-
ical-industrial civilization, in which the first priority is the pursuit of
wealth rather than the pursuit of virtue, on the false assumption
that the former generates the latter. That an inversion of these priorities would bring about a better world is an assumption of which
nobody need be ashamed; but it is very difficult to see how such an
inversion could be effected and it is impossible to foresee what the
resulting world would be like, if only because of the comprehen-
siveness of the changes involved, amounting to nothing less than a
complete and universal change of heart. That is something that
planning, however intelligent and well-intentioned, cannot even
attempt to bring about. It is evident that, in this connection at least,
the situation has passed beyond deliberate human control. We must
therefore again move back in order if possible to obtain a more
comprehensive view.

A situation in which anxiety and fear prevail is bound to produce reactions against itself, and many such are in evidence today,
some more intelligent, some less. They have little cohesion or unanimity and are mostly concerned with finding palliatives to particular aspects of the situation considered more or less in isolation, with
more concern for symptoms than for causes. In total they are much
more likely to be adding to confusion than alleviating it. Among the
more intelligent may be mentioned those movements that are concerned with the conservation of natural resources, with pollution,
and with agriculture in relation to health. In so far as these or any
other movements tend towards a re-orientation of the aims of civilization, away from an unrestrained pursuit of wealth towards a less
greedy, more restrained and even more humble and "neighborly"
attitude, not only between man and man, but also between man and
Nature (for Nature, considered as the source from which we obtain
what we need, is indeed our "neighbor" in exactly the sense of the
definition of the word that follows the parable of the good
Samaritan)—to that extent the movements in question, or some of
them, are favorable to the attainment of virtue. On the other hand,
to the extent that their real aim, professed or otherwise, is a
resumption of the present course of civilization after a pause necessary for the removal of some unexpected obstacles, they will accomplish nothing towards the removal of the causes of present
discontents. They will only deceive their adherents into supposing

that they are doing something useful. In almost all these movements there is one thing that remains no less axiomatic than it is in the civilization that has produced them. It is an assumption to the effect that the physical survival of mankind as the dominant inhabitant of this planet is, and must ever be, the first concern of humanity as a whole. Is it possible that this assumption is not fully justified, or is justified only conditionally? This question leads to our final point, which is either the key to the situation or is the most pathetic of delusions. The reader who has come this far must make his choice; for it must be one or the other; he must at the same time be prepared to accept that the truth is the only thing that counts in the end, even though it may not at first sight seem to point to any particular immediate course of action, for the truth alone is practical, since, in the nature of things, it must prevail in the end.

The instinct for the preservation of the species is universal among the animals, and man is, physiologically speaking, an animal. Is he then no more than an animal with exceptionally highly developed mental powers by which alone he has achieved his present dominance, and on which alone he must rely for his preservation ? Such is precisely the view implicit in the outlook of modern civilization; it is implicit in almost everything we do whatever we may profess to think. We behave as if man were self-sufficient and existed in his own right, and as if the fulfillment of his destiny depended primarily on the improvement of the environmental conditions under which he lives. We call that improvement "progress", and hope that we can ensure its continuance by increasing our knowledge of our environment with a view to a more complete control of it. This behavior implies, among other things, that our vision of the destiny of mankind is limited to the creation of a terrestrial utopia, peopled perhaps by supermen who, with all their desires fulfilled and freed from the anxieties that plague us, can devote themselves to the enjoyment of their situation.

All such views of our situation and destiny are relatively new; they are incompatible with an alternative view that will be recognized as being anything but new. The latter has however become so unfashionable that its first principle must be restated in its essentials as briefly as possible. It is to the effect that the destiny of man is spiritual and not terrestrial, eternal and not temporal, paradisal (or infernal) and not utopian (or cataclysmic); also that this is true despite the fact that the goal is inevitably beyond the scope of an imagination derived wholly from terrestrial experience, and is *a fortiori* inaccessible to scientific investigation or proof. Let us follow up this proposition, for if it is substantially true, our situation cannot be correctly envisaged unless it is taken fully into account, since all our motives must be conditioned by it, and it is they that dictate what we do, just as our motives today are conditioned by the view we now take of our situation. If our present view is false we can hardly expect our best intentions to be realized effectively, and there is no occasion to be surprised at the occurrence of exceptional difficulties in our civilization.

Even the practice of the behavioral virtues could become of no effect if it were undertaken with a terrestrial and not a celestial end in view, for the function of the virtues in the fulfillment of the destiny of man is primarily the purification of souls so that the light of the spirit may enter into them. Purification is indispensable, but it is not everything. The virtues cannot by themselves supply the impulse that sets men on the way, nor the guiding light that keeps them on it. In that sense, indispensable though they be, the function of the behavioral virtues is as it were not directly productive, so that they are not by themselves sufficient; the positive and decisive factor that makes them spiritually fruitful is of a purely spiritual nature, and it cannot therefore be objectified; its presence in an individual implies an orientation of the whole being—not a mere desire—directed towards the absolute, the infinite, the eternal, towards that which is "not of this world"; an orientation manifested in a love of God—much more than a mere belief—that secretly permeates every thought and every act and makes it fruitful, so that it can play its part in the fulfillment of man's true destiny. If the souls of men are orientated in that sense, so also will be their civilization considered as an entity. This kind of fulfillment of his destiny is the true function of man. It alone is the justification of his life and the glorification of his death. But more than that: man is not alone in the world; he cannot exist apart from it, nor can it exist apart from him, for he occupies a "central" position in it. Man is a "microcosm" a "little universe"; all the possibilities of the universe are reflected and "concentrated" in the human state. His collective function is that of "mediator" between God and the universe, between the spiritual and the physical. The manner in which he carries out that function necessarily affects not only himself but all creatures, whether living or non-living, whom he represents before God. Hence, for instance, the "dominion" accorded to him in Genesis 1.26; or his specific appointment as God's "representative" (Khalif) in the Koran; or, in Buddhism, the vow of Amida "not himself to enter Paradise until the last blade of grass should have been saved". Conversely, the abandonment or weakening of the exercise of the true function of mankind involves, not humanity alone, but also the whole world, living and non-living, in disturbances of equilibrium of many different kinds. They puzzle us simply because their prime cause, namely, our failure to fulfill our spiritual function, does not enter into our calculations, or if it does, it is only as if it were but one of a vast complex of factors, economic, psychological, political and so on, and one of the least calculable of those factors. It is of course inevitable that most of our problems should have to be tackled singly by people who are specialists in one way or another, but a piecemeal approach, however inevitable, well-intentioned and well-contrived it may be, can only be effective if society as a whole is unified and stabilized by a single ultimate aim that takes full account of the supremacy of the spiritual principle that is the origin, sustainer and end of the universe and all that it contains. The beginning of trouble lies in the natural incapacity of humanity to live fully in accordance with the nature of that principle, and trouble reaches a maximum when manifestations of the principle are mistaken for the principle itself, or in other words, when the appearance is mistaken for the reality, the accidental for the essential, the perishable for the eternal.

At present, for the lack of a right aim, the energies and the goodwill of mankind, both of which are available in abundance, have become dispersed and frustrated. We do not know where to look for guidance—as if the guidance offered by earlier self-revelations of the changeless spirit had itself changed! What has changed is only some of the interpretations put upon the scriptures and traditions associated with those revelations by modernizers in absurd attempts to "bring them up to date", that is to say, to bring them into conformity with the blatantly anti-religious and anti-traditional tendencies of the times. The essentials remain what they always have been. The door will be opened, as it always has been and always will be, to one who knocks; nevertheless he will for the present be acting very much on his own, since he will get little help from his surroundings. In accepting the guidance of a revealed religion he must not gloss over its aspect of severity; he must accept the implications of the universal scriptural and traditional prophecies concerning the inevitability of an end to be followed by a new beginning; he will understand that a direct intervention by the changeless spirit alone can restore all things, and that this implies that whatever is incompatible with the presence of the spirit must first be destroyed. Meanwhile, he will be ready. That is all that is possible for him, and that is all that is expected of him.

Our powers are much less than we seem to think. We cannot become other than what we are; we cannot shift the "here and now" in which we find ourselves; we cannot predict, and still less can we contrive, the future. We cannot conserve what is by nature perishable for more than a very short time, and both our civilization and we ourselves are by nature perishable. There is one thing in particular we can by no means do, try as we may, and that is to escape from or to destroy the spirit which alone is imperishable.

In exalting our own powers over Nature we diminish ourselves, for the realization of our full potentiality does not depend on the development and exercise of those powers for our own terrestrial advantage; it depends entirely on the fulfillment by us of our spiritual function; for that alone can keep us in touch with the imperishable and finally bring us into union with it. Such is our appointed destiny, and only to the extent that we follow it for its own sake and without ulterior motive can harmony between man and man and between man and Nature become a reality, and with that harmony a civilization that is worthy of the name, and is at the same time as fully protected from corruption and dissolution as any collective human organization can ever be.

Acknowledgments

Grateful acknowledgment is expressed to all of the authors for granting us permission to reprint their essays in this book. The essays published in this collection have been extracted from the following books and journals:

To Have a Center by Frithjof Schuon
To Have a Center, by Frithjof Schuon, World Wisdom Books, copyright 1990, pages 3-38.

Loss of Our Traditional Values by Thomas Yellowtail
Yellowtail: Crow Medicine Man and Sun Dance Chief, by Michael O. Fitzgerald, University of Oklahoma Press, copyright 1991, pages 187-193.

Modern Psychology by Titus Burckhardt
Mirror of the Intellect, by Titus Burckhardt, Quinta Essentia, copyright 1987, pages 45-67.

Man in the Universe, Permanence Amidst Apparent Change by Seyyed Hossein Nasr
Studies in Comparative Religion, Volume 2, Tomorrow Publications, copyright 1968, pages 244-252.

Lucifer by Tage Lindbom
The Myth of Democracy, by Tage Lindbom, Wm. B. Eerdmans Publishing Co., copyright 1996, pages 113-130.

The Mystery of the Two Natures by James Cutsinger
Sophia: The Journal of Traditional Studies, Winter 1998, pages 111-141.

Do Clothes Make the Man? by Marco Pallis
The Way and the Mountain, by Marco Pallis, Peter Owen Publishers, copyright 1991, pages 141-159.

Holy Fools by Patrick Laude
Sophia: The Journal of Traditional Studies, Winter 1998, pages 142-169.

Work and the Sacred by Brian Keeble
Art: For Whom and For What?, by Brian Keeble, Golgonooza Press, copyright 1998, pages 74-90.

Acknowledgments

The Role of Culture in Education by William Stoddart
Studies in Comparative Religion, Volume 17, copyright 1985,
pages 19-23.
Every Branch in Me by Kurt Almqvist
Studies in Comparative Religion, Volume 15, copyright 1983,
pages 194-196.
On Being Human by Joseph Brown
The Spiritual Legacy of the American Indian, by Joseph Brown,
The Crossroad Publishing Company, copyright 1982, pages 123-
129.
The Vocation of Man According to the Koran by Jean-Louis
Michon
Fragments of Infinity: Essays in Religion and Philosophy, edited by
Arvind Sharma, Prism Press, copyright 1991, pages 135-152.
The Forbidden Door by Mark Perry
Sophia: The Journal of Traditional Studies, Winter 2001, copyright
2001, pages 139-185.
Even at Night the Sun is There by Gray Henry
Parabola: The Magazine of Myth and Tradition, Spring 1993, The
Society for the Study of Myth and Tradition, copyright 1993,
pages 60-65.
Outline of a Spiritual Anthropology by Frithjof Schuon
From the Divine to the Human, by Frithjof Schuon, World
Wisdom, copyright 1982, pages 75-86.
The Prodigal Returns by Lilian Staveley
Studies in Comparative Religion, Volume 15, copyright 1983,
pages 155-159.
Hope, Yes; Progress, No by Huston Smith
Forgotten Truth: The Primordial Tradition, by Huston Smith,
Harper Collins Books, copyright 1976, pages 118-145.
The Survival of Civilization by Lord Northbourne
Studies in Comparative Religion, Volume 7, copyright 1973, pages
21-30.

Contributors

KURT ALMQVIST, a philosopher and poet, was editor and translator of the Swedish journal, *Tidlos Besinnung I besinniglos Tid—ur Frithjof Schuons Werk*. In addition to teaching Romanic languages, including Spanish, Latin, French, Catalonian and Provençal, and writing many poems, he published a Swedish anthology of quotations from the works of Frithjof Schuon and René Guénon.

JOSEPH EPES BROWN was Professor of Religious Studies at the University of Montana and a renowned author in the field of American Indian traditions. A vital interest in the traditional life ways of the American Indians led him to the renowned Lakota holy man Black Elk, who recounted to him the sacred rites of the Oglala Sioux, which served as the basis for his most well known book, *The Sacred Pipe* (1953). His other publications include, *The Spiritual Legacy of the American Indian* (1982), *Animals of the Soul* (1992) and *Teaching Spirits* (2001).

TITUS BURCKHARDT was an eminent member of the Traditionalist school who published many distinguished works in the fields of metaphysics, cosmology, art, architecture, alchemy, symbolism, and traditional civilization. A prolific author, he devoted all his life to the study and exposition of the different aspects of Wisdom and Tradition. His chief metaphysical work is *An Introduction to Sufi Doctrine* (1976), whilst his *Sacred Art of East and West* (2001) is an enunciation of the traditional doctrine of art as it is found in civilizations such as the Christian, Islamic, Hindu, Buddhist, and Taoist. An anthology of his writings, *Mirror of the Intellect* (1987), is particularly notable for its exposition of a wide range of subjects on traditional science and art, as well as an acute critique of their modernist counterfeits. Titus Burckhardt died in Lausanne in 1984.

JAMES S. CUTSINGER is Professor of Theology and Religious Thought at the University of South Carolina and Secretary for the Foundation of Traditional Studies. A widely recognized authority on the Traditionalist school of comparative religious thought, he is best known for his work on the Swiss philosopher Frithjof Schuon, and in this regard has published the acclaimed *Advice to the Serious Seeker: Meditations on the Teaching of Frithjof Schuon* (1997). His keen interest in ecumenism has led to his editing two books on religious dialog: *Reclaiming the Great Tradition: Evangelicals, Catholics, and Orthodox in Dialogue* (1997), and the recently published *Paths to the Heart: Sufism and the Christian East.* He is currently editing the Collected Works of Frithjof Schuon.

GRAY HENRY lectures and writes on the spirituality of the world's sacred traditions and has published in this field for many years. Founder and trustee of the Islamic Texts Society and former director of Quinta Essentia Publications, she currently directs Fons Vitae Press and is a consulting editor for *Parabola.*

BRIAN KEEBLE is co-founder of Temenos Academy, a teaching organization dedicated to the arts and imagination, and founder of Golgonooza Press, a publisher of important books on the subject of sacred art from authors such as Titus Burckhardt, Ananda Coomaraswamy, Philip Sherrard, Kathleen Raine and Wendall Berry. He has long been devoted to the promulgation of the traditional arts and crafts in Britain and is best known for his book *Art: For Whom and For What?* (1998).

PATRICK LAUDE is Professor of French at Georgetown University and the author of numerous articles, translations, and books on the relationship between mysticism, symbolism and literature. His works include studies of important spiritual figures of the 20th century such as Jeanne Guyon, Simone Weil, Louis Massignon, and Frithjof Schuon. His most recent publication is entitled *The Way of Poetry: Essays on Poetics and Contemplative Transformation* (2002).

TAGE LINDBOM was one of the intellectual architects of the Swedish Welfare State before undergoing a profound intellectual and spiritual change. In 1962 he published *The Windmills of Sancha Panza,* a book that rejects the assumptions behind Social Democracy. Thereafter, Lindbom published many books in Swedish, most of which explore the tension between religion and modern secular ideology. Two of his most notable works have appeared in English:

The Tares and the Good Grain (1983), and *The Myth of Democracy* (1996).

BARRY MCDONALD serves as Managing Director of World Wisdom Press. A strong attraction to authentic spirituality led him to many parts of the world and brought him in contact with spiritual authorities from several traditions. Thomas Yellowtail, the venerable Medicine Man and Sun Dance Chief, adopted him into his Crow tribe. His graduate degree is from Indiana University and he is also a published poet.

JEAN-LOUIS MICHON is a Traditionalist French scholar who specializes in Islam in North Africa, Islamic art, and Sufism. He received his Ph.D in Islamic Studies from the Sorbonne in Paris. With a keen interest in traditional Morocco, he served for many years as the Chief Technical Advisor to the Moroccan government on UNESCO projects aimed at the preservation of the cultural heritage of the Maghreb. His efforts were particularly influential in the rehabilitation of traditional Moroccan handicrafts, under siege from encroaching industrialization. His works include *The Autobiography (Fahrasa) of a Moroccan Soufi:Ahmad ibn 'Ajiba (1747-1809)* (2000).

SEYYED HOSSEIN NASR is University Professor of Islamic Studies at George Washington University and president of the Foundation for Traditional Studies, publisher of *Sophia: The Journal of Traditional Studies.* He is the author of over thirty books and three hundred articles on topics ranging from comparative religion to traditional Islamic philosophy, cosmology, art, ecology, and mysticism. Among his most notable works are *Ideals and Realities of Islam* (1966), *Knowledge and the Sacred* (the 1981 Gifford Lectures), *Sufi Essays* (1991), and *Religion and the Order of Nature* (1996). The Seyyed Hossein Foundation propagates traditional teachings in general, and the various facets of traditional Islam and other religions in particular.

LORD NORTHBOURNE was a frequent contributor to the British journal, *Studies in Comparative Religion.* His books *Religion in the Modern World* (1963) and *Looking Back on Progress* (1970) are considered by many to be especially good introductions to the Perennialist outlook.

MARCO PALLIS was widely respected as a teacher and writer of religious and metaphysical works. He was also a gifted musician and composer, as well as a mountaineer, traveler and translator of Traditionalist works. For many years he corresponded with the eminent Traditionalist writers Ananda Coomaraswamy, René Guénon, and Frithjof Schuon. His writings include the best selling *Peaks and Lamas* (1939), an account of his mountain experiences in Tibet, and *The Way and the Mountain* (1960), a collection of articles on Tibetan Buddhist themes, informed by a universalist outlook. He also wrote many articles for *Studies in Comparative Religion,* some of which appeared in a compendium called *A Buddhist Spectrum* (1980). Marco Pallis died in 1989.

MARK PERRY is the son of the eminent Perennialist author Whitall N. Perry. He has contributed articles to the journals *Connaissance des Religions,* and *Sophia,* as well as to an anthology of writings on Frithjof Schuon, *Le Dossier H: Frithjof Schuon* (2002). Fons Vitae has recently published his book, *On Awakening and Remembering* (2000). Currently, he is retranslating all of Schuon's books from the original French into English.

FRITHJOF SCHUON is the foremost expositor of the Perennialist perspective and is best known as a philosopher in the metaphysical current of Shankara and Plato. He has written more than 25 books on metaphysical and religious themes as well as having been a regular contributor to journals on comparative religion in both Europe and America. Schuon's writings have been translated into over a dozen languages, and have been consistently featured and reviewed in a wide range of scholarly and philosophical publications around the world, respected by both scholars and spiritual authorities alike. Frithjof Schuon died in 1998.

HUSTON SMITH is widely regarded as one of the most accessible contemporary authorities on the religions of the world. He was the Thomas J. Watson Professor of Religion and Distinguished Professor of Philosophy at Syracuse University. His classic, *The World's Religions* (1991) is the standard work for comparative religion in many universities. His many books include *Forgotten Truth: The Common Vision of the World's Religions* (1976), and *Beyond the Post-Modern Mind* (1989). His discovery of Tibetan multiphonic chanting was lauded as "an important landmark in the study of music," and his film documentaries of Hinduism, Tibetan Buddhism, and Sufism have all won international awards.

LILIAN STAVELEY was the author of two works that reveal the spiritual insights of a mystically inclined contemplative soul: *The Golden Fountain* (1982), and an autobiography, *The Prodigal Returns*, both written in complete anonymity from family and society in the early twentieth century.

WILLIAM STODDART has made a life-long study of the great religious traditions of the world, and in this connection has traveled widely in Europe, North Africa, Turkey, India, and Sri Lanka. Dr. Stoddart studied modern languages, and later medicine, at the University of Glasgow in Scotland, and obtained his M.D. there in 1949. For many years he was assistant editor of the British journal *Studies in Comparative Religion* and is the author of the introductory works, *Sufism: The Mystical Doctrines and Methods of Islam* (1976), *An Outline of Hinduism* (1993), and *An Outline of Buddhism* (1998). He has also translated several of the works of Frithjof Schuon and Titus Burckhardt into English. His current book, *The Essential Titus Burckhardt*, will be published by World Wisdom in 2003.

THOMAS YELLOWTAIL was Medicine Man and Sun Dance Chief of the Crow tribe, raised with the old timers who knew the freedom and sacred ways of the pre-reservation era. As the principal figure in the Crow-Shoshone Sun Dance religion during the last half of the twentieth century, he perpetuated the spiritual traditions of the Crow tribe as one of the last links to the pre-reservation days. His biography, *Yellowtail: Crow Medicine Man and Sun Dance Chief* (edited by Michael Oren Fitzgerald) was published in 1991.

Index

Index